3rd edition

Psychological Report Writing

NORMAN TALLENT

Prentice Hall, *Englewood Cliffs, New Jersey 07632*

Library of Congress Cataloging-in-Publication Data

TALLENT, NORMAN, (date)
 Psychological report writing.

 Bibliography: p. 252
 Includes indexes.
 1. Clinical psychology. 2. Report writing. I. Title.
[DNLM: 1. Psychology. 2. Writing. WZ 345 T147p]
RC467.T34 1988   808'066616021   87-12550
ISBN 0-13-732553-3

© 1988, 1983, 1976 by Prentice Hall
A Division of Simon & Schuster
Englewood Cliffs, New Jersey 07632

Printed in the United States of America

10 9 8 7 6 5 4 3 2 1

Cover design: Suzanne Bennett & Associates
Manufacturing buyer: Ray Keating

ISBN   0-13-732553-3   01

PRENTICE-HALL INTERNATIONAL (UK) LIMITED, *London*
PRENTICE-HALL OF AUSTRALIA PTY. LIMITED, *Sydney*
PRENTICE-HALL CANADA INC., *Toronto*
PRENTICE-HALL HISPANOAMERICANA, S.A., *Mexico*
PRENTICE-HALL OF INDIA PRIVATE LIMITED, *New Delhi*
PRENTICE-HALL OF JAPAN, INC., *Tokyo*
SIMON & SCHUSTER ASIA PTE. LTD., *Singapore*
EDITORA PRENTICE-HALL DO BRASIL, LTDA., *Rio de Janeiro*

This book is lovingly dedicated to Shirley,
who suggested that I write it.

Contents

Preface

As with earlier editions, the purpose of the present work is to set forth ways to make the psychological report a responsible and an effective communication.

From the standpoint of the report writer, this means having guidelines on how to identify substantive information for the report and how to organize and share it. From the point of view of the report consumer, a report meets the criteria of responsibility and effectiveness if it is understandable, not burdensome to read or listen to, and if it contributes to answers to current or potential questions about the person who is the subject of the report. The psychological report writer can best realize these practical objectives when he or she conceptualizes each case against a background of relevant assessment theory and research.

The increasing use of professionally gained psychological information to deal with human issues prompts the inclusion of three new chapters. The first addresses the sizable area being staked out by the "psychometric machine." Of particular concern is the construction of computer reports, the circumstances and the manner of their use, and some overarching ethical concerns that pertain to psychological evaluation by computer. One new chapter (Chapter 7) examines such basics of computer-generated psychological reporting and discusses guidelines to the use of electronically processed information.

Another new chapter (Chapter 8) explores relationships between psychological assessment and psychological therapy. Drawing on a wide-ranging literature, the thesis is presented that the psychological report can be (and in many settings is) a helpful tool in planning and carrying out psychological interventions. Appropriate psychological information, appropriately used, merits more of the sort of recognition now disproportionately accorded to technique and technology.

Chapter 9, Forensic Psychological Evaluations, was added to this edition to provide some reference points for the growing number of psychologists who are involved, or for students who are moving toward involvement, in the legal forum. Forensic psychological reporting follows the basic principles of report writing that are presented in this book, yet there are a number of special considerations to which the psychologist must attend. Shortcomings or deficiencies that might be overlooked or tolerated in school or clinic can surely be devastating in the courtroom.

A special point of emphasis of this book, particularly in Chapters 5 and 9, links psychological reporting more closely with *assessment* than with *testing*. Assessment principles are presented as integral to the development of a psychological report whose concern is with the needs of an individual, whereas a *testing* orientation that does not incorporate assessment principles requires merely that the psychologist transmit test data together with (nomothetic) statements linking the data with empirical correlates. *Assessment* is here preferred over *testing* because of the greater richness of information it may yield, as well as the ability of this approach to focus its powers on finding solutions to the identified (idiographic) problem areas of a person.

Dr. Galen S. Marburg, Dr. Barry L. Mallinger, and Dr. Mari G. Irvin have read the manuscript and made a number of meaningful suggestions for changes. My heartfelt thanks to all of them.

1
The Psychological Report

PURPOSE AND CONTEXT

The psychological report is described as a practical and relevant document that is used to improve our understanding of individuals. A grasp of the basics involved in developing the report will increase its value. Discussed in this chapter is the defining of a mission for each report that is written, thus structuring the assessment procedure. Also introduced here are the topics of optimizing the role of the psychologist and how the psychologist's awareness of the personal and interpersonal dynamics of the staff can have a favorable impact on the report.

Practical and relevant understanding of a person is the substance of a psychological report. Typically, reports are the psychologist's conclusions and reflect the outcome of tests, direct observations of behavior, other inputs of information, or a combination of these. Similarly, when therapy is conducted, the therapist's initial notes plus subsequent progress notes are psychological reports. How effectively a psychological report is written may be very important for the individual who is the subject of the report.

MISSION

The psychological report, then, is seen as an active contribution to a broad mission. Whether in a private or an institutional context, the purpose of that mission may be summarized by such terms as *therapy, growth, remediation, skill acquisition,* or *jurisprudence.*

    The purpose of schools is to educate and to enhance their students' quality of life. Hospitals and clinics deal broadly with problems of health—physical, mental, or emotional. Juvenile training schools are charged with rehabilitating youthful offenders. Courts are concerned with dispensing justice.

Psychologists in private practice deal with a wide range of issues centering on personal problems.

Subsumed under such general missions are the specific missions with which a psychologist must deal. Each mission generally involves an individual, although groups and the interaction of individuals may also be proper topics of concern. Whatever the problem, the psychologist brings to bear the resources that are available and delivers needed information in the form of a psychological report—written, oral, or a combination of the two.

The question with which the psychologist is asked to deal may necessarily be quite general. What is wrong? A child is doing poorly in school. Why? Is there an intellectual problem? Brain damage? A personality disorder? Autism? Excessive anxiety? Lack of goals or interests? A problem with authority figures? Situational stress in the home? An abnormally high intellect to which the curriculum does not cater? And so on. Or the psychologist may be asked to deal with an employee who is in frequent conflict with superiors, performs poorly on the job, and is prone to absenteeism. What is the problem? Can the employee be salvaged? How?

A commonly occurring problem is the need to establish a diagnosis for a patient newly admitted to a mental hospital. What sort of difficulty appears to be present? Does he or she suffer from a borderline personality disorder or from a schizophrenic disorder? Or perhaps the picture is sufficiently vague to render an early differential diagnosis impossible. Beyond general definition of the problem, which is the function of a formal diagnosis, much specific information is needed. Answers may be sought to such questions as a person's problems in living, inner conflicts, major defenses and how effective these are, the extent to which depression may be present, the possible existence of acting-out tendencies, and whatever else would appear to be of practical significance.

In various settings, as the individual is better understood, increasingly specific questions may arise. Thus, "There is reason to suspect that this student's intellectual level as established by group testing is not representative of his true abilities. Please evaluate individually." "From what sort of therapy is this person most likely to benefit?" "The patient's family indicates that a suicidal threat was made prior to admission. Are there any further indications that he might be potentially suicidal?" "Six months ago the psychological examination showed disturbances of the formal thought processes. The patient has since improved considerably. Are the thinking disturbances noted still present?"

Beyond generating descriptive material on an individual, the possible decision implications of the data must always be kept in mind and may be transmitted in the form of recommendations. These may be entirely implicit, such as when the psychologist reports to a somatically oriented physician on the presence of a generalized anxiety disorder, a dysthymic disorder, or a schizophreniform disorder. The accepted chemotherapeutic options for treating each of these conditions are limited, and the competent physician will prescribe accordingly. On the other hand, where psychotherapy is available, the psychologist may judge a person to be a suitable candidate for such treatment, and it is important to spell out some of the specifics of an approach to therapy that is most likely to be helpful. Will the patient probably do best in group or in individual therapy, or should both be considered? Is a behavioral strategy indicated, or should we go the insight route? Should efforts be primarily supportive, or is the essential need of the person practical guidance? How should staff react to the individual? To what extent, for example, should a student be coached, or to what extent should the youngster be encouraged to remedy educational deficiencies through personal initiative? Should staff listen one-sidedly to a person's marital difficulties? Might this reinforce some unconstructive viewpoints and help to rationalize self-defeating behaviors? Might this approach keep the person from seeking competent marriage counseling with his or her spouse?

A variation of mission exists in the case of screening or routine evaluation. Here the report may be based on impressions gained from group testing, individual testing, or both. The goal is to generate a data base and to identify salient features such as problem areas, intelligence level, insight, and motivation for change. These data may then suggest the need for further evaluation. Subsequent events may also give rise to specific questions that require answers.

The behavior therapist may approach the mission by listing target symptoms or other behaviors to be changed and the treatment strategy to be followed. A bioenergetic therapist may take a similar tack. A humanistic-existential approach may include a report to be shared with the client as a vehicle of interaction between therapist and client.

In the community mental health movement, naturalistic observation can be more important than testing. Concern is likely to center on environmental rather than intrapsychic forces, since a community model of psychopathology stresses etiological factors that are "outside" rather than "inside" the individual. Although testing may not be central to a mission—it may in fact be eliminated or minimized, especially when the psychologist's clinical assessment skills are high—psychological instruments are typically a valuable resource. The competent psychologist, of course, can never overlook social and cultural factors and must be wary that what is derived from psychological instruments does not lead us to neglect the individual's unique situation.

Not to be overlooked is the teaching value of the psychological report. Every report written should add to the psychologist's skill and knowledge. A well-written, well-conceptualized report, depicting a person in his or her individuality, similarly enriches the serious reader of the report. When psychological reports are prepared for a case conference, and especially for a training seminar, the teaching mission of the report is even more important.

Psychological reports, then, may be designed to contribute to various outcomes. Considering that therapy is a major activity of large numbers of psychologists, brief psychological reports in the form of *progress notes* should be specially commented on. The following observations are adapted from Mosak.[1]

Purpose of Progress Notes

The purpose of progress notes varies with the mission. We may think in terms of an institutional mission, when the psychologist is a member of an organization such as a school, a hospital, or a clinic, and the responsibility for the mission is shared by the staff. Notes written in such a context may variously emphasize administrative content or therapeutic matters. Other notes, often written by a therapist for personal use, are structured as therapeutic tools.

First, let us consider institutional notes. These are of two sorts, the *status documentation* note and the *administrative note*. The status documentation note records the client's condition, progress, or course of illness. Typical statements are of the sort "Patient continues to hallucinate," "The client is appreciably less depressed than she was at intake," or, simply, "No change." The administrative note documents actions that have been taken or are contemplated. Thus, "Psychological assessment completed," or "The patient will probably be ready for transfer to an open ward in a few days."

Progress Notes as Therapeutic Tools

Mosak identifies centers of emphasis in progress notes that may be helpful to the conduct of therapy. These notes may be identified by their salient contents. The centers of emphasis are:

Topics discussed   The purpose is to serve as a reminder of the most recent topics of therapy, or, "What's going on now." Example: "Parents asked John to move out of the house. Most of the session spent discussing feelings and options."

Topics to be discussed or other reminders   Here the therapist wishes to have a reminder so that there will be continuity between the previous session and the next. Example: "Discuss marital relations next week." Important intervening events or developments in the client's situation may, of course, lead the therapist to ignore such entries. The therapist may also want to have a reminder on points to be made, conclusions to be "tied up," questions to be asked, or tasks to be set for the client, "homework."

Behavior   Behavior, in or out of the therapy situation, may command interest as a record of progress or lack of progress, or as a matter of future

[1]Harold H. Mosak, personal communication.

concern. Examples: "The client is more assertive this week," "Beatrice still wanders in her communication," "Ms. F. relates a dream about me, emphasizing a scene in which I scolded her," "Bill promised himself and me that he will stop drinking, attend A.A. regularly, and control his destructive behaviors."

Dynamics   It frequently is helpful to record an impression of a client's dynamics, because these have implications for treatment. For example, what might be the implications of the analysis of transference? Or, can a knowledge of a client's dynamics be of value in dealing with his or her maladjustive behaviors? At times a note about dynamics may indicate a therapist's uncertainty at the stage of therapy when it is written. Thus, "I can't understand the patient's reluctance to talk about his aunt during the early years of his life when she cared for him. Watch for clues."

Summary/overview   An inclusive impression of the client and therapeutic guidelines typically are of value both at the initiation and at the termination of contacts, and may serve an administrative as well as a therapeutic function. An initial note might be concerned with such topics as an impression of the nature of a presenting problem, including prognosis, the possible need for additional early assessment, the client's expectations of therapy and motivation for change, initial goals discussed with the client, and the therapeutic strategy that is contemplated. A final note might review the highlights of treatment, record a reassessment of the client's psychological status, including the gains made during therapy, and make an estimate of the outlook.

INITIATION OF
PSYCHOLOGICAL ASSESSMENT

Psychological reports are the product of an assessment procedure. Individuals become involved with psychological assessment in various ways, commonly on the basis of a referral to the psychologist from another professional person. The manner in which the request for assessment is made might well be a potent factor in the quality of the psychological report that will be received by the referral source.

As we have seen, in many settings some sort of routine initial workup is requested. In a school it is often a teacher, a counselor, or a principal who feels the need for psychological information. In a hospital or a clinic it may be a nurse, a social worker, or a therapist. A psychologist who functions as a hospital ward administrator may decide which patients are to be assessed. In traditional psychiatric settings psychological assessment (probably called *psychological testing*) typically has been initiated at the request of a psychiatrist.

In many instances the psychologist initiates psychological assessment, as in routine screening or in the practice of behavior therapy. When such is not the case, the mechanics of referral, the manner in which requests for evaluation are made, may have much bearing on the usefulness of the psychological report. The request for evaluation is the means, or should be the means, by which the psychologist is charged with a mission. When the psychologist understands the specific problem to be dealt with and can choose the most relevant and economical approach, the person making the referral will be most likely to benefit from the psychologist's efforts. In turn, the psychologist must know well the mission of the referring person and also the general mission of that person's profession. In an institutional context the psychologist must have a comfortable knowledge of the workings of the institution.

Often the request for psychological assessment comes in general terms when the raising of specific questions would be more appropriate. The overly general referral may come from psychologically unsophisticated personnel who have difficulty pinpointing the individual's problems and who possess inadequate knowledge of the psychologist's skills and procedures. Such a referral may read, "Psychological examination," "For psychological testing," "Psychological survey," "Have the psychologist test this patient," or "Give this patient a Rorschach and see what you get." On the other hand, the psychologist is likely to be displeased with certain requests for specific information. Not welcome may be requests for formal diagnoses to be used largely for administrative record keeping rather than as a basis for treatment; equally unwelcome, in a psychiatric setting, are requests for IQ determinations, particularly when such information is asked for on a recurring basis or is the only sort of information requested.

When the psychologist receives a request for assessment in terms that are inappropriately general, several options are available. The psychologist may simply ask the person who initiates the request for assessment for more specific information on the problem. Or the psychologist may try to guess what is needed or wanted, with unpredictable results. Some psychologists prepare a general report that is likely to be both stereotyped and overly inclusive, hoping somehow that one or more of the plethora of statements will hit the mark. Such documents commonly are referred to as "shotgun reports," with pejorative meaning intended. When the reason for referral is not well formulated, it is difficult for the psychologist to be on target.

In sharp contrast to such reports, we advocate *case-focused* reports. Case-focused reports start with case-focused questions and attempt to reveal the unique aspects of persons; hence, the psychologist tries to avoid stereotypes, theory-dictated and test-dictated conclusions. Statements in the report are interrelated, just as personality features in an individual are interrelated. Uppermost, the focus is on the mission; the client's problem(s) and the helping measures that should be taken are spelled out as recommendations or are clearly implied. In most situations recommendations should be explicit. The advice for which the psychologist in a school setting, for example, is consulted is far more important than are general statements about the child. In a psychiatric situation, however, where the psychologist and the psychiatrist are in a close working relationship and there is good mutual understanding and frequent contact, specific statements of recommendation can often be redundant. Thus, after suggesting to a psychiatrist that a patient is suffering with bipolar disorder and has recently experienced a full manic syndrome, it would be gratuitous to recommend that she or he be treated with lithium. The options for treatments are broadly implicit.

The development of case-focused reports is illustrated in Chapter 5. Examples of this approach are presented in Chapter 6.

The psychologist should encourage the making of specific referrals, when these are appropriate, and should discourage those that do not seem to define a mission, especially those requesting that a certain procedure be carried out. If such a request is made, the reason should be stated. A general request may simply be an example of poor communication—that is, the writer fails to express the underlying thoughts that prompted the referral. Several surveys (Lacey & Ross, 1964; Tallent & Rafi, 1965; Tallent & Reiss, 1959a,b) indicate that many clinical workers have definite ideas of what sort of information they wish to receive through psychological assessment. Perhaps they assume psychologists know how they can best render services to their associates.

Although we stress the value of the specific referral, cases definitely exist where a referral cannot be based on a circumscribed problem. Sometimes not enough is known about a person to raise specific questions. Or circumstances may reveal an *apparently* clear-cut problem. "Is this patient homicidal, suicidal, depressed, likely to act out antisocially?" "Is his conduct attributable to mental deficiency; to brain damage?" "Is he ready for discharge from a hospital or clinic or from office treatment?" "Can he be rehabilitated, and to what extent?" "Will he profit from psychotherapy; if so, from what approach?" Often, however, the problem is not specific.

An example of a nonspecific problem may be presented by a patient who appears anxious, depressed, or schizophrenic. She evidences certain deviant behavior. It is too early to crystallize definite problem areas. Is it not legitimate in such a case to refer the patient for psychological assessment? Implicit are a number of questions about the patient concerning, perhaps, relevant history, the dynamics of the situation, or defenses, ego strength, reality perception, thought organization, severity of the condition, impulse control, central conflicts, goals, fantasies, interpersonal relationships, the psychoeconomic value of symptoms, probable outcome, and indications for various sorts of intervention. If the psychologist is personally aware that the referring person has such questions in mind, we have a broad but definite mission. Such an assignment will be more of a challenge than a general referral that appears to represent a lack of reflection or acumen.

Daigle (see reference to Vernon, 1955) suggests that the emphasis should be away from *what* is to be known about a person and in the direction of *why* certain information is important. He refers to the first as charging the psychologist with "testing for areas," the second with "testing for alternative means of management." The suggestion appears to have merit. It is important that the psychologist know the alternative procedure that might stem from assessment so that the pertinent information can be specifically sought and the conclusions be presented so as to be most meaningful practically. Of course, this does not mean that "testing for areas" should or can be abandoned. The point Daigle makes has to do with emphasis. Often the test battery may be modified only partly, or not at all, because of an awareness of why certain information is needed. Daigle's recommendation applies partly to how the request for referral should be made and partly to how the findings should be presented by the psychologist.

From the foregoing it should be evident that the psychologist and the person who refers cases to the psychologist must make a special effort, when necessary, to "educate" one another. Smith and Gabbard (1980) point out that "a common frame of reference with the same language concepts and views about treatment is an enormous asset." Along with such abstractions there are some very mundane issues, such as what the psychologist can and cannot do. What constitutes a proper referral is a related matter.

The referring person must be cognizant of some very practical clinical realities that, although they might seem trivial, are important. For example, a student or a patient is often referred to a psychologist with no idea of why the referral is being made. To explain why it is a good idea to "see" a psychologist might help to set the person at ease and to facilitate the establishment of rapport. In an institutional setting it is all too common for a patient to arrive for an appointment, only for the psychologist to find that testing cannot be done because the patient has inadequate vision and lacks corrective lenses. Another problem that can be nipped in the bud by the referral source stems from sending medicated patients for psychological assessment. It is well known that psychoactive medication frequently modifies behaviors of concern to the referring person (as it is supposed to do!)—for example, the extent and the effects of anxiety and depression that typically characterize a patient. When possible, it is a good idea to withhold psychoactive medication until the psychologist's assessment has been completed.

Request for psychological evaluation may be made with various degrees of formality. In private practice and in many institutions, a phone call or direct personal contact is often most expeditious. The important thing is that the needs of the referring person be set forth clearly. This objective can best be accomplished when there is a close working relationship between the person referring the case and the psychologist, whether referral is in writing or transmitted orally. Ideally all cases should be discussed prior to evaluation. In this way the points to be explored can be jointly developed and differences in understanding the nature of the problem(s) can be resolved.

A written referral form may be most appropriate in a large setting or when there is a forensic aspect. In many institutions requests for specialized evaluations, medical or psychological, for example, are by regulation printed on standard consultation forms on which the report may be typed. Many such forms are extant. A sample, "homemade" form (from a medical setting) on which psychological evaluation may be requested appears below. No particular claim is made for its merit: Changes would perhaps have to be made in terms of the mission of any particular setting. The main consideration for a referral form is the conscientiousness with which it is used. Most important are the detail and the explicitness with which the nature of the problem is stated.

Request for Psychological Evaluation

To: _____

Name of Patient: _____

Age: _____ Sex: _____

Provisional or Established Diagnoses: _____

Nature of Problem: _____

(Reason for Referral) _____

Special Characteristics:

Psychological

Untestable _____

Poor Cooperation _____

Assaultive _____

Unduly Suspicious _____

Mute _____

Aphasic _____

Poor Understanding of
Language _____
(Why?)

Other _____

Physical

Limitation of Movement Which
Might Hinder Testing _____
(Specify)

Hearing Loss _____
(How Serious?)

Poor Vision _____
(How Serious?)

Is Visual Defect Properly
Compensated? _____

Speech Impediment _____
(Specify)

Other _____

Patient is Ambulatory _____
            In a Wheel Chair _____
            Confined to Bed _____

"TYPES" OF PSYCHOLOGICAL REPORTS

Both the content and the format of the psychological report change in response to new concepts and tools. In the early days of Binet testing, the emphasis was on recording a child's IQ and a listing of the subtests or items that were passed and failed and their year levels. Psychologists also began to determine whether the IQ was representative or optimal and gave reasons for making such judgments based upon the cooperativeness and motivation of the child or upon such detracting factors as poor hearing or faulty vision. These "results" were regarded as directly useful for understanding the child in a school situation.

There appeared to be some slippage of rationale when psychologists became IQ testers in mental hospitals, since there was little correlation between a patient's IQ and the treatment prescribed for him or her. The same may be said of the psychologist's diagnoses and dynamics, the latter probably following a Freudian orientation. (This writer's early reports "out-Freuded" Freud, and the reader would be in line for laughs as well as instruction if any could be located.) Many fine dynamic reports were produced to no particular purpose, however. "They all get shock anyway" was the cynical but accurate observation.

Dynamics, an understanding of the motivations of the individual, became increasingly important (in the opinion of many) as psychotherapies multiplied and psychotherapy became widely practiced. However, the decision on whether to test depended, and still does, on the orientation of the therapist. There is similar disagreement on the matter of diagnosis. We are among those who insist that diagnosis often does make a difference. It makes a difference to know if a child's school deportment is related to a brain dysfunction or to something else. It makes a difference to know whether a person is suffering from schizophrenia or whether others are suffering because of his or her histrionic personality. Misdiagnosed people are likely to receive faulty treatment. Diagnosis in the broad sense of making descriptive statements about a person routinely enters decisions made about him or her. Most psychological reports today consist largely of such descriptive statements.

In recent years psychological reports increasingly reflect a rationale. Many reports now are sharply focused and highly prescriptive. What is the problem, and what can we do about it? In this tradition the behavior-oriented report is strictly a no-nonsense, businesslike approach. Psychopathologically oriented reports increasingly reflect the fact that certain classes of medication target certain behavior symptoms.

It is because the need for a guiding rationale for psychological reports is widely recognized that psychological reports now are seen in protean form, and properly so. Their content and organization obviously reflect the orientation of the writer and the use to which the report will be put. Thus a behavioral report would be quite beside the point for a psychoanalyst, and an analytically oriented report would probably not be acceptable to a humanistic therapist. Early Binet and psychoanalytically oriented reports were about the individual—what is "inside" the person, so to speak. Current reports may heavily emphasize social and cultural factors in a person's life, and personal circumstances.

Reports also vary in the degree to which they are "traditional"—that is, built on early school and mental hospital models that stressed matters of the intellect or dynamics and pathology. The case-focused report may be regarded as a refinement of the traditional report based on explicit rationale. Behavioral reports generally differ from the traditional report according to the specific understanding of the therapeutic approach. Humanistically oriented reports may also depart from tradition for different but equally valid reasons. Because narrative, case-focused reports are highly flexible, they can accommodate both behavioral and humanistic orientations.

In general the psychological report may be defined as a document written as a means of understanding certain features about a person and current life circumstances in order to make decisions and to intervene positively in a problem situation. Commonly the reports are prepared by a psychologist for others, such as a teacher, a psychiatrist, or a court, but a psychologist—a behavior therapist, for example—might prepare a report for personal use in outlining a treatment approach. Subsequently, for the same client, the psychologist may record changes in the person and in the treatment approach in progress notes.

Originally the psychological report was a vehicle to transmit test findings. In many current reports information gained from testing is minimal or absent. Originally the psychological report took the form of a narrative. Now reports may consist of a terse listing of problems and proposed solutions. Computer-derived reports may consist of sequential statements or a profile of characteristics. Checklists of statements or adjectives are a form of report. Clinical notes are reports. The oral relating of impressions also constitutes a report. A physician may ask a psychologist who has just completed two hours of testing, "Do you think he can make it?", to which the psychologist may respond with a nod, a horizontal shake of the head, or a gesture of uncertainty. Such is also a report.[2]

Of increasing importance is the *feedback* of test-derived interpretations to clients. This may take the format of a written narrative report (pp. 210–216) or of an exchange of test responses and interpretations in a psychological assessor-client interaction. Or it may consist of an interaction in which psychologist and client jointly arrive at interpretations of the client's test productions (for example, Fischer, 1970, 1972; Allen, 1981; Dorr, 1981). Such approaches involve many of the principles of psychological report writing as discussed in this book. For example, ethical responsibilities are uppermost in the psychologist's mind, and he or she is selective of the content that is offered to the client and uses only concepts and language that the client can grasp. In Chapter 8, then, we find it helpful to regard such feedback as in the nature of psychological reporting, and suggest that the technique not be used by those who have not mastered psychological report-writing skills.

---

[2]The expression "psychological report *writing*" is retained in a generic sense. Most still appear in that form.

Custom-written narrative reports probably continue as the most-used form. Most typically they are written by a psychologist for others.

THE TEAM APPROACH:
FROM "TEAM" OF ONE TO TEAM OF N

Team is a loosely structured concept that ordinarily refers to the multiple input and interaction of two or more persons who share responsibility in dealing with clinical-type problems. There is no immutable definition of what personnel constitute a team, their roles, specific functions and interrelationships, or the power structure of the group. Teams may appear to have a central core composed of key, highly active, influential workers, plus a more peripheral membership, some of whom become involved in specific cases and absent themselves from others. A diagnostician/therapist may carry out the functions of a team.

A psychologist serving as a team member is commonly expected to play a key role through contributing a report, observations, and other inputs. She or he may be "teamed up"—permanently or on an ad hoc basis—with teachers or with a counselor, a lawyer, a probation officer, a psychiatrist, or a pediatrician. In a mental health clinic the core team may consist of a psychiatrist, a clinical psychologist, a social worker, and perhaps one or more nurses. In a psychiatric hospital the team is likely to be rather extended, consisting of a psychiatrist, a clinical psychologist, a psychiatric social worker, one or more nurses, one or more nursing assistants or mental health technicians, and various counselors and therapists. This by no means exhausts the list. A parent or a spouse may be asked to participate, and the patient may also be regarded as a team member actively participating with staff in deliberating on remediation and plans for the future.

In schools the responsibility for identifying children in need of special education and entering them into special education programs is vested in a specially designated team or committee. Such teams are given various labels in different jurisdictions; some names currently in use include: Placement Committee; Admission, Review, and Discharge Committee (ARD); Core Evaluation Team; Case Conference Team; Staffing Team; Guidance Team; Pupil Personnel Service Team; and Student Study Team.

Various persons, both within and outside the school system, may serve on the team, and the team's composition can vary, depending on the nature of the problem under consideration. In preparing the basic evaluations leading to an education plan for each child, the child's teacher is responsible for the educational assessment, the school psychologist or counselor for the psychological assessment, the social worker for the home assessment, and the physician for the medical assessment (the physician is sometimes represented by a registered nurse who transmits and interprets the medical assessment, if necessary). The school principal may become involved early in the evaluation process (depending on such factors as the size of the school), determining what preassessments should be made. Preassessments might include systematic classroom observation, reading evaluation, or special diagnostic evaluation by the social worker or school counselor.

The child's teacher delivers key input based on academic performance, classroom behavior, or other pertinent information, such as information gained from parent-teacher conferences. Other staff members, such as a speech therapist or a reading specialist providing services to the child, also contribute pertinent information. The parent is asked to join the team as a key member. The Student Study Team leader may coordinate the efforts (if time and duties permit) and make necessary referrals to specialists.

Specialists function in the capacity of consultants. They may include various medical personnel such as a psychiatrist, an orthopedist, an ophthalmologist, a neurologist, or a gastroenterologist. Again, the nurse may transmit and interpret the findings and recommendations of medical specialists. A neuropsychologist may supplement the team's efforts through evaluation of a child's brain function. A behavior therapist may be asked to evaluate a child's potential to profit from one or more of the techniques in behavior therapy's array of treatments.

Special education team members, then, bring to bear on a child's educational difficulties a wide range of backgrounds and orientations, from layperson to specialist. All have the task of making themselves understood and understanding the input of others. (Tallent, 1980)

One of the most unusual teams coming to the author's attention is known as the *Forensic Psychiatry Clinic.* Based at the University of Virginia, its staff includes three psychiatrists, a psychologist, two members of the law faculty, a psychiatric social worker, researchers, and students. With a total input of about 20 to 30 hours per case, citizens involved in both civil and criminal law actions are evaluated. The team is available to courts and lawyers in Virginia and neighboring states.

Another team format, a psychodiagnostic/therapeutic team, has been developed by the author in collaboration with nursing colleagues (Tallent, Kennedy, Szafir, & Grolimund, 1974). Situated in a psychiatric setting, the essence is to involve in the diagnostic process the nurses and the nursing assistants who are in daily therapeutic interaction with patients. Conceived as an expanded role for nurses, in accordance with evolving nursing concepts, all test administration and initial interviewing are carried out by nurses and assistants trained in these functions. This accomplished, the psychologist meets with the nursing staff, the test protocols and other inputs are collaboratively evaluated, and tentative conclusions are reached. The patient is next interviewed by the team. Then, in further discussion, conclusions are reached on the nature of the patient's problems, indicated treatment, and plans for the future. These are immediately incorporated in the nursing care plan and are orally transmitted to the psychiatrist and discussed before the report is written.

The roles that the various team members play, the power structure of the team, the interpersonal dynamics of the team members, and personality features of the psychologist and the nursing staff, all help to determine the quality of the psychological report and how effectively it and other of the psychologist's inputs will be used. Teams that function in psychiatric settings are particularly instructive in these regards.

Such teams have traditionally been headed by a psychiatrist member—the captain of the team, as this clinician has sometimes been called. Traditionally medicine has had an authoritative role, particularly with nonmedical associates—so-called ancillary persons. The former practice of a well-known and respected setting is illustrative. Here a rigid seating arrangement was enforced at staff meetings. The senior physician occupied the chair at the head of the conference table, with physicians of lesser rank arranged in order, toward the far end. Next were seated the various ancillary personnel, by profession (from the highest on "down") and by rank within profession; the individuals at the far end of the table could thus entertain few illusions about their status.

Such hierarchical team structure is now largely in disrepute. A more democratic arrangement is widely endorsed and operates to a greater or lesser degree in many settings. It is sometimes referred to as a *wagon wheel,* because all members occupy a comparable position, and none is more distant from the hub of power than any other. In reality the dominance, other personality features, or qualifications of the persons involved come into play, and regardless of discipline, some are closer to the power center than others. Only in the sense of the lip service to the democratic ideal do all have equality. If the truth be known, a psychologist, a social worker, or a nurse in a medical setting may wield more power than does the physician in reaching some sort of group consensus on the nature of the problem and the treatment indicated. A determined physician sometimes falls back on the legal aspects of responsibility for making a "medical" diagnosis and prescribing treatment.

ROLE OF THE PSYCHOLOGIST

The role of the psychologist has evolved considerably since the emergence of the "testing movement," the high-water mark of the 1920s. At that time the psychologist, identified with an oversold IQ, was commonly known as a *mental tester.* Even when projective techniques had well overshadowed psychometrics in many settings, Schafer (1954), writing from a psychodynamic perspective, persisted in referring to the psychologist as the *tester,* a term also retained by Rosenwald (1963) and Appelbaum (1970), both psychodynamically oriented psychologists.

The proper role for today's psychologist, when functioning as a professional who provides information to others, is that of consultant, as explicated by Towbin (1960), formulated by Matarazzo (1965), and endorsed by Holt (1967). This is in sharp contrast to the role of tester, who is on a par with a laboratory technician—a fact that takes on immense social importance in the computer age (Matarazzo, 1986). This matter is approached in Chapter 7 in terms of the responsibility of the clinician when computer testing is used as an evaluative procedure.

The laboratory technician functions in a limited, circumscribed role for which the formal and practical preparation is much less lengthy and rigorous than that required for full professional functioning at the Ph.D., Psy.D., Ed.D., or M.D. level, for example. The training of the technician is always in accordance with the principles and the needs of a professional group, and the parent group, through various direct and indirect means, influences the training program: The students are trained explicitly to serve the group. The technician is asked to make a particular determination; the procedure will be the same regardless of the purpose. The technician does not interpret findings, make a judgment on which findings are relevant and which are not, or make recommendations. The technician is not sought out by the person who made the referral to discuss possible implications of findings or the need for additional tests or subsequent retests. It is sufficient that the technician gives results along with some indication of their reliability. The report of a psychological technician may contain such material as an IQ, various other requested scores, ratios, profiles, psychographs, or whatever raw responses might be requested by a supervisor.

The consultant, by contrast, is a product of advanced scientific and professional education designed to prepare an individual for high-level, responsible functioning. The consultant must have a grasp of both broad and specific knowledge and the ability to reach decisions that may be of major importance. Such training is under the sponsorship and the direction of the discipline of the consultant, who claims a unique role. Thus, the psychologist is thoroughly familiar with concepts of human personality, carries out psychological techniques with expertise, and works from a background of relevant research orientation. He or she must be familiar with the nature and the background of the problem at hand and the alternative decisions that might be influenced by the psychological report. On this basis the consultant must then decide on what kind(s) of data to seek, which findings have relevance, and how these can be most effectively presented.

The distinction between professional, or consultant, and technician is sometimes unclear to the psychologist's associates. One reason is that some perceive the psychologist as a "tester." Testing, in turn, may be understood as a mechanical procedure that yields totally objective "results." The emphasis, more properly, should be on interpretation. Tests can't think, as Schafer (1954) points out. In problems involving disorders of personality, or of personality functioning, we do not have instruments that can be routinely administered and interpreted by subprofessionally trained personnel.

In the clinical-type situation both the objectivity and the validity of our tools have meaning as they relate to specific problems and to the confidence the psychologist is able to place in the relevant conclusions that can be drawn from them. Published indexes of validity obtained through the use of particular research designs are but rough guides, for the psychologist must make judgments of clinical validity and meaningfulness in each particular case. Many tests, particularly tests of personality, are subjected to interpretive procedures that yield information not available from standard usage of the instrument. Both knowledge and clinical acumen enter all phases of the assessment process and, inevitably, some psychologists tend to be more effective than others in their clinical judgments (see Thorne, 1960, 1961). How does one assess validity of a test in an actual assessment situation, since assessment is not accomplished by tests alone, but by psychologist-test data–interview data (test data typically referring to the information deriving from administration of a battery)? The input of other team members must also be taken into account. It is a meaningless abstraction in the individual case to speak of the validity of (for example) the Rorschach, the TAT, or the Affective Adjective Check List. Evaluation more reasonably involves the basic assessment units of "Rorschach-Psychologist A," "TAT-Psychologist B," "SOMPA-Psychologist C," "Neuropsychological Questionnaire, Luria-Nebraska-Psychologist D," and more typically, such units as "Rorschach, TAT, AACL, Interview, Staff Input-Psychologist E."

PERSONAL AND INTERPERSONAL DYNAMICS OF THE STAFF

Schafer (1954) discusses at length the dynamics of the psychologist and how these bear on relationships both with the person who is being assessed and with the psychologist's colleagues. He lists no fewer than eight "types" of psychologists, types in the sense of salient personality failings. He discusses, for example, the psychologist with a defective self-concept, the rigidly intellectualistic psychologist, the psychologist with unresolved dependency needs, the masochist, and the sadist. All these failings influence the sort of report produced.

The sadist, for example, is a "chief inquisitor" who concentrates on the shortcomings and weaknesses of the subject and whose report reads like an "exposé," or a "denunciation," what is called in this book "the prosecuting attorney brief." But overly critical approaches to carrying out assessment may also stem from personality assessment's roots in the study of abnormal behavior. Thus, overpathologizing, a long-prevalent fault in psychological assessment, has led Zubin (1972) to call upon mental health workers to mend their ways. This group has behaved, he observes, "like bookkeepers who had only red ink available. It is high time the assets of patients were counted as well as their liabilities!" This topic is discussed more fully on page 56.

Although the personality of the psychologist has frequently been emphasized as a factor in his or her ability to function as a therapist, in our preoccupation with tests and our zeal to establish their validity too little has been written on the psychologist's personality as a significant factor in assessment. One of the greater concerns with the psychologist's personality has been with the tendency of some examiners to confuse their own problems with their clients'.

Perhaps an even greater source of difficulty is the confusion of the self-needs of a psychologist, particularly role needs, with the needs of the task. It is readily acceptable that one's occupation be a factor in bringing about a sense of personal fulfillment. However, in dealing with people who have major problems, who perhaps find themselves in a life-crisis situation, the psychologist must avoid intruding personal adjustment problems. Typical are difficulties with the self-concept; this may become evident in role aspirations that are hardly compatible with the specialized, technical functions of psychology. The psychologist may step outside the role of professional psychology. Sometimes this sort of problem detracts from effective contribution because the psychologist encroaches on the prerogatives of others rather than gathering the sort of information the team needs.

There are various other problems that seem to detract from the psychologist's function. These include attempts to seek insight through clients and thus effect self-therapy, to see oneself as superior to another (the client or the report reader), and to take advantage of the opportunity presented for catharsis, voyeurism, exhibitionism, and hostile expression. Sometimes the problem may be an ineptitude for psychological diagnostic work; sometimes the difficulty is one of lack of personal integrity. These latter deficiencies could go hand in hand, since the psychologist who cannot produce what is required may try to conceal inabilities as an assessor. One often-effective maneuver is to slant the report in a manner designed to please the individual who has referred the case. Klopfer (1960) refers to such a document as the "Madison Avenue Report."

Any of these personality difficulties may find its way into, and be readily identified in, the psychological report. Often the report reflects self-conflict. Sometimes there is an expression of interpersonal or interprofessional conflict, with the report itself serving as a battleground. Both offensive and defensive maneuvers will be evident, the aggressiveness being called up by defensive needs. Thus, the report that is exhibitionistic and authoritative in tone, displaying apparent knowledge of words and theory, may be a way of saying, "I am as good as you, even better." (It has also been suggested that words and theory may be used to hide ignorance.) But defensiveness in other respects may be even more obvious. The excessively detailed omnibus personality description ("shotgun report") is an example, as is the heavily hedged report.

Needless to say, the mission is best advanced when team members are comfortable with themselves and with one another. There should be mutual respect and compatibility (obviously only a goal in many settings), and each member of the team should have a good understanding of the function of the others. Even under favorable conditions, the psychologist needs to interact with colleagues in a persuasive manner. The psychologist is often able to make highly confident statements that are at variance with the impressions of other team members who operate without the benefit of psychological tools. Because of this the psychologist has a selling job to do in the interest of the client. Appelbaum (1970) suggests that a psychologist must also be a sociologist, a politician, a diplomat, a group dynamicist, a salesperson, and, if you please, an artist. Sales ability, Appelbaum advises, ". . . may denote high pressure, 'activity,' hucksterism; and, indeed, there may be clinical situations that do require some of this. Usually, however, the test report is more akin to institutional advertising, a low key presentation of evident factualness."

CONTINUITY, CHANGE, AND EVOLUTION IN THE PSYCHOLOGICAL REPORT

Today's psychological *Zeitgeist* is quite different from that of the early years of Binet and Wechsler testing. Many of our key instruments, however, have shown no particular evolution over the years. The newer Wechsler scales, for example, are built essentially as was the Wechsler-Bellevue of 1939, and the standard Rorschach cards are identical to those that Hermann Rorschach bequeathed to us in 1921. Our understanding and use of these instruments have undergone a veritable revolution, however. The Rorschach *experiment,* for example, is now conceived as the *Rorschach systems* (Exner, 1969), systems that have traveled far from Rorschach's own modest estimate of the worth of his blots. The most obvious addition to the current assessment scene is the vast interest in, and proliferation of, behavioral and cognitive approaches. Also widespread is the adaptation of older instruments to computer interpretation and the development of new instruments specially designed for computer analysis. The uses of assessment and how the psychologist's mission may be conceptualized have also undergone vast change. It should be instructive to note Wechsler's (1944) view of the first duty of a psychologist in a psychiatric hospital: ". . . to define, as an expert, the patient's intellectual level and to indicate whether the I.Q. obtained represents the true or merely the present level of functioning."

In just one 11-year period, Dollin and Reznikoff (1966) noted a decline in interest in formal diagnostic labels. In 1956 some 64 percent of the referrals received requested that a diagnosis be made, whereas in 1966 only 29 percent of the referrals asked for a label. In another study of referral questions, Korner (1962) found that over an eight-year period requests to clarify diagnosis dropped by some 60 percent, while questions pertaining to ego functioning and defenses increased by 50 percent and requests to assess organic deficit quadrupled. Studying the topics discussed in psychological reports, Korner noted many changes. Discussion of ego defects climbed from 30 to 72 percent, evidently in response to the changes in referral questions just noted. Discussion of diagnosis dropped by a factor of five and anxiety by a factor of two. Talk of aggression dropped from 42 percent to 18 percent, and discussion of sexuality fell from 48 percent to 12 percent. Since we may assume that eight years could not possibly make much difference in how aggressive or sexual people are, we might conclude that the interests of the psychologists who wrote the reports had changed. In 1950 clinical psychology was a rather new profession with a preponderance of youthful practitioners. Perhaps, as practitioners mature, they become more mellow and less voyeuristic. However, an alternative explanation might emphasize change in both the general and the psychological culture. Freudian concepts, in many settings, have yielded to other interests. Sex has lost much of its glamour, and aggression is all too prominent in our awareness.

In this context of flux there remain a number of persistent, nagging problems, among them the questions of validity and of the utility of psychological assessment. The latter pops up occasionally in the literature and continually in some settings where such assessment is carried out. The issue is not only the utility of psychological reports for traditional psychotherapists but also their utility for some of the newer therapies, particularly the behavior therapies and the humanistic therapies. These questions are addressed in Chapter 8.

Modern economics being what they are, the cost of preparing a psychological report—from the initial handshake to the last period of the report—is an increasingly important, if underdiscussed, problem. As a specific example, we may read with nostalgia Odom's (1950) paper on the time required to do a Rorschach examination and be transported back to that halcyon era when a psychologist's time was not worth very much, a fact confirmed by his or her income. Odom concludes: "The consensus is that the average test requires a little more than four hours, but that the total time required will sometimes be less than two hours, and at other times over eight hours." Even a leading practitioner like Beck spent, at that time, ". . . on the average, from three and one half hours at the minimum to about nine hours at the maximum in completing a Rorschach test." As an exercise, let's translate that into today's costs. And remember that, typically, the Rorschach is only part of a battery. We could just price ourselves out of the market.

USEFULNESS OF PSYCHOLOGICAL REPORTS
IN MAKING CLINICAL DECISIONS

Psychological assessment is predicated on the thesis that the reports of such assessments are useful working documents. There is a dearth of studies on this important topic, however, and the limited evidence available is contradictory and can be interpreted in various ways. Note the varied conclusions that derive from the following representative studies on utility.

Dailey (1953) reported that psychological reports contributed to clinical decisions in 26 percent of the cases referred for psychological evaluation. Cole and Magnussen (1966) state: "Traditional diagnostic procedures are only loosely related, if at all, to disposition and treatment." Breger (1968), examining psychological testing in clinical settings "in terms of its history and underlying assumptions," concludes: "Serious questions are raised about the clinical usefulness, logic and validity of practice." He refers here to the notion that diagnosis is a valid prerequisite to treatment and to psychology's emphasis on assessment and selection. Hartlage, Freeman, Horine, and Walton (1968) found that a sample of psychological reports ". . . was evidently of little value in contributing toward any treatment decisions for the patient." However, these studies also concur that this state of affairs is remediable, and make suggestions accordingly.

Studies by Dana, Hannifin, Lancaster, Lore, and Nelson (1963), Affleck and Strider (1971), and Hartlage and Merck (1971) reach quite encouraging conclusions. Studying routine psychological diagnosis and treatment planning in a juvenile probation department, Dana et al. report as follows: "Predictions of prognosis were made from psychological reports with 80.5% accuracy. When recommendations contained in these reports were followed, 82.5% accuracy of predictions was obtained."

The Affleck-Strider study also revealed high utility of psychological reports. The authors observe: "About two-thirds of the requested items of information were seen as either providing new and significant information or as providing information which confirmed information previously suspected, but which was not well-established." Further, ". . . it was found that 52% of the reports altered management in some manner, 24% had a minimal effect or confirmed current thinking, 22% had no effect, and 2% were felt to have an erroneous or detrimental effect."

The study by Hartlage and Merck is particularly instructive. It is not, these authors find, a basic lack of interpretive skills that detracts from the utility of reports. It is nothing more profound than a lack of reflection by report writers on what might be useful to report readers, a simple failure to use common sense. They note, ". . . reports can be made more relevant to their prospective users merely by having the psychologists familiarize themselves with the uses to which their reports are to be applied." And, "It appears that merely having the psychologists who write reports to consider the value to users of some of the statements that they commonly make in their reports can have a significant salutary effect on the value of these reports." Also, ". . . psychologists learn to test and write reports in an academic setting and that in the absence of any external stimulation they tend to persevere in a somewhat theoretical, non-decision-oriented approach to handling test data." Accordingly, they advise that psychologists need ". . . to evaluate their own reports in terms of what these reports contribute to the operation of their unique settings rather than to continue to grind out reports with good theoretical consistency but little decisional value." We agree. Case-focused reports are tailored to the setting as well as to the personal requirements of a case.

With the exception of the studies by Dana et al. and Hartlage and Merck, all these studies were either done in or had reference to a psychiatric setting. One way to evaluate their significance, then, is to compare their findings against what little data are available on the utility of other diagnostic procedures in such settings. These are entirely impressionistic; the practical utility of such inputs as the anamnesis recorded by the psychiatrist, the mental status examination, the social history, and nursing notes has not been systematically studied and established. But even if only 26 percent of psychological reports make a difference in patient management and disposition, we might regard the psychological report as a very effective instrument indeed. Most of the diagnostic procedures done in psychiatric hospitals, although expensive, have in most cases little bearing on treating the mental or emotional problem for which the patient was admitted to the hospital.

DeNelsky and Boat (1986) suggest that reliance on diagnoses based on the prevailing medical model is a limiting factor in the application of psychological assessment to practical problems, such as in therapy. Official psychiatric thinking is consistent with their position.

> Making a DSM-III diagnosis represents an initial step in comprehensive evaluation of a treatment plan. Additional information about the individual being evaluated beyond that required to make a DSM-III diagnosis will invariably be necessary. (American Psychiatric Association, 1980, p. 11)

The usefulness of psychological reports may be determined by how well they fulfill their mission in the context of the frame of reference in which they are produced. DeNelsky and Boat propose a Coping Skills Model (CSM) as more comprehensive and functional than the medical approach for psychological diagnosis and treatment. The CSM is based on the concept of adaptability and is applicable to the assessment of interpersonal relationships, thinking and feeling, and approaches to self and life. These three general areas are further divided for assessment purposes into 11 coping skills categories, thus defining with some precision the areas of function where intervention is needed.

2
Pitfalls
in Reporting

Psychological assessment, the results of which are formulated and conveyed in the psychological report, is widely accepted and sought as a contribution to the case study. In the opinion of many, however, psychological evaluation frequently could be of more value were the psychological report made a more effective practical document. There are many ways in which the report can fall short of its potentialities. Although these pitfalls are a hardy breed, most can be corrected. A first step in the right direction is to examine the criticisms commonly made of reports. We must, however, recognize that some of the problems in report writing stem from limitations in the field of behavioral science itself, and from shortcomings in our knowledge of how to apply it to practical issues.

With a positive purpose, this chapter discusses the negative aspects that are extant in many psychological reports. The concentration of negative comments that follows shortly is an artifact of presentation, and the reader should not reach a pessimistic conclusion about psychological reports, which are widely regarded as doing a needed and valuable job. Rather, the purpose is to highlight those difficulties, often unrecognized, that many psychologists incorporate in their reports and that might be eliminated.

The categorized problems in psychological reporting presented in this chapter are based on returns from a large-scale survey of clinical workers in interdisciplinary settings that resulted in an unusually high rate of response— 97.7 percent of psychologists, 81.2 percent of psychiatrists, and 97.2 percent of social workers, a rate achieved with the help of two follow-up mailings (Tallent & Reiss, 1959a,b,c; 1960), and a number of other pertinent studies that followed. Of slightly more than 1,400 workers who returned the Tallent-Reiss form, over 700 also completed an appended "optional" sentence (or paragraph) root, "The trouble with psychological reports is . . . ."

The product of this invitation to tell what is wrong is now in the author's files—118 single-spaced pages of pitfalls, which, to be sure, contain numerous instances of overlap. Interestingly, even this slanted sentence completion item, designed to draw negative comments, resulted in a number of favorable, even laudatory, observations from nonpsychologists. Mingling with critical, occasionally caustic, remarks are statements like "No trouble at all. They are useful and helpful," "I like 'em," "I find the psychological reports written at this hospital excellent," and "The trouble with psychological reports is . . . there are not enough of them." More neutral are comments that better approximate the author's outlook in that they recognize values, shortcomings, and greater potentialities: "A lot of work to be done, but still valuable," and "I appreciate whatever help they give and would allow their improvement to stem largely from the psychologist's own efforts." Perhaps the most favorable observation to be made is that, of those who contributed their time and thought to completing a lengthy form, almost half did not see fit to complete the sentence root that "pulled" for negative comments.

The primary purpose in trying to find out what writers and users of psychological reports think is wrong with such reports is to develop a rationale for practice. The gathering of such opinions is an example of searching for a rationale by means of the "popularity" approach (Tallent, 1956). This method has certain shortcomings. A compendium of opinions should not lead automatically to conclusions, and certainly not to a systematic approach to practical issues. Reflection on the overall problem of report writing and additional pertinent research are required. The major asset of the popularity approach is that numerous insights may be obtained by "talking" with hundreds of workers through a survey form. Yet, just as in talking face-to-face, the person seeking the benefits of the experience and observations of others must weigh and measure the information received and act accordingly. In the present instance it is well not to be seduced by the expressions of praise for psychological reports, however well deserved. Several respondents who made favorable comments indicated that they had the good fortune to be associated with excellent psychologists. In other instances there was a suggestion that the respondents were not sufficiently versed in the methods of psychology; they assumed that psychologists know their work and are beyond criticism by members of other disciplines.

The hundreds of negative comments received are particularly interesting. They are a sample of impressions gained by practicing professionals who have had experience in variously constituted psychodiagnostic/treatment settings, and need to be seriously considered. Although much of the criticism may appear valid to many psychologists, some of it obviously stems from disparity in training and orientation among members of the team; solutions to the difficulties noted would appear to lie in the direction of greater interdisciplinary contact and understanding. It is also interesting that some of the comments are mutually contradictory; what are regarded as superior report-writing practices by some workers are seen as wretched by others. The solicited comments give much food for thought, and the reader of them must be the judge. Thus, the author disagrees with some of the criticisms as suggesting practices contrary to the effectiveness of the mission. Indeed, whereas in our sample an appreciable number of workers, mostly psychiatrists, criticized the offering of diagnoses, prognoses, and recommendations, Siskind's (1967a) group of psychiatrists questioned whether such practice should be criticized. The justification for accepting, rejecting, or modifying any sincerely made criticism is to be sought in the implication it has for fulfilling the psychologist's mission, which itself is an evolving function.

A second purpose in studying what others have identified as shortcomings of psychological reports is to gain a better understanding of the image the psychologist presents to associates. Indeed, as we would expect, some of the comments made about psychological reports better reflect concepts that are held of psychologists. Such remarks bear on the entire group of psychologists working in clinical-type settings and on the psychologist's role, attitudes, theories, and procedures, as well as on individual skills. They thus afford awareness of certain value judgments made about both psychology and psychologists by their associates.

A number of respondents suggest or imply as a base issue the individual psychologist's personality or a conflict of personalities among staff persons: "The trouble with psychological reports is . . . psychologists," "The trouble with psychological reports is . . . they try hard to be an M.D.," and "The trouble with psychological reports is . . . many are influenced by psychiatrists' diagnoses and comments." In practice, relations between psychologists and team associates range from those characterized by cordiality, mutual respect, and interdependence, to those characterized by hostility. A paper by Moore, Boblitt, and Wildman (1968) cites examples of the latter, more offensive (and amusing) than any received in the Tallent-Reiss survey. The authors report the following two examples: "[Psychologists] lack training in the basic sciences of medicine and Freudian psychology," and "Psychology is to psychiatry as astrology is to astronomy." (!) Many other illustrations suggesting personality shortcomings of psychologists will be found under various headings of criticism that follow later in this chapter.

A comment offered by a number of workers made no reference to the quality of reports as such, but pointed out that they often arrive too late to be of maximum use (Mussman, 1964; Smyth & Reznikoff, 1971). This complaint should be borne in mind as the rationale of psychological reporting is studied. Might better practices allow the psychologist to deliver more punctual, and thus more practical, reports?

THE PERSISTENCE
OF PITFALLS

The discussion starting on page 27 is a compilation of pitfalls the report writer should be wary of. (We believe the listing is rather complete but hope that our readers will inform us of any we have overlooked.) Although training may tend to reduce the incidence of errors in report writing, in general, available research suggests that errors are a hardy breed. Each generation of psychologists must be taught anew. Both human traits and the nature of language itself tend to perpetuate errors. Only by conscientious effort at avoiding them can they be reduced. Other pitfalls will tend to continue, minimized only by diligent concern with certain problem areas, until research provides better solutions.

Thus Lacey and Ross (1964), in a poll of workers in child guidance clinics, turned up a number of the same complaints noted in the Tallent and Reiss (1959c) study, although the percentages varied. Olive (1972) compared psychoanalysts' opinions of psychological reports in two different years, 1952 and 1970. Her general conclusion was that there is a disenchantment with the psychologist both as a tester and as a writer of reports. In both 1952 and 1970, the analysts' criticisms included "lack of clarity," "vagueness," "excessive use of jargon," "theoretical bias," "unreliability," and "overgeneralized." The 1970 survey revealed, additionally, "bias to pathology" and "overlooking the patient's potential for change" (which is dealt with in the next chapter as the "prosecuting attorney brief" [Tallent, 1958]), "too pat," and "too intellectualized." Rosen (1973), in a delightful contribution entitled "Alice in Rorschachland," also points out psychologists' concern with pathology to the neglect of health factors. He further takes issue with those psychologists who "restructure reality along Rorschach dimensions of personality and terminology."

In a similar vein are the conclusions of Holzberg, Allessi, and Wexler (1951), Garfield, Heine, and Leventhal (1954), Cuadra and Albaugh (1956), and Smyth and Reznikoff (1971). Though differing in point of focus, a common denominator reported by these investigators is the frequent occurrence of shortcomings in reports. All these articles may currently be read with profit. Similarly Foster's (1951) succinct half-page of counsel to report writers is as pertinent today as when written. Just as teachers of rhetoric through the generations have been making the same corrections on their students' papers, so too has this writer noticed that students today tend to make the same errors as did students 20 years ago.

The persistence of pitfalls is well established in the faulty use of language. In a classical study Grayson and Tolman (1950) studied the definitions of clinical psychologists and psychiatrists for words that commonly appear in psychological reports. The first 20 words on the list were

Abstract	Bizarre	Defense	Father Figure
Affective	Bright Normal	Dependent	Hostility
Aggression	Compulsive	Depressive	Identification
Ambivalence	Constriction	Ego	Immaturity
Anxiety	Control	Emotional	Impulsive

The authors conclude that "the most striking finding of this study is the looseness and ambiguity of the definition of many of these terms." In a replication of this study 15 years later, Siskind (1967b) found that there was no decrease in the ambiguity of the same 20 terms. A stury by Auger (1974) in which clinical personnel matched behavior descriptors with psychologists' definitions suggested that "either the behavior descriptors lacked specificity, the definitions were ineffective, or both."

Such problems are also noted in the practice of school psychology. Rucker (1967) and Shively and Smith (1969) reported poor agreement on the meaning of terms that are commonly used in reports. In Shively and Smith's study, teachers, counselors, and students, using a four-item multiple-choice format, were asked to select the best definition for terms such as *aphasia, borderline intelligence, cortical involvement, neurological impairment,* and *perseverate.* Counselors tended to disagree significantly with both students and teachers, more than a third of the latter group failing to understand a number of terms that are presumably related to learning problems. Rucker's sample of teachers similarly showed poor agreement between school psychologists and teachers when they sought to define educational terms that appear in psychological reports.

Report stereotypy (pp. 51–56) continues to be a potent danger. This topic is discussed at length in Chapter 3. The psychologist needs to be vigilant in guarding against stereotyped material entering the report, and the psychologist's colleagues should be wary of accepting it.

That many psychological reports are written so as not to be very useful, so as not to contribute to decision making, is a complaint that just won't go away. Dailey (1953), Cole and Magnussen (1966), Breger (1968), and Hartlage, Freeman, Horine, and Walton (1968) all conclude that many reports exhibit this deficiency and suggest solutions that are considered in the following three chapters.

Ziskin (1981), in a heavily documented work addressed to lawyer colleagues, seeks to spread an awareness of all the preceding shortcomings to those in the legal profession who have occasion to cope with psychiatric and psychological testimony. Being at a disadvantage in contributing to the legal process is only one of the problems that saddle psychologists who ignore the perils of allowing pitfalls to find their way into reports. For psychologists in forensic settings, many of the pitfalls discussed in the following sections might just as well be called *downfalls.* This problem is discussed in Chapter 9.

But the ultimate problem is the limitations of science and profession, aptly put by Holtzman (1964) in the title of his paper, "Recurring Dilemmas in Personality Assessment." His major points are (1) that personality assessment is hampered by lack of a clear, adequate, and consensual definition of personality; (2) that there is no agreement on what are the units and combinations of units needed to understand a person; (3) that personality variance and method variance are not readily separable; (4) that personality and personality assessment are overly culture-bound; and (5) that there are built-in moral dilemmas arising out of the individual's right to privacy and the investigative probing needed to understand the client's personality. The psychologist's awareness of such shortcomings might make for a more cautious approach to assessment.

Ziskin is particularly attuned to problems of science and profession, especially those having to do with such mundane issues as validity and reliability of tests, diagnoses and predictions, standardization, and practical usefulness.

PITFALLS BY CATEGORY

The solicited comments on "The trouble with psychological reports . . ." are classified under five major headings and numerous subheadings. The first four pertain specifically to the performance of the individual psychologist. Problems of science and profession (Category V) have to do with issues that psychology and the other human science disciplines must identify and cope with. The matter of role conduct is particularly commented upon by psychiatrists, a reflection of a situation that can negatively affect treatment in some settings.

Problems of Content (Category I)

The psychological assessor seeks to convey a body of information or content that will contribute to a mission. It is important, then, that we examine how report content frequently falls short of being what is needed to carry out that mission.

Raw data   Whether or not the psychologist ought to include raw data in reports, or whether current reports contain too much or too little raw data, is an issue of major importance. To a large degree opinions on this matter are distributed along professional lines, the psychologists tending to be critical that there is overinclusion of such content, the psychiatrists being concerned that reports offer too little raw data, and the social workers being divided on the matter but perhaps siding somewhat with the psychiatrists. How one views this issue is an individual matter, and there is widespread disagreement on whether the liberal quoting of clients' responses is a major asset or a distinct liability. From a plethora of comments, just a few are needed to capture three basic points of view. First consider these two opposing statements, reflecting as they do differing role concepts. They were written by a psychologist and a psychiatrist, respectively.

> They are too often descriptive rather than interpretive, leaving this job to the reader when really the psychologist is in the best position to interpret results.
> They do not contain enough selected raw material to permit the psychiatrist to draw his own conclusions.

A social worker pleads a lack of qualification to deal with data that are not meaningfully interpreted.

> Reference to specific psychological material in reports has little meaning to nonpsychologists.

And similarly, from another social worker:

> When reference is made to test cards, formulas, etc., the reader is often not familiar enough with the tests to understand what significance they have.

Improper emphasis   Many workers, especially psychologists, criticize that reports are written with improper emphasis. The implications of such a shortcoming might be far reaching. It would seem to suggest, for example, that the report is not geared to the specific purpose(s) for which it is needed, a criticism mentioned many times and examined at greater length under another heading of this chapter ("Not practical or useful"). Improper emphasis may also suggest a faulty or an incomplete knowledge of personality or behavior, and of clinical operations—for example, what sort of finding is likely to prove clinically rewarding and what sort is not. The occurrence of such errors might indicate a deficiency of clinical judgment. Some psychologists evidently do not discriminate among findings. The following comments show how report readers are likely to evaluate reports with regard to the appropriateness of emphasis.

> They seem to emphasize the personality state of an individual whereas I think more emphasis should be placed on the functioning of an individual in terms of what that person is doing to and with other people. If the patient is to be seen in psychotherapy, the psychological report should include some predictions about how he will probably act toward the therapist, how he will see the therapist, some goals for the therapist, and how the therapist might try to accomplish these goals and why he might do it in the way suggested. If the psychologist knows something about the limitations of the therapist who is to see the patient, then he should take these into consideration before he includes some of the goals of treatment.
>
> The report of dynamics and structure of the personality is very good. There should be more attention to the strength of defenses or pattern of adaptation, i.e., how well will a reaction formation stand up under stress, for example.
>
> Tendency to emphasize the unconscious to the neglect of the conscious goals and values.
>
> Not enough emphasis is given to conscious, practical controls.

And an impassioned protest:

> Too much pressure on sex. I know, I know, it is important, but, for heaven's sake, the world does not spin around the axis of . . . genitals.

Diagnoses, prognoses, recommendations   Offering a diagnosis, a prognosis, or a recommendation in a psychological report seems to raise numerous objections, almost all of them from psychiatrists. In a sense this reaction is surprising, since many of this group actively seek such information from psychologists (Tallent & Reiss, 1959a,b), but as already pointed out, preferences in psychological reports are an individual matter. The dissenting group evidently sees the offering of such content as an encroachment upon its role, although quite often this meaning was not spelled out. A few quotes are more than sufficient to clarify this position.

> In my opinion, the recommendation as to plan of treatment, chemotherapy, etc., is not appreciated.
>   They try to diagnose.
>   Recommendations should be excluded from psychological reports. It would seem more appropriate a function of a staff decision where other data can be considered.

Omission of essential information   Some readers and writers of psychological reports feel that reports omit essential information; that is, they evidently fall short of what is required for an effective psychological contribution. It is not certain whether this criticism is based chiefly on the supposition that a fixed body of content ought to be conveyed in reports, or whether reports tend not to have information necessary to specific cases. The following representative quotes, however, indicate what is meant as far as the individual respondents are concerned.

> They do not present specific and essential data which would be helpful to a team conference or individual attempting to formulate a plan of treatment and working diagnosis.
>   They usually do not give any practical recommendations.
>   Seldom do they make recommendations regarding treatment goals, nor do they specify areas of strength.

In view of the content of the previous section, the reader is probably wondering if it is possible to write a report to please everybody.

Minor relevance   The problem of data selection seems to have arisen in any number of contexts. Some of the content of psychological reports is criticized as being not necessarily inappropriate, but of minor relevance. The flavor of such comments is captured by these statements.

> Our prejudices often lead us to make statements which are of little import to the recipient.
>   They include data that I believe are not an essential part of the report, such as clinical description of the patient, social and medical data. This may be nec-

essary to the examiner conducting the tests in evaluating the responses of the patient, but I do not believe this should be included as a routine procedure.

Unnecessary duplication   The final criticism pertaining specifically to content, one made by a minority of workers, is that in some reports the same content tends to be repeated unnecessarily. There can be no dispute that where duplication occurs without good reason, such as to provide needed emphasis, its appearance is not defensible. Poor rhetoric can hardly be good psychology.

Problems of Interpretation (Category II)

Irresponsible interpretation   The psychological report frequently reveals weaknesses in various aspects of the assessment process. One of the more common of these evidently occurs before the psychologist begins to write the report. The phenomenon is that of eisegesis, a term long used to denote misinterpretation of scripture, and now apropos to indicate faulty interpretation of psychological data based on personal ideas, bias, and whatnot. Dana (1966) urges that eisegesis be trained out of student psychologists and suggests a way of doing so.

Several meaningful patterns of criticism of data interpretation emerged in the analysis of negative comments made about reports. So many different kinds of alleged interpretive errors were pointed out that they are best summarized as "assorted irresponsible interpretations." Of the workers who made any sort of negative comments on psychological reports, no less than 41 percent of the psychiatrists, 27 percent of the psychologists, and 22 percent of the social workers made criticisms placed in this category. An examination of some of the criticism is informative.

> Clearly written to please the psychiatrist for whom it is being written, often interpreting data to fit his known pet theories and thus rendered unscientific.
>
> Tending to find more or less schizophrenia in every case.
>
> They sometimes seem to reflect the psychologist's feelings about the patient rather than the data revealed by the patient's responses to the tests.
>
> They draw conclusions from insufficient data, lack objectivity.
>
> They are frequently too arbitrary, expressing theory as fact.
>
> They are not sufficiently related to the tests they presumably are derived from.
>
> The referral question is frequently vague, and psychologists frequently hate to admit it when the tests don't give much information, and so overinterpret what they have.
>
> Too much "Barnum effect" (see pp. 51–55).
>
> Too much . . . (unquotable) . . . invalid statements, overgeneralizations, stereotypy and evidence of lack of reflection and integration of the material into a meaningful picture of the patient as a person.
>
> Just as the TAT reflects one's feelings, attitudes, desires, conflicts, etc., so do our psychological reports; We project ourselves. If we are integrated then so are our reports; if not—then?
>
> We read in the reports the examiner's own conflicts. These are usually dis-

cernible after seeing a few reports in which certain phrases and ideas repeatedly occur.

Sometimes there is more of the psychologist than the patient in the test reports.

People who write them frequently feel they have to say something about all areas of the client's life, even those about which they have little or no information.

Occasionally they paint a darker picture than is true, possibly because not enough emphasis is given to conscious, practical controls.

Sometimes sweeping pronouncements are made, and I doubt that the best tests can support such big conclusions.

Overspeculation   A specific type of irresponsible interpretation frequently mentioned is overspeculation. From reading the criticisms, it is difficult to know what all of the speculating is about, or why psychologists feel impelled to do so much speculating. There is the definite opinion among report readers that many psychological reports are characterized by too much speculation, that this practice often irritates readers, and that in some instances it reduces respect for the psychologist's contribution. Just a few illustrations suffice.

. . . speculative assertions beyond the realm of the testing results.
Too theoretical and speculative.
Too much speculation, reading between the lines, personal interpretation rather than reporting facts as observed.

Unlabeled speculation   Many report readers are not particularly disturbed by speculation, provided that such interpretations are properly labeled. There do not seem to be group differences among the members of the team in this regard.

Facts, inferences, speculations are often mixed and not labeled.
The distinctions between reasonable deductions from the data, speculative extrapolations from the data, and the psychologist's clinical impressions are not clear.
If some indications were given for the bases for speculation and if clearly labeled as speculation.
Many speculate and do not so indicate until questioned.
Data is frequently overinterpreted. One can speculate but should label it as such.

Inadequate differentiation   Another apparently frequent problem of interpretation is that psychological reports sometimes deal in generalities. It is charged that such reports do not differentiate among those who are assessed. Psychologists seem to be roughly three times more cognizant of this difficulty than are their psychiatric and social worker associates.

Too little individuality of descriptions.
All too often they don't present a comprehensive, logical picture of a unique individual.

Very frequently they are made up of too many stock phrases which do not give any real feeling for the individual client.

They frequently involve too many generalizations about human behavior and fail to describe the specific person who is involved.

They tend to present generalizations that might apply to anyone rather than to the particular individual.

Typically, they present a rather stereotyped picture into which any number of patients—or other people—might fit, rather than describing the individual.

They report in broad generalizations that, although they sound quite profound, really would apply to nearly any patient.

Too often the generalizations are so great that one could visualize the same report having been made on the preceding dozen persons seen at staff. Reaching for psychoanalytic concepts too often is the reason (and I am psychoanalytically oriented).

They tend to rely on vague, psychoanalytically-oriented phrases which fail to convey an individualized picture of the client. Their vocabulary is excellent but what is lacking is a feeling for the client's individuality as a troubled human being.

Problems of Psychologist's Attitude and Orientation (Category III)

A number of difficulties in the writing of psychological reports were singled out as more or less direct reflections of the psychologist's attitude and orientation. That is, many of the criticisms seemed more meaningful in terms of the ultimate improvement of reports when emphasis is related to certain personal features of the psychologist than to the end product.

Not practical or useful   The most frequent criticism made of the psychologist's attitude or orientation is that the report is not written with a practical or useful purpose in mind. Psychologists identify the existence of such a deficiency far more frequently than do social workers and psychiatrists. The following examples reflect some of the more cogent observations regarding this difficulty.

Our prejudices often lead us to make statements which are of little import to the recipient and to ignore or deal lightly with the objective reason for the referral.

Their lack of function and value to the person.

Often lack of comprehensibility in terms of a real-life treatment program.

They are often written without a clear idea of the practical "users" or "consumers" on the receiving end.

In my view we need to write more in the spirit of an operational approach.

Many writers forget the purpose(s) of their reports and wander all over the psychic range, even when they are asked for a relatively clear-cut opinion.

They're too sophisticated, too impractical for the people who rely upon the information they dispense.

They are not pertinent to the purpose desired.

They seem at times very professional but useless in terms of the personality of the patient.

They are too often written to satisfy the interest of the psychologist rather than for the clinical application and understanding.

Exhibitionism   That psychological reports are sometimes seen as exhibitionistic calls up a good deal of comment, especially from psychologists. A number of such comments refer to high-flown terminology in psychological reports but do not mention exhibitionism as such. Those so disposed, however, should find it easy to interpret this prominent dynamic in a number of psychologists via the following remarks. In fact, gratuitous interpretations are already built into some of them.

They are written in stilted psychological terms to boost the ego of the psychologist.

They are attempts on the part of the examiner to show what he or she can do rather than what the patient is.

Reports delight in including details of findings which are obviously comprehensible only to one who has made a study of psychological testing or is versed in the finer significance of statistical research expressions. Such reports occasionally produce the feeling that words of less than four to six syllables and sentences with less than two thoughts will convince the reader that the writer is too simple.

It is not necessary to impress the reader with the psychologist's mentality.

Their reports reflect their needs to shine as a psychoanalytic beacon in revealing the dark, deep secrets they have observed.

Reports should be concise and clear without an attempt to impress the reader with the erudition of the person who performed the test.

Too authoritative   Reports that convey an authoritative stamp may have a motivation similar to those regarded as exhibitionistic. Their effect on the reader, however, seems to be different. Reports that pontificate tend to irritate the reader even more than those that are merely regarded as show-offy, perhaps because an authoritative report is likely to be perceived as an affront, whereas the defensive motive of the exhibitionistic report is more transparent. Psychiatrists evidently take more offense at, or at least are more aware of, overly authoritative reports than are other workers.

They are too positive, confident, assured, as though they were the last word, irrefutable, authoritative.

Many reports are much too opinionated and obviously reflect the author's own biased viewpoints.

Some are too dogmatic.

They often are too definite in their interpretations and assume to have all the answers.

The psychologist feels too superior and will generally write a short summary of his interpretation forgetting that a psychiatrist reading the report might differ in interpretation. This feeling of superiority on the part of the psychologist has alienated many intelligent psychiatrists.

A lack of humility. I never cease to be amazed by the confidence some psychologists have in their tests and in their own abilities to interpret them. To accept such reports the psychiatrist would have to lose what little intelligence he or she is supposed to have [a psychiatrist's comment].

I have seen some reports which affected me adversely because of a tendency to sound pompous with the implication "This is the final word!" rather than "This is an opinion which is intended to be helpful in understanding the whole" (and) to be all-inclusive to the point of excluding the specific contributions of other disciplines—a sort of "I can do everything approach" which sometimes results in the clouding of the most important observations. A second, though no less important result, is the impairment or even destruction of the team function.

Test orientation versus client orientation   It is perhaps surprising that psychologists complain more frequently than do other team members that clinical reports are too test-oriented rather than client-oriented. It may be that since a number of workers from the other professional groups wish the inclusion of raw data, they do not find talk of tests offensive.

They usually talk about tests and test results rather than the client's personality.
Talking about the tests too much and the patient too little.
They often describe responses rather than people.
They are test centered too often rather than containing statements about behavior in the nontest environment.
Often the writers feel it necessary to include scoring and other quantitative detail at the expense of providing a useful and helpful picture of the person evaluated.
Psychological reports should reflect the judgment of the psychologist with all the limitations of maturity and experience. The psychologist should proceed as though he knows something about human behavior and tests are aids in his understanding. He should not act as though he is lost without his tests. I think other disciplines want us to give opinions which are free to open discussion and exchange.

Too theoretical   Sometimes criticisms indicate or imply that reports are not useful or client-oriented because they are too theoretical.

In general, they are too theoretical.
They concern vague hypothetic properties of people.
They often are too theoretical or academic in language to be comprehensible or meaningful in terms of future treatment goals for the client. They occasionally give us the feeling that no client was present at the time.
At times one has the feeling he is reading a biological dissertation on protoplasm rather than about a flesh and blood person.
Sometimes I come across psychological reports which are loaded with textbook phrases, but giving very little clear picture of the particular individual involved.
We sometimes get bogged down in vague, theoretical terminology which has little direct relation to the actual behavioral dilemmas confronting the individual. Also, we employ theoretical concepts reflective of basic psychological processes (e.g., oral sadistic orientation) which are so general and so removed from the level of behavior that we write more like textbook theoreticians than as psy-

chologists confronted with the task of making some sense out of a client's behavior.

Overabstract   Similar to the criticism that some psychological reports are too theoretical, and also that they are not practical or useful, is the complaint that they are overabstract. Criticisms that reports are too theoretical and overabstract frequently occur in the same statement.

At times they become too difficult and abstract.
They are sometimes too theoretical and/or abstract; and on the other hand, too concrete—as reports of exact performance on tests as such. Ideally, there should be a happy medium.
They are too often lofty abstractions or concrete banalities. In either case, they fail to offer a meaningful, readily grasped, exposition of the subject's psychological condition.
The more abstract and/or intellectual the report is, the more likely the examiner is either defensive or projecting his own conflicts into the report.
Some are unnecessarily involved, technical and abstruse so as to be virtually useless in planning disposition of the subject.

Fischer (1985) offers a workable solution with respect to this problem.

Saying what one means, both in speech and in writing, requires one to anchor abstractions in concrete examples. Ask yourself how you would explain what you mean to a 12-year-old. If you can't figure out how to do that, then you do not yet know what you mean—what your technical formulations come down to in terms of your client's life.

Miscellaneous deficiencies of attitude and orientation   There are a number of aspects of the psychologist's attitude and orientation we term "miscellaneous." Included are criticisms calling reports too intellectual, too academic, and too pedantic, comments which no doubt overlap those just quoted. Such features may stem from the transplantation of an earlier generation of psychologists from an academic to a clinical setting. At any rate the academic influence is noted by a number of observers who seem to feel it detracts from the practical utility of reports.

They are too studiously intellectual.
Too pedantic—obscure to other professions.
Usually too involved, pedantic.
In many instances psychological reports have the tendency to be too academic.
They are often esoteric to the practice of psychological testing.
Esoteric reference to statistical mechanisms.

A reluctance on the part of some psychologists to take on the consultant role, or to prepare psychological reports, is suggested by some clinicians as an explanation for blameworthy reports. In individual instances this shortcoming could stem from a lack of confidence in or confusion about psychological methods.

> Psychologists feel it is almost below their dignity to do them.
> [The trouble is] that you've got to write them.
> Psychologists appear to have lost confidence and/or interest in testing.
> I have a strong personal dislike for writing psychological reports, in spite of my recognition of their usefulness. Perhaps part of my feeling is due to the excessive length and detail of reports which are seldom read by anyone else, anyway. To me it is the most distasteful part of my job.

Problems of Communication (Category IV)

Many of those concerned with psychological reports oversimplify the matter in terms of communication. The negative comments already made about psychological reports demonstrate clearly enough that report writing cannot be divorced from purpose or context or from the basic technical competence of the psychologist. The communication aspect is but one of the vital problems to be singled out for study.

Hundreds of workers had one or more negative comments to make about faulty communication. More respondents were concerned with this kind of difficulty than with any other aspect of psychological writing or consultation. Accordingly there is a tendency toward overlap among the subcategories.

Word usage   The worst offender, according to our sample, is what is classified here as "Word Usage"—really a variety of offenses against the King's English. Thirty-seven percent of psychiatrists, 45 percent of psychologists, and 65 percent of social workers making negative comments on psychological reports had something to say on this matter. Deficiencies of terminology and wordiness were mentioned with great frequency. Some may be surprised to learn that psychoanalytic terminology is singled out as an offender with great frequency.

> A good report writer uses the language of the novelist, not the scientist unless he's writing for another psychologist. Analytic language is a language of generalities and thus loses the uniqueness we should be striving for.
> Often padded with meaningless multisyllable words to lengthen report.
> Gobbledygook [this expressive term was used by numerous respondents].
> Too much jargon [also a *very* frequently used term of criticism].
> I don't like reports which contain jargon which I can't understand.
> They do not take advantage of simplicity and ordinary words.
> Semantics have a tendency to creep in, and the phenomenon of "verbal diarrhea" occurs too often.
> The appearance of stereotyped phrases.
> They are too often written in a horrible psychologese—so that clients "manifest overt aggressive hostility in an impulsive manner"—when, in fact, they punch you on the nose.

Too much emphasis is placed on psychological phraseology and such when we could say the same thing quickly, efficiently, and simply.

They are not frequently enough written in lay language. I believe it requires clear thinking to write without use of technical terms.

What about describing the person's behavior in terms that one ordinarily uses in describing a person rather than a client?

Their value depends on whether the psychologist talks English or a special language of his own.

Vague, unclear, ambiguous   Many clinical workers are critical that psychological reports are vague, unclear, or ambiguous. No doubt a good deal of this difficulty stems from expressive deficiencies, although there are apparently other ways of writing reports that cannot be understood. How this occurs is a matter about which many respondents are not clear.

They sometimes are vague and unsubstantial.

They tend to rely on vague, psychoanalytically oriented phrases.

New words or new meanings to familiar words are used, leaving the reader confused as to what is meant.

Excessive wordiness which clouds the findings.

Perhaps some are a little "veiled" in meaning, so as to attempt to prove the psychologist is truly a professional.

Oftentimes the psychologist has to be interpreted.

They contain too many ill-phrased, hard-to-understand sentences.

Often lack of comprehensibility in terms of real life treatment programs.

They are intellectual vagaries.

They are not clear enough to be wrong.

Statements are made which could have more than one meaning, or are difficult to understand.

They suffer mainly from vagueness, double-talk and universality without enough of an attempt being made to specify more precisely what sets this person off from other people (and what does not).

Scores have little meaning even to the psychologist who understands their rationale, unless he also knows how they fit together in terms of cause and effect regarding behavior. To cover up his ignorance he resorts to the reporting of percentages, ratios, etc., and overwhelms his reader with such technical language that little information is conveyed.

Length of reports   The length of psychological reports comes in for a good deal of criticism. The consensus is that they are too long, but some feel they are too short. The latter scourge does not yet seem to be pandemic.

They are too lengthy—should be concise and to the point.

Many are too long. This usually teaches the reader to look for a summary and ignore the rest.

Too often the completed report is too long. Often I might go to the summary to get the gist of the examination.

Most of them are too long. Few people, if any, will take the time to read them.

Psychological reports should present specific data and specific interpretation. Too many contain omnibus recommendations and universal statements which apply to most people. I'd rather see brief reports with relatively little said than lengthy stereotyped reports which also say little.

A good report should stop when it has run out of useful data.

And one unhappy psychologist is concerned with length for what appear to be good reasons, and therefore would prefer to lessen the burden.

They are:
Over-imaginative,
Over-academic,
Over-syllabic,
And not over soon enough!

Too technical, too complex   A further plea for simplicity and straightforwardness is registered in comments that psychological reports are too technical and too complex.

The more simply the material is presented, the more useful it is.

I have made "Flesch counts" of quite a large number of reports and the level of difficulty tends to be much too high. Psychological reports should not be as difficult to read as our professional papers, but often they are. Many reports of this type are actually meaningless—a kind of polysyllabic illiteracy.

Too technical or too esoteric.

Technical terminology, particularly Freudian or statistical language, where these do not serve as highly specific communications, which implies writing a report for another psychologist or analyst.

I think that it is important that the person write in such a way as to communicate to those who will read the report. In some cases this will require that he write in a much simpler and more descriptive manner.

Documentation makes reports too technical.

It appears that the psychologist prepares the report for one of his own group rather than the benefit of other members of the team.

Style   Although style is generally regarded to be a rather individual matter, a number of workers believe there are certain necessary style requirements for effective communication. Psychologists are evidently more concerned with this matter than are members of other groups.

The reports tend to sound very much alike—to represent a personal "style."

Style is a matter of choice, but since we are supposed to be literate people, we should have certain standards of excellence to meet—too often this is not the case.

Too concerned with literary style.

The art of report writing should be akin to caricature.

They become too "flowery."

They all sound too much alike, as though the writers are adhering to a standardized model instead of allowing the form of their reports to be determined by the individual subject and the circumstances.

Too many reports follow a stylized form without due consideration to the real needs of the patient for which psychological testing had been requested.

Too often they seem to satisfy the writer's literary, "expressive" needs rather than communicate adequate description.

They give one more the impression of poetry than of scientific writing.

Under the guise of "capturing the flavor of the patient," appropriate scientific writing is sacrificed for style.

Organization   Psychologists are evidently more prone to the belief that psychological reports are not well organized than are other members of the team.

Often they are not coherently organized in terms of a personality or psychoanalytic theory and hence become meaningless jumbles of bits of data and information.

Frequently they are not organized—thought out—before they are dictated.

Too often they are so poorly organized that the reader has a difficult time to get a clear psychological picture of the client.

The analysis is in fragmented form rather than being integrated.

Write-ups frequently are not really organized, but formulations are "faked" in a sense by the use of syntax and grammatical construction.

They are often not organized around a central pattern characteristic of a person. Each paragraph seems a separate, discrete, unrelated part which could be clipped out and inserted in any other report.

When several tests have been administered, many psychologists cannot integrate the findings without giving separate results for each test.

Hedging   The final elicited problem of communication is that of hedging. A number of workers feel the psychologist should commit himself or herself at one level or another, and not straddle the fence.

Some writers refuse to take a chance and say anything definite. They beat about the bush, include every possible descriptive or diagnostic phrase.

Psychologists seem too often to "play it safe" and include so much in their reports (or so little) that they can never be wrong, refuse to make specific predictions, and therefore can never really be right either.

They too often are riddled with qualifications—"it appears that," "it may well be," "the test reports indicate." This is fine when speculation is being introduced, but many reports merely convey the inadequacy and timidity of the writer.

We seem to be afraid to commit ourselves in a few words; using too many qualifying statements and thus avoiding ever being wrong, but never actually predicting anything at all.

Can't they be more confident in their findings, i.e., when it might appear from testing that the patient may be homicidal or suicidal and may act this out, to say so clearly? It's better to know before than later—or too late.

Often no definite conclusions are reached and the reader of the report is left as bewildered as he was prior to requesting psychological examination.

Problems of Science and Profession (Category V)

Problems of science   In the Tallent-Reiss survey it was primarily psychologists who made observations to the effect that the trouble with psychological reports is not entirely the fault of individuals. Rather, many respondents saw the need for basic advances in areas such as psychological theory and the validity and applicability of tests. This latter problem is of great moment to many of the psychologist's team associates.

> *There is too little research on effective report writing. This would make an excellent thesis topic.* (emphasis supplied)
>
> I suggest that a "sociologist from Mars" would find the test reporting behavior of psychologists quite as "weird" as any of the rituals and customs and beliefs of many so-called primitive societies.
>
> There is lack of agreement, even among members of a small staff, as to how they should be written. Clinical psychology doesn't have an adequate basis, either in theory or tools, for writing simple, straightforward, meaningful reports.
>
> Most people, including psychologists, don't know what they are for or how to use them once they are written.
>
> It has never been convincingly shown that the type of information contained in a psychological report contributes information which can improve the validity of decisions beyond that possible on the basis of interview impressions and a good case history. The trouble does not lie so much with psychological reports as with the material we have to report.
>
> Primarily that their utility is unknown and untested. Few encouraging reports of prediction studies have been noted lately. Assuming validity and reliability (mighty big assumptions) psychologists are still in doubt as to the purpose of their own diagnostic efforts—particularly in a team setting.
>
> Their usefulness is limited by the validity of the inferences based upon test performance. Formulations of test findings in terms of some general conception of personality processes appropriate to the issues raised in the referral are always preferable in my mind to showing description of test responses and behavior in the test situation. Such formulations must, however, be explicitly tentative in the light of doubts one must entertain about the dependability of inferences drawn from test responses—especially in the area of projective techniques.
>
> Interpretation is too often based on theories which are yet poorly validated.
>
> Essentially the same trouble as is found with psychiatric and psychological theory and terminology in general. That is, theories and concepts are vague and of low reliability and validity. We have too many concepts, none of which can be regarded as demonstrably fundamental. Thus we write confused reports which depend on literary excellence more often than scientific knowledge.
>
> The greatest defect is inadequate and unsympathetic personality theory on which to hang our observations.

Consider some of the present realities of psychiatric diagnosis as suggestive of the scientific status that characterizes the study of mental disorders. Thus, DSM-III (American Psychiatric Association, 1980) and DSM-III-R (American Psychiatric Association, 1987), the eagerly anticipated advances of the 1980s for classifying mental disorders to the advantage of those who suffer with them (and for administrative and research uses as well), have long since become a matter of widespread public and professional controversy and criticism. With respect to the issue of objectivity, Faust and Miner (1986) argue convincingly that

> The methodological doctrine underlying DSM-III—strict empiricism—has not been achieved, and should not be pursued, at least in its extreme form.

And

> DSM-III's appearance of objectivity is largely illusory. Theory and inference have perhaps been reduced somewhat but eliminated nowhere—the document is replete with presuppositions and theoretical assumptions.

Problems of role conduct   An insight into psychological consultation, far broader in scope than the psychological report, is gleaned from an observation of comments classified as "Problems of Role Conduct." These relate to what is regarded as encroachment of psychology upon the functions or prerogatives of other professionals. It is the psychiatrists who feel most abused in this respect. An appreciable number of social workers also feel that the realm of the psychiatrist has been invaded by the psychologist, but some social workers see their own functions as assumed by the psychologist. Even more, a number of respondents are of the opinion that the psychological report encompasses the function of the entire team. None of the psychologists, however, indicated that there was psychological encroachment upon the duties of any of their associates.

> Too enterprising, perhaps too flavored with clinical feeling.
> Many psychologists tend to digress in other fields.
> They frequently do not mind their own business and go beyond their ken—invading territory properly allocated to the M.D.
> Some reports go to the extreme of becoming a clinical summary of the client, including social and personal history and mental status.
> They often contain medical and/or psychiatric diagnoses, prognosis, and at times, treatment.
> Some even suggest medical and other treatment.
> They often try to give purely medical advice to physicians.
> They make specific recommendations that an M.D. or a psychiatrist should do, and psychoanalytical insights of formulations that a psychoanalyst should do.
> There is a tendency to avoid the very purpose for which psychological testing exists. Namely, to present laboratory data codified in its original terminology so that the physician who has requested such testing for his own purpose of treating the patient may add to his clinical estimate of the patient. In my opinion, the recommendation as to plan of treatment, chemotherapy, etc. is not appreciated. Psychological testing and reporting is certainly a highly specialized and technical field which adds a great deal to the doctor's knowledge of the patient and should confine itself to this area.

They tend to make diagnoses rather than furnish specific data supporting a certain diagnosis. They are requested by the M.D. to help him make the diagnosis, prognosis, etc. The M.D. is not interested in what the psychologist thinks but why he thinks so. History and behavior are already available on the patient. The skilled psychiatrist knows how to interpret the data. If the psychologist feels his M.D. does not know what all this means, he should first give the data and follow it with a polite interpretation beginning such as "This data suggests . . . etc. . . . ."

Some psychologists seem to take offense and think it too menial to perform I.Q. tests. Their reports reflect their needs to take over the functions of a psychiatrist.

The psychologist tries to do everything else but an evaluation of intelligence, which is what he is best equipped to do. I personally feel that psychiatric diagnosis does not fall within the realm of the psychologist.

They try to make psychiatric formulations instead of assist.

The frequency with which the psychologist attempts to be a psychiatrist and does not use his legitimate observations from his testing materials to provide a picture of one or more samples of behavior. Most psychiatrists feel psychologists and their tests have value as such. Why don't psychologists feel this way?

They are too much concerned with matters unfamiliar to the psychologist and familiar to the psychiatrist. Thus the reports are too often replete with amateur psychiatric data, and deficient in psychological data, which had been requested and presumably are needed by the physician. On several occasions, I have been surprised, if not shocked, to see included in psychological reports "Patient should be helped by E.C.T."

On the other hand, one psychiatrist sees the "trouble" as quite the opposite from that expressed by some of the psychiatrists just quoted. This is definitely a minority opinion.

Too many psychologists are afraid they'll tread on M.D.'s toes. The properly trained psychologist will prepare better psychological reports as soon as he is liberated from the fear of overstepping certain unwisely defined professional bounds. Once liberated, he will have no need to fill space with social data. His reports will then reveal his full understanding of the patient based on observation, experience, plus the skillful interpretation of special tests.

When social workers make comments on the psychologist's role conduct, they are likely to be concerned with the same matters that trouble many psychiatrists. They feel, for example, that an invasion of social work territory, the taking of social histories, has occurred. One social worker, however, sees a problem of role dissatisfaction that affects a number of groups.

Our hospital has six psychologists and many student trainees. They have a wide range of duties and responsibilities but can't keep inside their own yard! Our staff has six social workers, one researcher, and an anthropologist.

The social workers all want to be psychologists.
The psychologists anthropologists.
The anthropologists social workers.
And only God knows what direction we are all going in.

A SUGGESTION
FOR AVOIDING PITFALLS

An awareness of the pitfalls discussed in this chapter will become most useful as the reader searches them out in their native habitat—actual psychological reports. Those reports in Chapter 6 that we suggest are not to be emulated provide examples of a number of the problems just discussed. The Quality Check of the Psychological Report provided in Appendix A can be useful to the reader in locating pitfalls in report writing as they occur in academic and practicum training and in the writing of reports in applied situations.

3

Responsibility and Effectiveness

The effectiveness of the psychological report may be enhanced by attention to a number of factors. With an eye to responding to practical needs, the psychologist is equally attuned to ethical considerations and legal constraints. He or she must provide an individualized report rather than one heavily saturated with some form of report stereotypy. Responsibility also demands that the psychologist focus on a number of workaday issues and carefully consider the use (or nonuse) of raw data, and decide on proper terminology and report length. If the report is to be an effective instrument, the psychologist must even take into account its cost and its timeliness.

Primum, non nocere—First, do no harm. Those words have been widely recognized as the sage admonition of Hippocrates to his medical students, and they are equally applicable to psychologists today. Typically psychological assessment occurs when intervention in another's life is taking place or is contemplated, an awesome responsibility. The psychological report thus may be a powerful instrument for good or ill. The points that the psychologist makes and how effectively they are communicated may influence such decisions as the sort of school or vocation an individual is to enter, the treatment that will be offered, or the client's living conditions. In the formative years of childhood, the school psychologist's understanding of a child, together with the ability to effectively convey that understanding, may contribute importantly to shaping the child's future. At times an individual's very life may be at stake. It is a matter of some moment, for example, when a psychologist is able to identify a client who appears to have suicidal propensities and is able to relate this impression unambiguously and convincingly to colleagues. The currently accelerating concern with social accountability reflects in part a recognition of the need for psychologists to deal competently with such matters.

Principle 1 of the *Ethical Principles of Psychologists* (American Psychological Association, 1981), Paragraph f, reads in part, "As practitioners, psychologists know that they have a heavy social responsibility because their recommendations and professional actions may alter the lives of others." Having reference to assessment, and specifically to the assessment of intelligence, Matarazzo (1981) recounts the contributions of Binet and Wechsler thus:

> . . . the fruit of their creative minds and the simplicity of the practical tools of measurement and assessment produced by Alfred Binet and David Wechsler would touch the lives and influence the careers of the majority of people who were born during the 20th century. Probably the work of no other psychologists, including Freud or Pavlov, has so *directly* impinged upon the lives of so many people.

In this chapter we deal with two rather basic issues: (1) the responsible development of data and (2) in an ethical, and perhaps also a legal, context, the presentation of these data using the principles of sound rhetoric. There is a logical relationship between knowing what one means and saying what one means, as Flesch (1972) reminds us in his book *Say What You Mean*. Knowing what one means must precede putting words on paper. In the course of recording what we mean, however, we also more fully develop the theme that we are setting forth, thus further clarifying for ourselves and for our readers what we do mean.

Style or rhetoric, then, contributes to (or detracts from) the psychological report. As a basic point, it is well to point out to the psychologist the words of Sydney Smith: *Everything which is written is meant either to please or to instruct. The second object is difficult to effect, without attending to the first.*

The psychologist who needs to improve writing skills, as many do, had better study the topic, perhaps from a good book on rhetoric. We are somewhat partial to Flesch's *Say What You Mean* and to his earlier work *The Art of Readable Writing* (1949/1974). What appeals most is the emphasis on simplicity, directness, and good common sense. Of particular interest in *The Art of Readable Writing* are scales for measuring the ease of reading and the level of interest of content.

Responsible interpretation, however, has many facets, the most basic being a well-trained, knowledgeable interpreter. The psychologist must understand the mission, his or her colleagues, the client, the client's circumstances, and available resources for dealing with the client's needs. The psychologist must have a good grasp on theory of personality and behavior but not be ruled by it, must know what *can* be interpreted and what *should* be interpreted, and must be able to present the client as an individual—with individual needs and goals—and not travel the easy road of stereotypy.

ETHICAL AND LEGAL
RESPONSIBILITIES

One might suppose that a definition of the assessment psychologist's responsibilities would be adequately covered by the ethical principles of scientific and professional associations and by the concern for ethics as enacted into law, and frequently this is so. However, Bersoff (1975) also points out that ". . . codes of ethics and the law may present competing demands" and that the onus for such incongruity lies with the ethical codes. He explains:

> 1. A basic reason for the failure of ethical codes to provide adequate bases for behavior is their ethnocentrism . . . codes represent the professional group's point of view and are rarely developed with help from the consumers who receive the professional's services. Psychologists may be living under the false presumption that their ethic is shared by the people they serve.
> 2. . . . ethical principles are formulated on such an abstract level that they merely provide general guides to actual behavior; practitioners rarely understand how those principles are to be applied in specific situations."
> 3. . . . the value of codes may be perceived solely as a means of providing practitioners with a symbol that they are truly professionals. . . .

Developing this position and pointing out some special vulnerabilities of school psychologists, Bersoff suggests that "it is apparent that psychology's codes are insufficient protections against increased scrutiny by the courts." And, ". . . while psychology may permit different interpretations of its ethical guidelines, the courts may not be so benevolent. They do not find it at all difficult to disregard a profession's claim to autonomy when the behavior of its practitioners is perceived to interfere with the rights of individuals or the public at large."

In formulating his thesis Bersoff quotes Principle II(c) of the ethical code of the National Association of School Psychologists (1974): (Regarding assessment) ". . . the emphasis is on the interpretation and organization rather than the simple passing along of test scores . . . ." To implement this abstract principle (in the sense of item 2 in the preceding list of ethical code shortcomings), much of the content of this book may be understood as offering practical explication and exemplification of the precept. Also following the theme of responsibility, Principle V(c) of the NASP code calls for getting the students' parents involved with their children's problems through ". . . frank and prompt reporting . . . of findings obtained in the evaluation of the student," an injunction that is paralleled in law (p. 49). *Effective* involvement requires that the parents understand the psychologist's conclusions.

In a related context there is a court ruling that requires that clinical records be written so that they are understandable and serviceable as guides to care providers (*Wyatt* v. *Aderholt,* 1974). In a suit brought in U.S. District

Court for the Middle District of Alabama pertaining to the constitutional guarantee of the right to treatment of persons civilly committed (not committed on a criminal charge) to state mental institutions, the court found that "evidence established that the hospitals failed to meet the conditions of individualized treatment programs." The evidence referred to was expert testimony that ". . . the patient records kept at the hospital were wholly inadequate; that they were written in such a way as to be *incomprehensible* to the aide level staff that had prime responsibility for patient care; and that they were kept where they were not accessible to the direct care staff particularly in need of them" (emphasis supplied). Clearly, both ethical and legal constraints are involved in the preparation and use of psychological reports; society is an interested consumer of our work.

In terms of the number of people affected—in excess of eight million at any given time—the Education for All Handicapped Children Act of 1975 (Public Law 94–142) sets a far-reaching precept for psychologists who are involved in the implementation of this act. For both educators and psychologists, the key term of this law is *individualized.* Calling for an *"individualized* education program" for each handicapped child, the psychologist's preparation of an *individualized,* case-focused report is most likely to be helpful in the preparation of an *individualized educational plan* to guide the course of instruction for each child. We submit that individualized, case-focused reports also are more effective than are reports written in general terms in contributing to effective (therefore ethical) psychotherapy and to management of clients (emphasis supplied).

Sharing Reports
with the Client and Other Persons

To share or not to share the psychological report with the client is a long-standing issue. Brodsky (1972) summarizes both sides thus:

> Traditionally the sharing of a client's files with the client himself has been only minimally considered, and when discussed at all, the practice has been seen as unethical, irresponsible, or at least questionable. Contrary to such traditional views, we suggest here that specific ways of sharing results with a client are a means for effective involvement and the assumption of appropriate professional responsibilities and roles.

The traditional position is well set forth by B. Klopfer and Kelley (1946) and by W. G. Klopfer (1954). The earlier formulation reads:

> It should be considered an unalterable role of professional conduct *never* to give a written Rorschach interpretation to the subject himself, since psychological terminology is so readily misinterpreted even by persons who should be familiar with it (emphasis supplied).

> [Also,] when the Rorschach expert deals directly with a subject without any professional intermediary, a completely new problem arises. No one should be permitted by his own professional conscience to give to another person as penetrating information about his personality as the Rorschach provides, unless he has specific psychotherapeutic training. Any person who violates this rule of professional conduct uses the Rorschach method in an irresponsible way.

In 1954 the topic continued to be approached with the greatest of caution.

> . . . if particular concern is expressed by the patient about test results it is best to give fairly superficial kinds of interpretation, which are apt to be consciously acceptable to the individual and not particularly anxiety provoking. In these cases it usually has been found that an emphasis on the intellectual aspects of the personality, thought contents, characteristic ways of reacting to stressful situations and the like can be discussed most easily. It should be kept in mind that some aspects of the Rorschach are apt to be of an unconscious nature, dealing with repressed material, and should not be brought out except in the context of intensive psychotherapy, and after the establishment of substantial rapport. It need hardly be stated that giving a written report to a patient is an extremely dangerous and harmful thing to do and may cause much grief, both to the patient and to the psychologist.

Proscription of sharing is a feature of a number of current approaches to reports, particularly of computer-generated reports that are widely available to professionals (Chapter 7). Here the concern stems from scientific caution and tentativeness as well as from concern with the welfare of clients. Thus Western Psychological Services prefaces the Personality Inventory for Children (PIC) report with the statement "This report consists of a series of hypotheses that may serve to guide further investigation." The WPS MMPI report is similarly introduced, with the additional suggestion that "this report is a professional consultation and should not be shared with the client." Reports printed by the Interpretive Scoring Systems Division of National Computer Systems supplies the following caveat with reports based on the Millon Clinical Multiaxial Inventory (MCMI): "Inferential and probabilistic, this report must be viewed as only one aspect of a thorough diagnostic study . . . it should not be shown to patients or their relatives."

However, some reports have long been addressed directly to the client. The Kuder Preference Schedule (1948), indeed, is designed to be scored and profiled by student clients, who are also furnished with instructions for interpreting the profile. The Strong-Campbell Interest Inventory (1984) similarly involves the client in the interpretation of his or her interest pattern. Behaviordyne makes available an MMPI report composed in the second person for personal study by the client.

Today reports written by psychologists about clients might well also be written *for* clients. Such a disposition was strongly represented in a 1971 APA symposium entitled "Shared Results and Open Files with the Client: Professional Irresponsibility or Effective Involvement?" A group of papers in the Fall 1972 issue of *Professional Psychology* (Brodsky, 1972) favors such an approach, as does the practice of many contemporary psychologists—for example, Craddick (1972, 1975) and Mosak and Gushurst (1972). Fischer (1970, 1972) involves the client as a coevaluator of data, as does Dorr (1981), who prepares both oral and written reports for clients (Chapter 8). Allen (1981) emphasizes the therapeutic aspect of psychological diagnosis and the need to "build a diagnostic alliance." In seeking this goal he invites the client to tell how testing might be helpful and what questions might be explored. Similar to the approach of Fischer and Dorr, Allen invites the client to participate in test interpretation. Richman (1967) and Aronow and Reznikoff (1971) also report the sharing of test data to be therapeutically advantageous.

Psychologists now widely accept that feedback to clients is both proper and useful. Berg (1985) believes this practice is justified because it rests on ethical and legal concerns that have "established the rights of patients to full disclosure" and also because providing feedback offers diagnostic advantage to the psychologist and additional therapeutic benefit to the client. The psychologist will be attuned to how well the client accepts feedback, on the basis of which he or she might add to, modify, or even discard earlier diagnostic impressions. Indeed, both psychologist and client might come to view matters differently. Berg comments specifically on how the client's response to feedback can provide diagnostic information in areas such as "the patient's capacity for self-reflection, synthetic functioning, anxiety tolerance, defensive flexibility, and the conditions under which he can accept help."

Wright (1981) proposes that clients be shown their reports, but for other than therapeutic reasons. He believes that when reports contain material that the client might view as unpleasant or as blocking an opportunity (for example, promotion, a chance for probation), the client, should he or she eventually become aware of the report content, might decide to initiate a malpractice suit. He believes that sharing findings and recommendations with the client can perhaps defuse a potentially dangerous situation. The client will not be faced with unwanted "surprises" sometime in the future and has an opportunity to digest the findings and work through reactions to them.

Regardless of the preceding opinions and practices, our actions are now governed by a number of laws that permit access to clinical reports: the Privacy Act of 1974, the "Buckley Amendment," various state laws, and PL 94–142. These laws mandate the terms under which clients and others with legitimate interests—for example, parents—may request to see records and the responsibilities of those who hold the information.

An inevitable question, then, is whether the disclosure of clinical material might be harmful to clients. "The federally appointed Privacy Protection Study Commission, after conducting extensive inquiries and holding hearings . . . has reported that 'not one witness was able to identify an instance where access to (one's own) records has had an untoward effect on a patient's condition.'" The commission further reported that ". . . clients' potential access to the files actually improved the quality of the notes, because . . . personnel were striving to enhance accuracy and exclude irrelevancies" (Plotkin, 1978).

In a study of psychiatric inpatients, Stein, Furedy, Simonton, and Neuffer (1979) report that patients who were given access to their records said that they were better informed and more involved in their treatment. Similar to what the Privacy Protection Study Commission found concerning record keeping, Stein et al. also note increased staff conscientiousness in this respect. Roth, Wolford, and Meisel (1980) permitted psychiatric patients to read their records in the presence of a staff member to explain the contents. Access to the complete record was not provided to all patients, however. Under such conditions of limited access, the authors report ". . . a generally positive experience for the patients, and harm has not ensued."

How clients subjectively experience having access to their records is probably at least as important an issue as whether they are permitted access. Smith (1978) advises that reports focus on the questions raised, and that simple language—as opposed to jargon and technical language—be used. But no matter how clearly the clinician writes, it appears to be a good idea that a professional be available to explain the report. Hammitt (1982) reports on 100 consecutive admissions to Madison State Hospital who were tested for word recognition and reading comprehension. Some 54 percent of the patients scored below the seventh-grade level, from which she concluded that large numbers of state hospital patients are "functionally illiterate." However, intelligent, well-educated persons may also experience problems in understanding when their own psyche is the topic.

Confidentiality

The sharing of information with clients may be a less troublesome issue than making records available to nonclinical personnel. The danger is that of breaching confidentiality. The psychologist must be aware that records may become involved in legal proceedings, even though they were not prepared for any such purpose. He or she obviously is in a difficult position when a court orders the disclosure of information that was received with the explicit understanding that it would be held confidential.

Therefore, the psychologist should be familiar with the law as it pertains to *privileged communication* of *psychological* records—the right of the client to bar personal information given to a professional person from being made available in a legal proceeding. (Psychiatric—that is, "medical"—records may be regarded differently by the law in various jurisdictions.) The mere awareness that such records might be subpoenaed should make the psychologist cautious.

The presence of the ubiquitous computer sounds a further note of caution. For example, information must be submitted to insurance companies as a condition of payment for psychological services. Such information routinely is stored in computers. Unfortunately, persons with no legitimate right to confidential information have been known to gain access to computer memory.

THE CLIENT IS AN INDIVIDUAL

In the diagnostic/treatment situation the psychologist's reason for being is to represent the client in the relevant terms of unique behavior, overt or covert. Perhaps the meaning of uniqueness as used here should be defined in terms of an orientation to human behavior. This is based largely on the idiographic approach, which stresses that each human being has a personality and behaviors that are different from those of all other persons; this individuality distinguishes relevant psychological features of one person from another as do fingerprints. Widespread traits, factors, clusters, constellations, complexes, types, pathological dispositions, and temperaments can be identified and ascribed to persons, but such descriptions must remain general and tend to omit much of what is important. Concern with these descriptions is only the first step in understanding an individual. The clinical approach, with its interest in the generally recognized human qualities, stresses that these are different in strength, in idiosyncrasies (which may be subtle but of the greatest importance), in terms of level and configuration, and in forms and occasions of expression.

In a previous publication the writer summarized some of the more common practices involved in general as opposed to individual clinical descriptions (Tallent, 1958). What is probably the most common of these is termed the *Aunt Fanny Description*. This designation seems appropriate because the report reader, on noting the characteristics ascribed to the client—what the client *has*—might well think, "So has my Aunt Fanny!" Thus, "The client has traits of immaturity," or ". . . he has dependency needs," or "has latent homosexual strivings." Such statements can hardly differentiate among people or point up what is unique—a person's specific needs, deficiencies, strengths, or stresses, or implications for the treatment of a troubled person. A study by Davenport (1952) lends support to this impression held by many psychologists. This is not to say that all statements in a report need be of differentiating value in and of themselves, for even the most objective statements take on additional meaning as they are appropriately modified and integrated with other findings. For example, you don't really know much about a person when told, "Her IQ is 115." This statement is true of millions of people (or at least would be if we tested many millions of people). The information is not sufficient to judge whether the person might make a superior teacher or regularly get lost between the bus stop and her house. However, when a statement about an individual's IQ is appropriately linked with other information—interests, attitudes, goals, defense mechanisms, formal thought processes, memory function—the contribution can become highly meaningful.

The following "psychological report" is a hoax. It was prepared by Dr. Norman Sundberg (1956) along with an accompanying explanation and is reproduced with permission. It was selected as a good example of the Aunt Fanny technique. Overlooking the fact that Fanny is a female appellation, this particular case report is, at least to a degree, applicable to many schizophrenic persons. Dr. Sundberg comments, "We had a lot of fun presenting it and discussing it at the Oregon Psychological Association meeting. It was quite impressive how it seemed to fit the case when it was actually presented."[1]

COMPLETELY BLIND ANALYSIS OF THE CASE
OF A SCHIZOPHRENIC VETERAN

—Norman D. Sundberg

(Written before knowing *anything* about the patient except that he was a new admission to the Roseburg VAH and was to be worked up for an OPA meeting.)

This veteran approached the testing situation with some reluctance. He was cooperative with the clinician, but was mildly evasive on some of the material. Both the tests and the past history suggest considerable inadequacy in interpersonal relations, particularly with members of his family. Although it is doubtful whether he has ever had very close relationships with anyone, the few apparently close relationships which he has had were tinged with a great deal of ambivalence. He has never been able to sink his roots very deeply. He is immature, egocentric and irritable, and often he mis-perceives the good intentions of the people around him. Projection is one of his prominent defense mechanisms. He tends to be basically passive and dependent, though there are occasional periods of resistance and rebellion against others. Although he shows some seclusiveness and autistic trends, he is in fair to good contact with reality. Vocationally, his adjustment has been very poor. Mostly he has drifted from one job to another. His interests are shallow and he tends to have poor motivation for his work. Also, he has had a hard time keeping his jobs because of difficulty in getting along with fellow employees. Though he has had some affairs, his sex life has been unsatisfactory to him. At present, he is mildly depressed, although a great deal of affect is not shown. What physical complaints he has appear mainly to have a functional origin. His intelligence is close to average, but he is functioning below his full capacity. In summary, this is a long-time inadequate or borderline adjustment pattern. Test results and case history, though they do not give a strong clear-cut diagnostic picture, suggest the diagnosis of schizophrenia, chronic undifferentiated type. Prognosis for response to treatment appears to be poor.

This completely blind analysis is based on the following assumptions:

1. The veteran being referred for psychological testing is not likely to be an obvious or clear-cut diagnostic case. There is no need for testing unless there is some indecision. Consequently, hedging is to be expected on a report anyway.

---

[1]Personal communication.

2. This is a schizophrenic case. Given the general class of schizophrenia, one can work back to some of the characteristics which belong in that class and have a fair chance of being right.

3. There are some modal characteristics of patients coming to VA hospitals. In placing bets on what the patient is likely to be like, the best guess would be a description of the modal personality. For instance most of the veterans coming to Roseburg are chronic cases who have not succeeded in jobs or in family life. Also, the best guess on intelligence would obviously be average intelligence, but since the person is a psychiatric patient it is likely that he is not functioning at his best.

4. There are also certain modal behaviors of the clinical staff. They use certain words, certain jargon; they have a preference for certain diagnoses. Oftentimes, a large percentage of the cases wind up with the diagnosis of schizophrenia, chronic undifferentiated type.

5. There are some "universally valid" adjectives which are appropriate for almost any psychiatric patients, such as "dependent," "immature," "irritable," and "egocentric."

6. In the less clear areas where modal characteristics are not known, it is more safe to write a vague statement or one which can be interpreted in various ways. Readers can be counted on to overlook a few vague misses and to select the descriptions which jibe with their own preconception.

7. All this is intended to say that we have much in common with the old fortune teller, and that what we need is better ways of dealing with individuality. Knowing modal personalities is very useful; it certainly adds to ease of social communication; however, we are sometimes fooled into thinking that we know persons when actually all we know is our own stereotypes.

A good definition for the Aunt Fanny description might note that " . . . descriptions from tests are made to fit the patient largely or wholly by virtue of their triviality; and in which any nontrivial, but perhaps erroneous, inferences are hidden in a context of assertions or denials which carry high confidence simply because of the population base rate, regardless of the test's validity." It is, however, Meehl's (1956) definition of the *Barnum Report*. We prefer the definition of the Barnum Report in the next paragraph. It is derived from D. G. Paterson's original Barnum Report (quoted on pp. 54–55), the essence of which is to give the "customer" a palatable report. The use of high base rate statements is but part of the technique. Paterson's Barnum Report also sought acceptance by the use of flattery, which is not a feature of Aunt Fanny statements. If there is a real distinction between Aunt Fanny and Barnum, it is important that such distinction be recognized for the implications it might have both for research and for teaching psychological report writing. We can also sometimes note a negative Barnum Effect, as, for example, when a psychiatrist or an administrator is "sold a bill of goods" to confirm a negative impression of an individual. Such a ploy might be an instance of Klopfer's (1960) *Madison Avenue Report* (p. 17).

The Barnum Report is viewed by the present writer (Tallent, 1958) as a method "to describe a personality by using a few mildly negative generalities which are quickly neutralized in a matrix of acceptable, even flattering remarks, both types of comments being apparently applicable to almost everybody." In short, a Barnum Report is readily "validated" by the subject about whom it supposedly is written. This was demonstrated to the writer's satisfaction when he passed out Professor Paterson's original Barnum Report to members of a college class, with the explanation that it was an individual personality analysis the instructor had arrived at through inspections of samples of the students' handwriting. The report was unanimously accepted as accurate by all 39 class members, with the exception of two students who indicated very slight error. The potency of the evaluation was punctuated by several of the more startled (or least inhibited) students making exclamations like "Uncanny!" and "This is me all right!"

This sort of "validation" has been studied under more exacting conditions by Forer (1949), Sundberg (1955), Carrier (1963), Ulrich, Stachnik, and Stainton (1963), Manning (1968), Richards and Merrens (1971), Snyder (1974), Snyder and Larson (1972), Bradley and Bradley (1977), Snyder, Shenkel, and Lowery (1977), Green (1977, 1978), Snyder, Handelsman, and Endelman (1978), Jackson (1978), Layne (1978, 1979), Petty and Brock (1979), Shenkel, Snyder, Batson, and Clark (1979), Snyder and Cowles (1979), and Layne and Ally (1980). However, it should be noted that all the Barnum literature to date reports on studies of the acceptability of high base rate statements to the persons who supposedly are described by such stereotyped material. Still needed are studies of the extent to which clinicians accept as valid such material when it is written about their clients.

Paterson originally used the Barnum Report as a lesson to business executives on irresponsible personnel evaluation practices. Passing out copies to groups of executives, he obtained excellent results by asking how many recognized themselves in "their" personality descriptions. (Professor Paterson's report is reprinted here by permission.)

Abilities: Above average in intelligence or mental alertness. Also above average in accuracy—rather painstaking at times. Deserves a reputation for neatness—dislikes turning out sloppy work. Has initiative; that is, ability to make suggestions and to get new ideas, open-mindedness.

Emotions: You have a tendency to worry at times but not to excess. You do get depressed at times but you couldn't be called moody because you are generally cheerful and rather optimistic. You have a good disposition although earlier in life you have had a struggle with yourself to control your impulses and temper.

Interests: You are strongly socially inclined, you like to meet people, especially to mix with those you know well. You appreciate art, painting and music, but you will never be a success as an artist or as a creator or composer of music. You like sports and athletic events but devote more of your attention to reading about them in the sporting page than in actual participation.

Ambitions: You are ambitious, and deserve credit for wanting to be well thought of by your family, business associates and friends. These ambitions come out most strongly in your tendency to indulge in daydreams, in building aircastles, but this does not mean that you fail to get into the game of life actively.

Vocational: You ought to continue to be successful so long as you stay in a social vocation. I mean if you keep at work bringing you in contact with people. Just what work you pick out isn't as important as the fact that it must be work bringing you in touch with people. On the negative side you would never have made a success at strictly theoretical work or in pure research work such as in physics or neurology.

The practice of writing personality statements that will be readily accepted by those for whom they supposedly are composed is an old one. M. Brewster Smith (1986) has turned up a "phrenological analysis," prepared by a distant relative, that bore the date of July 12, 1889. Familiar to modern clinical workers are such not-hard-to-take report statements as

> You are friendly but still guarded in making friends but what friends you do make you are very devoted to. You are very fond of pets and animals.
> Your constructive talent is very good and you have much inventive genius.

What may be called the *trade-marked* report (Tallent, 1958) has long been commented upon. This is a report that may overemphasize the psychologist's personal concerns, conflicts, interests, dynamics, or shortcomings at the expense of accurately describing the client. It is an example of eisegesis gone wild. Some psychologists are known in their organizations for always including and loud-pedaling a specific theme—hostility, heterosexual immaturity, homoerotic impulses, compensation for inferiority, presentation of a false facade, or conflict with father, mother, or authority. That this phenomenon exists seems well established (Filer, 1952; Hammer & Piotrowski, 1953; Robinson, 1951; Robinson & Cohen, 1954). Keller (1971) reports preliminary findings that there are three "types" of Rorschach interpreters: the *optimizers,* who emphasize health and play down pathology; the *intrapsychic pathologizers;* and the *interpersonal pathologizers.* The latter two fit the *prosecuting attorney* or the *maladjustment bias* stereotype (discussed in the next paragraph). Woody (1972) relates an anecdote of his meeting with a colleague, both psychologists having had the experience of attending workshops delivered by a certain Dr. X, but separated by a ten-year interval. The colleague tells Woody, "I attended that same workshop about ten years ago," and then proceeds to query, "Tell me, does the good Doctor X still find 'paranoid schizophrenics with latent homosexual tendencies' in every clinical record?" It is perhaps some comfort that such disposition to paint everyone with the same brush appears to be shared by clinicians of various disciplines. Observed at a staff conference was a nonpsychologist who appeared to interpret sex as the crucial dynamic in every case but could not seem to "see" the role of "hostility." The nonpsychologist impatiently asked a psychologist, who had just read his report, where he "got" all the hostility. The instant reply: "The same place where you 'get' all the sex."

Nonindividual reporting may also be seen in psychodynamically oriented reports in what has been called the *prosecuting attorney brief.* "Such reports are saturated with . . . negative dynamics . . . but give little or no attention to positive features, to commendable conscious strivings, socially valuable compensations, and other well-used defenses. These reports consistently reflect the motto 'always interpret at the lowest possible level of psychosexual fixation or regression.' They are prepared by psychological simians who hear no good, see no good, and report no good" (Tallent, 1958). This sort of reporting is what Klopfer (1960) calls the *maladjustment bias.* These observations, of course, refer to the extent to which reports are saturated with pathology. It goes without saying that a patient in a clinical setting does in fact have severe difficulties, impulses, and strivings that we may regard as unfortunate, and maladaptive defenses. These should be reported as they are meaningful. The point is that *appropriate* emphasis ought to be given to *relevant* positive features. But certainly all the favorable qualities are not relevant. One probably need not write of a neurotic patient as being "in contact," as showing no thinking disorders, as having a satisfying heterosexual adjustment, or as having an IQ of 135 (if intelligence is not a factor in the person's clinical situation).

POINTS OF VIEW ON INTERPRETATION
OF PSYCHOLOGICAL DATA

One of the major issues in the writing of psychological reports centers on the presentation of raw data or of incompletely interpreted data. If raw data are to be offered to the person who referred the case or to other team members, the next questions are: How much raw data? How shall such raw data be selected? For what purpose(s) shall raw data be utilized in the report? Or, from a different viewpoint, To what extent shall the psychologist interpret data for consumers of the report? On what basis may the psychologist decide what is to be interpreted and what not interpreted? Shall only interpreted data be reported? At the other extreme, shall no interpreted data be offered? Does the presentation of raw data obviate the need for its interpretation, or should (or may) an interpretation be accompanied by raw data either in a supportive or in an illustrative role?

Before attempting to cope with these questions, a definition of raw data and the range of possible "rawness" should be considered. English and English (1958) define "data/raw" as "data not yet submitted to logical or statistical analysis." In working with an individual client, it is the logical analysis of data that concerns us. Thus the data with which the psychologist deals differ vastly in terms of how much logical analysis is required before they can be viewed as meaningful or can contribute to useful action.

At one extreme are data that require highly skilled interpretation and have to be considered only in the context of a battery protocol. What competent psychologist would offer an interpretation of 4 Rorschach M responses without considering also their form level, popularity or originality, whether "easy" or "hard" M, the cards where seen, possible associated determinants, preceding and succeeding responses, the content, the particular verbalization of the content, color usage, pathognomonic signs, intelligence level, fantasy content, and so on? At the other extreme are responses that require minimal interpretation. Such responses often occur in interview, on sentence completion tests, or on other self-report or other report forms, which are, in effect, controlled interview situations. Thus the completions "Most people I know . . . can't be trusted," and "Those I work with . . . are out to get me" are apparently quite simple matters for interpretation. Similarly with such "critical items" from a parent's responses to the *Personality Inventory for Children* (Wirt, Lachar, Klinedinst, & Seat, 1977): "The child hardly ever smiles," and "The child is usually rejected by other children." Yet even here the psychologist must utilize some logical analysis, such as judging whether the parent is sincere, seeking to bring about some action with respect to the child, or otherwise trying to create an impression; how consistent the particular responses are with the full test protocol and other available information; and what significance the material might have. Data perhaps intermediate in the level of interpretive skill required are represented by statements such as "On four TAT cards the hero was depicted as in conflict with a father figure." Commonly appearing in psychological reports, statements of this sort are really descriptions of raw data, not basic raw data. To offer statements of this sort, the psychologist must use professional judgment; hence, some degree of interpretation takes place. We may also speak in this vein of "incompletely interpreted data." Other statements in this class are "loose use of color," "concrete thinking," or "syncretistic thinking."

Psychologists do not generally present raw data without what they consider an adequate interpretation of such material. Thus taken from a report, "Rorschach responses such as '. . . Two wolves . . . they both have their teeth dug into some person as though they're trying to tear him apart . . . a person who has taken on the wings of a butterfly . . . deformed embryos inside the womb . . . an infected vagina . . . a faint suggestion of evil spirits inside the womb . . . octopuses with horse's heads . . . two snakes seem to be trying to gain access to this vagina-like symbol'—are evidences of a severe formal thought disorder when personal material is involved. This is marked by primitive, symbolic, and dream-like associations and percepts, and by an accompanying loss of appropriate distance from stimuli which results in his making poor judgments in terms of the total situation."

Even though there are copious amounts of such raw data in some psychological reports, psychologists tend to feel that the appropriateness of including them depends on their purpose. There is widespread feeling among this group that it is all right to present material such as in the preceding example, but for illustrative reasons only. Had the conclusions preceded the data here, it would have been more evident that they were meant to illustrate conclusions, not to carry the freight. On the other hand, themes like the following are currently taboo among many psychologists, although other team members might find them more acceptable.

> On the Object Assembly subtest, the patient seemed at a loss as to where to begin. He picked up pieces at random and attempted to fit the parts together in an unplanned fashion. Finally, he stated his inability to solve the problem and gave up the task.
>
> This patient's verbal IQ is 91 and his performance score is 105. The Comprehension score (11) is five points greater than Information (6). The high subtest score is on Object Assembly, the weighted score being 14, while his lowest is a 3 scored on Arithmetic.

A number of psychologists feel threatened by the idea that they must present such data to others presumably more qualified to make the proper interpretations. Similarly there is widespread objection to being required to support one's conclusions with data, since this procedure might also imply that other professional groups have qualifications to judge the adequacy of the psychologist's interpretation of data.

There is a case frequently presented for the use of raw data in psychological reports. Some psychiatrists point out correctly that it is traditional for the physician to coordinate findings from diverse sources—the physician's own examination, consultants' reports, laboratory findings, social history—and to reach conclusions through the integration of all such data. He or she accepts responsibility for these and for the actions stemming from them. The medical consultant therefore helps a clinician by presenting a narrative report that makes liberal reference to the data on which impressions are based. Notice by way of illustration the ratio of raw data to interpretation in the following report written by a pathologist for a surgeon.

> Specimen consists of a 2 cm. cyst lined with soft cheesy material.
> Microscopic: Section reveals the cyst to be lined with flattened epidermis and the contents to consist of hyalinized, lamellated, desquamated, keratinized, epithelial cells.
> Impression: Skin, sebaceous cyst.

It therefore particularly behooves the psychologist who is working in a medical setting to examine whether a departure from what physicians do is justified.

The experienced psychologist is in a position to cite a number of pertinent differences between medical and psychological consultations. Most obvious, personality-behavior is made of stuff that is patently different from physiological-anatomical variables. Meaningful findings are deduced only after hundreds of bits of discrete data are sifted, pondered, and studied for consistency and the meanings of apparent inconsistencies, and after all the data units are studied as they are given significance or are modified by the data of the entire protocol and other pertinent information.

The logical extreme of presenting raw data to support conclusions or to help the person who referred the case independently to reach conclusions is of course to present *all* the data available on any given client. This practice would yield an unwieldy document of many pages, with little practical utility. Most psychologists would oppose such use of data, even when offered to associates highly trained in personality, contending that test data should be interpreted only by those who are expert in personality *and* psychological assessment methods.

A potent objection to presenting raw data so that the person who made the referral can make independent interpretations, "follow" the interpretations of the psychologist, or judge their correctness is simply that the practice is not valid. There is not a one-to-one relationship between datum and interpretation; neither is there universal symbolism that would permit translation from test material to client. The raw data on which interpretations are really made are far more extensive than test data. They include an experienced knowledge of the stimuli that elicited the data, an awareness of the relationship and effects of test stimulus and examiner stimulus, all sorts of behavioral variables, such as the person's tone of voice and facial expression, the entire context in which responses occurred, and all other relevant data.

A major factor pertinent to the question of presenting raw data—a factor that should be disconcerting to the clinician or some other consumer of the psychologist's services who would use the data to draw independent conclusions or to check on the psychologist's conclusions—is that the psychologist in the presence of volumes of raw data must, of necessity, be selective. And herein lies a telling criticism of such a procedure. It is the psychologist's judgment that determines *what* raw data should be selected for presentation—certainly an uncontrolled procedure of questionable validity. The psychologist cannot decide on what raw data to include in the report until *after* weighing the merits of some particular data. Unfortunate selection could come about through insufficient competence or be used nefariously by one having need to present certain conclusions and to justify them.

There is considerable feeling that raw data may legitimately be used for illustrating conclusions, perhaps linking the two in such fashion that the source of the conclusion is explicit (Mayman, 1959). This procedure may often have much to recommend it and in some instances may be as close to imperative as any rule for report writing can be. Particularly vivid or transparent material, judged by the psychologist to be a valid illustration of the conclusions it is intended to bolster, can be most effective—for example, "All the cards remind me of death, just sorrow and death." However, a response like "two bears with their tails cut off" may be transparent to the psychologist, particularly in the light of other data, but all readers may not reach similar conclusions. There is a danger that the use of such material may "backfire," a reader gaining quite a different conclusion from the psychologist or feeling that the illustration is not sufficient to support the psychologist's conclusion. Since the material is selective, the reader should be made aware that the illustrations are not fully supportive of the conclusions they advance.

Raw data may be required when conclusions rest largely on quantitative input—for example, in the diagnosis of mental retardation. The assessment of deficit based on neurological or other factors may also be documented with scores. Neuropsychological testing commonly generates volumes of data, and many psychologists find it helpful to put them in an appendix attached to the report.

A frequently safe and helpful procedure is for the psychologist to share raw data with an interested associate on a personal basis where the material may adequately be discussed. The central principles involved in the offering of raw data are (1) careful attention to the appropriateness of the circumstances of the procedure, with the wisdom of the illustrations used considered carefully from the standpoint of both validity and effectiveness, and (2) the inability of the psychologist ethically to relinquish responsibility for conclusions. The situation is parallel to what is seen in medical practice, where the physician, for good reason, is charged with coordinating all available clinical data and reaching conclusions based on them. The psychologist must coordinate all psychologically relevant material and reach independent conclusions.

THE FLAVOR OF THE REPORT

What may be called the "flavor" of the report comes in for a good deal of attention, from the readers if not also from the writers of psychological reports. The significance of the flavor is that it may readily influence the attitude of the reader. Such attitudes, positive or negative, may then contribute to what the reader derives. In addition, the flavor is inextricably enmeshed with such other matters as technical level and orientation, terminology, psychologist's attitude, and role concept. All of these have implications for the acceptance and effectiveness of the report.

Background, training, self-needs, and personality idiosyncrasies all may influence the flavor of the report. These contribute to reports that may be described by such adjectival expressions as "abstract," "theoretical," "academic," "intellectual," "erudite," or "learning theory oriented." Typical are reports with a concrete psychometric emphasis or reports that are more or less behavioral or psychoanalytic. There are also reports that exude an authoritative tone or are exhibitionistic. Although any of these flavors may arouse disapproval, disinterest, or antagonism in the reader, the latter two are regarded as particularly defeating professionally, not only because others are not likely to respond kindly to them, but also because such writing is incompatible with scientific tentativeness and modesty.

Styles of Reports

Psychological reports are sometimes categorized into one of three basic styles, although it would be easy to nominate others. These may be called the *clinical style,* the *scientific style,* and the *literary style*—which at the extreme may perhaps better be labeled "dramatic" or "flowery." No general agreement exists concerning the relative merits of each, but one does overhear comments, and the opinions of clinical workers may be formally surveyed (Tallent & Reiss, 1959b). For example, the following statement, intended as a specimen of literary writing of a somewhat dramatic sort, achieved significant popular support from clinical workers, yet many others did not feel that it suited their taste: "Crushed and defeated by telling setbacks, the patient feels unable to continue to fight what she sees as an oppressive environment."

The clinical style focuses upon pathology, maladjustment, deficiency, and equilibrative processes, and some would say that the report more nearly describes a case than a person. The orientation, of course, is basically medical and normative. An emphasis in this vein might make it hard to account for such behavioral variables as attitudes, sentiments, or relationships, unless these are diseased or associated wtih disease. The report on pages 142–143 is an attempt at clinical style, replete with test jargon, theory jargon, and psychopathological jargon.

The scientific style, by partial contrast, is more closely related to the academic psychologist's discipline. This approach stresses the normative, and sometimes also the pathological. It differs from the clinical most in its relation to a conceptual scheme of personality or to a theory of assessment. This style would apparently be particularly compatible with approaching a personality through its segments or part processes and dealing with these in some detail. Here the psychologist becomes involved with what, for convenience of study, might be regarded as discrete functions—intellection, perception, emotion— or finer divisions of these—much as the physician may be concerned with units of clinical study like the cardiovascular system, the genitourinary system, or the neuropsychiatric system.

This approach is subject to attack from a number of directions. It would seem to do violence to the concept of personality unity (this most important matter is considered in Chapter 5) and may also appear to many to be overly "cold" and impersonal. This approach may cause the reader to feel there was no person present at all. We must be aware that many clinical workers, particularly those in disciplines other than psychology, do not have empathy with scientific-sounding reports. Another hazard is that a scientific presentation with an unusually strong laboratory flavor may reinforce the commonly held impression that psychology renders laboratory rather than consultant services.

The scientific emphasis of modern experimental and quantitative psychology is the basis on which many clinicians and others, in and out of psychology, argue that the psychological report is a scientific document. As such, it is thought proper that the report be exclusively concerned with the "findings," that which is factual; any mention of application, or of an emphasis on application, is regarded by some as latter-day sophistry. However, a great distinction needs to be made between science and its application to workaday purposes. The psychological report is a practical document, and when it is not designed to be effective, its very purpose may be defeated. It is understandable that the more palatable and comprehensible the report, the more usable it is. To merely present ideas or conclusions is not enough; they must be "brought home" or "gotten across" to the reader or they are lost, and the psychologist's mission is aborted. The psychologist must write in whatever style is appropriate and effective, using literary, clinical, and scientific styles in whatever combination is necessary, using material that is objective, phenomenological, or whatever, again, as it appears to be effective and appropriate.

As with so many clinical issues that the modern psychologist faces, Freud was "there" first. Though obviously a bit uncomfortable with literary style, at the same time he saw scientific gain in this approach to recording his observations.

> It still strikes me myself as strange that the case histories I write should read like short stories and that, as one might say, they lack the serious stamp of science. I must console myself with the reflection that the nature of the subject is evidently responsible for this, rather than for any preference of my own . . . A detailed description of mental processes such as we are accustomed to find in the works of imaginative writers enables me, with the use of a few psychological formulas, to obtain at least some kind of insight into the course of that affection. (Freud, S. [1895]. *Studies on hysteria*. S.E. 2)

Archibald MacLeish suggests that the purpose of education is to weld the fact with the feel. The function of the psychologist is perhaps similar, the task being to present an integration of technical material with a feeling for the person. Many psychologists presumably operate on this premise. Recoiling from the scientific, they tend in the direction of, and sometimes get lost in, the literary. They sometimes fall into the style of the previously given example of literary writing. Here and there a literary twist may help in capturing the flavor of the person, but to do this effectively, using facts to instill a feel for the person, means presenting him or her as an individual. This objective is accomplished partly by the fortunate use of language, but mostly by developing the proper content, by understanding what the clinically relevant personality processes are and how these relate to one another, and finally by organizing these so that what is most vital stands out and what is less vital supports the essence of the presentation. The psychologist has to understand the person (a much bigger job than test interpretation) and then to convey that understanding to another.

The Use of "Human Interest"

We may profitably borrow from the newspaper people some methods of conceptualizing and presenting a theme. The traditional news item is a cut-and-dried affair concerned only with the "facts." Generations of cub reporters have learned their five W's—Who, What, When, Where, and Why—and the accounts of two reporters assigned to cover a fire on Main Street would probably read very much alike. Psychologists might even commend such similarity as evidence of a high degree of interobserver reliability.

But all newspaper stories are not the same; some strive for effect, for deeper understanding, or even for the development of understanding in the reader through "human interest." The latter can be valid enough, not detracting from the accuracy of the story and sometimes contributing to it.

Writing can, and often ought, to include both factual and affective elements—a point that Flesch (1949/1974) has developed well in his book on readable writing. Each field must develop its own styles. However, since the subject matter of psychology, like that of journalism, commonly involves the emotions of people, these can be incorporated in the report to describe people effectively and more realistically than when the emotions are exsanguinated in the objectivity of a specimen analysis. Even writings about scientific events, new machines, or industrial processes can be "humanized."[2] We shall see in Chapter 5 how even some engineers knowingly allow the intrusion of subjectivity both to color their reports and to aid them in conceptualizing their tasks. Indeed, great scientists like Einstein may rely heavily on the subjective and even the intuitive. He writes: "I very rarely think in words at all. A thought comes, and I may try to express it in words afterwards . . . During all these years there was a *feeling* of direction, of going straight toward something concrete. It is, of course, very hard to express that *feeling* in words; but it was decidedly the case and clearly to be distinguished from later considerations about the rational form of the solution" (Wertheimer, 1945, emphasis added).

In view of the objections raised here to literary, clinical, and scientific approaches, the reader might wonder what style would be suitable. Why not a simple, matter-of-fact approach based on everyday expository writing? Such an approach can readily incorporate scientific information as necessary, give pathological manifestations appropriate representation, and retain the flexibility or even sedate license allowed in any creative writing. A psychological report is, or at least should be, a piece of creative writing. There is no logical

---

[2]For a fine and powerful example see Tracy Kidder, *The Soul of a New Machine* (Boston: Little, Brown, 1981).

reason why the tone may not approximate the conversational or the journalistic.

An overly specialized tone seems to be a barrier both to communication and to understanding, and it not infrequently antagonizes the reader. The demand is for simplicity. This, of course, is distressing to some psychologists. It disturbs them to consider that the complexities of human behavior revealed by the psychologist's probing can be expressed in something less than an involved presentation, that personality functioning might even be made comprehensible to the psychologically unsophisticated. It is likely that large numbers of psychologists, because of training or for reasons of conviction or personal dynamics, cling to these views.

ORIENTATION OF THE REPORT

An issue related to the problem of flavor is that of orientation, particularly person orientation versus test orientation. The person-oriented report deals with the functioning of the person and with such real, pertinent matters as the outlook and recommendations that might prove helpful. The test-oriented report, by contrast, places its emphasis on test responses, on test scores, and perhaps on relations among test scores. The first kind of report talks about the person, the other about the person's performance on tests.

Although the test-oriented report is still quite common, there is considerable feeling that reports ought to be person-oriented (Chapter 2). Test orientation probably harks back to the early days of psychometrics and school psychology, when the IQ was at a premium and the various successes and failures on test items supposedly had some obvious and practical meaning.

The early days of clinical psychology in psychiatric settings again saw "mental testers" very much concerned with scores and proficiency levels. The orientation was essentially that of a technician, where the data were delivered to a clinician for interpretation—an entirely unacceptable procedure in personality assessment in a contemporary psychologist's point of view. However, many psychologists have carried over from early psychometric procedures to modern instruments a propensity to talk about tests rather than about people. At worst, test talk may be used as a veil to conceal the examiner's lack of understanding of the client or lack of ability to present conclusions effectively.

THE MANNER
OF PRESENTING CONCLUSIONS

The reporting of conclusions must be from the standpoint of a psychologist who has achieved certain impressions, or has *not* achieved impressions, about areas of the client's life that are of professional interest. In any event the psychologist's report ought to concentrate on what is known, not on what is not known. It is hardly necessary that the psychologist recapitulate the agonies of weighing data, accepting conclusions, rejecting conclusions, and holding other tentative impressions in abeyance. There is no need to hedge or to be indecisive, or even to "let the reader in on" the decision-making process. The process is complicated, but the major contradiction to a democratic approach is that it would take too many pages to convey the gross and subtle data that could permit the qualified reader to retrace the psychologist's steps. (As already indicated, however, it is desirable, when the personal relationship permits, to discuss such matters with team associates.) It falls upon the psychologist to state conclusions, together with appropriate modifying terms to indicate verbally the degree of confidence with which they are offered.

Speculation

Speculation refers to tentatively held conclusions for which adequate dependable evidence does not exist. Sometimes the psychologist's basis for such conclusions is little more than "impression," which might even stem from features of one's own personality or from one or two test responses that are interpretively equivocal. Hence, speculation refers to conclusions offered at a low level of confidence. One of the greatest sins a psychologist can commit is to fail to point out what is speculation.

In perusing the thousands of negative comments made about psychological reports (some of which form the basis for Chapter 2), one might readily conclude that a major job activity of psychologists is speculating. If there is truth in such a conclusion, so much the worse for psychology. Then what is the occasion for speculating? Legitimately, speculation may be in order when few definitive data are available and an important issue requiring attention is raised by the person making the referral, or when the psychologist becomes aware of such an issue during examination of a client. An uncertain answer may be better than none in *some* cases, particularly if it is not misleading. Blank (1965) suggests that ". . . waiting for ironclad proof [not an event occurring with great frequency] leads to a sterile report." It may be important in certain cases to speculate about such matters as suicide, homicide, antisocial sexual behavior, cerebral pathology, or rehabilitation potential. Inadequate information about such matters may suggest the need for further investigations by a social worker, a medical specialist, or another who might be able to throw light on the topic. However, speculation about matters that are not especially relevant may not be defensible. An example of this might be speculation about developmental events in a patient who is being seen in a setting where treatment is almost entirely by medication.

Transfer of Responsibility

A final comment on the manner of presenting conclusions pertains to the transfer of responsibility for conclusions from the psychologist to tests— for example, "Psychological testing reveals . . . ," "The Rorschach shows

. . . ," "Stories given to the TAT point up a person who . . . ." It is hardly quibbling to insist that psychological tests reveal or indicate nothing. The psychologist uses tests but reaches conclusions that involve clinical judgment (and theory) as well (Chapter 5). (Typically, in fact, conclusions are based more on a battery than on individual tests.) Sometimes quotes such as the preceding are little more than a manner of speech, but in other cases they reflect a psychologist's lack of confidence in self or in conclusion(s). The psychologist is hiding behind tests. The effect on the reader might not always be what the psychologist desired. In fact, this way of presenting conclusions might prompt referrals asking for administration of certain tests because of the sort of information they are thought to reveal. The belief of nonpsychologically trained readers—lawyers or judges, for example—that decisions affecting a person's life turn on a test (whose validity might be challenged in the literature and consequently in courts of law) rather than on a psychologist, a responsible human, may lead to some unsought outcomes. Ulrich, Stachnik, and Stainton (1963), in a study of gullibility to generalized personality interpretations, point to results that indicate ". . . the awe with which personality tests per se are viewed by the naive student or others of comparable test sophistication"— that is, many readers of psychological reports. Snyder and Larson (1972) report similar findings.

PRIMARY PRESENTATION
OF THE REPORT

The intended mode of first presenting the report may influence how it is written, although this need not be so. Many persons find it easier to absorb technical material by eye than by ear. When a report is requested for oral staff presentation or is likely to serve this purpose, special attention is necessary in the preparation. Reports heard in staff meetings may often be characterized as "involved," "complex," or "saturated," and many are difficult to understand when presented orally. However, it is often possible to derive meaning, sometimes important meaning, on reading these same reports. It would be a worthwhile objective, then, to write reports suitable both for written and for oral presentation.

TERMINOLOGY IN THE REPORT

Everyone probably agrees that a piece of writing ought to be comprehensible to its intended readers. Psychological reports are read by persons with various kinds of training and backgrounds, and it is not possible to know in advance who all the readers might be. Terminology obviously is one of the matters related to comprehensibility, and the question of appropriate terminology has not yet been settled. Psychological terminology is viewed by many as highly technical and specialized, complex, and esoteric (Tallent & Reiss, 1959c). Is it possible to substitute something simpler? A historical review of this issue reveals contrasting opinions.

Sargent (1951) believes that we must retain specialized terminology, together with its complexities. At least in writing for consumers familiar with psychological constructs, she observes that, in the context of relating "the degree and kind of abnormal psychological functioning . . . technical terms and concepts are . . . considered to be more economical and cogent carriers of meaning . . . than if they were to be translated into everyday language." Hammond and Allen (1953) go further. They contend that "technical vocabulary is indispensable for three reasons: first, it is precise; second, it can communicate concepts that are virtually impossible to convey in ordinary language; and third, it is economical." These writers do point out that the amount of technical verbiage used should be gauged by the ability of the intended reader(s) to understand and should be appropriate to the context, but for communicating "complex technical concepts with precision to a qualified reader," such a vocabulary is "indispensable."

A case can also be made against the use of technical terminology. Hammond and Allen themselves discuss frankly the shortcomings of such language as used in psychological reports and suggest some remedies. These writers effectively point out the difficulties the psychologist may face in the use of such words and the lack of understanding or the misunderstanding they may cause in the reader(s) of the report. Cited are variability in sophistication and orientation among the readers, the specialized meaning of certain terms, and the multiple meanings as well as technical meanings that differ from lay meanings. There is also a demonstrated tendency for professional persons to assign nonconsensual meanings to words commonly used in psychological reports. Here the work of Johnson (1945) and of Grayson and Tolman (1950) is pertinent. As an example of word ambiguity, Grayson and Tolman classified definitions of *anxiety* contributed by psychologists and psychiatrists—a word that appears in a very high percentage of psychological reports—into no fewer than seven categories of meaning. It would seem that the psychologist must indeed step lightly!

Another meaningful study that gives some understanding of at least the current effects of using technical verbiage is reported by Davenport (1952). She found that interpretive statements taken from case reports frequently did not differentiate adequately among persons and were ambiguous, with psychoanalytic-type expressions the worst offender. This observation calls attention to a special problem about technical words—the issue of analytic terminology. Many psychologists are sharply against its use. Writing that incorporates analytic terminology is more fashionable in some quarters than in others; in some settings it seems to be the expected mode of expression. However, the inexact, nondifferentiating use to which such a vocabulary may be put has caused considerable discussion. There has been for some years now a trend away from psychoanalytic terminology, and even many dynamically oriented psychologists may find it fashionable *not* to use it.

It may be true that technical words are precise, but such precision is to be found only in a carefully defined context associated with *discrete* orientations. It would be a prodigious task to train all writers and readers of psychological reports, even those at the professional level, to accept and learn some common meanings for several hundred words. At present, report readers—teachers, administrators, legal and correctional persons, medical people, and even psychiatrists and psychiatric social workers—typically do not have a large technical *psychological* vocabulary. Further, the multitude of schools, orientations, and loyalties that abound in the psychological domain would be a telling barrier. Nor would the eclectic, whose understanding reflects a number of viewpoints and glossaries, some of them contradictory, fare any better. Indeed, the same writer may use the same word with different meanings. Freud, for example, uses *ego* in various senses. Erikson uses *identity* somewhat differently in different contexts.

What about the argument that technical words "communicate concepts which are virtually impossible to convey in ordinary language" and that they are "economical"? Hammond and Allen point up specific examples: the words *empathy, rapport,* and *subliminal.* These words are said to be "virtually impossible to express in plain English: They may, by means of a lengthy paraphrase, be approximated, but the communication thus achieved is far less complete and *satisfactory* than that produced by use of the terms themselves *when they are fully understood by the reader*" (emphasis supplied). It does seem that paraphrased technical terms would be longer; how much longer would be determined from the context. The question is, Who finds the technical terms more "satisfactory," since the study on "The Trouble with Psychological Reports" compels the belief that very large numbers of readers, and writers, do not? (Tallent & Reiss, 1959c; see Chapter 2, particularly pp. 37–38.) The crucial phrase is, "when they are fully understood by the reader." The findings of the Grayson-Tolman study are too overpowering to suggest that such conditions are readily attainable. The answer to the question of economy is, Can fewer words be regarded as economical when they fail to do the job?

Technical psychological words used in a theoretical or a general context are wholly different from what is required in clinically oriented usage; even in a theoretical context such words are meaningful only when they are in a consistent, theoretical framework. Theories, by definition, deal with general phenomena. Clinically oriented psychology deals with the application of specific knowledge of general phenomena to persons. Technical names are certainly appropriate for abstract ideas or occurrences or for scientific notions or occurrences that are subjected to special study. Technical names are appropriate for many ideas or concepts or for phenomena, the understanding of which can suitably be modified with words to meet the individual instance. Individual personality study may be importantly different because of the numerous ways and occasions in which generally identified behaviors or other psychological phenomena are expressed.

Consider the example of *empathy.* To the extent our knowledge of an individual permits, we may describe specific situations in which particular usages of this word are permissible and contributory to the understanding of a unique person. We may glibly talk of an empathic person, but does the person exhibit empathy in all situations—empathy for a Hitler or for modern-day terrorists? It would be better to talk of the surface correlates of empathy, of the depth of the experience, of the kinds of situations that call forth empathic experiences, and perhaps of the kinds of situations in which the "empathic" person experiences feelings quite different from empathy. This approach to personality description is appropriate to clinically oriented psychology. Clinical description has to be specific because it is supposed to be useful, a basis for decision and action. In clinical prediction, where there may be a question of assaultive behavior or suicide, it does not help much to talk of generalized and somewhat ubiquitous psychological phenomena like sadomasochism, hostility, narcissistic wounds, or inadequate empathic development, because Aunt Fanny and perhaps her psychotherapist, too, may "have" these.

In the clinically oriented mission it is often necessary to spell out each conclusion in terms of the occurrences, levels, nuances, and interrelationship of events with the rest of personality. Such an approach is less economical of syllables than is one that relies on technical words to transmit insights. A more careful approach, in fact, may utilize technical verbiage to help establish a set or emphasize a personality component, but not really as organic to the description. For example, "This patient is narcissistic *in the sense that* . . . ," or, "He has little confidence in himself and is dominantly oriented to seeking all sorts of support, guidance, and reassurance, essentially an oral person." Notice that the ways in which the person is "oral" are spelled out. In how many ways, grossly, subtly, disguisedly, can one be "oral"? In our view words like *oral, narcissistic, masochistic, immature, compulsive,* and *schizophrenia* are often more concealing than revealing.

Technical words do not cause, but readily lend themselves to, imprecise or incomplete thinking. There is the *error of nominalism,* wherein we simply name a thing or an occurrence and think we understand something of the real world. Of course, this patient is anal, or immature, or insecure, or sadistic. But really, what is this living person, Mary Jones, *like* when she is anal, or immature, or insecure, or sadistic, and what does she *do,* overtly or intrapsychically? Do the terms differentiate, make for understanding? Cannot two persons have dominant traits of sadism, one of them awaiting capital punishment stemming from this characteristic, the other the respectable warden charged with carrying out the sentence? It may be countered that if the psychologist is careful to define the term *as it is used in a particular case,* then the term *would* differentiate among persons. However, then the term itself would become superfluous except, as suggested, that it might be used to help establish a set or emphasize a personality component. In this sense, *sadistic* may be employed as a strong word of dramatic quality to help focus on a central personality theme of personal or social significance. Too many such words obviously cannot be used in one report.

Several questions follow from this position. First, Would it be desirable to write reports in lay language? It is criticized that such writing permits the least common denominator to set the level of the report. In a sense this is true, but since even professionals trip over technical terms, plain English would seem to meet the need for a clear understanding shared by all readers of the psychological report.

Since technical language is often presumed more scientific, it is well to note Block's (1961) rejection of this point of view and his use of lay language in a quantitative research method (Q-sort technique). He notes, "The orientation of the presently proposed descriptive language is, as Lewin would say, a 'contemporaneous' one. *The subject is described as he appears and is understood by the observer at the time of observation.*"

Technical language is sometimes defended as necessary or at least useful as a "professional shorthand." If so, does it have a place in psychological reports, many of whose readers have not been trained in this shorthand? Worse still, in view of the Grayson-Tolman study, showing as it does intraprofessional variation as well as interprofessional variation in the understanding of professional terms, it becomes necessary to redefine the various symbols.

Providers and consumers of psychological services have an appreciable tolerance for terminological looseness, and unambiguous usage of technical words is not yet the rule. It seems to cause little concern to label as *paranoid* one who is defensive and cautious in interpersonal relations, and as *compulsive* a person who is careful, conscientious, ethical, and reliable. You may even hear that all psychologists or all graduate students are *compulsive*—that one has to be in order to negotiate the curriculum.

Such loose usage raises an additional question. What is *technical language?* Is *compulsive* still a technical word? Or *paranoid?* Or *identity?* These terms have drifted into the language and are freely used in everyday life, sometimes no more carelessly than by some psychologists. They may be used in psychological reports, if used responsibly and meaningfully as suggested in the foregoing discussion. On the other hand, *intratest scatter, critical item, cut-off whole, sex shock, position response* certainly are technical terms, test talk. They can only confuse or befuddle most readers. They have no place in most psychological reports.

There is a common-sense approach to the use of words. Words can be our servants or our masters. They are supposed to stand for real phenomena, things, or ideas, and as such they can help us to conceptualize our reports in terms of real events, or we can allow them to confuse us with generalities, vagaries, ambiguities, and imprecision. There is not necessarily a one-to-one relationship between word and referent, as *a* stands for the side of a given triangle. These facts are further complicated because many words—big words, little-known words, impressive-sounding words—have long been used by psychologists as currency and have an appeal not based on their communication value. How we use such "psychobabble" and "why we do it" are explored by Della Corte (1980). Her poignant observations are perhaps sufficient to make some of us stop "doing it."

Having noted all this, we might as well conclude that at least in the present state of the science and the art of psychology, and of language, our word usage is going to be something less than perfect—even as is word usage in many everyday documents. It is difficult in our field not to use at least occasionally such stock-in-trade words as *anxiety, defense,* or *affective,* even though there is inadequate consensus on their meaning. Knowing this, however, we can be careful how we use them. In-context usage well might result in less ambiguity than the out-of-context studies that identified these terms as ambiguous. We may also rationalize that we are still far from perfection in many other areas of human endeavor. Our interpretations are often not perfect either, and we are too aware of the many pitfalls that await the unwary psychologist. The responsible psychologist can produce an effective psychological report, however.

This discussion of terminology, then, is not intended to be totally proscriptive of technical terminology, but the heavily technical reports that were all but universal yesteryear (and which, alas, linger on here and there) are clearly not appropriate to most practical missions. We use some technical terms *in communicating among professionals who can be expected to know these terms* simply because there are no substitutes. In the report on Henry Dennis (p. 165) terms like *form constancy* and *position in space,* and the scores obtained on these, are highly meaningful to the intended reader, but the psychologist attenuates the technical psychological material in reporting to the child's physician (pp. 165–166). It is difficult to document an organic brain syndrome (or to do without the term *organic brain syndrome*) without using some technical material. Diagnostic terminology is frequently appropriate in a psychiatric setting, school terminology in a school setting, counseling terminology in a counseling setting. Even though there is insufficient understanding of schizophrenia with accompanying semantic confusion about the term *schizophrenia,* we have no substitute. (*Split personality* will hardly do!)

UNFAMILIAR CONCEPTS
IN THE REPORT

The use of unfamiliar concepts or materials from the psychologist's tool box can be as great a barrier to effective communication, and evoke much the same personal reaction, as the use of unfamiliar words. Unfamiliar concepts that psychologists are prone to use, to the detriment of the clinical mission, stem from (1) theory, (2) tests, and (3) statistics.

Theoretical concepts that give trouble are often carried into the report by equally troublesome words. Many readers remain unenlightened after reading about projection in the classical Freudian sense, "an inverted oedipal complex," "unconscious fantasy," "an external super-ego," "intermittent reinforcement," "the A-B situation," or "identification with the aggressor." Simply recording test results may suggest that the reader should gain information from these data, when, in fact, he or she does not understand what the psychologist is presenting.

Other unfamiliar matter presented to the reader presupposes familiarity with the physical nature of tests and score sheets. This includes talk of the client's performance on the Object Assembly test, a particular response to Card VI (Is that the one with the butterfly?), or a clear spike on the psychopathic deviate scale that is accentuated by unusually low scores on the neurotic triad. Some thoughtful psychologists try to take the reader into consideration by a description intended to be meaningful: "On a test involving the assembly of pieces such as in a jig-saw puzzle . . . ," or "On a card showing two male figures commonly seen as father and son. . . ." It is uncertain to what extent these humanitarian essays bring the reader closer to understanding.

Statistical expressions cause a certain amount of dismay, too, although this is not as widespread. Unfortunately, but understandably, reporting in terms of T-scores or percentiles would not be appreciated (Tallent & Reiss, 1959b), although from a technical standpoint these have much to commend them. These concepts can be used effectively, however, even with laypersons, in the context of an oral report if they are explained. Talking about people in terms of norms, standardization data, or standard deviations will probably not be confusing to the untrained inasmuch as such persons will not become sufficiently involved to become confused.

THE LENGTH OF REPORTS

A certain business executive likes to relate the anecdote about the occasion when he assigned a new employee to prepare a report for him. In due time a voluminous piece of writing was returned. Dismayed, the executive pointed out that the required information could be presented on one page, or certainly on not more than two pages. "But sir," pleaded the young man, "I don't know that much about the matter you assigned me to."

On purely impressionistic grounds there does not seem to be a necessarily positive correlation between the length of documents and the quality of their content. Some observers insist that in the case of psychological reports, the relationship is a negative one. At any rate, report readers tend to dislike overly long reports, even when they are otherwise good.

The often-noted "length compulsion" probably has a multiple etiology. Teachers often demand long pieces of writing, probably with the idea that this will lead to coping thoroughly with the assigned task. Is it possible to assign a term paper to a college class without a hand going up and a student asking how long it must be? The present-day psychological consultation also seems to encourage long reports. The nonspecific referral is one factor; another would seem to be a defensive attitude in many psychologists that gives rise to unnecessary inclusiveness of topic coverage, heavy detailing, hedging, and superfluous qualifications that are wasteful of space. The long document may then be identified as the "exhaustive report" or, more commonly, the "shotgun report."

Some common-sense considerations might help to reduce the length of reports. But when is a report *too long? It is often too long when it is not conceptualized in terms of the mission.* It probably is too long when the psychologist is unhappy over the length of time required to write it and experiences difficulty in organizing a multitude of details for presentation. It is too long when it contains content that is not relevant or useful, when the detailing is greater than can be put to good use, when low confidence statements (speculations) are presented without an excellent rationale for their inclusion, when the writing is unnecessarily repetitious, when the organization does not evidence "tightness," and when the reader is irritated by the length or limits reading of the report to one or more smaller sections like a summary, a diagnostic impression, or a statement of recommendations.

The Ten Commandments are expressed in 297 words. It took 300 words to write the Declaration of Independence and 266 words to compose the Gettysburg Address. Surely the modern psychologist can try to approach this standard.

4
Content of the Psychological Report

There is presently little consensus on the appropriate content for a psychological report. To start with, the psychologist might question the purpose to which the report will be put and the role that various items of content might play. With this orientation, how well does the "traditional" material of reports stand up to scrutiny? It should become apparent that although certain issues that are commonly discussed in reports are never appropriate, other "traditional" items of content may frequently be incorporated in the report to advantage. The choice and the appropriate emphasis of report content always depend on the case and the mission.

The psychologist in the assessment role is an important source of information about people. Such information, in large measure, is typically based on the interpretation of test performance and on observation of clients.

Some, however, think the task of the psychologist should be merely to pass along "test findings." Such a view suggests that the process of clinical communication is a more basic matter than the issue of what to communicate. Quite to the contrary, adequate guidelines for determining what content the psychologist should communicate can be discussed only in general terms; they must be developed for each individual case in terms of specific assessment missions and the settings in which psychologists work. The assessment goal becomes, then, the development of report content that is pertinent to each individual client. The identification of such content is the purpose of this chapter.

THE MULTIPLE PURPOSE OF REPORT CONTENT

The uses to which psychological reports are put dictate that content be developed in accordance with (1) the needs of the immediate mission, (2) the anticipation of questions and future needs, and (3) the creation of a record.

Needs of the Mission

The immediate mission must be regarded as having the highest priority, for this is understood in relation to a felt need and is therefore the only purpose (other than research, or sometimes training) that justifies the seeking of psychological information. Unfortunately the full scope of the mission is not always easy to define, particularly when the psychologist is in the consultant role and information is not requested in specific terms. However, the request for information, even when quite specific, does not necessarily circumscribe the mission. The specific request or statement of problem may profitably be modified as a result of discussion between the psychologist and the person who has referred the case. Beyond this, the psychologist must exercise judgment and decide how to understand the case in terms of personal experience, background, and theoretical and value systems.

Anticipation of Needs

Often the psychologist might wish to increase understanding of the mission in anticipation of further immediate or short-term uses that might be made of the report, or of further questions that might arise in current work with the case. If, for example, a psychologist in a medical setting feels that a patient is likely to present problems in nursing care, these might be explored in anticipation of difficulties. Similarly problems might be foreseen in the areas of psychotherapy, rehabilitation, social behavior, or diagnosis. Suggestions might be included on the best approaches in psychotherapy, in occupational therapy, or in diagnostic interview techniques.

Creation of a Record

The final, but essential, purpose of the report is the creation of a record for long-term use. A record is valuable as a means of comparing a person's condition from one assessment period to another. The psychologist must anticipate further questions and uses, but such anticipations are more easily found in short-term considerations of the case than in projections of its uses over the long run. A person who had earlier been regarded as showing a functional reaction may, some years later, be examined for organicity, and the psychological record searched for earlier evidences of suspicions of such a disorder. Or an earlier record of a person who commits an act of violence might be consulted for an understanding of personality tendencies that might help explain such behavior. The psychologist's record may eventually be used for research, in a court case, or for its further direct contribution to a case, as in a patient's readmission to a hospital. The difficulties of anticipation may therefore appear to be great, but it is hoped that the discussions of relevance and appropriateness later in this chapter will make the task easier.

DEFINITION AND CLASSIFICATION
OF CONTENT

Before delving further into the topics of *content,* we should differentiate among the various meanings of the term. Content can be thought of in a rather broad sense or in a more limited way. In a broad sense, content is anything the psychologist writes into the report—perhaps statements on such topics as the reason for referral, why a person is under treatment, how well a child cooperated, an IQ, an F percent, a diagnostic impression, recommendations for treatment, a discussion of scatter, what the client saw on Card II, or the fact that the client had to be excused twice to go to the bathroom. In the limited sense, content refers to the conclusions that are transmitted to the person who has referred the case.

It is perhaps most useful to think of content in the limited sense as the *primary* content of the report (the essential information to be conveyed) and everything else as *secondary* content (that is, supportive or explanatory information). This makes it easier to concentrate on the mission and to relegate other material that the psychologist feels ought to be transmitted to its rightful auxiliary position. Making the distinction will help to highlight the conclusions and to de-emphasize whatever else is required to make the report complete or effective.

The primary content may also be thought of as the psychological core content, since it is a basic (and original) contribution the psychologist makes to the case study. In many instances all or a substantial part of such content may be congruent with the findings of others. When this occurs, so much the better! The psychologist's contribution is original, not necessarily for the information it supplies—since psychological information may be gained in a number of ways against a number of orientations—but because conclusions derive from expertness in utilizing psychological methods for understanding the personality of individuals. It is as much a contribution when the psychologist, in agreement with a child's teacher, suggests that the child's poor classroom deportment is a desperate attempt to achieve recognition (which the teacher might make a direct effort to provide) as it is to report that a child's reading difficulty is based on brain dysfunction.

Various items of secondary content round out the report. Such material is not vital in the sense that the conclusions are so regarded. Nevertheless, the information may be useful in developing and supporting the conclusions, and just as a fortunate choice of words and pleasant readability add effectiveness, so information of secondary importance can help to "put across" a report. Such nonorganic items as the date the evaluation was made and the reason for referral can be important at some future time.

Orienting Data

First to be considered are orienting data. These refer to judiciously selected items of information (probably available elsewhere) that may help put the conclusions in appropriate context. For example, it may make a difference on how the conclusions are understood if the reason for referral or something of the client's social or educational background is given. A prosaic matter like the client's age may be highly relevant, since behavior or goals that are fully appropriate and expected at one age may be regarded as inappropriate, ludicrous, pathologic, or socially incongruous at another. To illustrate further, a request for vocational appraisal is often a straightforward matter, but sometimes it is not. How shall we understand the findings that might be obtained on a 35-year-old woman who appeared at the writer's office and asked for "vocational guidance testing"? Asked the nature of her vocational and educational background, she disclosed that she had just been awarded a Ph.D. in anthropology.

Illustrative and Persuasive Content

Illustrative material, the use of which has already been discussed in a more general context (pp. 59–60), may also be regarded as secondary content. At some indefinite point such matter shades into persuasive writing, which, at the extreme, is neither objective nor scientific. Some would argue that readers should be allowed to reach their own conclusions. A good thought, until we consider the process of reaching conclusions and the ingredients that go into these. The psychologist is responsible for forming conclusions, and to the extent there is confidence in them the psychologist has the responsibility to try to be an effective contributor to the case study. Appelbaum's (1970) suggestion that persuasion has a role in psychological reporting is therefore well taken (p. 18).

Subconclusions

Judiciously used illustrative material may be considered secondary content on a par with the necessary subconclusions that contribute to one or several of the major conclusions of the report. Major conclusions require support, not in the sense that raw data may validly support conclusions or that the psychologist's impressions are otherwise suspect, but because these conclusions are more comprehensible and useful when presented in the context of their components. It would be unthinkable, for example, to suggest, for no apparent reason, a diagnosis of schizophrenia. Mention should be made of such observed deviancies as a formal thought disorder, bizarre content, pervasive and exaggerated suspiciousness, and grossly inadequate insight. Nor would it be well to suggest that a patient is capable of destructive behavior without first pointing to such (possible) factors as severe undercontrol of thought and conduct, a tendency to projection and strong accompanying hostile ideation, and belligerence in the examination situation.

SOURCES OF CONTENT

A number of sources of content are available to the psychologist, although there is little agreement on what constitutes the proper sources of content. Three of these sources are directly available to the psychologist through examination: test data, interview material, and observed behavior. In addition, the psychologist may observe the client in nontest situations, possibly even know the person as a member of the community. Finally, there are a number of nonpsychological sources of information ordinarily available to the psychologist. These may include a social history, psychiatric and medical reports, nursing notes, staff conference proceedings, reports from various therapists, police records, or discussion with a physician, psychiatrist, teacher, principal, lawyer, probation officer, nurse, attendant, therapist, or social worker.

Contributing to contradictory views on the sources of proper content for the psychological report are divergent understandings of what psychological diagnostic instruments are. Korchin and Schuldberg (1981) clarify the issue in terms of how broadly or how narrowly the focus of a test is conceived. Thus a test, such as the Rorschach, may be employed as a narrowly focused instrument, psychometrically refined and emphasizing theoretically relevant scales. Such an application makes the Rorschach "more of a test" (than it has been). Other clinicians, however, following Zubin, Eron, and Schumer (1965) conceive of the Rorschach more as an interview than as a psychometric tool—hence, as "less of a test." Those who regard their instruments as "more of a test" are likely to look to them as the crucial device in a psychological case study. Those who employ their instruments as less of a test are likely to set more modest goals for them, and consider it both legitimate and desirable to supplement their "test results" with nontest data.

Some workers, both nonpsychologists and psychologists who are strongly committed to using tests only as psychometric tools, do not look at all kindly upon the practice of the psychologist seeking out and using data other than that elicited through testing. Those who hold this attitude in its most extreme form would have the psychologist do fully blind diagnoses and not see the client or know anything about the person. This position is held because psychological tests are regarded by these workers as fully objective tools, and the psychologist's function is seen as "testing"—a laboratory procedure where extraneous information might bias the "readings." Besides, expressing interest in the data or conclusions of others, or even in the psychologist's own interpersonal observations, to some coworkers smacks of dishonesty or calls into question the competency of the individual psychologist or the validity of testing. Presumably if it is not practicable for one psychologist to test the client and turn over the protocol to a colleague for interpretation, then at least the tester should attempt to maintain objectivity in the light of observations that might be made while testing the client.

Psychologists who incline to the "less of a test" position flatly reject this point of view, pointing out that blind diagnosis is (1) a training device, (2) a stunt, and (3) a research method. They agree, however, that blind diagnosis can supply pertinent information. Some psychologists might wish to examine the protocol in the presence of minimal data available from other sources before completing the assessment by utilizing all pertinent material. A comparison of conclusions arrived at blindly with data available from other sources may permit the psychologist to estimate the proper confidence that may be placed in various aspects of integrated conclusions based on test data *and* other material. In general, where practical decisions are to be made that may have temporary or lasting effect on a person, that person should have the benefit of being assessed by the psychologist under conditions where conclusions and recommendations are most likely to be realistic, accurate, or helpful—a matter of basic human ethics. The psychologist who functions in this manner is clearly a high-level professional, not a technician.

A position that incorporates validated psychometric approaches and also techniques that are "less of a test" appreciates that all psychological diagnostic tools are merely devices to help understanding. They represent contrived samples of behavior, some of which can responsibly be regarded, with a good degree of confidence, as having meaning for more typical life situations. Others, however, are of more tenuous value. In general, and within practical limitations, the more behavioral samples observed in the psychologist's office and elsewhere, the better, and the more meaningful and responsible the conclusions. Tests help us to understand the meaning and purpose of behavior in the person's everyday life situation; knowing something of a person's life in advance adds meaning and significance to test performance, thus increasing its practical implications. Tests are predictors of significant behavior only in the sense that they show potentialities; otherwise there would be a one-to-one relationship between test response and behavior, or between test interpretation and behavior. A Rorschach protocol may suggest a potentiality for behavioral undercontrol, but seen against a background of the person's history with regard to this variable, a more precise and practical estimate of future conduct, or an understanding of present or past conduct, may be offered. The value of testing is based only partly on tests and partly on the circumstances of testing and the collateral material available to the psychologist.

Certain cautions are necessary in using data that are or may be available elsewhere. The danger is repetition or unnecessary duplication, which is wasteful of time, increases report length, and may be offensive to those who feel that certain kinds of information—for example, clinical appearance and behavior, or social history—are more properly identified with professions other than psychology. The psychologist should therefore reflect on what such material adds to the report.

What, for example, does the psychologist tell Frank's teacher that has not been observed over and over since he has been in class, the psychologist's last observation, incidentally, being the reason the child was referred?

Frank is a neatly dressed, eight-year-old boy whose left eye constantly squints. He is courteous, perhaps overly courteous, and is most cooperative. When he doesn't know an answer, he becomes noticeably upset, sometimes appearing to be on the verge of tears.

What is added to the psychologist's contribution to the case study when the following is submitted on Patient A?

The patient says he came to the hospital because for the last three months he has become extremely "nervous"—couldn't eat, couldn't sleep, "started hitting the jug again," has been quarreling with his wife, his boss, and fellow employees, and last Tuesday night struck his wife during an argument although he "didn't mean to do it."

This information is no doubt available from the intake or initial examination interview. What is added to the case study when a psychologist in a psychiatric hospital writes the following on Patient B?

The patient enters the office with apparent apprehension, glances furtively about the room and asks if it is wired. He several times inquires about the examiner's purpose with questions like "What's this for?" He is guarded and evasive in responding to questions.

Isn't such material routinely noted in the psychiatrist's report? And, of course, it is usually the physician or the social worker who reports:

The patient is the youngest in a family of five children, the four older sibs being girls. All during school he was teased by his classmates because of certain effeminate ways, and he was taunted with the name "sissy." He admits that he doesn't have much interest in girls and thinks that this is why he was rejected by the army. He volunteers that the medical examiner asked him, "Do you go out with girls?"

There is great distinction to be made, however, between repeating or duplicating what is usually the property of others and utilizing such material *in the context of a new integration.* This sort of content can be employed for strengthening conclusions and insights suggested by tests, for understanding the practical significance of behavioral trends as indicated by test data, for showing how underlying psychological factors may relate to overt behavior that is of concern, or as illustrations for presented conclusions.

Thus for Frank:

This child's perfectionistic strivings, if not modified, can become a way of life, crippling spontaneity and ability to relate with warmth and satisfaction. He could develop a very serious breakdown as early as adolescence. He has the feeling that catastrophe awaits him if he does not achieve at an exaggeratedly high level, that somehow such performance is expected of him. Seeking to minimize fear, he sacrifices the positive feelings and true interest in his scholarship, for being correct is what is important to him and not the meaning of the work. This child has need for warmth, kindness, and acceptance—especially when he does not know the answer. He needs to learn that he can be accepted for himself rather than for his performance. He should be involved in play therapy, particularly in contact and rough-and-tumble games where getting dirty is assured. Finger painting might also be helpful.

For Patient A:

. . . anxiety centering largely about his sex role, conflict over his adequacy as a male, and dependency needs for which he cannot secure adequate gratification is most usually not too troublesome to him because a pattern of life emphasizing order, meticulous attention to details, and achievement tends to prevent the experiencing of acute distress. However, this defensive pattern is currently not sufficiently effective to control either strong subjective responses—anxiety and tension—which are apparently evidenced in his being "nervous," in his inability to eat or sleep well, and in drinking. Similarly, rather pervasive negative feelings toward others, about which he usually has no particular awareness, are now associated with an acting out potential. He currently ascribes his own antagonistic feelings to others and perceives people as a threat to him. Though according to the information now available he has expressed hostility only verbally with the exception of one temporary lapse of control when he struck his wife, he is seen as potentially capable of serious assaultive behavior and he should be closely observed for these tendencies particularly during his period of acute upset.

It should also be pointed out that the medical data of a physician influenced the writing of this passage, although there is no direct reference to it. The "nervousness," insomnia, and eating difficulties that the patient reports could have a physiological basis, but since the medical examination was essentially negative, these symptoms may tentatively be ascribed to the psychological state with which they are consistent.

Consider the following passage written about Patient B.

. . . he ascribes these unbridled hostile impulses to others, which causes him to experience his relationships in a context of severe threat. With the loosening of ties to reality he seems to see threat everywhere and is beyond rationality in his suspiciousness, a factor which no doubt aggravates his ability to function socially. This was observed during the examination where he was guarded and evasive, queried the examiner several times with "What's this for?" and especially when he entered the office, furtively looked about the room and asked if it was wired.

This integration of test conclusions with clinical observations makes real and alive the psychological defense maneuver of hypersuspiciousness and its social consequences. The purpose here is hardly to tell that Patient B is paranoid, which everyone knows, but to present the condition in a context where it is more understandable and its severity illustrated. This presentation differs from the still-common but regrettable practice of noting clinical behavior prior to offering test conclusions and then reporting the latter without reference to the patient's clinical behavior, which is kept separate from these (exclusively test) conclusions. The psychologist may feel the need to put forth much effort to illustrate or support an "independent" (test-derived) conclusion that Patient B is paranoid. This may be accomplished by offering test data, the meanings of which are less obvious (and also less valid) than the overt paranoid behavior of the patient. The reporting of such overt behavior blends nicely with test-gained diagnostic material. In practice, however, some psychologists build their entire case on tests. Thus, "on the Rorschach he sees a number of faces and the rear end of a bee; on the figure drawing there is eye emphasis, spearlike fingers, and concern is expressed over the size of the buttocks on the male figure; and one of his TAT stories depicts a character as an F.B.I. agent." This practice may be likened to determining a person's job qualifications by giving him or her an aptitude test, when actual job performance records on the subject—the sort of criteria against which the test is validated—are available.

This discussion of the source and the appropriateness of the content that the psychologist puts into the report should be understood in the context of an adequate, functioning team and in relation to a setting. In a traditional psychiatric setting, for example, it is not the psychologist who is usually charged with integrating the total data of the various disciplines. In other kinds of settings—school, counseling, forensic—the psychologist, by choice or not, may do many things usually regarded as not part of the psychologist's role in traditional psychiatric teams. The psychologist in current team practice often may be selective and utilize the contributions of others, or data ordinarily in the province of others (medical data, for example), only as these help to round out and make more useful the basic psychological conclusions.

SELECTION OF CONTENT
IN TERMS OF RELEVANCE

The problem of what is relevant for a given psychological report often is not broached. This is because of the tendency of psychologists to see their role as reporting the "findings"—whatever their tests happen to yield, such as IQs and other raw and partially interpreted data—rather than developing and interpreting content in terms of a specific mission. What content goes into a given report may depend on any or all of the following: (1) the orientation of the psychologist, (2) the orientation of the person who makes the referral, (3) the particular immediate problem that is under consideration, (4) the anticipated use(s) for the findings, and (5) habit.

The psychologist generally has the option to select content on the basis of a firm rationale and within liberal limits to be the sole judge of relevance. On the other hand, the psychologist may be subject to pressures from other team members, and the person who makes the referral may take quite an active role in the determination of relevance. If the latter is a Freudian, there may be obvious interest in getting data on such matters as psychosexual development, drives, and dynamics; the unconscious in general; the client's defensive structure and ego strength. If the orientation of the person making the referral is primarily descriptive, there may be heavy emphasis on diagnosis or classification and an expectation that the psychological report will work toward these ends.

Despite the strong orientations of many readers of psychological reports, the interests of the client and the goals of the setting should receive priority. In a setting where rehabilitation is emphasized, depth evaluations often detract from the main purpose. Instead, what is probably needed is information to help the staff understand the client's personal and social skills, attitudes toward rehabilitation and attainment of greater independence, and perhaps the client's interest or the ability to learn new skills. In settings where psychotherapy is practiced, it is often desirable to learn through psychological assessment of the individual's ability to profit from this form of treatment, the nature of the defensive structure, the basic personality integrity (ego strength), and hints to the psychotherapist. Where mental retardation seems to be the problem, a detailed qualitative and quantitative evaluation of intellectual and social skills might be in order.

Because of the possibly differing orientations among psychologists and other staff members, and also because of the wide range of problems that clients may present, there may exist a difference of opinion on what might be relevant information in a given case. A conference between the psychologist and the person who makes the referral, or indeed a preliminary staff conference, might be the best way of determining what kind of data are needed. Of course, after the psychologist starts the examination, pertinent material not previously seen as important might emerge.

The determination of relevance is a very practical problem when we consider the scope and the complexity of personality, to say nothing of the various ways in which we try to understand it. The full personality can hardly be approximated in a psychological report, even when the psychologist resorts to the presentation of an exhaustive list of conclusions. Nor would it be easy in practice to visualize where full or global coverage might be desirable, apart from the economic difficulties such an attempt would entail. Reports that include more content than is necessary require too much time to write and to read. They impose on the reader the task of separating that which is essential from that which is not—a duty that really belongs primarily to the psychologist to the extent that it is possible to anticipate what is needed.

What sort of conclusions should the psychologist report? There is no general answer to this question. The sort of information that might be indispensable in one case is probably superfluous or quite out of place in another. It is often appropriate to report on such matters as the self-concept, how others see the person, intellectual prowess or shortcomings, interests, life goals, frustrations, anxieties, defenses, and interpersonal and sexual adjustment factors. Frequently it is not. Sometimes it is well to discuss brain dysfunction, false notions held about the self, acting-out potentialities, self-destructive tendencies, impairments, relative skills, range and qualitative features of affective response, diagnostic category, intellectual level, or intellectual functioning, but often it is wasteful and an imposition on the reader to do so.

Fortunately it is possible to be more specific than this. Much of the remainder of this chapter discusses the sort of content often found in reports. We can assert quite definitely that certain kinds of content sometimes found in reports *never* belong there, and it is not at all likely that any particular primary content category ought to be represented in *all* reports. It is constructive to talk about the kinds of content that are frequently appropriate. Further, we often should not think about content on an all-or-none basis, but in terms of how much emphasis ought to be given to various kinds of content in specific case situations.

AN EVALUATION
OF COMMON CONTENT CATEGORIES
IN "TRADITIONAL" PSYCHOLOGICAL REPORTS

A systematic evaluation, specifically of psychological report content, might begin with an examination of what constitutes the "traditional" psychological report. The "traditional" report apparently came into its present form by accretion rather than by formulation and development of a rationale. This fact was of concern to Taylor and Teicher, who in 1946 noted that "clinical psychology . . . appears to have given little systematic study to the manner in which test findings are organized and formulated to provide necessary records and to render the data easily and fully understood by professional associates." Their solution to the problem was to offer a report-writing outline quite similar to the many now in existence. Apparently there was then no concern with what content is appropriate for *specific* reports, since the authors made reference only to the "test findings" and to "the data." Tests, presumably, provided all the information that might be necessary.

Many current psychological reports contain abundant "archeological" indicators of the origins of psychological practice. The early school background and the influence of the testing movement are evident in the prominent concern with matters of the intellect, and especially with the exalted position of the IQ. A more recent layer of development (1939) building on the Binet-Terman foundation is seen in the assignment of three IQs per person rather than one, and in the eager interest in which of the client's skill groupings—verbal or performance—is better. With the appearance in this country of the inkblots and the publication of the TAT, prominent new foci were what the person sees and the stories that are made up. After the association of psychology with psychiatry, Freud was welcomed into most clinics, and the emphasis shifted to personality, albeit one aspect of personality—such impalpables as the drives that trouble the individual and society, defenses, and retrospective developmental reconstructions. All these accretions commonly make up modern reports, prominent exceptions being found in many behaviorally oriented and neuropsychological reports where, for example, analytic concepts typically are absent. Just as taxes, once enacted, are hardly ever repealed, content categories, once they find their way into a report, are likely to be with us for some time.

Test-by-Test Reporting

Test-by-test reporting has lost favor with many psychologists and report readers, and integrated, battery reports are in widespread use. Particularly in the reporting of personality data are we likely to find interpretations from different tests blended into an integrated presentation. In the case of Mr. A., pages 125–132, there is a blending of material from personality tests and a test of intelligence.

Some psychologists anchor their major conclusions to the tests from which they were primarily derived. This need not detract from presenting the client as an individual or from the focus of the report. In the case of the school report (Eve) on pages 167–171, the report sequentially discusses WISC-R data, Illinois Test of Psycholinguistic Abilities data, and data from drawing tests, essentially three discrete areas of data. Similarly with the school report (Richard Swensen) on pages 171–173 where diverse tests are first interpreted individually and then flow together into a set of meaningful recommendations.

Reporting in Terms of Part Processes

Another type of broad content categorization still finds acceptance in many settings. This is the report that focuses on part processes—for example, intellection, drives, dynamics, affective responses, defenses, or sex adjustment. Objection is raised to this kind of report usually because some readers have difficulty in reconstructing the "whole person" from the segments. This kind of reporting predetermines what categories of content are important in *all* cases, largely relieving the psychologist of the necessity of questioning which conclusions are relevant and which are not.

Content Categories in Traditional Reports

The more typical traditional reports tend to contain a number of narrow content categories and two major categories, the first major category (typically appearing first in the report) labeled something like "Intellectual Aspects," and the second "Emotional Aspects," or simply "Personality." These common content categories may serve as a stable reference point against which revised categories may be compared.

Preliminary Part of Report

The first item of a report is often a statement of the reason for assessment. This can be a valuable piece of information, since the psychologist's mission is (or should be) largely defined by some presenting problem. A statement of the reason for assessment, therefore, may orient the reader on the sort of material likely to follow. This information commonly is supplied by someone other than the psychologist, such as a clinician who refers a case to a psychologist for assessment.

Following this statement may be a section on clinical behavior, various kinds of identifying information, or social data. Sometimes these heterogeneous classes of information are combined, appearing under the same heading or the same section of the report.

What the client does or says in the psychologist's office is commonly reported under a label like "Clinical Behavior," "Behavioral Note," "Behavioral Observations," or "Clinical Observations." The length of the section ranges from a few lines up to perhaps two single-spaced pages, and the sort of material found in it may vary widely from report to report and from psychologist to psychologist. In addition to behavioral information, this section often contains identifying information (for example, age, city of residence), descriptive information (for example, dress, attractiveness, how makeup is used), impressions (for example, the client has an underlying hostile attitude), matters of social history (for example, the person ran away and got married at 16), or the reason the person is being seen in the clinic, in the counselor's office, or wherever, in the individual's own words. In many instances such information is unjustifiably repetitious (for example, the date of admission to the hospital, height, body build, or what is elsewhere conveniently available), and such data are usually raw, uninterpreted, and often of doubtful value. Thus, "The patient readily entered the examining room and took the chair assigned" (few patients are dragged in, even when they are negativistic about being examined; in a school setting, however, a child's approach to an examiner is sometimes such as to challenge the validity of intelligence test results). Another example: "He wore a loose-fitting, faded blue bathrobe" (the one issued to him) "and was unshaven" (the patient is not permitted to shave himself and is shaved by an attendant three times weekly).

The behavior commented upon may be normal behavior (the patient responded appropriately to questions, showed appropriate affect, or gave no evidence of delusions or hallucinations); pathological behavior (the patient sat staring off into space, but with some difficulty could be induced to respond); common behavior (the patient smoked four filter-tip cigarettes during the two-hour testing session); or distinctive behavior (the patient was unusually ingratiating). Verbalizations commonly appear here, too. ("He spoke at length about his war experiences: 'I can still see the way the sergeant looked with his guts hanging out.'")

Presumably the material selected for reporting has some interpretive meaning that is best translated into clinically significant conclusions by the reader of the report. This abrogation of responsibility is, of course, out of keeping with a responsible professional role. Such practice goes so far at times that it strains the interpretive resources of even the most imaginative clinician ("The patient wore a bright red tie," or "The patient was excused during the testing period to go to the bathroom"). It should also be a matter of concern that there is no rational or consensual basis for what should appear in this section; this becomes obvious when we consider how much irrelevant and unoriginal data are found here.

There is apparently more rationale in reporting on the client's test behavior and test attitudes ("The client moved the blocks about in random fashion, sometimes forming a correct beginning for the required design, but then breaking up the pattern and starting over"; or "The client usually responded overly quickly, often being in error, and then usually asked for permission to correct her answer"; or, "He was vehement in his objection to testing, referring to the procedure as 'brain picking,' and 'in violation of the spirit, if not the wording, of the Fifth Amendment'"). Here too, however, the psychologist is asking another to interpret data that are clearly part of psychological training and competency. It may be very wasteful of such significant data to present them uninterpreted and apart from the important conclusions to which they may contribute.

Sugarman (1981) objects to including a section on clinical behavior at the beginning of the report for two powerful reasons: (1) the ease with which the examiner's description of the client's behavior is distorted by way of the examiner's countertransference reactions and (2) the distortion of the person in the mind-body dualism implied in the separation, for discussion, of the behaviors that are directly observed by the examiner and the characteristics that are elicited with the aid of psychological tests.

> Many graduate programs and treatment facilities teach testers to begin each test report with a description of the patient's behavior. Although there are many reasons to focus on nontest variables (some legitimate and some suspect), such a format allows the examiner's affective response to the patient to creep into the report in an unintegrated fashion. Such reports usually read as though behavioral attributes and the responses they evoke in others are distinct from internal attributes which have been assessed through the test responses. This separation reflects the mind-body quandary that has plagued psychology since Descartes and that impedes a holistic understanding of the patient.

Fresh fish sold here   Before proceeding further, a word of caution and logic may help reduce the sort of superfluous content that can work its way into reports. It should be a rule that the psychologist ask about each bit of content presented: "Does this contribute useful information?" Both in the preliminary section and throughout the report, superfluous, totally useless material can be nipped in the bud. The psychologist is not really contributing, as a psychologist, in reporting on such matters as the client's age, number of sibs, the presence of an accent, or the amount of hair that remains on the scalp.

There is the tale of the young man who went into the fish business. He rented a store, erected a sign, FRESH FISH SOLD HERE, and acquired merchandise.

As he was standing back admiring his market and his sign, a friend happened along. Following congratulations, the friend gazed at the sign and read aloud, FRESH FISH SOLD HERE. Of course it's *here.* You wouldn't sell it elsewhere, would you? Impressed with such astuteness, the young man painted over the obviously superfluous word. The next helpful comment had to do with the word *sold.* You aren't giving it away? Again impressed, he eliminated the useless word. Seemingly that was it, but the critic then focused on the word *fresh.* You wouldn't sell spoiled fish, would you? Once more our hero bowed to the strength of logic. Finally he was relieved that he had a logic-tight sign for his business: FISH. His ever-alert friend, however, audibly sniffing the air for effect, made a final observation: "You don't need a sign."

"Test Results"

Following the preliminary part of the report—such content categories as "Reason for Assessment," "Reason for Referral," "Descriptive Data," "Identifying Data," "Social Information," and "Clinical Behavior"—psychologists commonly shift gears and move to another realm of reporting that employs a sharply different flavor and vocabulary and examines the client on a wholly different level. This section of the report may be introduced by a heading such as "Test Results," "Findings," "Test Interpretation," or "Evaluation." Whereas the report up to this point made obvious reference to the client in various concrete ways, it is in this section that the consumer of the report frequently reads about matters like tests and theories, with the client an incidental, a vehicle to carry information about the psychologist's instruments and beliefs.

This broad content category is then commonly subdivided into two smaller categories. Let us call them, as they often are, "Intellectual Aspects" and "Personality" or "Emotional Factors."

"Intellectual Aspects"

Almost always found in the section on intellectual aspects is an IQ—or more usually, IQs—along with considerable discussion about the number(s) offered to the reader. Commonly it is thought important to let the reader know whether the number is truthful or not, but to report a number in any event. Thus, the writer once saw a psychological report prepared on a poorly accessible patient; the obtained IQ quite obviously did not have meaning or utility in its usual sense and was no indicator of the person's potential under more fortunate circumstances. Nevertheless, the psychologist, feeling constrained to report the expected IQ, wrote, "The patient obtained an IQ of 58, which is regarded as invalid." Then why present it? Is it not like the old technique of the late comedian Jack Benny, who always reported that he was 39, the humor residing in the fact that everyone understood this to be a broad falsification? (This is not to deny the pathognomonic significance of the impaired intellectual functioning.)

Also prominent in this section of the report, if one of the Wechsler scales is used, is a statement about the variability or "evenness" of intellectual functioning (scatter), about the patient's relative proficiency in the verbal and performance areas, and in certain heterogeneous skill groupings that may be subsumed under various descriptive headings, such as visual-motor function. Frequently there is no apparent rationale for the inclusion of such material, and what are presented as conclusions are more akin to raw data. Heavy scatter, for example, as determined either by inspection or by a quantitative index, is without any necessary meaning, even though there is a tendency for a high scatter index to be associated with schizophrenia (Trehub & Scherer, 1958). Nevertheless, the prudent psychologist will not conclude that a patient is schizophrenic solely on the basis of scatter; other data must also be weighed. On including a report about scatter, the psychologist must therefore consider what conclusions readers might reach from such raw datum. If a report of scatter is intended to support a conclusion, then it is also necessary to report the other main components that brought about that conclusion.

Some psychologists report in this section personality implications of intelligence test findings, matters like personality organization and factors related to adjustment. This meaningful approach, however, poses problems of content organization, since many such conclusions are less matters of the intellect than what is generally considered, report-wise, to fall under "personality." But some psychologists are not very much concerned about such matters and report *all* conclusions gained from intelligence tests under "Intellectual Aspects" and *all* conclusions derived from general tests of personality under "Personality"—even basic information on intellectual function gained through, for example, the Rorschach.

"Personality" or "Emotional Factors"

The section often entitled "Personality" or "Emotional Factors" may cause discomfort to the purist solely because of terminology. The objection is that personality is generally regarded as encompassing a larger field of study, perhaps something like ". . . the dynamic organization within the individual of those psychophysical systems that determine his unique adjustments to his environment" (Allport, 1937). To exclude what may be vital information on the role of cognition in adjustment (excluded because it is already neatly tied up in the previous section in a discussion of levels of test achievements, assets, shortcomings, and impressions about abstract heterogeneous skills) is hardly to give an adequate picture of personality. As for the term *emotional factors,* it should be obvious that much of the vital personality material described here—goals, interests, psychological characteristics of the parents, or cultural factors in the home—are not necessarily more related to emotions than is the intellect or the IQ.

The sort of content that appears in this section may vary somewhat among psychologists, but stereotypy is frequent. Commonly written about are such topics as psychopathology, unconscious drives, attitudes, conflicts, frustration, guilt, anxiety, defenses, psychosexual factors, and significant relationships. These topics may frequently be related to the mission, but often they are not. In many instances this section does not integrate significant environmental factors, the content of consciousness, and surface behavior with the deeper elements of personality.

"Diagnosis"

In many diagnostic/treatment settings the psychological report commonly gives some attention to a formal psychiatric diagnosis, usually after the discussion of "Intellectual Aspects" and "Personality," and somewhere toward the end of the report. As we have already seen (Chapter 2), the contribution is sometimes not appreciated. This objection apparently does not relate to psychologists' ability to diagnose, for it seems that they are as well qualified as are other experts in this respect (Wiener & Raths, 1959). Indeed, behavioral and neuropsychological diagnoses are almost exclusively in the realm of psychology. The issue seems rather to be one of role and of responsibility. Psychiatric diagnosis has long been considered a medical prerogative and is sometimes based on information not ordinarily available to the psychologist or on information that the psychologist cannot competently or ethically utilize (for example, neurological findings, or a laboratory procedure such as the dexamethasone suppression test). "Official" psychiatric diagnosis has traditionally been legally entrusted only to physicians. In practice, in a team setting the formal diagnosis frequently reflects the contributions of various team members.

Many psychiatrists are not offended by a psychologist's diagnostic impression or by a suggested diagnosis. It is possible to be overly obsequious in suggesting a diagnosis: "Such a pattern is commonly found in patients diagnosed as schizophrenic." This apologetic suggestion of a diagnosis may imply either (1) that the psychologist is convinced that this is a case of schizophrenia but hesitates to say so or (2) that diagnoses stem from tests and not from psychologists. The verbal maneuver is not necessary. Some psychiatrists might be offended only when the psychologist authoritatively indicates that schizophrenia *is* the diagnosis, thus usurping what some psychiatrists consider to be their function. It is hard to know why there is so much concern over formal diagnosis, particularly since many psychologists and dynamic psychiatrists minimize, or are even critical of, this contribution to the case study.

There are obvious instances where the psychologist's reporting of classificatory material is superfluous, even in settings where diagnosis is an administrative requirement or a matter of firm orientation. One occasion of this sort is when the person presents clear-cut classificatory characteristics or is already well known or "well diagnosed." Another occasion when the psychologist's suggested diagnosis contributes minimally, if at all, is when the emphasis is on understanding some personality characteristic—for example, when it is more important to know the meaning of a symptom than to know that the client's behavior merits some particular diagnosis.

Diagnosis, assessment, and *evaluation* are terms sometimes used interchangeably, in which case *diagnosis* usually includes much more than a formal classification. In such cases the term often refers to a major evaluative conclusion. Sometimes such contributions may consider what is appropriate as a formal diagnosis in a discussion context rather than offering a clipped nosological entity. In all cases the appropriateness of this diagnostic contribution depends partly on its pertinence and partly on the psychologist's qualifications to render it. In no case is the psychologist qualified to render what is properly a medical diagnosis.

Consider the following quoted material, taken from a discussion in Sarbin, Taft, and Bailey (1960). A 17-year-old girl had been referred to a psychiatric clinic because of "hysterical manifestations" after the examining physician could find no organic basis for her complaints of abdominal pains. As part of the total evaluation process the patient was seen by a psychologist who reported, in part, "the patient's unresolved oedipal conflict is apparent in her responses to the Thematic Apperception Test. The 'abdominal pains' *are* at one and the same time an identification with her departed father and a way of getting love from her mother" (emphasis supplied). Unfortunately for the patient, and for the validity of the psychologist's diagnostic statement, she was soon found to have a far advanced cancer in the region of complaint and succumbed to this condition the day following its discovery.

Now it may be that the psychologist's psychodynamic explanation was based on a sound understanding of the person. In fact, we are told that the girl's mother reported that her daughter had always been given over to dramatizing her problems and that she had been close to her father, who died as a result of a perforated ulcer. Such collateral information about the girl is similar to what the psychologist concluded from tests, but it should have been regarded in the light of the original medical findings only as *suggestive* of the nature of the girl's ailment, what it *might* be. How much better it would have been if the psychologist had not rendered an unqualified opinion on the nature of a bodily complaint, but had offered the opinion that the findings were consistent with a functional complaint, or even, in the light of the medical conclusion, suggested that "hysteria" was a *possible* explanation of the complaint.

"Prognosis"

Prognosis often follows diagnosis, as is frequently the case in medicine. Again, the objection from some psychiatric associates rests on how the content is presented. Certainly the psychologist's understanding of an individual's personality permits the making of certain predictions about future behavior. The psychiatrist may welcome these. What the psychiatrist may object to is wording to the effect that the psychologist is charting the presumed course of a *diseased* state. When behavioral deviancy is regarded in this manner, clearly a declining point of view, the psychologist is evidently wrong. Hence, the manner in which predictions are made—even the headings under which predictions are recorded—may influence the reader's perception of just what sort of content is being reported. (Try *outlook,* for example.) What can seem to be subtle differences are sometimes of great practical moment. In any event, many readers of psychological reports, such as educators, corrections personnel, and rehabilitation workers, welcome whatever glimpses into the future psychology can offer.

"Recommendations"

Recommendations often appear as one of the final content categories of the report. In many settings—in schools, for example—psychological consultation is sought for the help the psychologist can give in dealing with a problem. In other settings, however, notably some psychiatric settings, there is dispute about the psychologist's offering of such content. Some psychiatrists actively solicit this kind of material, whereas others denounce it as inappropriate and an encroachment upon medical function. There is no doubt that the psychologist does have information that can be translated into practical terms that have meaning for treatment, disposition, or other special considerations. And, in responding to a referral, the psychologist's purpose is specifically to present the content that meets the needs of the person making the referral. The manner of presentation, particularly the tactfulness of presentation, must be reemphasized. Thus, "Psychotherapy along with treatment directed at symptomatic reduction of depression may be beneficial" probably is a more palatable statement to most psychiatrists than "This patient ought to have psychotherapy and be started on Ludiomil 50 mg. b.i.d."

The working relationship will determine in part "just how far the psychologist should go." In the context of many relationships it is probably appropriate to write something to the effect that "the prominent and incapacitating depressive features in this patient suggest that she might respond to E.C.T." But it is doubtful that a recommendation such as ". . . the patient should be started on a course of insulin therapy with participation in group psychotherapy and occupational therapy . . . ," appearing in Garfield's (1957) textbook of clinical psychology, would be well received. Insulin treatment can have serious physiological consequences (the recommendation, incidentally, does not specify whether subcoma—"subinsulin"—is being prescribed or whether the psychologist wants the patient to have comas—"deep insulin"). Treatment with insulin requires intimate medical and nursing control, and the hazards of "deep insulin" have long since been one of the reasons for discarding its use in most settings.

"Summary"

Generally the report is concluded with a content category labeled "Summary," or sometimes "Summary and Conclusions," which may imply that new major material not dealt with in the body of the report, perhaps a diagnostic formulation or a recommendation, is being introduced. It is hard to argue against the use of summary content since this is so well entrenched in writing practice and since many clinical workers seem to feel the need for such a statement (Tallent & Reiss, 1959a,b). However, the use of a summary may often be injudicious, and it should be considered for use with discretion.

The major objection raised against the use of a summary is that it may serve with some degree of effectiveness as an antidote to an otherwise inadequate report. Such seems particularly true of reports that are inadequate because they are too long, too difficult, and too involved, the summary by comparison being readable. The reader is soon trained to ignore the report proper and to be content with the summary, even though by definition this section can hardly be expected to carry the legitimate freight of the report. The fact that a number of readers are apparently content with first perusing the summary suggests that perhaps this briefer version of a report often more closely approximates the felt requirements of report readers than does the main body.

An opposite objection to the use of a summary may be made when the summary concludes an otherwise succinct report. There is a tendency among some psychologists to present a concise, content-loaded report, although without omitting the traditional summary. The result may appear ludicrous, at least visually if not also logically, when the length of the summary approaches the length of the report. In terms of actual measurement, one may find reports six, seven, or eight inches in length to which is appended a summary statement of three, four, or five inches!

When a summary statement is used, Hammond and Allen's (1953) suggestion for an "opening summary"—what is sometimes called an *overview*— is well taken. This technique seems to be used effectively in journalism, particularly in feature articles, in scientific journals, and with book chapters. It is thought that presenting the essence of the material at the beginning will create in the reader the proper set needed for understanding and will entice the reader to delve into the main body of writing. By contrast, many are of the opinion that a summary at the end, when read first, tends against turning back to the text proper.

FREQUENTLY APPROPRIATE CONTENT

From consideration of the traditional report, we may profitably turn to a discussion of the kinds of psychological content commonly thought to be helpful to clinical workers. The original data that form the basis for the ensuing discussion are from the survey reported on in Chapter 2 (Tallent & Reiss, 1959a). No doubt some of the expressed needs reflect familiarity with traditional reports, but many who offered advice on appropriate content had ideas of their own. All the categories suggested with a degree of frequency are examined closely in terms of their positive and negative potentialities and with a view to their proper usage. The kinds of content mentioned are not appropriate for all reports, since each report is a highly individual matter. Nor is it implied that reports should be limited to these categories, which are meant only as general guidelines. It is better to think in terms of what sort of content is *frequently* appropriate.

Clinical Behavior
and Descriptive Material

Report readers are interested in a broad range of behavior, both current and potential, and the reporting of the client's clinical behavior and other descriptive material continues to find favor among a number of them. This area of data, dealing as it does with overt material, presents the hazard of duplicating the contributions of other team members. Such observations are best presented—if relevant to the evaluation goal—in a unique context elicited in some special way, or one that offers some special insights (for example, in response to test stimuli or in association with unique psychological findings).

Three subcategories of such material are specifically mentioned as appropriate: appearance, general behavioral observations, and a description of the examiner-client interaction. Of these, a discussion of a client's appearance (probably noted elsewhere, particularly if highly unusual) is least likely to be fruitful. This is especially true of those aspects of appearance without apparent psychological correlates or not reliably interpretable.

General behavioral observations are frequently unique material because of the inherent differences between a psychological examination and the contacts of other workers. A psychological examination involving a full battery is, in general, more time-consuming than are other examinations or the interviews carried out by the psychologist's associates. This longer period of observation offers the possibility of noting behavior that might not occur in procedures that are cursory by comparison. The length of examination also presents opportunities for noting variations in behavior, particularly when the client is seen over a period of two or more days. Unique behavior is frequently elicited because aspects of the psychological examination are ambiguous to the client. Many clients find it hard to understand the role of the psychologist, the purpose or rationale of the tools that are used, and the procedures. The psychological examination is a projective situation to which people make diagnostically useful responses.

The examiner-client interaction is a vital datum, especially to those psychologists who stress the role of interpersonal relationships in the understanding of personality. Knowledge of this interaction is regarded as valuable, since it is a sample of a role the person tends to take in certain social encounters and of some of the person's more typical behaviors. This is particularly important for the psychotherapist in need of gaining a firmer understanding of transactions with his or her client (p. 197). Thus the unique personality of the psychologist is as much an examination stimulus as are the various test stimuli. The client's test productions are quite reasonably regarded as based in part on the interaction between examiner and client (Masling, 1960). This situation, skillfully understood, can contribute valuable conclusions to the case study.

From the point of view of the current presentation, all such behavior description is generally best offered as interpreted material, except where it is used for its illustrative value. Some readers of the psychological report ask for the psychologist's impressions, which are, in effect, interpreted observations. Such interpretation no doubt involves a greater subjective element than is often regarded as proper in the interpretation of test data.

Intellectual Factors
of Personality

Various intellectual factors of personality continue to be of interest to clinical workers in nonschool or nonrehabilitation settings, although the specific things they want to know sometimes differ from the information found in the traditional report. Their concern with intellect often has less important consequences than does the concern of the teacher or the rehabilitation worker, for example. Yet some workers are particularly interested in learning about the intellectual assets of their patients. Such data would seem to be most valuable to school personnel, when rehabilitation measures involving training or placement are at issue, and sometimes under other circumstances, such as when forensic matters are at issue. They may be helpful, in fact, when any change in a person's life situation is contemplated, since cognitive resources are definitely a factor in adjustment. Include here matters of cognitive style as well as of intellectual level, both of which may be of interest to the psychotherapist (p. 197).

Intellectual liabilities seem to call up interest among clinical workers, perhaps because of the "maladjustment bias" that is so often found in the diagnostic/treatment setting. Data on low intelligence, however, may help to explain the person's frustrations or other problems of significance to the case study. Planning for the future is thus facilitated. Similar interest centers on acquired intellectual deficit—various earlier resources that are no longer available to the individual. This type of difficulty may present problems, particularly vocational, academic, and social adjustment problems. Of importance here are the nature and the extent of deficit and the requirements that are placed upon the person. An isolated statement of deficit may not be very valuable practically, since persons can often carry on adequately in well-practiced areas of function, sometimes even in occupations involving a fair degree of responsibility, in the presence of appreciable loss.

Information about another aspect of deficit, that of the premorbid intelligence, is spontaneously requested by clinical workers far less frequently than such discussions occur in samples of psychological reports. An estimate of premorbid functioning, or of the relationship of current to premorbid functioning, is mainly of value as a crude, nonspecific index of the extent of psychopathology and is perhaps best expressed in qualitative terms. Figures presented on deficit frequently lack practical clinical meaning, particularly when they are presented out of context of the functioning personality.

The interest of many clinical workers is in some specific aspect or aspects of intellectual functioning that they feel is of importance. A psychiatrist or a social worker may wish further information on such matters as abstract ability, memory function, or the ability to learn. Such more or less specific requirements point up the desirability of specific referrals. Many workers nevertheless express a general interest, such as in the "current intellectual status." Presumably such a request gives the psychologist latitude in deciding which findings about the intellect ought to be reported.

Surprisingly, when asked about the sort of content that ought to appear in psychological reports, 58 percent of the replies from psychiatrists indicated that an IQ or the intelligence level be specified, whereas only 1 percent of the psychologists so replied. This finding is surprising because a much higher percentage of psychologists *do* apparently give this kind of datum high priority by presenting it before there is any discussion of other findings. Is it possible that psychologists do not really believe in this generous offering of the IQ but are under the impression that it is supposed to be done? The psychiatrists' apparent eager interest in numbers purporting to tell how intelligent their patients are is also surprising, since it is often uncertain what practical use they make of this information. It may be that this interest is a residual of the great emphasis psychologists and educators had put on the IQ in an earlier era, or it may reflect the interest in intelligence emphasized in the middle-class cultural background of many psychiatrists.

Whatever the sources of differing opinions on the need for various kinds of intellectual data, it is appropriate that we reexamine the role that knowledge of the intellect plays in the appraisal of personality in practical (clinical-type) situations. There should be almost universal agreement that knowledge of the functioning of the intellect offers information on (1) skill-interest-motivational complexes of efficiencies, (2) the functioning of various personality processes, and, as a special case, (3) the kinds and degrees of both functional and organic disruption of the personality.

The relatively infrequent need for detailed knowledge of efficiencies and inefficiencies, in many diagnostic/treatment settings has already been mentioned. The common use of individual intelligence tests that require over an hour to administer, score, and interpret would hardly be justified in many cases were the main purpose to determine intellectual level. There frequently are more economical ways of obtaining such information.

On the other hand, individual intelligence tests of the Wechsler group are being used effectively to gain personality information of the sort presumably related to intellectual function but usually thought of in a noncognitive context. Information on personality, such as dependency traits, attitudes toward society, suspiciousness, impulsivity, and defense mechanisms, may be gained through intelligence tests. The manner in which such traits are intimately tied up with the client's intellectual resources often constitutes valuable datum for the person who makes the referral. Information of this sort, however, generally is best discussed along with personality features other than the client's skills and efficiencies.

An analysis of intellectual functioning is sometimes the key contribution the psychologist can make to the case study. This contribution commonly is arrived at through a study of deficits, both quantitative and qualitative. Certain quantitative deficit patterns, often considered together with observations of functioning on an intelligence test, may be identified as the effect of brain pathology. This item of information is of particular interest to many teachers, psychiatrists, and neurologists, as well as to psychologists, and is regarded as one of the more valuable contributions of the psychologist.

Psychiatrists are often interested in learning from the psychologist about the formal thought processes. The official criteria for the diagnosis of the schizophrenic psychoses include alterations in the thought processes (Spitzer and others, 1980), and these are often best evaluated through psychological procedures. Sometimes, in fact, this kind of malfunction is not evident in samples of well-practiced interpersonal relationships and is seen only in performance on psychological tests—intelligence tests and other psychological tests. Similarly the full effect of a neurotic process or a personality disorder often is better understood through the effects on the cognitive processes.

Nonintellectual Factors
of Personality

Those personality factors generally considered nonintellectual are requested as proper content by large numbers of report readers, although sometimes one professional group places more emphasis on certain classes of data
than do others. The separation of these data from intellectual operations is
merely a habitual way of thinking, a result of the artificial dichotomization
of the personality in psychological reports (or perhaps more basically of the
"isolation" of intelligence from the rest of personality years ago). Many clinical workers mention as proper content a "general personality picture."

Interest in psychopathology is widespread in psychiatric settings, and
there are a number of discrete areas that are often specified. These include
general description of the psychopathological process, discussion of the areas
of disturbed functioning, behavioral symptomatology, reality contact, and
etiological information, although perhaps significantly it is primarily psychologists who seem to value such content in reports. Now that the *Diagnostic
and Statistical Manual* of the American Psychiatric Association (Spitzer and
others, 1980, 1987) is essentially "atheoretical," many users of the manual perhaps are also inclined to be "atheoretical" in their diagnostic formulations
and do not seek etiological information. It is difficult to believe, however, that
dynamically oriented psychiatrists, or others, will alter their position on the
basis of the conceptual underpinnings of DSM-III and DSM-III-R.

The underlying psychological processes are regarded as an appropriate
topic by all professions of the classical clinical team. Many think in terms of
a partial dichotomization of evaluative function between psychologists and
other team members, the former being charged with illuminating deep activities of the psyche and psychiatrists and social workers with focusing on more
palpable behaviors—historical information, affect, or stream of consciousness, with some inferential penetrations into the unconscious. This view is
inaccurate and unfair to all concerned. All levels of behavior are the province
of psychology, and psychological examination is often invaluable in describing
important but essentially overt manifestations of behavior, functions such as
memory, behavioral control, the intensity of surface hostility, and the channels
through which it is expressed. The psychologist who seeks an integrated view
of the client explores the unconscious, too, often contributing valued information. Instruments such as the Rorschach frequently contribute to a significant advantage in subsurface explorations, but the psychologist holds no deed
on this section of the personality.

One of the more vital content areas, in the opinion of many workers, is
the conflicts of the patient. Presumably both unconscious and conscious conflicts are alluded to here, although the unconscious conflicts are generally considered the more important ones in shaping psychopathology. The adjustment
variable most frequently suggested as proper content, however, is the defenses.

The defensive structure is truly one of the major highways leading to an understanding of personality. A knowledge of the defenses permits one to gauge the stability of a person and may also have a direct relationship to psychotherapeutic activity. The sort of controls exercised by a person, and their effectiveness, can be of key significance. Some think it may be advisable to discuss the appearance or the role of anxiety in adjustment.

The motivational factors in personality also come in for a good deal of attention. Again these would seem to be of central importance in understanding the personality and its key problems. In general, there is much stress on the importance of drives or dynamics, but some point out the importance of motivational elements that are largely conscious, such as the person's interest areas and goals. It certainly would be remiss of the psychologist not to emerge occasionally from the depths of the unconscious to assess the molding power of forces about which the person has awareness and which are probably significant to an individual's life.

The personality assets and liabilities of the client, aside from purely intellectual assets and liabilities, are commonly proposed as important psychological contributions to the case study. Interestingly psychologists who were questioned suggested far more frequently the appropriateness of reporting on assets rather than on liabilities. This opinion contrasts with the notion that many psychologists show a "maladjustment bias" in their reports. Psychiatrists and social workers in particular comment on the importance of learning from the psychologist about the person's "ego strength," an item of information that would be especially important when psychotherapeutic intervention is contemplated.

Perhaps surprisingly, social workers indicate that they look for a discussion of social variables in psychological reports. Since it appears that social workers are sensitive to encroachment on their function and could hardly be sympathetic toward reports that parallel and duplicate their own material, it is likely that they favor the thesis presented here: that social variables ought to be presented in the psychological report, but only when they are integrated with newly developed personality data. Of particular interest to social workers is information on interpersonal relationships. How clients relate to significant life figures is a key topic of interest to social workers.

Interpersonal perceptions are suggested as another key topic. Psychologists understand that a person's perception of the environment is vastly more important than the physical facts of the environment. This personality topic frequently is central to adequate case study, on a par with the self-concept.

Diagnostic Material

The reaction of many psychiatrists to the offering of a diagnosis by the psychologist has already been presented in several contexts. It is well to note the other side of the coin, the expressed *interest* of psychiatrists in obtaining diagnostic information from the psychologist. The existence of such differences would seem to emphasize the individual focus of psychological work. Much of the diagnostic information sought, however, is not formal or in terms of an official classification. Many psychiatrists, for example, often would like a psychological opinion on the presence of an underlying psychotic process.

The medical orientation of many psychiatrists is particularly evident in their interest in securing from the psychologist diagnostic information concerning a possible organic mental disorder—their requests for psychological assessment often reading "rule out organicity." It is good both that many psychologists are able to deliver an informed opinion on this important topic and that psychiatrists are aware of this fact.

Predictive Material

The cautions mentioned with reference to the offering of diagnoses also apply to predictions. Particularly the giving of a prognosis may be a delicate matter, as already noted. Social workers, however, seem to be more accepting of such contributions than are psychiatrists, hardly a surprising finding. Social workers also emphasize the practical and the environmental in the way of predictions and ask for such information as the vocational and educational outlook. Thus the reception of various areas of prediction is an individual matter among report readers. Many are interested in several of the different forms of acting-out potential, such as homicide, suicide, or paraphilia, and others want to know about treatment prospects.

Recommendations

The objections raised to the psychologist's offering of recommendations have also been noted. Some potential strain is seen in clinical relations because psychologists in general seem to want to make recommendations more often than their team associates, particularly psychiatrists, might wish to have them. Thus in the Tallent-Reiss survey (1959b) 74 percent of the psychologist sample suggested that it is appropriate to offer recommendations regarding treatment, whereas only 14 percent of the psychiatric respondents spontaneously mentioned the need for such help. Teachers and others who so eagerly seek the help of psychologists must find all of this strange.

What is appropriate content for a psychological report depends, then, on the workers involved in the case, on the reasons for which the person is referred, and on the available conclusions from which the psychologist has to select.

INAPPROPRIATE CONTENT

It is far easier to make pronouncements on what is never appropriate in a psychological report than to offer opinions on what may be appropriate. The most helpful generalization is that the psychologist never renders conclusions that are outside actual or defined limits of function or competence. Admittedly the borderlines are sometimes vague and subject to personal interpretations that may be at variance with group consensus. The overall psycho-evaluative competence of the psychologist is not generally challenged, however, and at this late date is not likely to be. Yet the establishment of certain conclusions based on personality data—for example, the making of medical treatment decisions—are functions legally proscribed to the psychologist. Thus there exist some clear external guidelines that show what is beyond the psychologist's qualifications or functions. This observation is consistent with the fact that psychologists may be, and are, asked to contribute information or opinions to decisions that are ultimately outside their scope.

Then there are matters that are within the broad purview of psychology but that may be beyond the competence of a given psychologist. Generally the decision here is based on the psychologist's awareness of personal limitations of training and experience and on adherence to ethical principles, particularly Principle 2 of the *Ethical Principles of Psychologists* (American Psychological Association, 1981). A psychologist not skilled in the Rorschach ought not to present conclusions based on the use of this instrument. A psychologist not enlightened or practiced in psychoanalytic usage ought not to present conclusions in such a framework. Many psychologists cannot give sound direct treatment suggestions in cases of speech disability or reading disability, but psychologists who have had adequate training and experience in these areas might be specifically employed for their ability to render conclusions on such problems.

Another basic ethical constraint follows Principle 5a of the *Ethical Principles of Psychologists*. In accord with this principle the psychologist must not write into the report statements that are not germane to the evaluation or that are an undue invasion of privacy.

THE APPROPRIATE EMPHASIS
OF CONTENT

In report writing it is helpful to think not only in terms of what to include or exclude but also in terms of what contents to emphasize or de-emphasize. The topics composing the psychological report should, according to our present frame of reference, try to meet perceived and anticipated needs of the client. This requirement ought to be true of the various emphases in a report, too. If we take into consideration the different orientations held by psychologists, however, it is understandable for the psychologist to present findings in terms of a personal approach to understanding personality and behavior. This is probably not wrong *as long as the psychologist is still able to fulfill the mission as perceived.* This argument is not meant to defend the habitual emphases of a psychologist who has no clear-cut orientation or who emphasizes certain kinds of material solely because of a misguided impression of how psychological reports are supposed to be written.

We may consider, for example, emphasis on developmental content versus emphasis on contemporary content. A psychoanalytic orientation might focus on developmental stages and apparently suit the requirements that prevail in an analytically oriented setting; even here, though, the therapist will probably be more interested in the strength of the individual's defensive structure and in other issues (see the discussion on pp. 202–203). When humanistic or somatic therapies are used, we should be aware that such treatments may deliberately be blind to the individual's developmental history. Even when traditional psychotherapy is the chosen approach, many therapists, including analytically oriented workers, now tend to believe that treatment centering on contemporary problems offers the greatest therapeutic leverage.

An emphasis on unconscious content often appears in reports to the exclusion of concern with consciously directed behavior, the content of consciousness, and surface behavior. Unconscious content is commonly related to the origins and to the deepest reaches of psychopathology. To dwell on such content may be unjustifiable in other than very dynamically oriented situations. Other significant clues to psychological problems—such as the precipitating factors and salient features of the condition, its future course, and therapeutic possibilities—can often be effectively approached through the content of consciousness and the surface behavior. The practical relevance of content may then properly dictate the emphasis. Consider, for example, the matter of drives or dynamics, or, as a specific instance of this, the term *hostility*, which appears so frequently in psychological reports. The form this ubiquitous trait takes may be central to the understanding of a particular problem—for example, "hysterical" behavior—otherwise it is often unworthy of emphasis or even of mention in a report. Much the same may be said of the common content categories of defenses and conflicts. A discussion of these topics can be crucial to the psychotherapist who wishes to strengthen a functioning personality and needs to know how well the client can cope with stress developed in the therapeutic situation. But of what value is the presentation of unconscious content to the symptomatically oriented chemotherapist?

5

Conceptualizing the Psychological Report

A flexible approach makes for better psychological reports. This view, along with some ways to implement it, is offered as a contribution to the old problem of how to organize reports. Apparently the difficulties involved in this task have not been alleviated by the various general report outlines that are presently available. What is proposed here is a new schema of the assessment process together with the suggestion that the report be case-focused and conceptualized in terms of the mission. In such a report the roles of issues like content selection, theoretical orientation, and organizational form will readily take on meaning.

The responsibility of the psychologist—to the client, to the person who makes the referral, to the team, and to society—is the central theme of this discourse. The foregoing discussions have dealt with many of the elements that make up such responsibility. This chapter ventures to round out the points already made and to suggest for them a framework to provide some additional rationale and further guidance for the preparation of an effective psychological report.

In an earlier chapter much space was given to the topic of pitfalls that, unfortunately, seem to be prevalent in psychological report writing. Additional pitfalls are exposed in the ensuing discussion, but there are differences. The pitfalls that were discussed earlier are, for the most part, of the sort that are common to poor rhetoric: inappropriate choices about what to write, insufficient self-criticalness of the writer and the consequent presentation of faulty and blurred ideas, inadequate consideration for the reader's needs, poor command of language, and the like. Only in our discussion of "Problems of Science and Profession" did we confront another sort of pitfall.

In focusing on the assessment process we reveal concern that many psychologists do not conceptualize well an adequate scheme of psychological assessment. When such is true, the development and implementation of assessment skills may be seriously impeded. The value of psychological input into the case may be in doubt.

THE EVOLUTION OF PSYCHOLOGICAL ASSESSMENT SCHEMES

The psychological report is the end product of the assessment process and a contribution to some sort of intervention in a person's life. To follow the thinking that leads to the report, we must first conceptualize a theory of the assessment process, from the development and integration of information to the emergence of pragmatic conclusions. Let us start the discussion by noting the role of the physicalistic model of assessment and then move to a model of clinical assessment that better reflects much of current practice.

Psychological assessment stems from, and *incorporates* features of, the psychometric model that has so long been prominent in psychology. Thorndike's logically sequential pronouncements are the basis: "If a thing exists, it exists in some amount," and, "If it exists in some amount, it can be measured."

Such a physicalistic position, equating psychological behaviors at all levels with *things,* a position that many find conceptually flawed, nevertheless has long proved useful in making individual and group predictions. Measurement of this sort is also the basis for norms that have such a crucial role in assessment. Group testers and individual assessors differ, however, inasmuch as the individual assessor develops or utilizes normative data only as these are consistent with and amplify other highly valued data. For example, a psychologist employing the Halstead-Reitan Neuropsychological Battery may encounter a high error score on the Categories test suggestive of conceptual impairment and a possible brain dysfunction in the client. But alternatively, the psychologist might be impressed that the client demonstrates good conceptual ability in other ways, or perhaps even that adequate motivation to do well on this rather demanding test seemed lacking. For such reasons a diagnostic impression of brain dysfunction may be neither conclusive nor convincing.

In the routine course of clinical psychological assessment, numerous problems are encountered for which the psychometric (physicalistic) model is not adequate. A new scheme of assessment must be explicitly set forth; clinical psychologists obviously have long followed leaders other than Thorndike. But even these leaders evidence some Thorndikian influence, at least in their word usage, employing such still-current expressions as *tester* and *test results.* Indeed, Ivnik (1977) points out that the term *psychodiagnosis* sometimes ". . . is primarily reserved for the use of psychological tests." There seems to be a discrepancy in that many who do not follow a physicalistic model routinely use physicalistic language.

Schafer (1949), in a research-oriented paper with broad significance for clinical practice, was, as a participant in the development of the Rapaportian tradition, among the first to contribute direction to the approach to assessment presented here. Indeed, many view his emphasis of psychologist over tests as a major distinction of modern practice.

> Scores are not meant to replace psychological thinking; they are designed to facilitate it, and as such they can be relegated to the background when this is warranted by the logic of the problem.

Also

> The alternative to considering the score the adequate meaningful micro-unit is considering the interpretation the meaningful unit. This approach recognizes that the same score can have different meanings and that the same meaning can be conveyed by different scores. It also recognizes the fact that scores in general do not adequately convey all the implications of a response or a set of responses.

Further, in the psychometric era of the 1940s, anticipating more nearly universal current trends, Schafer (1949) set forth the following as goals of psychological assessment:

> Identifying personality characteristics rather than diagnoses as clinical criteria.
>   Individual variations as a focus of interest along with group trends.
>   Blind qualitative analysis prior to statistical comparison.
>   Interpretation as micro-units of analysis and batteries of tests as macro-units of investigation.

Drifting further from the earlier physicalistic approach, Shectman (1979) argues that effectiveness of assessment must now consider personal characteristics of the psychologist (particularly shortcomings, covered in our earlier section called "Pitfalls") and interpersonal staff issues (see pp. 16–18). Additionally Shectman broaches the content of the referral question. With this issue the complexity of clinical psychological assessment starts to become evident.

How the clinician formulates questions to the psychologist is a related issue. The psychologist sometimes must interpret the referral source—that is, what does the referring clinician *really* want to know? Might one infer from the question as posed that the assessment psychologist is in a position to supply useful information that is *not* being requested, or is the referral question as posed impossible to answer meaningfully or usefully? Thus Shectman (1979) comments, ". . . the provider who responds to the referral issues alone and not to the person making the referral repeats Freud's mistake and that of diagnosticians who respond to referral questions as if they existed in a vacuum." Freudiana surfaces again as Cohen (1980) suggests that ". . . there is a manifest and a latent content to many testing referrals." The latent content very well may pertain to interpersonal factors among clinic personnel. One example, a personal anecdote cited by Cohen, reports on a case where the real issue was a disagreement over diagnosis between psychiatrist and patient, with Cohen finding himself more in the position of arbiter than of diagnostician.

Howe (1981) describes an evaluation schema that emphasizes (1) the need for meaningful referral, (2) "the differences between a diagnostic model of *testing* and dispositional assessment" (emphasis added), and (3) the need for ". . . the assessor to understand the treatment context as well as the client. . . ."

Shevrin and Shectman (1973) propose yet additional crucial features for an assessment schema. Such features are relevant, of course, in various diagnostic situations and not simply in the diagnosis of mental disorders of which the authors write: "In the diagnosis of mental disorders, the diagnostician, through the *medium of a personal relationship, elicits and observes* a range of *psychological functioning* which he considers *relevant on some theoretical grounds* for understanding the disorders so that he can make a *recommendation* which stands a good chance of being acted on as a basis for dealing with the disorders." Consideration of the personal role of the psychologist and of the psychologist's theoretical position leads to another powerful comment: "From our point of view, diagnosis is *not* the unsolicited functioning existing in a purely impersonal empirical realm unrelated to theoretical orientation and indifferent to outcome."

The Sloves-Docherty-Schneider Scientific Problem-Solving Model

A logical end point to the evolution of Thorndike's physicalistic thesis is based on Sloves, Docherty, and Schneider's (1979) adaptation of a scientific problem-solving model proposed by Comtois and Clark (1976). Such an adaptation is informed by their view that "the current state of affairs in psychological assessment is one of confusion, misconception, attack, and counterattack." The position of Sloves et al. suggests that the roots of this problem run deep.

Much of the confusion and misconception over psychological assessment is a result of the failure to differentiate between two conceptually distinct aspects of psychodiagnosis, referred to here as psychological assessment and psychological testing. Psychological assessment is defined as a variable process of problem solving, decision making, and evaluation procedures. The goal of psychological assessment is to "yield information relevant to treatment and . . . generate decisions which will be helpful to clients" (Peterson, 1968, p. 8). Psychological testing is defined as a set of skills, tactics, and strategies subsumed under the heading of psychological methods. In this view, methods represent the technical skills used as a means of carrying out a psychological assessment. Psychological assessment is systems and problem oriented, dynamic, and conceptual; whereas psychological testing is methods and measurement oriented, descriptive, and technical.

Lack of conception of such fundamentals has, in the view of these authors, resulted in the inability of ". . . many practitioners and trainers in professional psychology to distinguish between assessment and testing." This problem, in turn, ". . . has led to a tendency for the profession to focus its attention on the mechanistic and technical aspects of test administration and to ignore or slight the conceptual basis of the assessment process."

To counter this trend, Sloves et al. present their model in six steps:

Step one, *problem clarification,* is a reframing of the referral question. What are the needs of the referral source? To answer this seemingly simple question may require the posing of a number of additional questions and a study of the circumstances that have led to the making of a referral.

Step two is called *planning.* Responding to the statement of a problem, the psychologist forms hypotheses for testing. What might give rise to the problem and how might we establish that such is the case? Often there might be alternative explanations, and it might be wise to consider which of these apply.

Development, the third step, involves planning for implementation of the previous step. What data are requested? Will the administration and interpretation of tests in widespread use meet our purpose, or is the construction of an ad hoc tool, such as an instrument for the systematic recording of behavior, indicated?

The fourth step, *implementation,* involves all the particulars of what usually come under the rubric of "testing" or of the making of direct observations. Such details as preparing clients for assessment and explaining to them their legal rights are part of this step.

The fifth step is *outcome determination.* Here the effects of the psychologist's intervention are evaluated. Was the information deemed necessary for clarifying issues forthcoming? Were the hypotheses adequately tested? Responding to these questions involves a number of considerations, such as evaluations of "the level of expertise of the assessor, the instruments used, any biases of the instruments or assessor that may have influenced the reliability and validity of the assessment, and the reactions of the persons involved in the assessment." No small order! An accomplished, well-seasoned psychologist, we would hope, can take the responsibility for such a determination. Perhaps at times the collaboration of a colleague might also be helpful at this stage of use of the problem-solving model (or at any stage, for that matter). Certainly where a trainee is involved the role of the supervisor should be particularly conspicuous.

The final step, *dissemination,* involves report writing in the broad sense that we use it here and, as such, is concerned with many of the issues dealt with in this book. The authors define this step well in terms of "the com-

munication of *useful* information to those concerned with the assessment''
(emphasis supplied).

Although the authors see some drawbacks to the use of this model, they
nevertheless believe that its advantages ultimately overshadow initial difficulties and that it provides a training aid to the neophyte.

> By making the process explicit, of course, it becomes at once laborious to use
> and a gross simplification of the actual clinical process. However, it need only
> be used in this unwieldy manner until the model is internalized. The oversim-
> plification of the model is a characteristic of any conceptual model and can ac-
> tually be considered an advantage for the sake of training. Once the process is
> internalized, the clinician-trainee can begin to provide his or her own elaboration
> in practice.

An Interactional Schema
of the Clinical Assessment Process

Figure 5-1, the author's concept of the assessment process, would appear
to be compatible with the views formulated by Sloves et al. (1979). As these
authors indicate, assessment is not a linear event, and as described here, the
process is understood primarily as an interaction between the psychologist and
four key categories of information: (1) the reason for assessment (or the background of the case), (2) raw data, (3) frame(s) of reference, and (4) the psychological report. Only as the psychologist adequately develops, reacts to, and
integrates the first three categories (placed at the angles of the triangle) do his
or her activities lead to a set of meaningful conclusions that, when effectively
presented, make for an adequate psychological report.

Focusing attention on the triangle, the placement of the psychologist (Ψ)
at the center emphasizes a hierarchy of importance of the interacting elements.
As commonly observed, in psychological assessment the psychologist is the
chief diagnostic instrument. The reason for assessment, a matter to which the

FIGURE 5-1   Psychological Assessment Schema

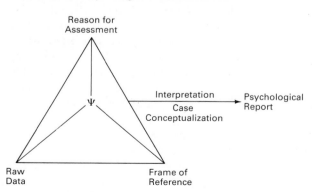

psychologist should always react, is a matter of importance secondary only to the psychologist and is shown at the apex of the triangle. Without an explicit and meaningful reason for assessment, an assessment needn't be carried out.

Frame(s) of reference should be considered to hold a somewhat lower position inasmuch as the reason for assessment commonly can be dealt with in the context of various frames of reference. For example, the solution to a problem may be sought in a behavioral approach, in various dynamic positions, in a humanistic or neuropsychological orientation, or perhaps even through some combination of these or through an open-ended exploration.

Similarly assessment data are in a subordinate position since these are developed by the psychologist in terms of both the reason for assessment and the frame(s) of reference. Test results may be placed in the category of assessment data: Test results are not the basic purpose of a clinical assessment and are not synonymous with the psychological report.

In the following paragraphs the components of the schema, of which the psychologist is an integral part, are explicated in terms of typical clinical practice. The operation of the schema guides the development and the formulation of the case of "Mr. A." presented later in this chapter.

Reason for assessment   The psychologist may carry out an assessment to provide guidelines for planning a therapeutic strategy. Or a therapist, a teacher, or an administrator may seek the help of a psychological assessor to gain understanding and an approach to working with a person. Regardless of who initiates the request for assessment, the reason for assessment in a treatment situation is always based on the recognition that some specific behavior or behaviors in a client may be changeable to the client's advantage.

Problems are most likely to arise when the referral source does not provide a reason for requesting an assessment or when the reason given appears to the psychologist to be unrealistic or not likely to yield the sort of information that might be helpful. The psychologist therefore cannot be merely the passive recipient of referrals. Often it is necessary for the psychologist to contact the referral source and clarify what sort of data should be sought in the assessment. The psychologist plays an active role in developing the consultation. The assessment procedure starts before the psychologist meets the client.

Raw data   *Raw data* consist of all observations and other information that are available to the psychologist and that may be pertinent in responding to the reason for carrying out an assessment or that otherwise might be judged by the psychologist to be useful. Included are direct observation of behavior (including the client's spontaneous actions and verbalizations) plus information supplied by others, such as parents or teachers. Behavior report forms may be completed by such persons or by the psychologist. The psychologist may also administer tests from which stem such data as scores, ratios, percentages, profiles, and verbalizations. Classically such material, together with a discussion of quantitative relationships among scores and a qualitative description of test performance, have been labeled *test results*. [The author's preference is to call such material *raw data* (pp. 56–60).] Currently the term *test results* is also used by some psychologists when various interpretive comments accompany a discussion of raw data.

Frame(s) of reference   *Frame of reference* refers to the personality theory (theories) plus the views on psychopathology and other behaviors that the psychologist holds. These, together with the reason for assessment, greatly influence the data that the psychologist seeks to gather and the means used to gather them. Shall the psychologist seek parents' and teachers' reports of a child's social behavior, for example, or is the content of the child's unconscious judged to be of greater pertinence? Is a behavioral report likely to supply the material we need, or should we look to the client's performance on projective techniques such as the Rorschach and the TAT? Finally, frame of reference determines the psychologist's recorded response (the psychological report) to the reason for assessment.

Interpretation   The translation of raw data into formulations that are meaningful and significant in terms of the reason for assessment and the psychologist's frame of reference is called *interpretation*. Such topics as why certain behavior occurs or antecedents or events associated with such behavior are part of the interpretation that is made. Implicit or explicit in the interpretation may be found suggestions for approaches to changing behavior. Interpretation always involves the relation of a client's responses to conclusions, but interpretation typically is not as simple as A (datum) = B (conclusion). The relations between test data and conclusions collected by Gilbert (1978, 1980) and Ogdon (1981) may be helpful to the neophyte psychologist but do not explicate the process of interpretation. As Levy (1963) suggests, an indefinable style may also affect whether one is a good or a poor interpreter.

Psychological report   The *psychological report* is the end product of the assessment procedure. It consists of a series of interpretive statements plus other comments, as discussed in Chapter 4. Omitted are those conclusions that the psychologist judges to be not pertinent to the reason for assessment or otherwise not relevant to the needs of the client. The manner in which conclusions are presented reflect the assessment skill of the psychologist and determine the usefulness of the report.

THE RATIONALE FOR FLEXIBILITY

"There is, of course, no one way to write a report, just as there is no one form or organization that will always suffice. *Each writer's personal characteristics will determine, in part, how he will attack his problem*" (emphasis supplied). The source of this quote is perhaps as important as the idea it expresses. It is taken from *Technical Report Writing* by James W. Souther (1957), a guidebook prepared for engineers. Engineering, as the nontechnically trained understand it, utilizes precise methods based on the physical sciences and mathematics. The sorts of things engineers write about in their reports are machines, factory or mine installations, or industrial manufacturing processes. Where should one be more systematized and objective? Yet engineers are trained to be flexible and to allow their personalities to color their reports, whereas psychologists are frequently exhorted to deny their participant-observer role, to standardize their report procedures, to be objective. We are frequently reminded from within and without our profession that the psychological report is a laboratory report or a scientific document.

General outlines for dealing with large areas of *personality* at various levels, as is typical with traditional reports, are to be regarded as Procrustean schemes, and none will be found on these pages. How can a rigid outline accommodate the protean complexities of personality and recognize the variability among people, circumstances, and practical needs? Such outlines, especially if well detailed, may be welcomed because they partly or totally relieve the psychologist of the necessity of thinking about how to organize an effective presentation. But they also force the psychologist to fit findings where they may not belong if optimal meaning and effectiveness are to be had.

When we deal with problem-oriented, prescriptive reports, the situation can be different. Here we deal with well-defined, circumscribed areas of behavior such that the psychologist is in a position to juxtapose problem areas or symptoms and plans for remediation. Such reports are of particular value in the behavior therapies. For example, Lazarus's (1981) categorization by the modalities that make up the "Basic Id"—*B*ehavior, *A*ffect, *S*ensation, *I*magery, *C*ognition, *I*nterpersonal relationships, *D*rugs/Biological factors (pp. 218–220)—exemplifies a highly functional approach. Computer reports, too, are an exception. Such reports present conclusions under predetermined categories. Thus the following main categories provide the conceptual framework for the MCMI Report: Axis II (Personality Patterns), Axis I (Clinical Syndromes), Noteworthy Responses, and DSM-III Multiaxial Diagnosis. Additional information is provided under the headings Psychosocial Stressors, Severity of Disturbance, and Therapeutic Implications.

However, Souther's observation still applies. Have you ever noticed how many psychological reports start the body of the report with a statement of IQ(s) and a stereotyped discussion of intellectual functioning? Why? Is it because these are the most important findings about the client? Is it because such matters appearing later in the report after a discussion of more meaningful personality content would be anticlimactic and are thus best gotten out of the way as soon as possible? Or is it that this is the way we have been doing it for over a generation and don't really know what else to do? In any event, second (or third) generation generalized report outlines continue to place, after

"Test Behavior" or "Behavioral Observations," a report of the IQ and data on intellectual functioning (for example, Carr, 1968; Lacks, Horton, & Owen, 1969; Sturm, 1974; vanReken, 1981).

Let's look at it this way. The psychologist has a creative, custom job to do and, following an outline, approaches the mechanical filling out of a standard form. Perhaps the engineers can help us again. Dr. L. B. Headrick (1956) of RCA advises, "Consider the writing of a technical paper as an engineering problem. Analysis of a problem is essential to understanding and to an organized plan of attack." Souther amplifies this point while presenting a rationale and general guide to the kind of report he proposes.

> The point of attack is always identification of the problem and analyzing the writing situation. Material must be gathered and evaluated, and the report must be designed and written. Failure and confusion often result because the writer starts in the middle of the process or overlooks major considerations. Thus the application of the engineering approach to the solution of writing problems is certain to produce more effective reports, for a report, like any other engineering product, must be designed to satisfy a particular industrial function with its own specific set of requirements. If the analysis is accurate and extensive, the investigation complete and thorough, the design detailed and purposeful, and the application careful and ordered, the report will effectively communicate to its audience, play its industrial role, and fulfill its purpose.[1]

To which the psychologist can but meekly add, "Writing, communication itself, is also a psychological problem."

HOW TO ORGANIZE REPORTS:
AN OLD PROBLEM

The discussion to this point has extolled the merits of flexibility, albeit in general terms, and discouraged rigid outline schemes. "But how then are we to get help in organizing our reports?" the reader might be justified in asking. An unpublished survey of ours among student psychologists and psychologists at various levels of experience indicated that a prominent concern of report writers is difficulty in organizing their reports and that a prominent criticism of training programs is that they do not offer enough help on how to accomplish this task. (These observations in themselves would seem to imply that report-writing outlines are not felt to be satisfactory, for there certainly are enough of them to be had!) One cannot give a simple answer on how to organize the report. This depends on how the assessment function is conceptualized, which, in turn, depends on one's philosophy of the assessment function itself.

[1]From James W. Souther, *Technical Report Writing* (New York: John Wiley, 1957). Copyright © 1957 by John Wiley and Sons, Inc. and reprinted by permission.

WHEN THE PSYCHOLOGIST
IS A CONSULTANT

The psychologist, when serving as a consultant, is a contributing and interacting member of a professional group. Persons with psychological problems of various sorts are, in effect, assigned to the group with the expectation that it can help, in some degree, to overcome or cope with their problems, or even that it can manage or care for them better than they can do for themselves. To accomplish one or more of these goals, different kinds of information about the person may be required.

It is the psychologist who sets the goal(s) of assessment. Others may request answers to certain questions, but the psychologist determines the means of responding to those questions. There are times when the psychologist conceptualizes a problem differently from the way it is understood by others; during the assessment process the psychologist may even come to see a problem as something other than was initially the case. Nevertheless, an attempt should always be made to respond to questions that are raised, even though additional (not asked for) material may be offered. Thus a client may be referred to a psychologist for assessment of the extent of depression, but the data additionally are interpreted as showing the existence of a schizophrenic process. The report should comment on both the depression and the schizophrenia.

All findings are not reported, however. The psychologist selects from a reservoir of interpretations only those that might contribute to the mission and omits those that are apparently not relevant or that add unnecessary length and confuse the issue. The presence of deep castration anxiety—with which the person will no doubt die—would not ordinarily be pertinent when a patient's emotional stability is being evaluated to help determine the advisability of hospital discharge after a lengthy stay. In fact, the busy psychologist, on spotting raw data that would apparently not contribute to the assessment goal, might not wish to develop further interpretations in this area. In addition, it may be found advisable to eliminate low confidence conclusions or perhaps to retain them with appropriate qualifications only if they relate to pertinent issues.

At this point the psychologist will resort to some sort of weighing of interpretations, placing them in a hierarchy of importance and perhaps reevaluating a few of the conclusions earlier judged not to be relevant. Again the psychologist might well ask how much confidence should be placed in the conclusions and how pertinent they seem to be. In most cases only a few key conclusions constitute the essence of the report, and the minor conclusions often are best eliminated lest they add bulk and detract from the central theme(s) of the case.

The psychologist is now ready to set pen to paper. It is here that the problem of effective presentation might seem greatest. Chapter 4 discusses the problem of what content may or may not be appropriate and also broaches the topic of emphasis of content. Only in working with a specific case, however, does the psychologist concretely face the problem of which conclusions to report, their organization, and the composition scheme that will enhance the appropriate emphases.

SOME BASIC CONSIDERATIONS
IN ORGANIZING THE REPORT

Prior to organizing the case presentation with an eye to its effectiveness, the psychologist must review the mission. Focus should be on what is important in the case (as illuminated by theory and the circumstances that are relevant to the mission), emphasizing that which needs to be emphasized and eliminating that which is not immediately or potentially useful.

Parsimony is basic to organization in addition to whatever other virtues it might have. Parsimony will not only save the time of the report writer and reader and cut down on bulk but will also eliminate some of the possible sources of confusion and misunderstanding in the report. Parsimonious writing will tend to emphasize the central problem(s) and personality issues for the psychologist and the reader, whereas shotgun reporting tends to dilute the main conclusions and place them on a par with matters of minor relevance. For example, for a patient who had been economically and socially successful but was now being evaluated for discharge following hospitalization brought about by an acute break, an unneeded recitation of the relations among intellectual skills would probably not add, and might detract from, attention to the main problem. We might similarly judge to be insignificant knowledge about psychosexual development, feeling of inadequacy as a male, fear of heterosexual contacts, or oedipal status in a patient who is being evaluated for protective institutional employment.

It is well for the psychologist to be committed to a theoretical orientation and to be aware of biases that might enter the report. There must be concern with what the psychologist can do for a specific person with a specific problem or problems, in the particular situation where a client is being assessed and treated. Often there is a temptation to conceptualize the consultation in terms of what the psychologist regards as ideal rather than in terms of the perceived limitations of the situation. A psychologist can think, perhaps rightly so, that psychotherapy (perhaps even a certain kind of psychotherapy) is the therapy of choice for most clients. However, it would be unrealistic to conceptualize the typical mission in terms of evaluating the indications for psychotherapy or specific recommendations for psychotherapy in a setting where the availability of this form of treatment is very limited.

The language in which the psychologist *thinks* is also a major issue, influencing as it does both the conceptualization and the presentation of the case. The inexactness and multiple meanings of jargon are well established. When the psychologist thinks in terms of these inexactitudes, can the writing be any more precise? Is it constructive to think through a case using words that are variously used and variously understood and then to *translate* these into words that have but one meaning and are in the experience of the report reader?

The same sort of consideration applies to the theoretical constructs in terms of which the psychologist *thinks* about clients, particularly if these are complex and removed from the experience or perceived requirements of associates. The psychological report is a practical document prepared for use by persons with various amounts of psychological knowledge. Many of them are not expected to be sophisticated in psychological theory. When the psychologist conceptualizes a case in terms of theoretical constructs to communicate to the reader, practical considerations might require that conclusions be translated, simplified, or diluted. Again the question is raised whether the maneuver of translating can be accomplished satisfactorily. Simplifying or diluting the conclusions might tend to call forth a condescending attitude on the part of the psychologist. Theoretical constructs are most useful when dealing with theoretical matters, and they are often helpful, probably indispensable, in making it possible for the psychologist to understand the client. Such use of theory, often implicit, is to be distinguished from publicly conceptualizing the case in terms of theoretical constructs. The psychologist may frequently turn to personality theory or to test theory to find meaning in the data. But one cannot dwell at this level, for the needs of the client in a particular situation are sometimes far removed from even clinically derived theory.

A direct counterproposal to theory-based case conceptualization is that the psychologist think about clients in terms of a simple descriptive and operational approach. Schafer's (1976) "action language," which is explicated and illustrated by Harty (1986) as it has implications for psychological report writing, is such a systematic approach to personality description. Following Schafer's explicit principles and rules of action language, Harty notes that "the tester's task is not to diagnose what the patient is, has, or contains, but rather to understand and convey as fully as possible what the patient is doing."

A hypothetical psychological report, written in an all-too-common mode, was prepared by Harty to illustrate the limited clinical usefulness of a metapsychological, jargon-laden presentation.

> The patient's obsessive-compulsive facade is crumbling under the impact of intense oral-aggressive impulses. His preferred defenses of intellectualization, reaction formation, and isolation of affect are badly strained, and more primitive projective mechanisns are now visible, especially under conditions of reduced external structure. There is an occasional intrusion of primary process material into his conscious thinking, and it is likely that occasional outbursts of poorly modulated affect may occur. Although probably a man whose relationships have always been distant, he now shows increasing signs of withdrawal and weakened

cathexis of reality. His failing ego functions leave him increasingly vulnerable to sadistic fantasies and panic attacks that may result in impulsive action.[2]

Translated into action language, which is comprehensible to a broad spectrum of readers, Harty suggests that such presentations of psychological information "force the test report writer to address the questions of greatest relevance to the therapist's work." Thus,

> The patient strives ineffectively to regard each situation as an intellectual puzzle, which he attempts to solve by reasoning out all the possible consequences of anything he or others might do. He approaches situations this way so that he will not interpret them as opportunities for seizing, consuming, and destroying sources of possible satisfaction, only to have punishments of equal savagery inflicted on himself. He does not currently use his preferred approach consistently, and on occasion he thinks consciously of inflicting or receiving violent damage. At such times, he also thinks illogically and inefficiently, in contrast to his more usual accuracy and precision. . . . [3]

In the interest of relevance a client may be largely described in terms of both current behavior and potential behavior. Presumptions about what the client does and might do are both likely to be important; sometimes current behavior, sometimes potential behavior, is of greater pertinence. Relevant behavior may be found in that which is overt and that which is covert, that which is in consciousness and that which is unconscious or preconscious, the molar and the molecular. Things that the person may *do* include the entertainment, at various levels of consciousness, of goals, ideas, beliefs, or feelings; the exercise of various intellectual and social skills, and other means of manipulating the environment; and the many possible ego defensive maneuvers. Behaviors that are habitual or part of a life style would ordinarily be of greater import than occasional behaviors.

Although potential behavior may sometimes overshadow current behavior in importance, often the two need to be jointly considered. Paranoid ideation may be a factor in potential assaultive conduct, but we may also be interested in the presence or the absence of such thinking because it is needed to fix a diagnosis, to determine feasibility for psychotherapy, or to estimate the client's ability to adjust to a certain environment. The psychologist can often predict potential behavior, such as improvement or retrogression, or socially significant actions when adequate indications are not otherwise available. Even though past behavior is often the most efficient predictor of future events, nevertheless, the psychologist can often point up unsuspected trends or tensions, the sort of stimuli that activate them, and perhaps even estimate the thresholds at which they are activated.

[2]From "Action Language in the Psychological Test Report" by Michael K. Harty, *Bulletin of the Menninger Clinic,* 1986, *50,* 456–463. Copyright © 1986 by The Menninger Foundation, Topeka, Kansas, and reproduced by permission of the publisher.

[3]Ibid.

With these several considerations in mind, we may now begin to think about the problem of organization. The very wording of this proposal indicates our bias of presentation in this book, at least as far as the presentation of personality topics is concerned: Personality ought to be contemplated as an organized whole, not as unorganized segments.

In this book the psychologist is exhorted to humanize reports, to think and write in simple operational terms, and to describe the client in functional language. In basic form this mode of delivering personality data approximates the manner in which one nonpsychologist describes another, without the loose methods of observing and reaching conclusions that some untrained persons employ.

Lay evaluation is organized into functional unities that focus on behaviors. Nonpsychologists concentrate, as the occasion demands, on areas of felt concern, such as an associate's intelligence, sincerity, friendliness, or "personality." They reach conclusions rather directly—come to the point and tell what sort of a person someone is. "He's the sort of feller you can trust. You can count on him when you need him. He'll go out of his way to help when you're in a jam." The narrator may then cite some empirical supporting evidence, or perhaps even intuitive knowledge. One can hardly be more succinct than the late president Lyndon Johnson who characterized a political rival as "a man who can't walk and chew gum at the same time." The nonpsychologist never segmentalizes a subject into predetermined and fixed discrete areas such as "intellect," "emotions," and "object relations." The lay listener might have difficulty in integrating such segments into some kind of a functional whole. Professional people sometimes have similar problems.

A segmentalized presentation of more or less static personality data may appear to be scientific and clinically functional because it suggests the existence of distinct, identifiable personality components that were isolated and measured, or otherwise assessed. However, we believe that personality is a functional interrelated unity, and we concur with those who believe that clinically important traits are largely specific, that a stimulus in a total situation is as relevant as the organism or its responses. A more extreme point of view holds that general traits may be invalid abstractions of transactional behavior. Even if we think in terms of psychometrically defined general traits, the personality segments ordinarily discussed in reports do not correspond closely with personality variables so established. Nevertheless, to some workers segments seem a convenient way of thinking about a person. A report composed of information on various a priori established segments may seem crisp and "scientific." It is crisp, but it is no more scientific than an integrated presentation.

The presentation of discrete segments to a report reader may be regarded as akin to presenting data having a certain degree of rawness. The whole is more than the sum of its parts, and the functionally integrated report has meaning not found in the separate information units with which the psychologist initially deals. It is logically the psychologist's duty to integrate data, if we accept that the purpose of psychological assessment is to present functional conclusions rather than mere elemental data. It is technically sound to entrust this responsibility to a psychologist who has a grasp of the data and is in a position to judge which of these should enter the report and which should be omitted. The psychologist ought to be able to formulate more meaningful psychological conclusions than can someone who has a less intimate grasp of the basic materials.

THEORETICAL CONSTRUCTS
AND THE REPORT

It is the task of the psychologist to translate the raw material of the protocol into a meaningful, useful picture of personality or behavior. This is the most difficult phase of assessment. Many theories—from Freud's to Skinner's to Kohut's—may be helpful; the same is true of theories of assessment and experience with assessment modalities. In general, clinically derived theories, especially Freudian psychoanalysis and its more socially oriented modifications, are pertinent to dynamically oriented psychologists, since they are concerned with human development and the major conditions of the maladjustment and readjustment processes. At the same time psychoanalysis is not particularly conversant with the assessment of skills, with many aspects of rehabilitation, or with behavior therapies, or with neuropsychology, or with current humanistic approaches. Other orientations, such as learning or conditioning theories, are also adapted to help understand human development, maladjustment, and readjustment. Increasingly a cognitive approach is recognized as very useful.

As helpful as systematic views of personality can be, they too often become unduly injected into a case and lead both the unwary psychologist and the reader astray, away from the individual and toward the generalities that characterize most persons. Personality tests can be interpreted in the framework of any number of theories. The Rorschach owes allegiance to no particular theory and is compatible with many. The Murray TAT can, of course, be interpreted according to the viewpoint on personality from which it emerged, but more often the TAT stories are assigned meanings contributed by various theorists. Responses to a psychometric procedure (for example, the WAIS-R) are freely interpreted as contributions to personality understanding.

Interpretation that closely follows a personality theory—for example, Freudian psychoanalysis—can be technically superb in terms of the congruence with theory of the insights offered, completeness and potency of presentation, and internal consistency, yet fall short of the case requirements. A protocol thus interpreted is likely to give workers who are sophisticated in analytic theory an excellent understanding of such matters as basic drive structure, psychosexual status, and developmental factors. Unfortunately an understanding of such matters may not be very helpful in working with a particular individual, whereas other information may be much more pertinent. Knowledge of early factors in the client's emotional development can be quite beside the point when the problem is one of attempting a community readjustment or treating the individual with available modalities such as electroconvulsive therapy, occupational therapy, or antidepressants. Many modern analysts, as well as other psychotherapists, do not rely very much on information about the person's early life, preferring in many instances to deal with how the individual copes with contemporary problems.

THE CLIENT'S NEEDS AND THE REPORT

What would seem to be required is a realistic point of view on what are the clinically important variables commonly found in the people we evaluate. The topics of concern must be established on the basis of judged relevance for each individual case, not on the basis of the topics prominent in some personality theory or on classes of content thought to be regularly made available through the use of various tests. At the present stage of our development, this task may be accomplished independently by psychologists through both experience and theoretical orientation. Theory is sometimes to an extent implicit and based partly on personal factors in the psychologist, hence perhaps less alterable than it should be. Regardless of the reason, some workers will stress the role of hostility, social influences, the role of the mother, the oedipal status, inferiority feelings, repression, or fixation at the oral level. An a priori list of variables acceptable to all would be extremely difficult to draw up, although systematic investigation might eventually succeed with this task.

The General Topics of the Report

Quite arbitrarily we can draw up a useful list of tentative general personality topics that could provide the basic elements around which the psychologist might conceptualize the case presentation. These may be regarded as "handles" with which the psychologist can come to grips with the mission in the presence of the mass of data accumulated about the client. Although something might be written on almost every one of these topics for every person (a systematic approach to shotgun reporting!), usually a person can be meaningfully and effectively described in skeletal form by focusing on just a few of them. In most instances the case presentation can probably be conceptualized around perhaps three to six of these topics. Occasionally seven or eight might be required, but at other times, particularly when a pointed question is asked, even one or two might suffice. The report can then be rounded out with subcategories also taken from the list.

This list of topics cannot be offered as complete, nor are all topics mutually exclusive. Each psychologist may wish to add those variables that seem to be generally pertinent.

Examples of General Personality Topics Around Which a Case Presentation May Be Conceptualized

Achievement
Affect
Aggressiveness
Antisocial Tendencies
Anxieties
Aptitudes
Attitudes
Aversions
Background Factors
Behavioral Problems
Biological Factors
Brain Dysfunction
Cognitive Functioning
Cognitive Skills
Cognitive Style
Competency
Conative Factors
Conflicts
Content of Consciousness
Contingency Management
Defenses
Deficits
Developmental Factors
Diagnostic Considerations
Drives, Dynamics
Emotional Cathexes
Emotional Controls
Emotivity
Fears
Fixations
Flexibility
Frustrations
Goals
Hostility
Identity
Imagery
Insight

Intellectual Controls
Intellectual Level
Interests
Interpersonal Relations
Interpersonal Skills
Life Style
Molar Surface Behavior
Needs
Outlook
Perception of Environment
Perception of Self
Personal Consequences of Behavior
Placement Prospects
Psychopathology
Rehabilitation Needs
Rehabilitation Prospects
Self-concept
Sentiments
Sex
Sex Identity
Sex Role
Significant Others
Situational Factors
Social Consequences of Behavior
Social Role
Social Simulus Value
Social Structure
Special Assets
Subjective Feeling States
Substance Use
Symptoms
Target Behaviors
Thought Processes
Treatment Prospects
Value System
Vocational Topics

The Concept of Case-Focusing

Related to the selection of general topics on which to report is another major but more specific aspect of the conceptualization of the report. This is the matter of selecting the appropriate focus of interpretation—the kind of conclusions to be derived from the raw data. Test manuals and textbooks, good as they may be, can suggest interpretations only in the general terms of the accepted meanings of such variables as test responses, scores, or quantitative patterns. The psychologist must adapt these general interpretive meanings to the specific case and mission, determine the central and pertinent topics with which to deal, and develop the interpretations (conclusions) in these topic areas as the mission requires.

There are several differences between interpretations made in general terms and *case-focused interpretations*. First, the case-focused interpretation is derived relative to a mission. We administer selected tests and search the elicited protocol for any information related to the assessment goal. Such data are emphasized to the partial or total neglect of other material. Second, interpretations are made according to their implications for action. The psychologist bridges the gap between the general interpretation and the perceived needs of the mission; in effect, *the conclusions, with greater or lesser directness, are recommendations*. The interpretations tell the report readers as much as possible about the practical meaning gained by the psychologist's unique approach. Finally, in the case-focused interpretation the psychologist is not content with reaching conclusions solely on the basis of the restricted assessment units (for example, tests, subtests, scores, ratios, profiles, indexes) on which validity research has been done and for which published interpretation guides are available. Following sophisticated clinical practice, whatever fortuitous data are available are appropriated. Thus the psychologist may probe the meaning of verbalizations or of symbolic productions, interpret sequences or combinations of responses or scores in a manner not authorized or explicitly set forth by the test manual. Meanings may be derived by comparing scores or responses cn one test with those on another (the battery approach), or conclusions reached from any of the preceding in the light of, or in combination with, such information as that provided by direct observation, anamnesis, other self-reports, behavior reported by others, or physical examination.

Let us consider a few brief examples showing the difference between general interpretation and case-focused interpretation. For meaningful, psychological work, general interpretations are incomplete interpretations that, too often, are of the Aunt Fanny sort. The mission of the psychologist is more closely related to knowing, for example, whether the client will act out than whether he is "hostile"; whether he requires treatment rather than whether he has "anxiety."

Here is a statement from a case report:

The patient appears to be an immature, dependent individual whose passivity and feelings of insecurity leave him with little capacity to initiate decisive action.

There are four Aunt Fanny-type statements in this example: "immature," "dependent," "passivity," "feelings of insecurity." These four sub-conclusions contribute to a final conclusion, ". . . leave him with little capacity to initiate decisive action," which may or may not have specific meaning to the reader, depending partly on what other information about the patient is available. The writer of the sentence, a student, on looking through his full report, some three single-spaced pages, found scattered through the document enough information to put together a more meaningful contribution:

The patient currently presents an apparent picture of self-assurance since he is socially deft, alert, and obviously knowledgeable. Nevertheless, an overprotective upbringing becomes apparent when he has to put forth directed and sustained effort such as evidently was required in his recent business venture which failed and preceded by a few weeks his admission with a diagnosis of major depressive episode. His need to achieve "success" is mostly a matter of his family's aspiration for him and is not congruent with his self-needs. Thus we find a person who does not at a deep level aspire to adult standards for responsibility and achievement. He would rather receive than produce. Hence when he finds himself in a position of responsibility he becomes fearful of his ability to perform as expected. Tension, confusion, indecisiveness, and depression are the results, the patient alternating between different courses of action but unable to take definite steps.

Another general interpretive statement gleaned from a report reads:

Tension, depression, aggression, and sexual conflict are evident in the protocol.

One hundred percent Aunt Fanny!
Maybe the patient is something like this:

This patient is deeply involved with a mother figure, and mixed feelings about this relationship seem to be associated with the symptoms for which the patient seeks help at the clinic. A dependent and overly close relationship with this parent has hampered his ability to assume a male role without conflict, and his mere urges to heterosexual expression cause him to feel anxious and tense, sometimes to a degree which incapacitates him for his everyday functioning. At the same time his sexual tensions and fantasy mean to him that he is going against his relationship with the mother, a feeling which ties in with other deep negative feelings which he has for her.

But this guess might be wrong. Possibly the next piece of fiction would be more descriptive of the patient who produced the protocol. Notice, incidentally, that an Aunt Fanny "sexual conflict" may fit both sexes.

The client is in conflict over what are the proper sex mores, the family and church teachings being on the one hand, and her liberated peer group standards and pressures being on the other. She initially complained to the counselor of an "inability to concentrate," and she does in fact seem to have a degree of tension which at times may hamper her studying. But she has always apparently become anxious when in conflict, and her present struggle to readjust to the standards of her new environment is hardly the basic cause of tension. What probably really brings her to counseling is a feeling that she is "letting down" her parents (a matter of truth at a fairly deep level where she does entertain rebellious urges). The implication this has to her for a vital relationship in her life has been causing her to feel unhappy.

And another illustration:

Thinking is syncretistic.

What does this mean for a particular patient? Perhaps that

Overt schizophrenic behaviors currently are not observed. Psychological examination of the thought processes, however, indicates an active psychosis, the nature of which suggests that if the patient is now returned to the community he might repeat the behavior which led to his hospitalization. It is true that the patient has better emotional controls now, but his thinking causes him to reach some unlikely, sometimes bizarre ideas because he is prone to illogically relate unrelated ideas in a manner which can cause social difficulties. It might be well to delay discharge and have this patient's thought processes restudied in three weeks or a month.

THE PROCESS
OF CONCEPTUALIZATION

In conceptualizing the presentation of a case, the psychologist might first imagine being asked to "Tell me about this person with regard to (*reason for assessment*)." In responding to such a request the report writer recognizes (1) the need to be selective of the information to be conveyed and (2) the need to organize this information meaningfully.

The first task takes cognizance of the frequent observation that the various aspects of a person's existence may be understood in terms of some kind of hierarchical order, and from this structure those traits that are of "central or dominating importance" may reliably be judged (Conrad, 1932). As a result of psychological study, certain features suggest themselves as predominant in the person's psychoeconomics. In our clients we may identify, in addition to overt behaviors of interest, organizing centers or central themes, which may relate to underlying tendencies or to modes of expression. Thus we become aware of the basic role of such issues as an inadequate self-concept, an attitude of interpersonal hostility, a need for achievement, a rigid control over emotional expression, tendencies to withdrawal, conflicts over sexual goals, or a pattern of achieving self-needs through the manipulation of others. A large number of such issues may be identified in any person, although there is perhaps a relatively smaller number of recurring themes that accounts for many of the topics found to be apparently relevant in case studies.

The organization of the central themes into a report may, for discussion purposes, be regarded as involving several different tasks. What the psychologist considers most important must be made to stand out, with the other material assigned an auxiliary role for the sake of completeness. Importance is gauged in terms of consequences, which might mean that the major emphasis is not accorded to the most central feature in the person's psychoeconomics—if this can be determined. Thus a hospital psychologist, for example, must think in such practical terms as whether obtained information will give the staff the sort of understanding needed to relate more effectively to the patient. The psychologist may have determined that dependency, hostility, and a poor sex identity are the central themes. A hierarchy of emphasis for these must be established. If depression and suicidal tendencies were also identified, the practical imperativeness of this finding would dictate that it be emphasized, even though sexual conflict was basic in undermining the patient's adjustment.

There are as many means of supplying appropriate emphasis to content as literary creativity will permit. For practical use, however, the more common techniques will generally suffice. These include the order of presentation, the skillful and appropriate use of adjectives, and the use of vivid illustrative material. Less often the psychologist might resort to the use of underlining, capitalization, dramatic presentation (such as is produced by a clipped statement), or an exclamation point. Sometimes the occasion presents itself when the psychologist can state in virtually so many words what is most important: "This man is best understood through a description of his deep dependency needs and his manner of attempting to gratify these."

The skillful use of repetition can also make for effective emphasis. This is perhaps best accomplished by weaving the central theme through all or a substantial part of the report, relating subsidiary themes to that which has been selected as the main point for emphasis. The dependency theme mentioned in the previous paragraph, for example, can be related to the other prominent and clinically relevant personality themes. Suppose that a person has strong but inexpressible urges, a tendency to perceive the environment as threatening, feelings of inadequacy and depression, deep anxieties about the adequacy of core gender identity, and the objective appearance of free anxiety. All of these may be more or less directly related to the crucial dependency problem, and the dependency theme might be presented in a number of contexts.

What this amounts to is that the psychologist should practice a mild form of caricature. This was also the intent when the principle of selectivity of content was advocated. We are charged with presenting a clinically useful picture, not an exact photograph. Admittedly by eliminating certain material judged to be nonrelevant to the purpose, we produce a distortion of the whole person; yet we might as well accept the fact that we cannot present an undistorted picture of the person—the full content is simply not available to us, and we may not be entirely accurate in what we do know. The shotgun report also deletes information, but its errors are more serious because its bulk can prevent the reader from recognizing the relative importance of the various topics and can thus lead to the development of a distorted image. Test-by-test reporting, segmentalized reporting, and traditional, non-case-focused reports, for various reasons, have similar effects.

Along with seeing the case in terms of its needed emphases, the psychologist must consider the detailed attributes of the central themes to be understood and presented. Each basic theme must be seen in terms of its role in the person's economy, its unique components, its social import, and associated personality information (for example, the relationship of a central theme of inferiority feelings to a subsidiary theme of deficiencies in heterosexual functioning). It is these that make the central themes take on the action characteristic of life.

On achieving an understanding of the client and the basic tactics of case presentation in terms of the overall guiding principles discussed here, the psychologist is ready to outline a report—preferably on paper, although this might not be necessary for some seasoned psychologists. The first step in this task is to select from a population of personality topics, such as that presented in the list on page 120, those that compose the central features of the case.

Outlining a Report

Here is an example of how a case may be outlined, together with the report that emerges. The report will serve to initiate a discussion of the often troubling problem of intraparagraph and interparagraph organization.

The client, a young man in his twenties, twice in recent months had come into difficulties that led to his arrest, the first time for "bookie" activities and the second time for threatening his parents with a gun after consuming "12 or 14 beers." The psychiatrist who examined the client on direction of the court referred the case to us, with the request that we probe the meaning of the antisocial tendencies.

We determined that the client had a basic conflict centering on passivity and dependency, these being associated with what the client perceived as a harsh father, and hence a (now generalized) need to rebel was developed. No fewer than four clinically relevant defenses were erected against this conflict: (1) a denial of personal inadequacy, (2) a denial of real events, which precludes effective or constructive action, (3) a renunciation of personal goals so as to gain support (and thus perhaps to be maneuvered by "bad company"), and (4) a hostile and an unrealistic fantasy life. The typical view he presented to others and the difficulties he experienced in cognitive functioning round out this picture.

The core personality topic outline might go like this:

    I.   Conflicts
   II.   Social Stimulus Value
  III.   Cognitive Functioning
  IV.   Defenses (1)
   V.   Defenses (2)
  VI.   Defenses (3)
 VII.   Defenses (4)

This preliminary outline form is both general and incomplete. Yet it presents an overall structure for the report, and the topic headings might well form the bases for paragraphs. In practice we would now simply translate these headings into more specific behavior referents and elaborate on the content to be discussed in these paragraphs. By drawing the following additional topics from the same list that supplied the material for the core personality topic outline:

Attitudes	Interpersonal Skills
Awareness	Needs
Cognitive Skills	Outlook
Conative Factors	Perception of Environment
Content of Consciousness	Perception of Self
Deficit	Personal Consequences of Behavior
Drives, Dynamics	Psychopathology
Emotional Cathexes	Subjective Feeling States
Emotional Controls	Social Consequences of Behavior
Frustrations	Social Role
Goals	Value System
Interpersonal Relations	

. . . the outline then becomes

   I.   Conflicts
       A.   Self-Perception
       B.   Goals
       C.   Frustrations
       D.   Interpersonal Relations
       E.   Perception of Environment
       F.   Drives, Dynamics
       G.   Emotional Cathexes
       H.   Emotional Controls

   II. Social Stimulus Value
- A. Cognitive Skills
- B. Conative Factors
- C. Goals
- D. Social Role

  III. Cognitive Functioning
- A. Deficit
- B. Psychopathology

  IV. Defenses (1)
- A. Self-Perception
- B. Needs
- C. Conflicts

   V. Defenses (2)
- A. Subjective Feeling States
- B. Attitudes
- C. Deficits
- D. Personal Consequences of Behavior
- E. Insight
- F. Subjective Feeling States
- G. Insight
- H. Social Stimulus Value
- I. Social Consequences of Behavior

  VI. Defenses (3)
- A. Interpersonal Relations
- B. Needs
- C. Interpersonal Skills
- D. Emotional Controls

 VII. Defenses (4)
- A. Content of Consciousness
- B. Needs
- C. Values
- D. Needs
- E. Social Consequences of Action

. . . which now, in more lifelike terms, still highly detailed for teaching purposes, becomes

   I. Conflict centering on dependency and passivity
- A. Feelings of inadequacy
- B. Frustrated personal goals (dependency and passivity)
- C. Faulty, unsatisfying relationship with father
- D. Father seen as cold, rejecting, punishing
- E. Rebellious tendencies which are generalized
- F. Control over negative impulses out of fear

  II. How others see client
- A. Intellectual level and skills
- B. Lack of will to function at optimum
- C. Fluctuating goal for self-achievement
- D. Social irresponsibility

  III. Cognitive functioning
- A. Deficiencies under stress
- B. Psychopathological aspects of deficiencies

  IV. Denial of felt inadequacy
      A. Negative view of self
      B. Need to feel "like everybody else"
      C. Conflict over adequacy as a male
   V. Denial and nonexperience of pertinent realities
      A. Partial avoidance of depressed feelings
      B. Naive attitude
      C. Inability to assess his behavior adequately
      D. Inability to correct own behavior
      E. Inability to understand problems
      F. Depressive tendencies
      G. Lack of full experience of depression
      H. Social masking of depressed feelings
      I. Relation of inner feelings to negative social behavior
  VI. Social maneuvers to gain acceptance
      A. Receptive orientation
      B. Need for support
      C. Techniques of gaining support
      D. Control of negative impulses to retain support
 VII. Fantasy as a basic defense
      A. Value of fantasy
      B. Needs as reflected in fantasy
      C. Deficiency of social values
      D. Need to appear in socially favorable light
      E. Fantasy content and deficiency of social values as a basis for unlawful activity

. . . and then, initiated by an opening summary or overview, is translated into the body of a report:

> This man is most readily understood in terms of his unusually passive, dependent approach to life and his attempts to overcome the deeply unhappy state brought about by his personality limitation.
>
> Mr. A. does not feel very adequate as a person, an attitude that is developed through experiencing a continual sense of failure in terms of his own goals, and that apparently is reinforced by others. In fact, his relations with his father very likely are the basic reason for such feeling. This person is seen by the patient as cold, rejecting, punishing, and unapproachable. He has an urge to rebel and fight against this person—an urge that has been generalized to all society, but he is afraid to give vent to his impulses. Whatever emotional support he does get (got) seems to be from the mother.
>
> As others see him, he seems to have the essential capacity to do well if only he would try. He scores at the average level on a test of intelligence (IQ: 106), he is able to learn readily, when he wants to, and on occasion can perform unusually fast and effectively. Yet he does not typically follow through on this advantage. His willingness, sometimes even his desire, to do well fluctuates, so that in the long run he could not be regarded as a constructive or responsible person.
>
> Other personality deficiencies also compromise his functioning. Under stress or when faced with difficult problems he becomes blocked, confused, and indecisive. His thinking does not show sufficient flexibility to meet such situations so that he would be regarded as inadaptable and unspontaneous.
>
> Mr. A.'s felt inadequacy causes him to feel that he is not as good as others.

By way of reassuring himself on this matter he frequently during examination makes remarks that he is "like everybody else." The feeling that he is inferior includes also the sexual area where he is quite confused about his maleness. It is likely that one or more sex problems contribute to his sense of failure, although, quite understandably, he denies this and indicates a satisfactory sex life "like everybody else."

He hardly experiences the full effect of his failures, however. He protects himself by denying many events of reality, by keeping many facts about himself and others unconscious, by a general attitude of "not knowing"—an attitude of naiveness. He can hardly take corrective action about himself because he does not understand himself or his actions, or recognize the nature of his problems. Oddly enough, as already stated, this is an unhappy person, but he does not adequately recognize this fact, nor does he appear to others as depressed. Yet on occasion this might be a factor in his behavior that could be personally or socially unfortunate.

This man's insecurity about himself forces him into a receptive orientation to other people. He must have friends to provide support. To achieve this he presents himself in a positive, correct light, tries to say the "right" things and even to be ingratiating and obsequious. It is important that he create the "right" effect and may resort to dramatic behavior to bring this about. "Friends" are so important to him that he sometimes must take abuse in order to hold them. He must always hold back hostile expression.

But it is perhaps in fantasy where the greatest satisfaction is derived. He dreams of being a "success" (his term)—accumulating enough money by the age of 35 so he can retire and effortlessly enjoy the comforts of the world. In his fantasy he is independent of authority, can openly express the aggression he ordinarily cannot, and flout society. He has no positive feelings about social rules (although he may profess to), but is concerned when apprehended for misconduct, possibly less for the real punishment than for how it "looks" to be known for doing what he is afraid to do. It is little wonder that he is easy prey for an "easy money" scheme.

The reader will note that the sections of the outline and the paragraphs in the report contain heterogeneous and occasionally repeated content. This is intentional. A report consisting of homogeneous paragraphs would be a form of segmentalized report (although perhaps not as artificial as the kind of segmentalized reports commented on in this book) and subject to some of the same censure. The psychologist should try to relate in the report those behaviors that occur together in the functioning context of the person. If sex conflicts hamper intellectual functioning, these related facts should be mentioned as closely together as they are in this sentence, not as unconnected statements occurring in different and possibly widely separated paragraphs. In a good report the beginning of a paragraph commonly announces the integrated theme of the topics that compose it.

Arranging Findings in a Report

There is a final and most important consideration pertaining to effective organization. How are the component findings to be arranged in a report? How, for example, was the scheme for the preceding report developed?

First consider the intraparagraph organization. The intention was to take the main integrated themes emerging in response to the imaginary request to "Tell me about this person"—the brief statement of the psychologist's findings that precedes the outline (p. 126). Thus each of the four basic methods of defense the client uses has some meaningfully interrelated components. Consider the derivation of the fifth paragraph of the report. That the client feels inadequate was one of the principal conclusions of the psychologist. In fact, the client's repeated statement that he is "like everybody else" strengthens this conclusion and also suggests how he tries to adopt an attitude to deny his feeling of inadequacy. The psychologist also had strong reasons to reach the conclusion that the client had several prominent sex conflicts associated with his feelings of inadequacy—a conclusion perhaps strengthened by the client's comment (to a sentence completion item) that he has a sex life that is "like everybody else." (Notice, incidentally, the emphasis to be gained by repeating this expression closely together in different but related contexts. The topics in the fifth paragraph obviously belong together.)

Or look at the third paragraph. From observations of samples of the client's intellectual functioning, it was apparent to the psychologist that he would impress others well in this respect, at least as regards capacity. Yet it was also clear by the client's performance on a number of tests that there was a fluctuating will and a consequent lack of goal-directedness and responsibility. It was further noted that he meets many of his problems through fantasy, but this possible way of elaborating on the theme of irresponsibility and its social effects was reserved for the emphasis that can be brought about by treating a topic in a final paragraph. In the third paragraph, however, it was thought appropriate to contrast his capacity with his output, since this discrepancy suggests that people would be critical of him, an important finding in view of what rejection means to the client. The theme was not "pushed" more strongly only because the conclusion was not judged to be sufficiently firm. If it were, it could easily have been developed in this paragraph.

There is one simple rule for deciding on the contents of a paragraph: functional relatedness. (What relatedness is there in the other paragraphs in the report on Mr. A.?) This criterion permits the intentional repetition of items of content in different paragraphs. Beyond this, the psychologist has to decide how to arrange the several items in the paragraph and how to word thoughts for effectiveness. The limiting factor in learning this skill is probably the basic prose style of the psychologist. Nevertheless, much of the ingenuity needed for this skill can be acquired. Perhaps most important are the terms in which the psychologist thinks. If the task is conceptualized in terms of communicating "findings"—perhaps that the client has anxiety, hostility, and narcissistic wounds—such content probably is precisely what will be recorded. But if the psychologist understands the case in terms of a practical mission, conceptualization of report content and the manner in which it is expressed are likely to be more functional.

The novice can learn how to make a paragraph hang together by studying samples of effective clinical writing. Supervisors are often in a position to make relevant suggestions in training conferences based on live case material. There are any number of writing techniques that can be adapted for specific effect. For example, in paragraph three the method of contrast was used. The client's capacity was contrasted with his productivity because of the social meaning and implications such a discrepancy may have. Some of the techniques that aid in interparagraph organization might also be useful.

The organization of paragraphs in a report is possibly more complex than the organization of conclusions within a paragraph, because the report is a larger conceptual unit. Moreover, the organization of each report must have its own rationale, although certainly other reports may have a similar rationale and be organized along similar lines. How do we arrive at a rationale for organizing a report? How, for example, was the rationale for the report on Mr. A. reached?

First, Mr. A. was understood in terms of an approach to life (central personality theme) that is not socially adaptive and leads to some personally unsatisfying results. The ways in which he tries to overcome some of the effects of his basic personality orientation bear rather directly on the reason for his being referred to us. By stating the central problem the client may quickly be introduced to the reader in general terms, with the understanding that the necessary details will follow.

The top priority then became the further development of the theme introduced in the first paragraph, hence the need to know about Mr. A.'s feelings of inadequacy. This topic led naturally to a discussion of what the client is "really" like in contrast to his misperception of himself. However, he is also objectively seen to have shortcomings, so the deficiencies mentioned in the fourth paragraph supplement those commented on in the third. So far we have presented the logically related topics of the client's perception of himself and an external evaluation of some of his qualities. All of this was thought to be pertinent to the problem for which he was referred.

The next four paragraphs are logically interrelated, since they serially disclose how Mr. A. copes with his feelings about himself. First, in paragraph five, is a discussion of the basic manner by which he tries not to feel inadequate. The theme is amplified in the sixth paragraph, which suggests a very wide scope of denial and the effect this might have. The seventh paragraph shows a social maneuver he uses as a defense for the same basic problem. The final paragraph suggests an additional defense for this problem, that of a fantasy life that seems to be closely associated with his long-term antisocial activities (being a "bookie").

The overall guiding principle was to present the man in terms of his personality as this pertains to his antisocial activities. Nevertheless, the relationship between what is described in these paragraphs and his social difficulties is not mentioned in every instance. It would be logical enough to do so, but a different scheme was used in preference to cluttering the report with what in this case would be speculations. Instead, the speculations were gathered together as a "speculative note" that was appended to the body of the report. Its purpose was to attempt to relate, more directly than responsible interpretation practices permit, the basic personality of the man to his unwanted behaviors.

SPECULATIVE NOTE

The client's antisocial behavior appears to be related to the personality problems noted here and to his method of coping with these. His negative attitude to authority (father), of course, would seem to be a basic ingredient. His need for support is another factor, and the support of a group of persons on the other side of the law might be as meaningful as support from another source. As we have seen, he will go out of his way (engaging in illegal activities?) to retain his "friends." His fantasy life of wealth and leisure would also seem to make unlawful activities appealing. Finally, his intellectual inefficiencies and his inadaptability might tend to give trouble in more straightforward enterprises. He does not genuinely feel he is wrong.

Concerning the gun incident, the client seemed to be trying to indicate to the examining physician that the weapon was used to try forcibly to extract sympathy and support that he could not get by passive means. The gun evidently made him feel powerful, and the reasoning was childish and incomplete. Apparently the act was impulsive. The client admits to consuming 12 to 14 beers before the event and this probably loosened his usually tight control over direct hostile expression. Further acts either against himself or against others cannot be ruled out, although no specific or immediate danger is foreseen.

Schemes for Organizing Reports

There are many possible schemes suitable for organizing reports. The total number is probably limited only by the psychologist's ingenuity and the variety of case material. The following suggestions pertain to some elementary organizing schemes. In many instances one of these will not be a sufficient scheme for a whole report; several strategies will have to be combined.

Regardless of the presentation scheme, an overview statement is commonly in order. In any event a clear focus and objective must always be established in the light of the available material and its significance. Sometimes it will be most effective to present a major conclusion at the beginning (a purpose often served by an overview) and then make supporting information available. At other times the psychologist may be able to build up to the major conclusion and present it more forcefully at the end of the report. It is difficult to generalize. Most often, when the psychologist is asked to contribute a diagnosis, this matter may be dealt with at the conclusion of the report after the relevant evidence presumably has been presented. However, a diagnosis may be offered at the beginning of a report for a good reason: "This is a severely schizophrenic patient whose homicidal fantasies and inability to control her behavior could pose a serious threat to the community."

1. The simplest approach to report organization is possible when it is necessary to deal only with a limited segment of behavior, such as might be the case when dealing with a circumscribed matter. Thus when dealing with intellectual efficiency, the report considers sequentially several pertinent aspects of this problem. Or if the problem is one of cognitive deficit, such as in a brain syndrome, it is necessary only to cite the related data contributing to the major conclusion—for example, that the deficit is present. Probably the relative seriousness of the signs, such as memory defect, inability to shift concepts, concreteness, confabulation, loss of mental control, confusion, and loss of orientation, will suggest a meaningful order of presentation and appropriate data groupings—for example, memory defect and confabulation would probably be closely linked.

2. With more complex material a quite simple, yet effective, approach is to present a general opening statement, an overview, or an introductory statement, followed by the necessary elaborations and whatever other pertinent information is required to round out the personality study. A report might start: "The dominant emphasis in Ms. B.'s life is manipulating others in order to realize a set of strong ambitions." The nature of these ambitions, why they are important to her, and her techniques of manipulation might then be commented upon. Finally, whatever else is important, such as capacity (for example, intellectual or social), situational frustrations, adaptability, or the effects of failure, could be woven into the theme.

3. Some reports might be essentially a buildup to a diagnosis or some major conclusion. What is required is that the psychologist present bits of evidence step by step, as these contribute to a final conclusion. A tightly reasoned report of this sort might be in order particularly when the conclusion is of far-reaching significance. Examples would occur when a diagnosis is an essential ingredient in a court decision, or when contemplated action like commitment to or release from a hospital might hinge on the psychologist's findings. Such an organization might be in order when the psychologist feels the need to convincingly present findings that are not at all apparent. Quite frequently, for example, clinical diagnosis may point to neurosis or personality disorder while psychological indicators suggest psychosis.

4. A cause-and-effect presentation can be useful when concern is with some symptom whose basis needs to be understood. Physical symptoms that are thought by a physician to be psychogenic are a common instance. This approach is also particularly valuable when a social symptom, such as misbehavior in school or criminal behavior, needs to be understood and identified with a set of dynamics or with pathology, such as a brain syndrome. It may be best at times to first explore the nature of the unwanted symptom and then to deal with its causes. At other times it may be appropriate to deal with the pertinent underlying psychological material and show how this relates to the issue of concern.

5. In many instances the order of presentation might be from periphery to center or from center to periphery, and the most effective approach can be a subjective matter. Frequently it is helpful to contrast the surface picture with what is not apparent. Reasons for doing this might be (a) to alert others to unsuspected personality features; (b) to contribute understanding as to why a person who is without evident pathology gets into difficulties; or (c) to contrast a superficial picture or facade with what a person is "really" like.

6. Sometimes it is appropriate to emphasize the subjective view of the individual if the writer feels it is important to understand the situation(s) as the client does. Contrasting the subjective picture with the external viewpoint can often contribute valuable perspective to a case. When the fantasy life, orientation, or per-

ception of environment is particularly important, the value of this approach becomes evident.

7. Contrast can be an appropriate organizing focus of a report. The nature of a conflict may be brought out quite effectively by contrasting its elements—for example, incompatible goals. Contrast can also be functional when different layers of behavior need to be understood in relation to one another. An illustration of this might be severely hostile attitudes sublimated in one who fights for social justice. This technique is also called for when the findings of a current examination are compared with those of a previous examination. The writer sets forth the important similarities and differences uncovered in the two examinations and whatever significance these might have.

6

A Workshop on Psychological Report Writing

HOW TO WRITE REPORTS
AND HOW NOT TO

The author's impetus for writing a book on psychological report writing relates, in part, to the large number of inferior reports that are still to be found in file cabinets. What better way to emphasize this point than to share a few of them with the reader? Fortunately, good, effective reports are also being written, and it is also well to share some of these with the reader.

REPORTS NOT TO EMULATE

Presented first in this chapter are examples of how *not* to write psychological reports. They were gathered from case folders over a period of time. Each case is followed by comments based on the principles set forth in this book.

Most of these reports were written by students; hence, in general they are a better source of instructional material than are the products of practicing psychologists. Nevertheless, experienced persons often have the same difficulties as beginners do. Some of the reports, particularly those personality-oriented reports written in test-by-test fashion, were selected to illustrate an approach that is fortunately much less popular than it was some years ago. Several of the reports are of the shotgun type, harking back to a time when it was common to encourage students to include as much as possible in their reports in order to demonstrate their competence to interpret test data. Although this teaching method is still in use, we strongly encourage supervisors to teach the writing of case-focused reports. Students can demonstrate their interpretive skills in supervisory conferences and their overall qualifications as psychologists in the writing of case-focused reports.

The approach is informal, and the criticisms that are made of the reports are similar to some of the observations that a supervisor might make. For self-instruction or assigned instruction, it may be profitable for students to apply the principles of the preceding chapters to the following selections or to samples of their own reports. While doing such exercises, it is well to be aware that some of the reports can be variously criticized, according to one's point of view. Thus a selection might merit the labels "academic," "theoretical," and "cold and impersonal" at the same time. Some readers will be more inclined to describe a piece of writing by one of these terms, some by another.

In most instances the reasons for referral of the cases that resulted in the following passages are not known. Most of the referrals were probably general. The overinclusiveness that is typical in the ensuing reports probably would not be much altered were the referrals specific, however. Unnecessary content is a major characteristic of many traditional reports.

The first exhibit is presented to illustrate a number of principles. It was selected also because of its uniqueness and for the question it poses: Can flexibility be overdone?

Behavior During the Examination

The patient, John C., appeared to be very alert and in good contact with his surroundings. He claimed that he was in the hospital because of his wife's threat to leave him if he did not come here and cure his chronic alcoholism. He also felt that his children would be hurt. The obvious omission in his statements is a reference to himself as having anything to do with his being in the hospital or acknowledging his desire to get well for his own sake. But the omission is understandable if we make the following assumptions: (1) He does not want to acknowledge any responsibility for himself; and (2) his problem is really his wife's problem. In support of these assumptions consider the following incident which occurred at the very beginning of the testing session between the patient and the examiner. The examiner brought an ashtray into the room. There may have been some question as to its decorative value but there really were no grounds for questioning its use as a supplement to smoking. Nevertheless, the patient asked, very timidly, if he could smoke. Now, if he knew the answer to his own question which was made all too obvious by the ashtray that the examiner had *just* brought in and placed before him, why did he ask it? Again, his behavior makes perfectly good sense if we assume that (1) he wanted the examiner to give him explicit permission for smoking, thus setting up the examiner in a judgmental role; (2) he wanted to appear inept and helpless in the situation, hoping that the examiner would then be inclined to intervene and direct him since he "obviously" could not direct himself with any measure of success if he were inept and helpless; (3) he was so self-absorbed that he was not attending to the situation and the ashtray was not in his perceptual field. However, since the question, "Can I smoke?", followed *immediately* upon the presentation of the ashtray, we may reject this assumption as not doing justice to the facts. Thus, there is a striking parallel between his expressed relation to his wife and the relationship he tried to establish with the examiner. In both cases he is told what to do ("Go to the hospital." "You can smoke."), and he disclaims responsibility for both ("I am in the hospital because of my wife." "I smoke because I have your permission.")

Consider another example in which two items of the patient's behavior which followed each other in close temporal succession *appear* absurd because they are mutually exclusive. The patient let the examiner know that he was enjoying the tests and that he found them very interesting. (We will disregard, for the moment, the rote fashion of his verbalization.) As often as he let the examiner know this, which was several times, he just as often followed it with an inquiry as to how many more tests there were left, leaving very little doubt in the examiner's mind that the patient wanted to leave and was trying to find out how much longer it would be before his "enjoyment" would be terminated. Again, certain assumptions make good sense out of what is, prima facie, an absurdity. These assumptions are that: (1) He would not permit himself to be interested in or to enjoy what he was doing, the product of a pathological predilection for discomfiture. Thus, he could not even say he was interested in what he was doing with any real conviction in his voice. But, this certainly does not explain why he should ever mention his "interest" and "enjoyment" to begin with. This brings us to the second assumption which ties together many loose ends: (2) The patient did not really mean he was interested at all as his voice, for one thing, indicated. His subsequent behavior (asking the examiner how much more time the testing would consume) gave the lie more certainty than ever to his preceding words ("I am enjoying this"). So why did he say he was enjoying the testing? He said it strictly for the consumption of the examiner. The patient's modus operandi vis-à-vis the examiner was to act the role of a "good" testee thus entitling himself to the examiner's charity in return. "Surely the examiner will be pleased with me and relax his gimlet eye if I flatter him as a purveyor of good things." This role, we may note, was part and parcel of a pervasive obsequiousness and servility that ran through all of the patient's behavior. Possibly, at a more dynamic level, we are observing a rigid reaction formation against hostility which has lost even its pseudo-adaptive quality and culminated in a sticky sweetness which is emotionally inappropriate to the situation.

Test Findings

The patient's intellectual functioning is in the normal range (Full Scale IQ 97). His almost total failure on the Arithmetic Subtest of the Wechsler suggests a severe defect in concentration. His Performance Subtests are generally better than his Verbal, suggesting an intelligence potential in the bright normal range. An overall educational retardation is suggested if, in addition to the low Verbal and Arithmetic scores (the latter score is, of course, too low to be *only* a matter of educational retardation), one makes a qualitative evaluation of the Information Subtest where the patient shows an inability to even closely approximate the population of the United States or the distance from New York to Paris.

Personality-wise, the patient is unable to relate to people. The intimacy implied in such relationships brings the danger of his experiencing hostile impulses toward the objects of his "affection." Thus, he relates to women, whom he conceives of as mother figures, by provoking them, thus externalizing (projecting) his hostility and setting up the situation so that the hostility is directed back at him. This seems to serve the triple purpose of (1) distorting the outer world as a hostile place and reversing the source of the hostility so that the net effect is for him to disown (repress) his own hostility, yet still define his relationships within a hostile context; (2) punishing himself to serve an expiatory need based on his own completely unacceptable hostile impulses; (3) forcing other people to take an interest in him, thus temporarily putting his isolation in abeyance and making his own need for human contact seem to be the need of the other person. His chronic alcoholism in this context seems to be an attempt to be taken in hand and punished for his derelictions toward his wife and family. His social naiveté allows him to think that an apology for wrongdoing ("wrongdoing" is used here not in its moral sense but to define something the patient does which he may depend upon to provoke somebody) will bring everything back to its ante-bellum status. The "peace" is maintained until, unable to bear his isolation and loneliness, and unable to relate to people because of his hostile feelings (exaggerated all the more when he realizes his need for them) he commits a social crime, e.g., infidelity or irresponsible alcoholism, to hurt his family. The crime naturally forces the intervention of some other people to take him in hand (usually the wife in her maternal role).

The dynamics of this particular patient's pathology seem more clear-cut than is usually the case. He was placed in a home by his mother as an infant. She could not maintain him because her husband was an alcoholic and made the marital relationship impossible to endure. He did not see his mother again until, as a grown man, he accidentally located her. In all probability the mother rejected the infant not because she could not maintain the expense, but because she looked upon the child as part and parcel of the hated husband. Thus, traumatic rejection experiences in the patient's background have severely warped his whole personality development. Affectionally deprived in a most basic way, he can find affection only by twisting his human relationships in such a way that he "finds" rejection everywhere. Is this also a way of finding his parents everywhere? In the most naively impossible way he tries to gain acceptance by being apologetic, an acceptance which is doomed to be very short-lived since it amounts to nothing but an uneasy truce with none of the relevant issues even hinted at. Thus he may be assured that the rejection will be forthcoming again, symbolically reconstituting the basic relation to the rejecting parents, the paradigm of all his relationships.

A therapeutic approach which has, in this type of case, succeeded, is the so-called relationship-therapy in the style of Jessie Taft or of the Rankian School. The basic premise and whole modus operandi of such therapies are focused on just such a barrier to establishing interpersonal relationships on a realistic basis as the patient has to break through.

Summary

The patient, John C., is a 35-year-old man. Intellectually he functions in the normal range with a bright normal potential which is not reached because of a severe concentration defect and what appears to be an overall educational retardation. The patient's pathology seems focused around a severe disturbance in interpersonal relationships based on traumatic rejection experiences in infancy. Rigid reaction formations against his tremendous hostility toward people, conceived of as essentially rejecting, prevent the possibility of any but the most pseudo-adaptive adjustment. Feeling intensely lonely and isolated, his need for people grows more urgent, as does his hostility toward them because he is so completely dependent on them. However, unable to acknowledge this need, he forces other people, primarily his family, to intervene in his life by committing some social misdemeanor (infidelity or alcoholism). Rejection experiences are compulsively sought after as a way of symbolically reconstituting the basic relationship to the rejecting parents, the paradigm for all his relationships. His attempt to break this relationship by a childish apology, usually to his wife conceived of in a maternal role, is as naive and shallow as it is abortive and unworkable. Yet he persists in maintaining a Pollyannish optimism. Thus, with his pathology firmly secured, he goes his self-defeating way.

Diagnostic Impression

Chronic Alcoholism in an Emotionally Unstable Personality.

Just glancing at this report, one may wonder if it is too long. On reading it, one may be sure that it is. The relationship of length to usable content is disproportionate. Too much space is devoted to building a case, as opposed to presenting pertinent conclusions. In fact, what are the pertinent conclusions?

This question cannot be fully answered without knowing the reason for referral, which unfortunately is not available. We do know, however, that the person is in a hospital and is regarded as an alcoholic, at least by his wife. What then might have been the basis for referral? What might have been the psychologist's evaluation goal? What might he have contributed to the case? We can't be sure, of course, but a contribution to the diagnosis could be of importance. That is, is the presenting symptom secondary to some other condition—possibly a condition that might be treatable? Perhaps knowing the role alcohol plays in the patient's economy could be a therapeutic lead. Or it might be useful to know something of the patient's "ego strength," or of his motivation for therapy.

How well does the psychologist approximate goals like these? As to diagnosis, he is impressed that this is a case of "alcoholism." This is a contribution of sorts in that he implies the absence of a number of other conditions, such as schizophrenic disorder, dysthymic disorder, or generalized anxiety disorder. He does, however, link the patient's drinking with an "emotionally unstable personality."

This diagnosis, no longer current, applies when ". . . the individual reacts with excitability and ineffectiveness when confronted by minor stress. His judgment may be undependable under stress, and his relationship to other people is continuously fraught with fluctuating emotional attitudes, because of strong and poorly controlled hostility, guilt, and anxiety" (American Psychiatric Association, *Diagnostic and Statistical Manual, Mental Disorders,* 1952). The accuracy of the diagnosis can hardly be challenged at this time, but the reader of the report has no warning that it is coming. The conclusion is in no way supported, and we in fact think that the content of the report better supports another diagnosis (passive-aggressive personality?).

The psychologist does considerably better in defining the role of the symptom that led to hospital admission in the person's economy, and this information, if accurate, might be of value to a therapist. Unfortunately we do not know if the man would be a good candidate for psychotherapy. The psychologist recommends a special kind of therapy, but the early part of the report suggests that the individual does not recognize that he has a problem and that there is no motivation to change. On the other hand, the report would seem to indicate that the symptom is an aspect of the person's basic psychic structure, and that the man can be successfully treated through "relationship therapy" has to be questioned. Apparently the psychologist himself is skeptical and seems to hedge here. He speaks of success "in this type of case" but does not prophesy success in the case of John C.

Looking at the case in overall perspective again, the composition is good, and the report reads smoothly. The organization is grammatically logical, in a sense, yet there is no apparent development of major conclusions in the interest of effectiveness. Intelligence is given priority in the discussion, although how the patient's intellectual level or his intellectual defects are related to anything relevant is not apparent.

The flavor of the writing is captured by words like "pompous," "exhibitionistic," "authoritative," "erudite," and "academic." Notice the deftness with which apparently insignificant events are made to yield their full portentousness. The reader should feel that he is being instructed in a method of clinical analysis as well as being informed. Most readers would probably also feel that the foreign expressions used in the report are a bit too show-offy for a clinical document, and the contribution about Jessie Taft and the Rankian School almost certainly is so. The reader might be self-critical for not being as smart as the psychologist, unless he or she concludes that the psychologist is now studying—or has recently studied—the various schools of psychotherapy. If the reader understands the matter this way, he or she may feel the comment to be gratuitous and more appropriate in a term paper.

The report seems to have been written by a prosecuting attorney who sees the patient, a not very honest fellow, as always up to some nefarious end. But he won't "get away" with anything. The manner of expression contributes more to this impression than does the content. How much of the jockeying for position and trying to outmaneuver the other fellow belongs to the patient and how much to the psychologist is hard to tell. This question might be easily answered, of course, if we had available other sample reports by the same psychologist. Nevertheless, how the psychologist feels about his patient is evident in talk of a "modus operandi," of receiving the "examiner's charity," and of behavior which "gave the lie." "Now I've got you, you son of a bitch," is the way Berne (1964) puts it. The patient is seen as a manipulator and a leech.

The report would seem to be patient-centered in the sense that the discussion is about the patient and only minimally (as reports go) about tests and test products, and the common Aunt Fanny stereotypy does not occur. Yet the feeling is strong that the psychologist is really more interested in juggling ideas than in meaningfully describing the patient. From the hundreds of words appearing under the title "Behavior during the Examination," we know with a good degree of confidence that "the patient appeared to be very alert and in good contact with his surroundings" (no doubt already observed by the staff), the patient's view of his hospitalization, that the patient asked for permission to smoke after an ashtray was placed before him (and presumably also before the psychologist), that the patient indicated enjoyment of testing but behaved otherwise, and that the patient's behavior involved obsequiousness and servility. With a lesser degree of confidence we learn something more about the patient, mostly on a dynamic level. With at least the same degree of confidence, we know more about the psychologist than about the patient from this passage.

The responsibility with which interpretations are made here is a matter of great concern. Near the end of the report we learn, with eager anticipation, how clear-cut the dynamics are. Then we find that the mother placed the patient in a home while he was an infant, an event that the psychologist unhesitatingly calls a "rejection" (we would need more evidence than presented here to be able to conclude that *the patient* felt rejected). Then the psychologist guesses that the mother "in all probability . . . rejected" the infant because she saw him as "part and parcel of the hated husband." There is no reason given why this guess was made, and there is no evidence offered that the patient's mother hated her husband, certainly not to such an extent that she also did not want their child. The fact (?) that the husband's drinking made it impossible for the marriage to endure does not necessarily indicate hatred. The mother may have had feelings of ambivalence, or possibly even some feelings of love for the man with whom she could not live. People are that way. Nevertheless, the psychologist accepts all of this without feeling the need to offer a bit of evidence, if he has it (the report writer does not impress one as being a devotee of parsimony), to make such far-reaching conclusions appear plausible, and to relate them to the patient's way of life as he (the psychologist) understands it—apparently to no small extent in terms of his personal and class values. Thus, unsupported events are brought together to develop one speculation; this is then accepted as a premise and another speculation built on it. The purpose of this is not certain, since the patient's "dynamics" as described are not clearly linked to the presenting problem (presumably alcoholism). We are told that his mode of life is symbolically to relive the rejection by his parents, but in the previous paragraph we find the symptom related to hostility and a means of getting himself taken care of (the opposite of seeking rejection). Quite evidently, this psychologist does not appreciate the difficulty of relating current behaviors to their distant causes, even when there seems to be an evidential link.

The responsibility of interpretation is also particularly suspect in the first sections of the report. The psychologist arbitrarily restricts the possible interpretations of the patient's behavior and then selects the ones that seem most reasonable to him. However, we can only wonder to what extent his obviously ill perception of the patient guides his interpretation.

The following text reads very much like a laboratory report.

Test Results — WAIS:

Verbal IQ.................... 114.		Full Scale IQ................. 119.	
Perf. IQ..................... 121.		Classified—Bright Normal.	

The patient is presently functioning at a Bright Normal level of intelligence (IQ 119) demonstrating a Bright Normal capacity on the verbal scale and a Superior capacity on the performance scale. There was a considerable amount of scatter on the verbal scale. On the performance scale, however, scatter was minimal. There was some intra-test variability. The patient's concentration and voluntary effort was good but capacity for abstraction and psycho-motor speed was inefficient. The test did show anxiety and depressive trends as well as some schizophrenic indications.

Draw-a-Person

The results of this test indicated that the patient manifested some degree of uncertainty in handling reality situations, and that his world is but vaguely perceived. Orality, anxiety, infantile aggression and dependence and guilt feelings are also present. There are some indications that the patient is attempting to compensate for an inadequate sexuality.

Rorschach

The tests show orality, anxiety, infantile aggression, and dependence and guilt feelings are also present. Color usage exceeds human movement responses, and the F percent is high (72). He no doubt converts tension into psychosomatic complaints.

Bender Gestalt

No severe pathological indications. There is evidence, however, of infantilism and regression.

Szondi

There is an open demand for love and affection. The patient is openly accepting his emotional outbursts. He is fond of pleasure and ease and accepts things from people.

Babcock Memory Paragraph

The memory paragraph was greatly rearranged, distorted, and poorly recalled. The patient's memory is not functioning freely and efficiently; there is a definite indication of pathology.

Projective Sentence Completion

The patient balked a great deal in doing this test. He repeatedly asked if he had to fill in all of the sentences and stated that many did not refer to him. He took an unusually long time to complete the test. The results indicated insecurity, evasiveness, anxiety, dependency on mother and ambivalence toward her. The possibility of latent homosexuality was also indicated.

Word Association

Many clang associations and close reactions were given indicating a lack of flexibility of thought processes. A poor psychosexual adjustment was indicated. A good deal of orality was present. On the whole, the responses were of a regressive, infantile nature suggesting a schizophrenic process.

Object Sorting

There were many rejects, narrow, and split narrow groupings as well as many concrete and fabulatory explanations. Capacity for abstract thinking seemed to be impaired. The results indicate a schizophrenic process.

Such test-by-test reporting with a lack of integrated conclusions and only feeble, manual-type interpretations goes beyond the laboratory technician's report of findings, but not greatly. Instead of WAIS, Draw-a-Person, and Bender Gestalt, we might have Urinalysis, Hematology, and Serology. Instead of the sort of data that appear here we can imagine under these several laboratory headings: Color-appearance—clear amber; Reaction—acid; Specific gravity—1.020; Albumin—neg.; Sugar—neg.; W.B.C.—8,000; Neutrophils—55; Lymphocytes—42; Eosinophils—2; Basophils—1; Hemoglobin—12.8; Hematocrit—42; Kahn—neg.; Wasserman—neg. These are meaningful bits of information, not for the laboratory technician who obtained them, but for one specifically trained to interpret and apply them.

From this point of view, consider, " . . . a Bright Normal capacity on the verbal scale and a Superior capacity on the performance scale. There was a considerable amount of scatter on the verbal scale," or "Orality, anxiety, infantile aggression, and dependence and guilt feelings are also present," or, "There were many rejects, narrow, and split narrow groupings as well as many concrete and fabulatory explanations." Would it not seem apparent that the writer feels less capable of interpreting this material than do the readers for whom it is intended? Or does the psychologist endow this material with an obviousness of meaning?

There is much test jargon ("rejects," "narrow and split narrow groupings," "concrete and fabulatory explanations") and some theory-derived language (for example, orality and latent homosexuality). Are we to assume that the readers of the report know as much about these things as the physician knows about basophils, the hematocrit, or the white blood cell count?

Perhaps the writer did not fully think so, for throughout the report there are *little* interpretations, jumps from raw data to partially interpreted data that are in the nature of general, unintegrated conclusions. For example, "The patient's memory is not functioning freely and efficiently . . . ," "The results indicated insecurity, evasiveness, anxiety, dependency on mother and ambivalence toward her." We can only wonder if such material meets the needs of the team, or if the psychologist felt she had a mission other than to report what the tests yield. What is this psychologist's concept of her role? There is throughout a tendency to attribute the conclusions offered to the tests rather than to the psychologist. If errors have been made, they presumably are the fault of the tests. In any event let us feel sorry for the report reader who *cannot,* no matter how bright or learned, interpret much of the content. Who knows, for example, in the context of the information given, the meaning of ". . . a considerable amount of scatter on the verbal scale," while on the performance scale "scatter was minimal." The further contribution that "there was some intra-test variability" would not seem to help.

The report is saturated with Aunt Fanny statements. Most of us, in our more candid moments, will admit to "anxiety," "dependence and guilt feelings," "orality," "insecurity," perhaps even to "dependency on mother and ambivalence to her," and to having "some degree of uncertainty in handling reality situations" (although use of the word *reality* makes the statement appear sinister). Nevertheless, much of the material may sound impressive, if not meaningful, to a nonpsychologist. But we should perhaps feel ashamed to write, "He is fond of pleasure and ease and accepts things from people," because this probably is also true of the reader of the report who may be made uncomfortable by the foregoing. It is also perhaps going too far to write, "The *possibility* of latent homosexuality was also indicated" (emphasis supplied). Not only may we not be enlightened to learn that the patient has latent homosexuality (because *it* is supposed to be well-nigh ubiquitous—though *it* has no meaningful, or highly consensual, frame of reference), but also we would have been surprised had the psychologist concluded that there were no possibility of such!

But however critical we may be of this non-case-focused report, it is probably largely accurate. With the exception of a few statements (for example, intellectual level, mention of pathological indications, and a diagnostic impression), the report is not specific enough to be wrong. Some of the statements are not transferable into demonstrable behavioral referents. We need to alert ourselves to the specific statements when they do occur, since it is only then that we may check for irresponsible interpretations. The psychologist is able to learn from the Rorschach that the patient "no doubt" converts tension into psychosomatic complaints. Other team members will either challenge the right of the psychologist to express this opinion or get an erroneous view of the prowess of the Rorschach.

Here is another test-by-test report.

WAIS

The patient is presently functioning in the Average range of intelligence, with a full-scale WAIS IQ of 102. This measure is, however, clearly not optimal. He refused to do either the Digit Span or Arithmetic subtests, saying, "You can't touch the darn numbers, Bill." The influence of impairing factors is also seen in inconsistent function. The patient's optimal capacity is most probably in the

Superior range. His tendency toward pedantry, and a careful attention to minute details indicates compulsive features in the personality. Many verbalizations are rather bizarre, and test performance in general reflects marked deterioration.

Wechsler Memory Scale

The patient refused to do more than a few items of this test. He gave his age as 34 (incorrect), and the year as 1971 or 2, but knew where he was.

Several other tests—Color Form Sorting, Memory Paragraph, Bender, Benton, and Szondi—were refused by the patient. For the Bender he said, "You can't do it Mac—I'll bet you don't believe it, it's all ended—It has to end after a while, Bill—I can't, Bill." He seemed to have difficulty in any tests which require symbolic manipulation of materials, i.e., where there weren't models or designs to be copied.

Object Sorting

The patient rejected two items on active sorting, had two somewhat loose groupings, and manifested a tendency to narrowing. Five concepts were essentially abstract in nature, two of them also reflecting functional and concrete thinking. One grouping in passive sorting was rejected, and two elicited syncretistic reasoning. One functional concept was given. The patient was able to offer abstract concepts for the remainder of the groupings, including some of the most difficult ones. Performance on this test would contra-indicate organic involvement, but the inconsistent and erratic function points to a severely pathological process, psychotic in nature.

Rorschach Examination

The large number of responses suggests an over-ideational individual, one who has emphasized intellectualization as a defense. The stereotypy and banality of content, however, indicate an impoverishment of constructive energies in the personality. In spite of the apparent productivity, constriction is a prominent characteristic. The presence of only three popular responses indicates the degree to which the content of the patient's thinking differs from usual modes. There are also signs of gross disturbance in the structural aspect of thinking, including neologisms. Reality testing in general is quite poor, although there is some residual ability to appraise the outside world.

Chronic difficulties in interpersonal relationships are suggested, with little capacity for dealing adequately with emotional stimulation. Inferiority feelings are seen in the presence of homosexual features and paranoid thinking. Compulsive signs are found, and there appears to be a depressive aspect in the personality.

While a schizophrenia is indicated by these test results, the subtype is not clear. Both paranoid and catatonic features are seen, as well as certain aspects of function consistent with simple type. In view of these intermingled aspects, the diagnostic impression is schizophrenic process, unclassified. Lastly, general test performance would contra-indicate the importance of an organic factor.

This report in some ways resembles the previous one, yet it is different. The patient's verbalizations give much more of a feeling that a live person was present. These comments are most colorful but unfortunately are not linked with conclusions that they might illustrate.

The report is inconsistent with respect to interpreting the data. There are some meaningful conclusions—for example, those about reality testing—but much material is not interpreted. What is the meaning of the discrepancy between current intellectual functioning and estimated optimal functioning, or what is the significance of the observation that the patient experienced difficulty with tests having certain characteristics, or what is the behavioral significance of the concepts demonstrated on the Object Sorting test (other than the obvious clinical fact that the patient is psychotic)? The patient evidently was confused about his age and orientation for time, giving an incorrect age and incorrectly identifying the year, yet we must read the analysis of other tests to know that he is not "organic." The psychologist felt it important to include some deviant findings yet not tell their meaning, although loss of orientation in two of the three "spheres" is frequently an organic indicator. Who then shall make interpretations from such inherently rich material?

This report includes much in the way of concepts and jargon that are likely to be unfamiliar to the report reader. The reader is expected especially to know about the Rorschach and the Object Sorting tests and to appreciate the significance of constriction, of three popular responses (how many should there be then, and what is a popular response anyway?), of loose groupings, and of narrowing. In general the patient is presented as an individual, although a few minor Aunt Fanny comments are to be found. Here note especially references to "inferiority feelings," "compulsive signs," and a "depressive aspect in the personality." These could all be spelled out with profit, as could the information on "homosexual features" if it is of any importance in terms of the mission.

The following report on a chronic state hospital patient attempts some segmentalization of personality and also illustrates a number of other faulty practices.

Intelligence, Memory, and Organization of Perception and Thought

The patient is presently functioning toward the lower limits of the Superior range of intelligence, with a full scale WAIS IQ of 120. Qualitative analysis suggests that anxiety, mild negativisms, obsessiveness, and excessive compulsivity may have had the effect of lowering the score somewhat from an optimal measure, which would probably fall higher in the Superior range.

It appears that there are temporary periods of preoccupation that may hinder the intake of presented material, but the memory function seems to be otherwise intact. There is a tendency for verbal material to be distorted, but this is mitigated somewhat by the patient's capacity for critical self-appraisal. So, while reality-corrupting factors are present, the patient is able to exert some degree of control over them.

Basic perceptual functioning is apparently largely intact—perceived figures are drawn in quite faithful reproduction.

In the sphere of thinking, particularly as reflected in the Object Sorting test, the level is not as abstract as would be expected in an individual of superior intelligence. Groupings are mainly assembled on the basis of functional and concrete concepts. This test further reveals the patient's over-ideational nature, and the severely obsessive-compulsive character of his thinking. The looseness of thought structure which is also observed here assumes more pathological proportions in this configuration. Looseness of psychotic degree is also evident in the Word Association test, where the patient gave distant, highly personalized, clang, and even neologistic responses.

Personality

Analysis of projective material indicates a passive-dependent, insecure individual with marked feelings of rejection, inferiority, and inadequacy, and with a strong felt need to be wanted and cared for. There is also a desire, on the other hand, to be active, assertive, and masterful, with the resultant incongruence contributing to a passive-aggressive conflict.

Hostility and its expression is a problem of magnitude for the patient. He harbors a great deal of such feeling, which is variously directed toward the father figure, toward females (who are regarded as castrating, rejecting agents), and toward himself. The extrapunitive feeling arouses a considerable amount of guilt, anxiety, and fearful apprehension of morbid proportions. The intropunitively directed aggression contributes to a marked depressive feeling-tone as well as other self-preoccupations of a more malignant nature. He pictures himself as being helplessly exposed to, and buffeted by, hostile environmental forces, with consequent feelings of futility. Worse than this, there are indications of feelings of self-disintegration and decay, which smacks of the apathy of the chronic, deteriorated schizophrenic.

It appears, in fact, that the patient is struggling, almost consciously, to achieve an emotional nirvana through schizophrenic apathy, but he has not been at all successful in this attempt. There are persistent signs of high emotional responsivity and lability, inner tension and turmoil, rather intense and apparently chronic anxiety, as well as the aforementioned hostility, guilt, and fearfulness.

All of these factors threaten the integrity of the patient's personality organization, and control over them is attempted by means of diverse defenses. Obsessive-compulsive mechanisms, principally intellectualization, predominate and result in thinking which may be characterized as over-ideational, obsessional, doubt-ridden, and ambivalent. He is extremely attentive to the minutiae in his environment, attempting to figure out the meaning and significance behind the details of events. This, in company with a somewhat suspicious criticalness, lends a strong paranoid flavor to the thought content. There is excessive ambivalence concerning almost anything which the patient considers he wants, but at the same time doesn't want, likes but doesn't like, etc. Other defensive mechanisms which the patient is utilizing include strong inhibitory efforts and repression, which give an hysterical aspect to the personality picture. These, together with observed oral material and negativism, could contribute toward catatonic features in the patient's behavior.

As a result of these various regulatory mechanisms, particularly the intellectual factors, the patient can probably succeed at times in presenting a facade which may make him appear more psychologically intact than he actually is. Large areas of thinking are apparently reality-bound, but this is achieved at the expense of rather severe constriction of personality resources. The patient has retained some ability to appraise his own thinking and behavior in order to keep it consonant to a degree with reality.

That the patient's attempts at control are not adequate is most apparent in the intensity and content of his morbid, autistic preoccupations. There is a marked, malignant self-preoccupation, indicating severe withdrawal—the patient is "all wrapped up" in himself. There is an inordinate preoccupation with his sexuality, which is undifferentiated and chaotic. Homoerotic tendencies are strong, but they are not recognized or welcome—as manifested by the extent to which the patient is absorbed with heterosexual problems. There is evidence, too, of guilt concerning autoerotic behavior. The possibility of perverse sexuality should be considered. Another area of preoccupation is religion, problems of good vs. evil, etc.

The patient's apparent willingness to talk about his problems, particularly in glib psychological terminology, would seem to indicate a high degree of positive introspection and insight. Certain test indices suggest, however, that his verboseness is a means of "covering up," of talking about topics of his own choosing. In more ambiguous, non-conversational situations he is cautious, careful, and evasive, thus enabling himself to avoid traumatic topics. This suggests that introspective capacity is actually somewhat limited and insight restricted.

His attitudes toward parental figures indicate marked residuals of unresolved oedipal problems. The father is the object of strong aggressive feelings, while the patient's attitude toward the mother has more warmth, but is still intensely ambivalent due to her rejecting qualities.

In conclusion, the foregoing description indicates a chronic schizophrenic process in an individual who has, nevertheless, retained some degree of reality contact. The type of defenses predominantly employed—i.e., obsessive-compulsive—suggests that paranoid features should be most prominent. The presence of hysterical mechanisms, plus other test indices, would suggest that catatonic features should also be in evidence.

Intelligence is discussed first, although problems of general personality functioning are obviously uppermost in this case.

In this report the headings announce that certain portions of personality are to be separated and treated apart from the rest of "Personality." The psychologist is not successful here (fortunately), for in discussing intelligence he talks about a number of "personality" features—anxiety, negativism, obsessiveness, compulsiveness. This is quite proper if there is a rationale for discussing the intellect in this report. The same holds true of the discussion of what the psychologist describes as the memory function. It is only the headings and the averred attempt to think of personality in terms of segments that are blameworthy.

The report is exhaustive, overdetailed—a shotgun report. What else can the patient have wrong with him? A chronic case, he is schizophrenic, apathetic, deteriorated. He is depressed, paranoid, catatonic, hysterical, and obsessive-compulsive. He is oral, and anal also, no doubt, because he is obsessive-compulsive, and he didn't do very well during the oedipal period either. He has homosexual problems, heterosexual problems, autoerotic problems, and maybe some other kinds of sexual problems. He turns aggression outward and inward because he is a hostile person. He also has guilt, anxiety, fearfulness, minor tension and turmoil, outward hyperresponsivity and lability. He feels self-disintegration and decay. He is passive-dependent, has feelings of rejection, inferiority, and inadequacy, with a strong need to be wanted and cared for. He hates his father and he hates females (they castrate and reject him). The environment is a hostile place.

What is the focus of all these impressions? What are the major conclusions? What is the supporting material?

All the faults written into the report would seem to suggest that the psychologist has a jaundiced view of the patient, but possibly some of this comes from close attention to a pathologically oriented theory. The various fixations, conflicts, and problem areas discussed by Freud are also discussed by the psychologist, the patient appearing to be the vehicle by which knowledge of the theory can be demonstrated. Had Freud lived longer, the report might have been longer. In accentuating the negative, the psychologist watches the patient closely lest he present an unjustifiably favorable image. The patient talks well (though sometimes glibly) and would seem to have much positive introspection and insight. But we mustn't be fooled. He is covering up. He is evasive. Then, too, "large areas of thinking are apparently reality-bound, but this is achieved at the expense of rather severe constriction of personality resources." This patient looks better than he actually is because he presents a facade.

Because theory is a matter of generalities, and because Aunt Fanny typifies the banal generalities of people, this report is very much of the Aunt Fanny type. To be brief, consider traits like orality, anxiety, nonoptimal intellectual functioning, oedipal problems not fully resolved, and an imperfect sexuality. This latter theme is entrenched in many psychological reports as firmly as the IQ emphasis. Psychologists, with the diligence and dedication of Diogenes, would seem to be searching for a person with a solid sex identity, complete acceptance of his or her sex role, lack of guilt or conflict over sex activities, lack of actual or fantasy indulgence in anything but true mature heterosexuality (this is wholesome and good), lack of id impulses that tend in any direction but the latter, and great enjoyment and fulfillment in coitus. Where might we find such a person?

The report has word jargon and test jargon. Terms like *intropunitiveness* and *extrapunitiveness* are not generally used clinical terms; they are associated with a test having low rank order in clinical usage. Nevertheless, the theory talk and the test talk may give the reader the impression of having been here before.

In the next report, which is shorter and contains fewer comments on pathology, the focus is somewhat clearer. At least it would seem that the patient is an intelligent schizophrenic person who is deeply troubled and has, along with several distressing problems, difficulty in controlling the expression of his feelings.

Intellectual Evaluation

Intellectual functioning is generally in the superior range (IQ 127), with very superior verbal intelligence and excellent memory, psychomotor performance, and motor learning. He shows an unusually low drop on social comprehension, however, which is out of keeping with his general performance.

Personality Organization

Objective personality data disclose a generally deviant personality profile with particular emphasis on "depression" and "psychasthenia" scales. Underlying these surface disorders one notes the presence of malignant mental processes in terms of schizophrenic, bizarre manifestations. Thus "Schizophrenia" and "F" scales also show deviant elevations. Disturbed psychosexual functioning is indicated by the elevated "Femininity" scale. Consistent with this picture of severe schizophrenic pathology, the Rorschach and other projective data show marked inner turmoil, multiple unresolved emotional problems, and loss of control of psychotic proportions. Uncontrolled aggressive themes on the Rorschach are exemplified by his percepts of "pelvic bone removed with blood" and "Fox's face." Also his percepts of "colored designs" on plates IX and X indicate reduced emotional control which is compensated by evasive defensiveness.

His thematic associations to the figure drawing suggest considerable concern about problems relating to vocational dependability and perseverence and ability to take care of one's family. His own reported difficulties of this type indicate that he is still ruminating and experiencing loss of self-esteem because of them. His sentence completions disclose other basic personal problems having to do with marital relations, attitudes and feelings about his parents, and general interpersonal relations. There are signs of continued angry depression, intropunitiveness, and reduced self-esteem.

Even though some useful conclusions are presented, the effectiveness of this report is, for several reasons, open to question.

First, there is a lot of test talk. If the reader does not have expert knowledge, or at least a working knowledge, of the MMPI, what is being discussed cannot be very meaningful (but it can still be impressive). In connection with this emphasis on test performance, as partially opposed to emphasis on the patient, is the seeming transfer of responsibility for conclusions from the psychologist to the tests. "Objective personality data disclose . . . ," "His thematic associations to the figure drawing suggest . . . ," "His sentence completions disclose. . . ." The MMPI scale scores apparently give conclusions automatically, and the presence of "schizophrenic, bizarre manifestations" are backed up with mention that " 'Schizophrenia' and 'F' scales also show deviant elevations." With this bit of instruction, other team associates may feel free to reach similar conclusions in the presence of such elevations or to question a psychologist who does not report such conclusions when there are elevations on these scales. Similarly with the interpretation of the elevated "Femininity" scale. In the discussion of intellectual functioning, there is mention of "an unusually low drop on social comprehension," but this is not interpreted. Presumably this statement has meaning in the context in which it is mentioned, and the reader will reach the correct conclusion. Finally, in reviewing the test talk we note the use of test content both to exemplify and to support conclusions. Is it really apparent that "Fox's face," seen somewhere on the Rorschach, is an uncontrolled aggressive theme? Does the isolated information that the patient saw "colored designs" on plates IX and X necessarily indicate "reduced emotional control which is compensated by evasive defensiveness"? All these observations raise questions about the responsibility of interpretation and about the impression given to associates on the way that psychologists reach conclusions.

In a passage taken from a longer report, the opposite of the battery approach is demonstrated; the findings of an individual test are summarized and a diagnostic impression is based on this one test. This is generally hazardous and unwise. In the case from which this excerpt was taken, all the various diagnostic impressions and other conclusions were integrated in the *summary*. This procedure may seem objective, but it sometimes forces the psychologist to arrive at far-reaching conclusions from too restricted a sample of behaviors.

WAIS

On this test, this patient attained a full scale IQ of 125, giving him a classification of "Superior" general intelligence. His performance IQ of 128 also places him in the "Superior" category, and his verbal IQ of 116 in the "Bright Normal" group. This discrepancy of 12 IQ points in favor of performance is considered very significant; this pattern would ordinarily tend to point to psychopathy.

Quantitative discrepancies of the type where easy items are missed and more difficult ones of the same subtest are passed, occurred in the following instances—he misses "movies" (0) and "land in city" (0), but gets "forest" and "child labor" on the comprehension subtest. Qualitative analysis of these and other responses on the comprehension subtest reveal some tendency toward psychopathy (he would leave the theater; his only concern would be to remain calm—he does not care about the others there) and some negativism and inaccessibility (taxes—"They're very necessary"—this is an inadequate answer considering patient's age and educational background).

There are no bizarre responses such as would indicate any pathology of psychotic proportions.

A scatter analysis shows significant negative discrepancy from the mean of the subtest scores for comprehension and digit span. The extremely low digit span performance points to an anxiety laden person; this impression is heightened by the discrepancy between digits forward and backward (5 vs. 3). The digit symbol subtest reveals a pervasive insecurity and some hostility (heavy lines).

Summary of the WAIS

This 31-year-old white male patient is now functioning at a "Superior" level of general intelligence (full scale IQ 125, performance IQ 128, verbal IQ 116). This score is taken to be a fairly reliable estimate, but patient probably has capacity to function on a Very Superior level as evidenced by his performance scores; a great amount of anxiety seems to be depressing his digit span and comprehension performance with a resultant constriction of his verbal ability. There is no indication of any psychosis.

Diagnostic Impression

Neurotic anxiety with pathological personality trends.

This psychologist seems to have faith in report readers' intimate familiarity with the test under discussion—with its items, the sort of responses it yields, and something of the scoring system, too.

The report writer also appears to be giving readers some unfortunate instruction in the interpretation of psychological tests. For example, a qualitative feature of performance on the Digit Symbol subtest is interpreted as indicating the presence of Aunt Fanny traits like "pervasive insecurity" and "some hostility." The interpretation of the patient's response to the "movies" and "child labor" items does not appear to be adequately substantiated. (What was the response to child labor?) Nevertheless, the report writer seems to be building toward the conclusion that this patient is a "psychopath." Progress toward this goal is thwarted, however, when it is noted that the Digit Span score is down—the patient repeated 5 digits forward and 3 backward, a result that could be due to various causes—and by the "pervasive insecurity" already noted from performance on the Digit Symbol test. Hence, the WAIS-based diagnostic impression now becomes "neurotic anxiety with pathological personality trends," an unofficial and ambiguous classification.

The strong need for a summary statement, even though the text is so brief, is interesting. It might also be noted that the summary contains a new integration of material. The meaning of the discrepancy between verbal and performance IQs was suggested in the text—with some hedging (". . . would ordinarily tend to point to . . .")—as a "psychopathic" indicator. Now, in the summary, comes a new insight. Anxiety is leading to a "constriction" of "verbal ability," and the patient is not a "psychopath" after all. The report reader, if able to follow the twisting path of this brief report, is being asked to contribute to the conclusion-making process, rather than being presented with firm conclusions.

Notice that the psychologist interprets a verbal IQ that is lower than the performance IQ as a "constriction of his verbal ability." What impression is the report reader supposed to reach? *Verbal,* in the WAIS sense, refers to tests in which the stimuli are auditory and the responses are made through speech. It is thus a limited technical term. In the usual connotation, *verbal* has to do with linguistic function, and apparently it was not a difficulty of this sort that resulted in a verbal IQ lower than the performance IQ. But even if the test were essentially a measure of verbal ability, a score that is a standard deviation above the mean probably should not be considered as evidence of "constriction."

The final "how not to" case is necessarily abbreviated. The request for assessment was made by a neurologist who requested a neuropsychological reevaluation, the original psychological assessment having been made prior to brain surgery. Much historical data recorded in the present report repeats information that was reported by the psychologist in the original report and is also recorded in other places in the patient's clinical folder.

The abstracted material that follows is from a report that approaches six pages in length, single spaced, plus two pages of raw appended data. The "Reason for Referral," as spelled out by the psychologist, approximates a page. "Behavioral Observations" cover two-thirds of a page. "Test Results" exceed two pages. The "Summary," which is a summary of the entire clinical course of the patient, including highlights of the surgical procedure she underwent and her postsurgical condition, is two pages in length. Then come "Recommendations" that cover half a page, short by comparison. Some excerpts follow.

Reason for Referral

Alice F. is a 46-year-old right-handed female office manager with no known familial left-handedness. On 12/21/81 she underwent a resection of a right mesial temporal arteriovenous malformation. The AVM was totally removed, and seizures were controlled with Dilantin. She was left with a dense left hemiplegia with increased tone and hyperreflexia, left hemianesthesia, left lower facial weakness, and loss of the right cranial nerves III and IV causing an inability to open voluntarily her right eyelid. After the operation she became confused about where she was. . . .

Behavioral Observations

About three to four months after surgery, Ms. F.'s mood was noted to improve. She showed constructive changes in Physical Therapy, Occupational Therapy, and Corrective Therapy. . . . Several weeks later, however, she was found to have a supply of sleeping pills, and on questioning she admitted she planned to use them to "end it all." Shortly after admission she had also threatened suicide. On testing, however, she was in a very good mood. This may be due to the fact that she is now able to get about for short distances with the help of a cane. But she is changeable, and ward nursing staff reports occasional outbursts since surgery. . . . Ms. F. was somewhat of a problem during testing, telling anecdotes, jokes, and posing riddles such as "What is the difference between a psychologist and a psychiatrist? Answer: Fifteen dollars an hour."

Test Results

Ms. F. is functioning at the average level of intelligence. Her WAIS-R IQ is 102. Her Verbal IQ is 116 and her Performance IQ is 76. Information, Comprehension, Similarities and Vocabulary are all in the High Average to Superior range (See Appendix of Scores) suggesting that this was her premorbid level. On Proverbs she is concrete, tangential and circumstantial. On the Wechsler Memory Scale immediate and 20 minute delayed recall was very good and on the Rey Auditory Learning Test she had learned 14 out of 15 words on the fifth trial. Her approach to the task was based on an active and effective strategy of encoding words into a story. Left-neglect is seen on the Bender and on Performance tasks of the WAIS, on the Visual Reproductions of the Memory Scale and in copying the Rey-Osterrieth Complex Figure Test. . . .

Summary of Current Results Compared with Preoperative Results

Ms. Alice F., a 46-year-old right-handed female office manager was referred for a postsurgical neuropsychological assessment following resection of a right mesial temporal arteriovenous malformation on 12/21/81. Following surgery she became depressed and then her mood improved when she was able to get about for short distances with the help of a cane. She then became depressed again over a strain in her marriage. Test results show a marked left-neglect on the Bender, on WAIS-R Performance tasks, on Visual Reproductions of the Memory Scale and in copying the Rey-Osterrieth Complex Figure Test. Cognitive processing of verbal material exceeds performance on visual-spatial material. Knowledge of Vocabulary words and cultural facts and social knowledge is superior. Logical memory and the ability to remember lists of unrelated words is excellent (14 out of 15 words by the fifth trial). . . . Such a pattern is indicative of right fronto-temporo-parietal dysfunction. . . . Compared to preoperative testing, test scores for old verbal knowledge is the same or improved. She is more impaired on tests of visual-spatial functioning since she had her CNS surgery. There was no left-neglect in preoperative testing. . . .

Recommendations

Ms. F.'s left visual-neglect impairs her reading ability, interferes with her ability to solve the visual-performance tests she was given, and impedes her ability to move around in the environment. In addition to the Corrective and Physical Therapy that is planned, she should have visual-spatial orientation therapy.

Ms. F. has a history of maladjustment with depression that dates to 1975. She has taken mood elevators and psychotherapy for this condition until she entered the hospital for her AVM problem. . . .

Severe repetitiousness, problems with organization, and test orientation are very obvious. The function to be served by the information contributed by the psychologist is not always clear. For example, the patient's neurological history and the CNS surgical procedure performed on 12/21/81 was already well documented, and dated where it should be—in her medical records, not in the psychologist's report. A psychologist in a large medical center (where patients with this sort of problem would be treated) does not have the responsibility to integrate the reports of the various specialists into a summary report. What end is served by returning to the neurologist neurological information with which he or she no doubt is thoroughly familiar? Similarly the patient's ward behaviors, certainly the material centering on suicide, is recorded precisely where one reviewing the case would look for it. Her behaviors during testing would appear to be diagnostically rich as an indicator of current psychological status, but the psychologist simply records them for the neurologist and others. The psychologist presumes that in addition to being good out-of-context interpreters of clinical behavior, these clinicians are well versed in the content of psychological tests and the significance of the content that they yield.

It is evident to this reviewer that valuable conclusions are mixed with a plethora of words, their volume being multiplied by repetition that has no clear rationale. In the context of all these words, then, what is omitted stands out boldly: an exploration of the patient's personality and psychopathology as opposed to a recitation of the skills she has retained and those she has lost. True, this topic was not broached in the request for assessment made by the referring neurologist, whose immediate interests may have been focused on topics of his or her specialty. The psychologist appears to have an awareness that affective disturbance and suicidal issues are of importance, but this theme is merely noted—largely by historical reference—not developed. Indeed, no testing was done to better define this obvious problem area, and no recommendations were made to deal with it. An adequate neuropsychological report may be required to deal with more than such typical issues as the retention or the loss of cognitive and other skill functions, the lateralization and the localization of brain dysfunction, and observations on whether the lesion appears to be static, progressive, acute, or resolving.

SOME CASE-FOCUSED REPORTS

Personality-oriented, Educationally-oriented, and Neuropsychological Reports

Contrast the preceding reports with the following case-focused reports, contributed by psychologists from a number of clinical and school settings. The first is on a 40-year-old skilled worker of moderate but comfortable means. He had made three suicide attempts, the last one involving a particularly serious gunshot wound to the abdomen. All the attempts were associated with drink. His psychiatrist referred him to us for an opinion on his readiness for hospital discharge.

Battery: Rorschach, TAT, WAIS, Bender, DAP, Sacks Sentence Completions, MMPI

Psychological Assessment: The most obvious personal and social trait of this patient is a remarkably poor tolerance for frustrating situations—a trait which is directly relatable to his multiple suicidal attempts. This man's need is for large quantities of love and acceptance, and he refuses to stand up to stress. When the going gets rough he will "pick up his marbles and go home." This type of behavior is to be understood as including suicidal attempts.

Mr. M. does not want to know the frustration of the real world. He thinks in terms of platitudes and seeks to avoid the unpleasant (even if this means killing himself). For example, he minimizes his suicidal behavior and seems to protest that such is a matter for casualness. He is clearly an alert and perceptive person (his current IQ is 108) but he is reluctant to use his intellectual powers to help him in his adjustments. It is far easier to believe that unpleasantries are always someone else's fault.

This negative social attitude in fact is a rather strong one. An attitude of hostility and impatience is always close to the surface and many life circumstances are sufficiently frustrating to him to cause these feelings to spill out in undercontrolled behavior. This may take the form of verbal aggression or of physical belligerence. As his behavior demonstrates, there is a proneness also to turn this hostility against himself (although there is reason to believe that such behavior is seen by him as self-righteous and as a punishment for others). Alcohol apparently facilitates such a reaction, so we may partially agree with him that it is the liquor which is to blame.

There are no indications suggesting any immediate suicidal threat, but there is also no reason to believe that he is inclined to eliminate self-destructive attempts from his behavioral repertoire. There are no particular evidences of depression, clinically or subclinically. Rather this patient is seen as having a probably unmodifiable characterological defect. This in combination with frustration can again lead to the sort of behavior for which he was hospitalized.

Some "full" psychological evaluations result in reports longer than this, some in shorter reports. A report of this length is probably about right for many referrals, although the necessity for wide variability needs to be recognized.

The approach to this case was to tell what sort of person this is, and then to relate these significant aspects of his life pattern to the problem under study. In focusing on the problem this way, much about the man is left out. Much could have been made of his hostility at the level of the id, and we could call him "oral" if we wished. However, a judgment has to be made on what sort of content to include and what to exclude. This can be done only when the psychologist focuses on the mission and understands what is relevant in terms of this requirement.

The attempt was to compose the report in an integrated, easy-flowing manner, a task that becomes increasingly difficult and time-consuming as report length increases. The language is unstilted, and the intention was that the report be comprehensible to all who have need to use it, such as physicians, social workers, nurses, chaplains, and hospital aides. Words like "frustration" need no longer be regarded as technical and, we hope, are used in the nontechnical sense in which most report readers probably understand them. There is no shame in using colloquialisms like "pick up his marbles and go home." Those who believe that technical words are economical and convey what cannot be communicated otherwise should be apprised of the economy and the forcefulness to be found in informal expression. Such must be used with discretion, however, and never forced or employed for its own sake.

In another case a psychological evaluation was requested on Mr. O. because his need for hospitalization was questioned by his ward physician. The possibility of a deep disturbance was raised, since it was noted that this patient is a professional person, bright and alert, and without much surface evidence of distress or deviancy. He had complained of "nervousness."

Battery: Rorschach, TAT, Sacks Sentence Completions, WAIS, Bender

Psychological Assessment: The central and prominent theme of this man's life is belligerence and rebelliousness. This negativeness has contributed to turning his marriage into a stormy affair and his job into an arena of bitter dispute. Thus two of the most vital areas of his life, family and career, now are sources of heavy situational stress.

Although Mr. O. is capable of dispensing rancor in many directions, the primary focus of discharge is against authority figures. The origin of this attitude seems to be in the early father-son relationship with the father being seen as unreasonable, not understanding, and overdemanding. In response to this situation the patient has become a great self-justifier and links his rebelliousness with a belief of almost pious self-righteousness. This is true even where his rebelliousness takes the form of flouting conventionality.

Mr. O. feels very anxious and tense at times, sometimes unsuccessful and unhappy, not only because of the stress at home and work, but because of a basic conflict in his personal needs. Stemming from his early home life is an ambition for achievement and the need to be conforming, but an even deeper need causes him to secretly yearn for passivity and to wish to overthrow, the values which are a part of him but which he does not want. Accordingly, merely fulfilling the role of a responsible male member of our society is a primary source of stress for him. If he could resolve the conflict one way or the other he would feel more comfortable.

His oppositional tendencies are a continuing source of guilt for him, and there is reason to suspect that he precipitates conflict with others so that they will retaliate, punish him and thus relieve some of the guilt. If so, this maneuver is not adequately successful for it does not sufficiently relieve deep doubts which he has about his personal adequacy. These are most readily observed in his need to present himself as a superior person.

This same type of compensating maneuver is seen in his marital infidelity. His basic sense of maleness is not strong, and he is unsure of his adequacy here, hence a need to demonstrate that he is a man. Such activity, of course, is also an expression of hostility against his wife and rebellion against his family standards. He probably would not have difficulty in justifying this kind of behavior. Thus, his pervasive negative feelings cause him to feel that others also feel obliquely toward him. He is on the defensive, feels abused, jealous and suspicious. It is very likely that at one level or another he is suspect of his wife's fidelity.

This is an intellectually bright person (his current IQ is 118) and he has a certain amount of appreciation of his difficulties. He recognizes that he is an openly hostile person and that this causes him trouble, but he also believes that he is "right." He therefore is not able to use his intelligence adequately in relating to others. It is easy to visualize his interpersonal conflicts as severe and ugly, since under stress he becomes impulsive, his judgment tends to give way seriously, and he cannot fairly see the other person's point of view.

This patient may be classified as anxiety disorder not otherwise specified (300.00) and Oppositional Defiant Disorder (313.81). There are important paranoid trends, but the basic respect for reality is good and there are no disturbances of the thought processes.

The personality conflicts which this person has should be amenable to a degree of resolution through individual insight-giving therapy of a moderately deep level, but his stay at the hospital might not be long enough to permit adequate time to reach this objective.

It soon became apparent to the examining psychologist that his patient sought hospitalization in connection with a "personality" problem, and it was necessary to study his social stimulus value and the underlying conflicts and adjustment processes on which this is based. An overview of the patient's (clinically pertinent) psychological self is therefore given in the first paragraph, the rest being elaboration. A formal diagnosis is part of the process of understanding the patient—that is, recognizing the extent of his anxiety and subjective stress. A diagnosis is also in keeping with the reason for referral, since, as noted, the possibility of an underlying psychotic process had been entertained.

There is a fair amount of negative comment made about this patient—negative in the sense that society regards hostility as a bad thing, and much attention is focused on his hostility (more than in an Aunt Fanny shotgun report, when we say the patient is repressed, anxious, conflicted, insecure, hostile, and withdrawn, and we can't be too concerned with the observation that he is hostile). Is this a prosecuting attorney report? The report was prepared with a knowledge of the socially negative nature of this patient's personality, and it was felt that to understand him we must highlight this trait. The psychologist felt the description to be accurate and individualized. There was no hesitancy in talking about an inadequate sense of maleness in the patient, this seeming to be directly pertinent even though prosecuting attorney psychologists commonly impugn the maleness of clients. The only way we can be sure whether or not a psychologist writes prosecuting attorney briefs, however, is to look at a number of his or her reports.

In yet another case an evaluation was requested on Mr. Q., who drinks too much. He periodically finds himself hospitalized as a result. The staff has seen other alcoholics, of course, but the questions nevertheless arise, "What sort of person is this? What can we do for him?"

Battery: Rorschach, MMPI, TAT, WAIS,
Sacks Sentence Completions, Bender

Psychological Assessment: This man's dominant orientation to life is characterized by a childlike passivity and dependency, with marked inadequacy in coping with the everyday stresses of life.

Mr. Q. has never really gotten into the competitive stream of life, but, without full awareness that he is doing so, inwardly wishes to be taken care of. Superficially he subscribes to the belief that a man should be responsible and productive, but his passive needs are stronger and he can readily rationalize his shortcomings. Thus he can work for only a few months at a time, then becomes unhappy and "exhausted" and finds relief in drink. He sees himself as physically weak, not having recovered from illnesses while in service, namely malaria, jungle rash, and prickly heat. Similarly, he would like to get married for the dependency gratification this might offer (his dependency needs are much more insistent than his sexual needs), but has not sought out a mate because a girl friend married another man 20 years ago and he has not yet gotten over it.

Mr. Q.'s mode of adjustment is fairly adequate except where he is required to come to grips with life physically or mentally, to put out any form of sustained effort. This is so because of his passive needs, but also because of defects in his intellectual functioning. Though of average endowment, he is very naive about life and about himself, and he is unconcerned either with the world of real everyday living or with the poor quality of his own thinking which so easily makes it possible for him to deceive himself. Beyond this, he is remarkably unsure of himself, and any external pressures to make him function responsibly would only lead to indecisiveness, tension, and no doubt drinking.

Psychodiagnostically, this patient would appear to be a case of alcoholism in association with a personality disorder. The latter is probably classifiable as Dependent Personality Disorder, but a reliable social history (the patient is not regarded as a reliable source of information about himself) could help to establish whether this is correct. It is not felt that psychotherapy can provide any real benefits, but there is a possibility that he might be helped by associating actively with Alcoholics Anonymous.

The focus is on personality description because this might be explanatory of the behavior that leads to hospitalization. It was not felt that going into the patient's problem of orality, at a psychoanalytic level, would add to this objective. Certainly it did not seem that simply to mention that he is oral would do much for the man or for the staff.

Being unable to state a precise diagnosis is not to be regarded as a deficiency. Frequently other team members contribute to the psychologist's diagnostic impression. It can be unfortunate when the psychologist feels the need to state an impression without qualification. Most people respect honesty, and the psychologist ought not contribute to a false image of omniscience.

The following report was made on Mr. T., who has an unsavory police record. In his early forties, he has been arrested 30 times in the past 15 years for drunkenness and brawling. No doubt this figure would be much higher were he not incarcerated so much of the time. He presents an appearance rather contrary to what one might expect from a person who spends so much time on the other side of the law. He was referred simply for a fuller understanding of his behavior, anything that would contribute to an understanding of why he is as he is.

Battery: Rorschach, MMPI, TAT, Bender,
Sacks Sentence Completions

Psychological Assessment: Mr. T. prefers to believe, and would have others believe, that he has a "nervous" condition which is directly attributable to war service. He does in fact experience anxiety and tension—which is quite evident, for example, in a speech blockage that he refers to as stuttering—and he does have a tendency to feel quite unhappy at times. An examination of his thinking shows blocking of thought that may be seen in temporary defects in memory and temporary confusion in dealing with problems. These too are definite indications of tension, but Mr. T.'s primary difficulty is one of social maladjustment.

Mr. T. is seen as an unusually self-centered person who feels markedly inadequate and insecure in meeting the requirements of living. He really does not try very hard to function up to the usual expectations that people have of others, and he certainly does not put himself out where sustained effort and perseverance are required. Rather, he leans very heavily on others for support to the extent that he has developed some rather effective techniques for getting such help. But this does not solve the basic problems which are responsible for his difficulties. In particular, negative feelings he has toward himself—the feeling that he is an inadequate person—and his need for support by others, as already mentioned, cause him readily to sense that he is being rejected. He reacts to this with markedly hateful feelings. Initially it was his parents who he felt were unreliable, rejecting, and making difficult demands on him, but now he tends to feel this way about people in general. In fact society itself now seems to be treating him as he felt he was treated as a child. This feeling of being "let down" by others and reacting to people with hateful urges is associated with inward feelings of guilt and unhappiness. He feels bitter toward the world, distrustful of people and suspicious of their motives.

Obviously then, this is a person who has never grown up psychologically, and one of his major apparent difficulties is in relating to others. This inability to relate to people on a mature plane is seen quite clearly in the sexual area. The patient admits that he does not feel attracted to members of the opposite sex, but he does have need for a woman because of the things she can do for him. This is one of those men who might be regarded as marrying his mother.

On the surface one observes a person with what would ordinarily be sufficient mental capacity to function quite effectively (IQ 106), but he has never adequately developed his intellectual resources any more than he has been able to mature more generally as a person. He has a good understanding of what society expects from people, and he is alert and able to acquit himself well in nonstressful social contacts. But he is not the sort of person who spends much time thinking. He prefers to do things with his body, to move around physically, rather than think. He is an impulsive person whose rash behavior does not permit him to deal constructively with everyday matters. And he has a lack of mental discipline which permits him from time to time to be unrealistic in his thinking, to deal with events as if they were different from what exists in reality. He just chooses not to see the unpleasant truths of his existence. This permits him to deceive himself about his personal motives and behavior, and to some extent probably to deceive others too, at least temporarily.

Socially Mr. T. is rather smooth, glib and ingratiating. He says the "right" things, sounding sincere and convincing. He readily volunteers that he has fallen short of even his own aspirations, but this is quickly explained as due to his childhood circumstances. Mr. T. is quite proficient in behaving in such a way that others might become sympathetic and lend support. As a matter of fact, in the testing situation before the examiner had an opportunity to understand the patient more objectively, he (the examiner) was moved to ask, more out of personal curiosity than clinical curiosity, how it happens that a person like himself has such an unsavory police record. This surface behavior is regarded as a technique of relating to others, and probably also of exploiting them, but under stress or frustration this gives way and his more basic nature emerges. He is a person who must have things on his own terms. He cannot tolerate strains or tensions very long and he must live out his needs.

Often this takes the form, when he feels abused by others (possibly as a result of misunderstanding others because of his own negative attitudes), of striking back with violence. This tendency, along with his drinking, is an unfortunate combination socially.

Notice how many traits Mr. T. has in common with much of the rest of the population. He is of average intelligence, narcissistic, impulsive, dependent, anxious, depressed, insecure, a "latent homosexual," and hostile. Yet it is possible to understand all of these as they have meaning for the patient in the context of his individuality.

Notice also the participant-observer role of the psychologist. Part of the impression gained of the patient was through the effect he had on the examiner. This is not in keeping with the principles of laboratory work.

The next two reports are reproduced with the permission of Dr. Donald N. Bersoff.

Richard was almost 17 years old when he was referred by the school guidance counselor because he was making repeated, almost continual, visits to the nurse's office for vague complaints that were never substantiated. The school was interested in knowing how disturbed he was emotionally and what could be done to help him (and, most likely, to help the school nurse rid herself of a disturbing child, although that was not given as a reason for referral).

Richard was administered the Wechsler Adult Intelligence Scale, the Minnesota Multiphasic Inventory, and the Rorschach Psychodiagnostic Test. Richard's mother was also seen, with her son, for a brief interview. (In addition, a long telephone conversation was held with the school counselor.)

Richard is an essentially normal boy with little evidence of overt, serious emotional difficulty. He does have a tendency, however, to exaggerate minor problems and embellish their significance. He then proceeds to brood, ruminate, feel all sorts of catastrophic events are about to occur and will consequently react to the perceived problem rather than to the problem as it is in reality. As his major modes of responding to problems in living are to escape rather than confront them, and to act quickly with only moderate forethought rather than to unemotionally weigh alternatives, he wants to find a workable expedient that will aid him in his escape.

He finds school aversive for several reasons: He is compared in his athletic endeavors unfavorably to his more adept brother; he is forced to comply to schedules; he is infinitely more interested in nonacademic activities and school time prevents him from engaging in those activities when he wants to; and finally, because he has little patience to work through or think through a difficult but manageable problem, he must then find a way to escape from this aversive stimulus. This he has done by, initially, finding his parents and the school infirmary vulnerable to somatic complaints. Thus, reinforced by sympathetic understanding and excuses from class, he has found the hypochondriacal route quite appropriate to his ends.

However, this behavior is quite amenable to extinction, both at home and in school. He simply needs to be refused treatment and classroom excuses (after a brief examination in case of genuine physical illness), and his "nurse-seeing" behavior will stop. There is no reason to be inhibited in doing this. As indicated earlier, he is not suffering from any severe emotional illness; he is neither psychotic nor neurotic, and most of his outpourings of grief are a histrionic display, easily eliminated. He is an intelligent boy (Full Scale IQ Score is 113—"Bright Normal" and better than 80% of the adolescents his age) and he has merely used his intelligence to find a convenient and feasible means for avoiding frustrating and challenging work. He might fuss and fume about this refusal because he does feel victimized and picked on, a sort of hapless victim of adult irrationality, but he also has a deep well of humor and is smart enough to give up when he understands that he cannot avoid limits being set. One final note of caution: he is also bright enough to try something else.

David was referred by the family physician, although a copy of the report was sent to his school. He was referred because he exhibited all the behaviors associated with those children typically labeled as "neurologically handicapped" and the doctor wanted to know if there were any psychological indications of brain damage. The boy was in the first grade and about six and one-half years old when seen.

David was administered the Stanford-Binet Intelligence Scale, Children's Apperception Test, Thematic Apperception Test, Bender Motor-Gestalt Test, Rorschach Psychodiagnostic Test and Figure Drawings. Both parents were interviewed, and a telephone conversation was held with the doctor.

David is an imaginative, talkative, active boy of high intelligence with no overt evidence of brain injury. His measured intelligence on the Stanford-Binet is 126, which places him in the "Superior" range of intellectual ability, ranking him better than 90% of the children his age. He is able to perform tasks expected of the average seven, eight, nine, and even ten year old. It is not until he is given problems appropriate for an average eleven year old that he shows consistent failure. His vocabulary, the best single indicator of intelligence and academic success, is equivalent to that of a bright eight year old.

His intellectual capacity, however, is not matched by his emotional maturity. When frustrated or overstimulated he is very likely to become hyperactive, impulsive, disorganized, and infantile. He is an intense child whose impishness can easily turn to annoying and seemingly negativistic behavior.

It appears as if general family relationships are good, but he tends to see his mother as more restrictive and punitive than his father. But, while he sees his father as protective and concerned, David is moderately angry about the fact that he is gone a great deal. At one point he responded to a picture of a little boy looking at a violin and said, "The boy isn't very happy. His Daddy won't fix his banjo because he doesn't have time." When the examiner asked what the little boy's father does for a living, David responded, "he fixes cars" (his real father's occupation). He also has been affected, more than most children by the birth of his next youngest sibling. The usual feelings of displacement and "being left out in the cold" seem to be heightened in David.

While the syndrome of hyperactivity, impulsivity, low frustration tolerance, and irritability are classically seen in the so-called hyperkinetic child and is usually associated with intracranial damage, demonstrable brain damage does not seem to be the etiological agent in this case. His visual-motor functioning is good and at least average for his age. Any deficiencies are not due to perceptual or motor disturbances but are attributable to his difficulty in sitting still or attending to many stimuli at one time. When stimulation is reduced (for instance, presenting one card at a time to copy on separate pieces of paper rather than having 8 or 9 copied all on one sheet) his performance is more controlled, accurate, and commensurate with his intellectual level. Thus, he cannot be expected, despite his high intelligence, to consistently react and behave like the average six or seven year old. It may be that high expectations both at home and school, demands made that he was physiologically incapable of fulfilling, and attempts at restraint that were doomed to failure, all served to increase his frustration and irritability beyond his control to the point where he has begun to be viewed in such negative terms as destructive, vicious, and uncontrollable.

He is controllable and will respond to discipline if a comprehensive management regimen is begun. His parents could use brief counseling of an educative nature, during which ways of reacting to him and ways of controlling his behavior can be detailed. He can be imaginative, clever, and a highly effective child both at home and school, and proper management and perception of his problem will be helpful in securing this goal.

The language in the fifth paragraph is technical, directed as it is to the referring physician. Dr. Bersoff indicates that he would have written this paragraph differently if the referral had come from a teacher.

The following is a progress report written by the psychologist in charge of a remediation program. It is addressed to the parents, who may become part of the treatment team and who have a right to know what is being done for their child and how he is progressing.

We have worked with Jeff in three areas this year: visual memory, academic subjects, and behavior modification. Jeff's progress has been extremely slow and we feel his attitude has been the chief cause of this.

Jeff has reached a satisfactory level of ability in visual memory. We feel that no further work is required here.

We worked with Jeff in the following academic areas: reading, spelling, math, and library skills. In reading we started with a review of vowel sounds and after becoming sure of these, Jeff worked on blending and syllable division. He was placed in the beginning of the Merrill Reader, Book 2. Gradually his oral reading grew smoother and his comprehension improved. Often Jeff randomly guessed at a word by its context rather than trying to sound it out. Consequently Jeff has moved very slowly through Book 2 and still has not finished it. Another academic area we worked in was spelling. We used the same list which Jeff used in school. He had difficulty in reading the words on the list. We would study as much of the week's words as Jeff could handle. Occasionally he could tackle the whole list and at other times only one or two words. Again, Jeff would prefer to guess rather than make a calculated attempt at the correct answer. In math Jeff would count on his fingers when doing multiplication or addition and subtraction problems. This slowed his responses down considerably. We worked on his remembering the multiplication tables, but Jeff was able to remember only up to the "three times" tables out of order without using his fingers. In the area of library skills we covered alphabetical order along with puzzles involving library vocabulary.

During the year we needed an increasingly more structured behavior modification program for Jeff. Toward the end of the year we gave him chips for: good work, effort, listening to directions, and for the completion of a given task. We took chips away when Jeff was late, wasting time, guessing wildly, and for failure to complete a task. We also gave him time limits for each activity and he received chips when he came within the time limits. Jeff's teacher was able to use a similar approach in the form of a "weekly report." Jeff received checks from his teacher for copying down his assignments, for correct answers, for good behavior, and he received a bonus for a perfect paper. He received minuses for bad behavior. After he accumulated a certain number of checks he was allowed to do a job in the classroom he enjoyed. We found this to be the most effective approach in encouraging Jeff to apply himself more in a learning situation.

Conclusions and Recommendations

Overall Jeff has shown only a small amount of improvement. He no longer requires tutorial assistance for his learning disability. We are concerned over Jeff's being below grade level and avoidance behavior in a learning situation. Outside counseling might help him a great deal. We feel he should continue to seek remediation at school.

It is also strongly recommended that a comprehensive behavior modification program be set up at home and at school. We would be happy to work this out with you and the school at your convenience.

The following two reports were written on the same child. The first is written for the clinic staff as a basis for advising the child's mother and the physician who referred the case. The reason for referral and pertinent history (his restlessness and distractibility are considered along with current findings in making a diagnosis) are given, then the findings are disclosed, a diagnosis is made (a diagnosis that has direct implications for treatment), and a conclusion on what must be done is offered. The scores are important. They are meaningful to those who work with minimal brain dysfunction children. The scores will be available at a later date should the child be retested; hence, there is a basis for measuring change.

The letter to the physician spells out the meaning of the scores and completes the picture with a description of the child's behaviors and the diagnosis. The psychologist has reason to believe that this physician knows little about MBD and its treatment, hence tactfully suggests appropriate medication together with its physiological rationale.

Re: Henry Dennis

Henry Dennis, aged 9 years, 2 months, was evaluated at the Center. Presenting problems were impulsivity, social problems, and poor school functioning. From Henry I understand he was tested at school this past year. A retest here on part of the WISC revealed Henry to have good average intelligence. He was noted to have poor attention span, concentration and memory. He was an extremely restless and distractible child. He has a history of hearing problems related to a familial pattern.

The Frostig gave the following results:

Eye-hand coordination:	5 yrs	-3
Figure-ground	8	-3
Form-constancy	3	-0
Position in space	5	-6
Spatial relations	8	-3

giving the basis for severe learning disability based on perceptual handicaps. The Wide Range Achievement Test yielded the following findings:

Reading	Grade 1.9
Spelling	1.6
Arithmetic	2.6

There was no real association between sound and symbol in reading and spelling. Arithmetic is weaker than the obtained rating. For practical purposes, Henry has not really mastered the first stage of literacy. Even the personality test (Rorschach) revealed severe figure-ground problems, inability to cope with percepts and, in general, the primary finding was that associated with a minimal brain dysfunction as the core basis of Henry's problems.

Our conclusion was that he will need special help to progress in school as well as an awareness of these special problems on an emotional level in order to keep Henry from becoming demoralized and so making worse his social adjustment. Mrs. Dennis was also referred to her physician for further consultation.

Re: Henry Dennis

Dear Dr. Prinz:

You referred Henry Dennis to us last winter for evaluation.[1] Major complaints were bedwetting, soiling, stealing, impulsivity, and "does not listen." Henry was seen in February and we had a family conference with mother on April 10. The school's and our testing of Henry revealed him to be of good average intelligence but with serious physical problems. From our history the difficulties became remarkable at 3 years when Henry developed high fevers, then a hearing disability. Concurrently he became over-active, difficult to manage. Psychological studies here revealed Henry to be indeed a hyperactive child, easily stimulated

---

[1]The recapitulation of case circumstances apparently is necessary. The referring physician would not necessarily be expected to have immediate recall of the case and cannot be counted on to review the details of the earlier psychological report.

and perseverative. Attention span and concentration were very poor; he was highly distractible by even tiny auditory and visual stimuli. He seemed to lack the ability to differentiate figure-ground not only in paper work but in general activity. He had no sense of body orientation, which presented continuous confusions to him. Tests revealed him to be four years below his expectancy in perceptual functioning. School achievement was still at Grade 1 level instead of Grade 3. The severity of his disabilities suggests a minimal brain dysfunction which would account for much of his basic difficulties, including the inefficiency of sphincter functions. Exacerbating these problems has been very poor parental management, leading to even greater confusion and disorganization.

We have found that children such as Henry often benefit markedly from medication (dexedrine or ritalin) by increasing efficiency of neurological functioning. Parental guidance was offered by the Center but the mother did not respond. The school is being alerted to Henry's academic disabilities and to the need for special tutorial help.

Sincerely Yours,

The following neuropsychology report, prepared on consultation with a mental health clinic, is presented essentially in telegraphic style and includes scores. Extensive data are presented concisely. The school psychologist may be helpful in interpreting them further, although the report explains well the subject's level of functioning. He or she may also help with an understanding of such terms as *contre-coup effect,* and with some of the technical terms that follow. The narrative is informative, however; it helps to explain why the student, a 16-year-old injured in an automobile accident, is having difficulties with his vocationally oriented program, which offers such courses as "shop," blueprint reading, and mechanical drawing.

Borderline defective general intelligence and neuropsychological test borderline performance consistent with moderately impaired brain function. The test findings are consistent with the presence of cerebral dysfunction. With regard to differential functioning of the cerebral hemispheres, there is evidence to suggest that the right hemisphere is functioning less well than the left. The test evidence suggests the presence of a mild, static lesion.

General Conclusion and Recommendations: This kind of picture is frequently seen in individuals with severe open head injuries. The deficits may be associated with the direct site of injury or might have resulted from a contre-coup effect. This young man has substantial visual-spatial deficits, which may be amenable to rehabilitative efforts. These might include intensive tutoring with visual-spatial material, bearing in mind that the lesion is mild.

Lateral Dominance Examination

Subject is left-handed.
Subject is left-eyed.
Subject does not have crossed eye-hand dominance.
Subject is left-footed.

Perceptual Disorders Examination	Right	Left	Wide Range
Tactile suppressions	9%	9%	Achievement Test
Auditory suppressions	0%	0%	Reading = 9.9 grade
Visual suppressions	0%	0%	Spelling = 8.8 grade
Finger agnosia errors	5%	20%	Arithmetic = 3.4 grade
Fingertip writing errors	30%	20%	10 years of education

Name of Test	Rating	WAIS Subtest Scores	
Halstead Category	3.	Information	6
Form-Board, Time	5.	Comprehension	6
Form-Board, Memory	1.	Arithmetic	3
Form-Board, Location	3.	Similarities	10
Speech Perception	3.	Digit Span	11
Rhythm	1.	Vocabulary	9
Tapping Speed	5.	Digit Symbol	4
Trails-B	4.	Picture Completion	5
Digit Symbol	4.	Block Design	4
Aphasia Screening	2.	Picture Arrangement	5
Spatial Relations	1.	Object Assembly	5
Perceptual Disorders	2.		
Average Rating	2.83	WAIS Verbal IQ	= 91
Percent of Ratings in the Impaired Range	75.00%	WAIS Performance IQ	= 69
		WAIS Full Scale IQ	= 80

Rating of 0 = Superior
      1 = Average
      2 = Mildly Impaired
      3 = Moderately Impaired
      4 = Severely Impaired
      5 = Very Severely Impaired

(Average score on each subtest is 10 and average IQ is 100. Higher values are above average and lower ones are below average.)

The next two reports were written in response to students' academic problems. The first deals with a child's lack of school achievement, the second with severe reading disability in a 20-year-old.

EVE

Reason for Referral

Eve was referred for reevaluation because of obvious lack of progress. Her teachers continue to be concerned about her lack of academic success, despite special programming. A complete educational reevaluation is therefore being done. An intellectual reassessment was also deemed necessary as an integral aspect of such evaluation since her current poor performance seems discrepant with earlier intellectual measurement.

Tests Administered

Wechsler Intelligence Scale for Children-Revised (WISC-R)
Illinois Test of Psycholinguistic Abilities
Children's Human Figure Drawing
Kinetic Family Drawing

Wechsler Intelligence Scale for Children-Revised (WISC-R)

Full Scale IQ: 76
Verbal IQ: 75
Performance IQ: 80

Verbal Tests	Scaled Score	Performance Tests	Scaled Score
Information	3	Picture Completion	6
Similarities	4	Picture Arrangement	4
Arithmetic	6	Block Design	4
Vocabulary	7	Object Assembly	11
Comprehension	9	Coding	9
Digit Span	7	Mazes	8

Test conditions were considered fair. Eve appeared comfortable with the examiner, but highly structured work sessions combined with frequent breaks had to be used in order to insure her involvement on the WISC. There were periods when Eve became exceptionally tense and hyperactive. During these times she rushed through, apparently unconcerned about an accurate performance.

Eve continually tried to talk the examiner out of giving her anything else to do. Open defiance and destructive use of materials occurred near the end of the test.

Eve's full scale IQ falls in the borderline range of intelligence. The WISC score shows her to now be significantly below the Stanford-Binet IQ of 110 she achieved 22 months ago.

The highest subtest scores Eve was able to achieve on the WISC included:

Object Assembly—involving putting simple puzzles together. Requires good spatial relations and knowledge of whole-part relationships.

Coding—involving visual perceptual skills in the learning and writing of symbols. Requires good manual dexterity as well.

Mazes—an eye/hand coordination task involving visual perceptual skills.

Eve also achieved a higher scaled score on the Comprehension subtest requiring the use of common sense to solve problems.

Eve was least successful on the following subtests:

Information—measuring knowledge gained from experience and education, as well as alertness to the world around her.

Similarities—requiring logical abstract reasoning and the use of comparative thinking.

Picture Arrangement—requiring attention to the details of pictures, interpretation of social situations, and sequential abilities.

Block Design—measuring ability to perceive and analyze patterns and requiring the use of whole-part relationships. Eve may have experienced frustration with Block Design because of the nonmeaningful nature of the patterns, whereas she was successful on Object Assembly, which involves some similar skills but uses material more motivating and meaningful to her.

Scatter in the Scaled Scores of the WISC-R appears to be not only the result of perceptual dysfunction, but attention problems and emotional disturbance as well.

Illinois Test of Psycholinguistic Abilities

Auditory Vocal	Age Score	Scaled Score	Visual-Motor	Age Score	Scaled Score
Auditory Reception	5-2	21	Visual Reception	6-7	28
Auditory Association	5-9	22	Visual Association	6-3	28
Verbal Expression	5-10	26	Manual Expression	10-4	42
Auditory Memory	5-3	28	Visual Memory	7-3	34
Grammatic Closure	7-0	27	Visual Closure	7-0	30

Composite Psycholinguistic Age: 6 years, 6 months

Eve was given the ITPA 22 months ago when she was 6 years, 9 months of age. Her psycholinguistic age at that time was 6-0. Those test results indicated strength in visual and visual-motor skills. Short-term visual memory measured significantly higher than auditory memory. Some disability was noted in the auditory sensory modality.

Present test results show Eve to have made only a few months gain in communication skills over the last two years. Her psycholinguistic age now measures at 6 years, 6 months.

Auditory skills continue to measure lower than visual skills. Eve's poorest scores were in auditory reception, auditory association, and auditory closure. As in the past, auditory sequential memory measures below visual sequential memory.

While the visual channel is Eve's strongest, her skills within this modality are variable and significantly below the expected performance for an eight-year-old child.

Eve scored significantly below age level in manual expression, requiring that she use gestures to express herself.

Children's Human Figure Drawing

Developmental Score:	2 (Borderline Level)
Emotional Indicators:	6
Poor integration of parts	
Stick figure	
Hands cut off	
Omission of feet	
Gross asymmetry	
Slanting figure	
Developmental Score:	2
Emotional Indicators:	5 (2)

Eve's drawing reveals the absence of three expected items (feet, two-dimensional arms, and legs). The Developmental Score is therefore 2, indicating that Eve is probably functioning in the borderline range of intelligence.

The drawing exhibits five emotional indicators and two other clinical signs of emotional upset. From the number and kinds of emotional indicators on the drawing it is apparent that Eve continues to have a great many emotional problems.

Specific indicators include:

Poor integration of parts—related to immaturity and impulsiveness.

Asymmetry of limbs—associated with poor coordination and impulsiveness.

Hands cut off—related to feelings of inadequacy and guilt over failure to act correctly.

Omission of feet—again related to a general sense of inadequacy, as well as feeling of insecurity and helplessness.

Genitals—this indicator is rare and occurs almost exclusively on the drawings of extremely disturbed children who are overtly aggressive. The presence of genitals is also associated with acute body anxiety and poor impulse control.

Eve's drawing also contained two additional likely clinical signs of emotional upset. She drew large detailed ears. Emphasis on the ears is often associated with sensitivity to social criticism and paranoid reactions. Eve's drawing contained a bed with "pretty sheets" and her teddy bear in it. Beds on children's HFDs have often been shown to be an expression of sexual concern.

Kinetic Family Drawing

Eve initially refused to draw her family. When she did produce a drawing, the figures were carelessly done and were not shown involved in any kind of action. Defensiveness and negativism are indicated by her reaction.

Eve's intelligence test scores are significantly below those achieved in her earlier testing. Her Full Scale IQ now falls in the borderline range at 76, compared to an earlier Stanford-Binet IQ of 110. In this examiner's opinion the significant drop in scores is due to a combination of debilitating factors including: social or emotional problems, perceptual dysfunction, an elevated activity level, and attentional deficits.

Recommendations

1. Individual and family therapy on a long-term basis.
2. Continued work in language development.
3. Special school programming. Eve requires much one-to-one and small-group attention with a teacher trained to work with emotionally disturbed and learning disabled children. Behavior management and carefully structured work periods should be used to assist her in making a more positive adjustment in class.

RICHARD SWENSEN

Richard Swensen, a ninth-grade dropout, was referred to this examiner for an evaluation of his reading skills. Richard has considered himself virtually a non-reader and the inconvenience and embarrassment caused has made a tremendous impact on his life.

Richard was eager to have this evaluation hoping to receive an explanation of the cause of the problem and the development of a plan for remediation. He was a very cooperative subject, and the results of the testing are seen as valid.

Tests Administered

> *Wechsler Adult Intelligence Scale*
> Subtests: Digit Span
> Block Design
> Object Assembly
> Digit Symbol

Gallistell-Ellis Test of Coding Skills
Orthographic Patterns Spelling Test
Durell Analysis of Reading Difficulty
Informal Evaluation of Word Recognition and Memory
Bender Visual-Motor Gestalt Test

Discussion

Richard's performance on the Block Design and Object Assembly subtests of the WAIS indicate above average ability and no deficits in the areas of organizing visually presented material. His scaled score of 11 on the Digit Span subtest also attests to better than average ability and no problems in auditory memory. However, on the Digit Symbol subtest, which is a paper-and-pencil task, Richard's lack of confidence in this area caused him to slow down and become almost compulsively careful. Since this is a timed test his score suffered and fell below normal. However, his short-term and long-term memory for the symbols was excellent.

The results of the Bender Visual-Motor Gestalt Test yielded no evidence of organicity. Again, his memory for the designs was good and showed no distortions. He did exhibit some impulsive and compulsive tendencies. The indications are that Richard's problems with reading are not due to organic causes.

On the Gallistell-Ellis Test and the Orthographic Patterns Spelling Test Richard exhibited a solid foundation in initial and final blends, short vowels, and one-syllable long vowel words. Some problems in sequencing and consonant reversals were noted. The complete tests were not administered since, in the opinion of this examiner, Richard's confidence in his reading abilities is minimal and care was taken not to present a failure experience. Diagnostically, the results are meaningful and indicate a point of departure for remediation.

The Word Recognition and Word Analysis subtest of the Durrell yielded a score of grade 3.5. Richard has some good basic word attack skills. However, on the Oral Reading test he competently (if slowly) read selections through the sixth grade level. His phrasing and comprehension were excellent, and he decoded many unknown words. The words that he missed were put on "flash cards"; and an hour later, at the end of the session, he still knew them.

Some informal evaluation of difficult words was conducted, and Richard is developing adequate sight vocabulary.

It was noted that at the end of a two-hour session which had been devoted almost exclusively to reading fatigue was evident. Richard puts a lot of energy—both emotionally and physically—into reading. It is a draining experience for him.

Richard has more solid basic reading skills than he thought that he did. (He may not believe it, either!) He has no perceptual or memory deficits, and the indications are that his intellectual functioning is above average. The block seems to be, at this point, an emotional one. He must be convinced that he can learn to read better and more efficiently than his current level. In the opinion of this examiner, the motivation is strong, and he is extremely "teachable."

Recommendations

It seems important that any remedial program that is initiated have the following aspects:

1. A well-trained tutor who has good professional qualifications. Richard needs to feel secure and to trust that this person "knows what he is doing."

2. Care should be taken to insure success and a minimum of frustration. Richard does not trust his own abilities to improve his reading skills, and he must be helped over this block. At this point he is a "fragile learner". He tends to be impulsive and compulsive and can quickly "overload" and fail.

3. Lessons must be sequentially structured and grouped into short tasks, especially at first.

4. It is important that spelling and writing skills be developed in conjunction with reading.

5. New word attack skills should be presented: i.e., syllabication, "r" controlled vowels, silent letters.

6. Sight vocabulary should be enlarged.

7. Time must be provided to read relevant material: i.e., newspapers, books of vocational interest. These could be approached from the "experience chart" approach.

8. Reading speed must be improved. "Homework" in this area would be appropriate. A controlled reader would be excellent.

Suggested Materials

1. The Gillingham reading method.
2. Merrill Linguistics—from about third-grade level.
3. The Dolch Word list

4. Flash cards
5. Any graded sequential spelling list.

In conclusion, Richard was a pleasure to meet and to evaluate. He is a good candidate for reading remediation, and if care and concern are exercised, he should be able to overcome his anxiety about his reading skills and improve them. Thank you for the referral. It was a challenge and pleasure.

The final report in this series is based on the Luria-Nebraska Neuropsychological Battery (Golden, Hammeke, & Purisch, 1980) and was contributed

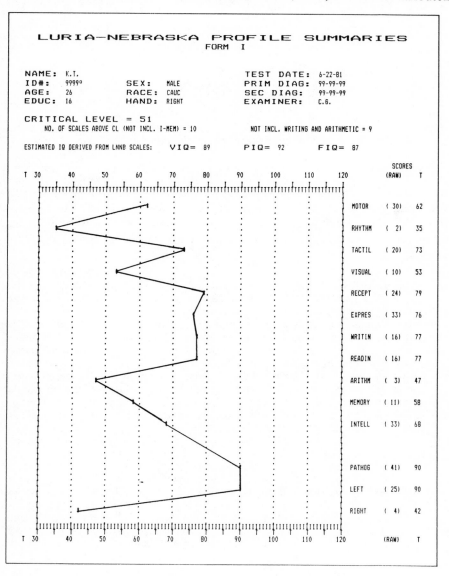

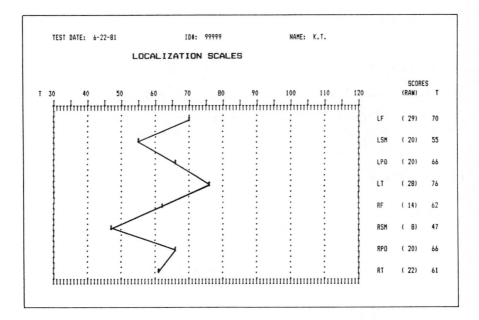

by Charles J. Golden and Charles Ginn. Included are (1) Luria-Nebraska Profile Summaries (p. 173), (2) Localization Scales (above), and (3) Factor Scales (p. 175). The item scores are not shown. This report was obviously written for a neurologically sophisticated reader who is familiar with the LNNB.

The patient is a 27-year-old Caucasian male who was involved in a single car accident in October, 1980. In the accident he suffered a closed head injury, fractured ribs, and a right pneumothorax secondary to the fractured ribs. He was semiconscious on admission to the hospital and was moving all extremities. Two to three days post-trauma, a right hemiparesis developed. This was determined to be the result of a CVA resulting from left carotid artery injury secondary to hyperextension of the neck. The CVA was confirmed by CT scan and carotid arteriogram. CT with contrast showed a wedged shape area of decreased density in the left parietal region. The arteriogram indicated occlusion of the left angular artery with marked slowing of the left internal carotid circulation. At the time of the accident the patient was doing graduate work in psychopharmacology. He has an undergraduate degree in psychology.

Test Instrument: Luria-Nebraska Neuropsychological Battery administered seven months posttrauma.

Findings: Evaluation with the LNNB revealed moderate to severe deficits across a number of areas of neuropsychological function. The severity of the injury was evidenced by the high peaks on the Pathognomonic and Left Hemisphere scales. The patterns of the deficits were consistent with damage involving the areas of the brain supplied by the left middle cerebral artery. His good performance on the Rhythm scale as well as the low Right Hemisphere Lateralization score suggested that the right hemisphere had been spared damage.

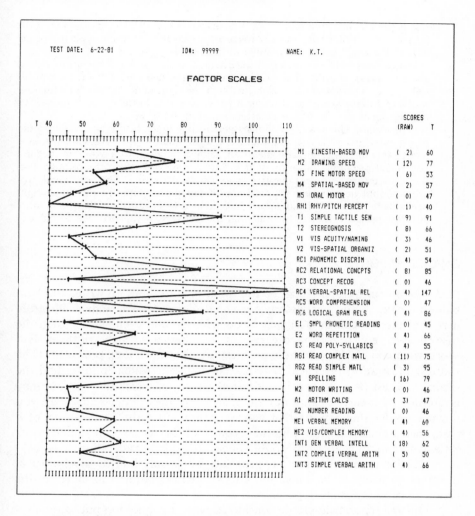

TEST DATE: 6-22-81   ID#: 99999   NAME: K.T.

FACTOR SCALES

		SCORES (RAW)	T
M1	KINESTH-BASED MOV	(2)	60
M2	DRAWING SPEED	(12)	77
M3	FINE MOTOR SPEED	(6)	53
M4	SPATIAL-BASED MOV	(2)	57
M5	ORAL MOTOR	(0)	47
RH1	RHY/PITCH PERCEPT	(1)	40
T1	SIMPLE TACTILE SEN	(9)	91
T2	STEREOGNOSIS	(8)	66
V1	VIS ACUITY/NAMING	(3)	46
V2	VIS-SPATIAL ORGANIZ	(2)	51
RC1	PHONEMIC DISCRIM	(4)	54
RC2	RELATIONAL CONCPTS	(8)	85
RC3	CONCEPT RECOG	(0)	46
RC4	VERBAL-SPATIAL REL	(4)	147
RC5	WORD COMPREHENSION	(0)	47
RC6	LOGICAL GRAM RELS	(4)	86
E1	SMPL PHONETIC READING	(0)	45
E2	WORD REPETITION	(4)	66
E3	READ POLY-SYLLABICS	(4)	55
RG1	READ COMPLEX MATL	(11)	75
RG2	READ SIMPLE MATL	(3)	95
W1	SPELLING	(16)	79
W2	MOTOR WRITING	(0)	46
A1	ARITHM CALCS	(3)	47
A2	NUMBER READING	(0)	46
ME1	VERBAL MEMORY	(4)	60
ME2	VIS/COMPLEX MEMORY	(4)	56
INT1	GEN VERBAL INTELL	(18)	62
INT2	COMPLEX VERBAL ARITH	(5)	50
INT3	SIMPLE VERBAL ARITH	(4)	66

   The patient had greatest difficulty in the understanding of language. This was especially so in tasks where a language related concept is tied to the comprehension of another language concept or of a spatial task. He has problems understanding verbal-logical, verbal-grammatical and verbal-spatial relationships. Problems were seen when the task was given orally to him and when he had to read the material for himself.

   While he was able to read and repeat phonemes and one-syllable words, more complex reading and repetition skills were not present. Tasks involving the coordination of verbal analysis, synthesis, and output of material were very difficult for him to complete with any degree of smoothness, speed, or accuracy. This was most evident when auxiliary words conflicted with the direct connotation of the order of actions or objects. For example, when he was asked to "Point at the pencil" or "Point at the key," he was able to do so with no trouble. However, when the directions went beyond the simple nominative function of words, he was not able to do what was asked of him. When presented with the instructions "Point with the key toward the pencil" or "Point with the pencil toward the key," he merely pointed to the pencil and to the key.

Deficiencies were also seen that were related to his residual hemiparesis. Speed and fine motor coordination were all but absent in tasks involving the use of his right hand. There also exist problems with the right hand in simple tactile sensation and in the synthesis of tactile input to identify objects by touch alone. His intelligence at present would be estimated at an IQ of 88.

Conclusion: This man is obviously performing much below that which would be expected given his age and education. Continuation with graduate school is inadvisable at this time. Considerations should be given to having him begin a vocational retraining program as it is doubtful he will regain the complex language necessary to be competitive in an academic setting. The vocational program should be designed to make use of his skills related to the intact right hemisphere. Retesting in six months would also be in order. At that time, more accurate predictions as to his potential for recovery of function can be made.

QUICKIE REPORTS

That psychological reports can be too long, take too long to write, and be a burden on the reader has already been well discussed. We wish to illustrate here that reports can be designed to be effective and even shorter than the case-focused reports presented earlier in this chapter—which are themselves short when compared with the typical reports that have long prevailed. (The shortest illustration presented here is that of Ellen, which follows, and the second shortest (K.C.J.) consists of but 41 words, of which the last four may be considered superfluous.) Before judging any of the examples adversely, you might consider that reports that concisely summarize the key features of a case, that are easy to read, and that require of the seasoned psychologist as little as five minutes to write would appear to merit consideration.

Quickie reports are most appropriate when only limited psychological information needs to be conveyed. Quickie reports require no more justification than do "global" reports.

Quickie reports should be considered when the question put to the psychologist is circumscribed and can be forthrightly responded to. An interim report in a school situation provides an example.

> Yes, Ellen's interest in school is diminished because she does not know what she wants to do on graduating high school. Work? What kind of work? College?
> We shall administer interest and aptitude tests and discuss possibilities with Ellen.

Quickie reports are optimal when initial impressions are needed, especially fast initial impressions, and when reports of current psychological status are needed. When "well-documented" cases are referred, little additional documentation may be necessary and repetition of earlier documentation could be irksome to the reader of the report. There are, indeed, a number of situations were psychologists might agree with Shakespeare's Polonius, who prefaced his observation of Hamlet's mental state with the observation that "brevity is the soul of wit."

Even shorter and more quickly written, yet no less serviceable, are many workaday progress notes. These often skimp on formality and take liberties with syntax, and they may make use of incomplete sentences, abbreviations, clinical shorthand, and jargon. Thus,

No change.

R/O OBS.

Mrs. K didn't feel like talking much today. Obviously depressed. Expresses a "What's the use?" attitude.

Bill angrily refused psychological testing. He said he had tests at Clearwater, where the psychologist showed him "a bunch of dirty pictures" and got him excited. The patient signed a release form and I called Clearwater for his records.

Frieda talked today for the first time about her stepfather. She reported that she had never told anyone of his incestuous contacts with her that occurred between the ages of 10 and 13 and ended when her parents were divorced. She sobbed a good deal but said she felt better to "get it all out." I suspect that she will have a great deal of working through to do on this matter.

The matter of quickie reports has been put in perspective by Souther and White (1977). Their message is addressed to scientists and engineers.

> . . . in reality, aren't some kinds of writing we produce quite adequate even if they are "quick and dirty"? Some of the things we write must, of course, possess as high a quality as we can provide.
>
> Many of the kinds of writing that we do, however, belong somewhere between these two extremes. It would be helpful if technical and scientific writers and their supervisors would discuss the degree of quality required for the different kinds of writing that the staff must produce. Definition of quality standards would do much to clarify the writing task, both for the writer and for the reviewing supervisor.

But these authors caution that the above is not a license for inferior work:

> We are not suggesting, of course, that writing can be unclear, ambiguous, distorted, or sloppy.

Several quickie cases and some comments follow.

D.R., AGE 12½

Debbie is a twelve-and-a-half-year-old girl from a broken home (father deserted six years ago and continues to upset the family by calling to complain to Debbie's mother about his present wife). Debbie is thought to be under-achieving in school. Her teachers see her as an angry, troubled child. Debbie herself complains that schoolwork overwhelms her, tires her out. The following report seeks to achieve an understanding of Debbie as a basis for taking further action.

> Debbie's intellectual status is above average. Her observations are accurate and there is originality of thought. She is an insecure child who has many fears. She fears the loss of her integrity, attack from others, and her own impulses. Debbie has a great need for acceptance and affection, but is inhibited by an overpowering fear of being rejected and hurt. There seems to be hostility directed to the mother. The relationship has not been mutually satisfying, often leaving Debbie frustrated. It is my impression that the mother's inconsistencies in handling the child may be a source of anger. Now she wants her own way and is conflicted about her dependency. Her attitudes to men are also unwholesome. They are seen as weak and mutilated. And she is confused about herself. She feels inadequate, and having a specific learning disability she requires more guidance and love than most children her age. However, not being able successfully to reach out to others has only left her more frustrated. Since Debbie finds it difficult to relate to people and because her own feelings are threatening to her, she withdraws to an immature fantasy world that provides little refuge. Even her fantasy is fearful, involving aggression and fear of being injured emotionally. Debbie is a very unhappy child.

D.J.H., AGE 52

> The patient presents a solid picture of histrionic personality disorder. The dominant defenses are denial and repression, with resultant naiveté, poor respect for reality situations, poor judgment, and a variety of socially immature behaviors. He is remarkably self-centered, employing exaggerated histrionic techniques in a continuous attempt to gain support. He is rigid, demanding, and potentially somewhat paranoid in defending what he regards to be his best interests. He thus finds himself involved in frequent interpersonal problems, particularly with those to whom he relates most closely; and low frustration tolerance, exaggerated and labile emotional response, and acting-out tendencies that he regards as "righteous" make for assaultive behaviors. He is preoccupied with sexual fantasy and somatic problems, seeking to live out the sex material in flirtatious behaviors. Marital problems are a source of stress, albeit he contributes to these problems, most recently through his flirtations. The outlook for significant change is not great.

D.J.H. was hospitalized on the "advice" of a judge after he was charged with assault and battery on his wife for the nth time during one of their battle royals. There is no "curable" condition, and (barring a minor miracle) only separation of the couple can put a stop to the presenting complaint. This report does not do justice to the polished histrionic behaviors of this man—a veritable Hollywood actor as he plays out the scenes that regularly take place in the home. But what if the report, with the investment of great effort and time, did a superb job of capturing the flavor of this actor, surely one of the most colorful people I have ever met? Would it make any difference at all?

K.C.J., AGE 49

This is a florid, chronic schizophrenic of the paranoid type. Delusions are un-systematized and involve ideas of influence and persecutory themes, all in a bizarre context. Thought and speech are quite loose, and neologistic expressions are noted. The outlook is guarded.

This man has been as described for a number of years, and the most promising approach would be antipsychotic medication, support, and whatever hospital programs he might fit into. It is well to document briefly the patient's status on admission as a baseline against which to evaluate possible changes in the future, since these might provide a basis for action. Pages detailing personality and psychopathology could be added, and we could have at least a paragraph of discussion on intelligence, but to what end? Indeed the comment on outlook is gratuitous.

B.F.K., AGE 21

This is a picture of a thoroughgoing "psychopath"—an antisocial personality with a history of disturbance extending far back into childhood. He is essentially an unsocialized individual with a hostile, nihilistic view of the world, capable of dispensing hostility, including assault and physical acts of destruction in many directions. Particularly when under the influence of alcohol and/or drugs is he likely to be destructive, and he may show psychotic-like behaviors. The possibility for any degree of improvement is slim; on the other hand, he could decompensate to psychosis.

Short, if not very sweet. It's telling it like it is. Anyone who claims to have special skills in treating character disorders may volunteer to be this man's therapist. Many nonpsychologists likely would "give up" on such a person, or already have. (Following the patient's discharge, a local district court judge ruling on his most recent transgression selected jail, over the hospital, for him.) Perhaps our random selection of cases contains a disproportionate number of "losers"; at any rate this was one person not benefited by our ministrations. We must remember that although modern treatment helps many, we don't win 'em all.

M.A.B., AGE 27

There are two opposing sides to this personality: on the one hand there are highly conventional aspirations, on the other, a "psychopathic" side that generally triumphs. This man is remarkably hedonistic (though his marathon sexual expression has recently become "hollow, not worth the effort"), self-indulgent, impulsive, and, in the presence of particularly low tolerance for tensions at the present time, is likely to live out his impulses. He further shows tendencies to schizophrenic behavior that evidently were lived out under LSD, and have at least some potentiality for emerging in stressful situations. He may be diagnosed in terms of his presenting complaint of drug dependence. He might profit from psychotherapy addressed not only to the direction of socialization, but also to deal with problems of hostility and anxiety about sexuality. In addition, there is psychometric evidence for an organic brain syndrome. His WAIS Full Scale I.Q. is 113, his Verbal I.Q. is 121, and his Performance I.Q. is 102. His Wechsler Memory Quotient is 73, with the greatest deficiencies in the areas of logical memory and in making and briefly retaining new visual and verbal associations.

This writer is evidently more hopeful for this man than for the previous one, but not very. The prognosis is built into the character structure. Key personality features and problems are identified, although not all in clinical terms. There is, for example, implicit depression in his "hollow" sex experiences. The nature of his sex anxieties is not spelled out but would quickly become evident to a therapist. He was assessed for a possible organic brain syndrome because of severe, prolonged drug abuse, and the level and quality of his intellectual functioning could be a factor in a rehabilitation program.

7

Computer-Generated Psychological Reports

In this age of high technology, the microcomputer has taken on a major role in psychological evaluation, from testing to scoring and report writing. The "psychometric machine" does the job of psychological testing well; it is fast, efficient, and economical, and it saves the human tester time and tedium. It can also contribute to the more complex process of psychological assessment. The psychologist must be aware, however, of the ethics and the procedures, and of some role changes, that are involved in computer evaluation. These topics have been codified by the American Psychological Association.

Computer-generated psychological reports are now in prominent use on the professional scene. One diagnostic service alone is estimated to have provided reports to approximately a quarter of the American psychologists and psychiatrists who are eligible to subscribe to computer reporting (Fowler, 1985). As this remarkable technology struggles out of its infancy, we are replacing our initial "gee whiz" admiration with hard questions, and already we have found some answers on how to live with the modern psychometric machine (Tallent, 1987).

Computer-generated reports are an efficient means of providing psychological information about individuals, efficient but entailing some important limitations. Both the value and the limitations of electronically developed psychological information are explored in this chapter.

Many of the questions raised by computer-generated reports relate to old issues, albeit in a new context. This was evident in early efforts by the American Psychological Association to adapt established ethical standards and test standards—particularly of validity—to computer report writing (Newman, 1966). Similar concern with ethics and test quality is highlighted in the more recent *Guidelines for Computer-Based Tests and Interpretations* (American Psychological Association, 1986), referred to throughout this chapter simply as *Guidelines*.

A second major point is that the advent of computer reports calls for a renewed emphasis on, and some modifications in, the traditional diagnostic role of the psychologist who becomes computer involved. Particularly demanded are a strong rooting in tests, and in test theory and research, and a knowledge of the application of psychological measurement to human issues (American Psychological Association, 1986).

Contrary to some early speculation that computer reporting would eliminate the diagnostic role of psychologists, it is now recognized that a qualified psychologist must function as a "middleman" in passing on to consumers information that issues from a computer. "There must be a clinician between the computer and the client" (Fowler & Butcher, 1985, p. 95). No technological unemployment here.

Even more surprising, computer reporting has led to a new, mandatory role for clinical judgment.

> Computer-generated interpretive reports should be used only in conjunction with professional judgment. The user should judge for each test taker the validity of the computerized test report based on the user's professional knowledge of the total context of testing and the test taker's performance and characteristics. (American Psychological Association, 1986, p. 12)

Computer reporting accentuates the need to distinguish between psychological testing and psychological assessment. They are different processes and they yield different products. But today's computer reports, mimicking the syntax of assessment, may belie that they are test reports, particularly since they may be more clinically flavored than test-flavored. Indeed, computer reports are sometimes referred to as "computer assessments," though, clearly, computers do not perform assessments (Tallent, 1987).

Computer reporting also may entail some special problems when used in the legal system. These are in addition to the normal challenges that psychological reports may meet in the courtroom (Chapter 9).

SOME BASICS OF COMPUTER PSYCHOLOGICAL REPORTS

The hardware and the software of computer psychological reporting are widely familiar, as are the printouts that are the outcome of the computer process. Access to the technology is simple, and the user of computer services has a number of options for generating responses to test material and having them interpreted, perhaps in conjunction with history, observations, or self-descriptive statements. Psychometric and projective instruments can be individually administered by a clinician, for example, or the client may record responses on an answer sheet. Data may be mailed or telephoned to a computer service or interpreted by an on-site computer. Or the machine can handle the entire operation of administering and scoring a test and printing out a report.

The basic rationale of computer reports has a long history; it is the recognition that the existence of predictable regularities between test scores, or test score patterns, and behavior can be established. The venerable MMPI *Atlas* (Hathaway & Meehl, 1951) is based on such recognition. It is the existence of regularities between test data and behavior that makes possible the "cookbook" (Meehl, 1956) approach to evaluating personality.

With the demonstration of statistical regularities, algorithms (a partly Greek term honoring the ninth-century Arab mathematician al-Khuwārizmi) are established. These are mechanical decision rules for arriving at interpretive statements. Thus an elevation on MMPI Scale 2 may lead to selecting from a statement library a sentence about depression, and a 4-9 pattern might indicate that the test taker has a possible problem with alcohol. If an MMPI Scale 0 score of 77 is achieved the decision might be made to present the test taker as "a shy, withdrawn person who tends to prefer solitary activities."

Such a straightforward approach typically is augmented with clinical insights and theoretical flavoring (for example, psychoanalytic). These are the contributions of leading diagnostic experts, so their potential to enhance the quality of interpretive reports could be great. There are problems, however, and we shall discuss some implications of this practice later.

FROM TEST MAKER TO TEST TAKER

Guidelines defines various participants in the computer approach to psychological evaluation. These are definitions that incorporate responsibilities as well as statements of role. Though even the position of the test taker in the evaluation scheme is spelled out, our focus in this and the next section is on the *test user,* the role of the psychologist or some other qualified professional who has the responsibility for delivering psychological information to another.

Test author   The computer reporting process starts with the development of a test by a *test author* or by test authors. This may be a conventional instrument, such as the MMPI or the WISC-R, or it may be an instrument such as the Millon Clinical Multiaxial Inventory (MCMI), designed for computer processing, particularly scoring and interpretation.

Software author   It is a *software author* who creates the algorithms required to put the instrument to use in producing information about *test takers* (students, clients, patients, job applicants, and so on). These include, in addition to the all-important algorithms for interpreting the test, less glamorous algorithms for test administration and scoring. (More sophisticated algorithms for test administration are on the cutting edge, however. *Adaptive testing* is an approach to tapping individual features of the test taker by administering items contingent on the examinee's responses to earlier items—as is done in Binet testing.)

Test or software publisher   The *test or software publisher* provides services to professional consumers on a commercial basis. Available from the publisher may be access to equipment that will process test responses and return processed data (for example, scores, profiles, lists of critical items) or reports or both, to automated testing/interpretation programs, and to test materials, software and manuals.

The professional consumer of computer services should be knowledgeable about the function of those who are involved in the development and distribution of services related to psychological evaluation. In an area of activity where ethical concerns are uppermost we should be familiar with the integrity and the reputation of the test developers and providers of computerized services whose input is basic to the evaluation process. The professional consumer should also know the assessment-related orientation of the test author(s) that underlies his or her development of tests and algorithms.

Test administrator   The *test administrator* is the person who is in charge of administering tests, either through direct supervision of those who take tests or through a proctor to whom the task of oversight is delegated. The test administrator in all cases retains responsibility for the proper administration of tests. This includes carrying out the testing in a physically congenial environment, making sure that test items displayed on the screen are legible and free from glare, and familiarizing the test taker with the computer equipment on which testing is done.

Test taker   *Guidelines* gives special attention to the *test taker* when that person is also the consumer of the interpreted test data, as, for example, when the test is a vocational interest inventory. In such instances the test taker is also the *test user* (next paragraph), and "special care is needed in providing an appropriate context for understanding the test results" (p. 6).

Test user   *Guidelines* defines the *test user* as a "professional" rather than as a psychologist, in the recognition that many test users are not psychologists. It is the test user who utilizes "test results"—that is, scored data or interpretive statements for the purpose of decision making. A variation of this role occurs when the test user passes along data or interpretations to another decision maker, such as a director of special education or a therapist. In such cases both the test user and the final decision maker are responsible for using the information properly.

On reading the *Guidelines'* statement of the user's responsibilities, rooted in the American Psychological Association's ethical principles and standards for providers of psychological services (American Psychological Association, 1977, 1981), one may conclude that many nonpsychologist test users do not have the training needed to meet those responsibilities. However, only members of the Association may be held to the following criteria.

The test user should be a qualified professional with (a) knowledge of psychological measurement; (b) background in the history of the tests or inventories being used; (c) experience in the use and familiarity with the research on the tests or inventories, including gender, age, and cultural differences if applicable; and (d) knowledge of the area of intended application. For example, in the case of personality inventories, the user should have knowledge of psychopathology or personality theory. (p. 8)

Ethics Guidelines should be understood as the application of established ethical principles and standards to the mechanical and technical characteristics, the powers, and the limitations of the modern psychometric machine. The user of computer services should, therefore, be thoroughly familiar with *Guidelines,* both to maximize the usefulness of computer-generated information and to be certain that she or he is following sound ethical practices.

Particularly compelling are the previously quoted criteria that the "qualified professional" must meet. These are requirements that are difficult to quantify. They might be met at an acceptable level through taking appropriate courses and gaining experience in the areas of testing and assessment.

The implications of ethical issues and provider standards are further spelled out on pages 8–13 of *Guidelines.* Under the heading *The User's Responsibilities* are listed the provider standard that pertains to the psychologist's knowledgeability and the limitation of practice to the areas of his or her competence, and the ethical principles that pertain to responsibility, competence, welfare of the consumer, and assessment techniques. The latter, particularly, underlines earlier discussions regarding the sharing of reports (pp. 47–50) and the report reader's ability to understand the report (pp. 49–50).

Thus, the interpretation of Ethical Principles 8a and 8c reads:

The direct implication of Principles 8a and 8c for the user of computer-based tests and interpretations is that the user is responsible for communicating the test findings in a fashion understandable to the test taker. The user should outline to the test taker any shortcomings or lack of relevance the report may have in the given context. (p. 9)

Under *Guidelines for Users of Computer-Based Tests and Interpretations* are the headings *Administration* and *Interpretation.* The first is addressed to the test administrator, who is charged with the responsibility to provide conditions "equivalent to those in which normative, reliability, and validity data were obtained" (p. 10). To that end the administrator must attend to (1) the equipment used in testing and the physical environment and (2) to the test taker's ability to adapt to and function adequately with computer equipment. Thus the test administrator should provide instruction or assistance as needed.

Spelled out in some detail in *Interpretation* is the very considerable role assigned to the professional and to professional (or clinical) judgment. Only a qualified professional is equipped to consider "the total context of testing," the appropriateness of a particular test for a particular person, and factors that might invalidate test results.

> It is imperative that the final decision be made by a qualified professional who takes responsibility for overseeing both the process of testing and judging the applicability of the interpretive report for individual test takers, consistent with legal, ethical, and professional requirements. In some circumstances, professional providers may need to edit or amend the computer report to take into account their own observations and judgments and to ensure that the report is comprehensible, free of jargon, and true to the person evaluated. (pp. 12–13)

Such a decision "must be that of a qualified provider with sensitivity for nuances of test administration and interpretation" (p. 13).

THE COMPUTER PRINTOUT:
TEST REPORT OR PSYCHOLOGICAL ASSESSMENT?

In Chapter 5 we introduced a basic approach to psychological assessment. Here we contrast *assessment* and *testing*. In a climate where such a distinction is not made there is a resultant inability of "many practitioners and trainers in professional psychology to distinguish between assessment and testing." This oversight, in turn, "has led to a tendency for the profession to focus its attention on the mechanistic and technical aspects of test administration and to ignore or slight the conceptual basis of the assessment process" (Sloves, Docherty, & Schneider, 1979).

The widespread use of computer reports, often referred to as computer assessments, makes it more important than ever that we make the distinction between the processes of testing and assessment. The test user, surely, must know when computer reports might be adequate to a particular clinical mission and when psychological assessment is the optimal approach.

We may examine some key features of psychological testing and assessment to show how they differ.

Psychological testing is physicalistic (mechanistic and quantitative) The basis for physicalistic testing (psychometrics) was presented in Chapter 5, page 104. It is the demonstrated statistical relationship between measured performance on test items of valid tests and nontest behaviors of interest that is the raison d'être for testing. Translating test performance to statements about nontest behaviors is a basic forte of the computer.

Psychological assessment is more encompassing than testing. Maloney and Ward (1976) make the point that assessment is a broader activity than testing by emphasizing that tests are only one of a number of means of collecting data.

A simple definition for an extremely complex process is that *psychological assessment is a process of solving problems* (answering questions) in which psychological tools are often used as *one* of the methods of collecting relevant data.

In the next quotation, Maloney and Ward drive home just how complex assessment is. Note that if this observation is correct, then computers, which operate in accordance with decision rules, cannot produce a psychological assessment.

Psychological assessment is a variable process, depending on the question asked, the person involved, time commitments, and myriad other factors. As such, it cannot be reduced to a finite set of specific rules or sets.

Observations by Sloves, Docherty, and Schneider (1979), presented in Chapter 5, pages 106–108, are consistent with those of Maloney and Ward, particularly with respect to the variability of the assessment process and to the subsidiary role of testing in the conduct of assessment.

Psychological assessment is problem solving.   The positions of Maloney and Ward and of Sloves, Docherty, and Schneider emphasize psychological assessment as a problem-solving activity. Schafer's (1949) position (pages 104–105) is similar as he challenges the exalted position that scores hold in psychometrics, and puts in their place the logic of the psychologist. It is logic that comes from study and experience. It is *psychological thinking.*

Psychological assessment is multiple and complex interaction.   The diagram in Figure 5-1 summarizes the multivariable, complex interaction involved in the assessment process. There is interaction with the person or persons who have referred the client, and with the client, whose personal behaviors might provide data as important as "test results." There is interaction with ideas—the psychological assessor's frame of reference—and with many facts—such as options for disposition, history, the family situation, health—and with various persons who might be able to supply facts.

The psychologist's knowledge, sensitivity, and ability to interact comfortably with the client, staff, or informants will greatly affect the collection of material that contributes to the assessment. The ability to *interpret* a colleague's referral question may yield important information not available through formal channels (pp. 105–106). An informal chat in the corridor following a formal case conference can focus material in a new light, or from an altered perspective.

Information given formally has a different character, if not content, than that given informally, as may be seen at the end of many meetings when people walk out together and say what is "really" on their minds. . . . Some people simply seem to need face-to-face discussion before they can understand or believe.

> Sometimes the consumers of the test report, those for whom it was written or spoken, have questions which were not covered in the formal report or which have occurred to them on the basis of the report and other newly acquired information. (Appelbaum, 1970)

Psychological assessment is an integrative task: Its focus is on the individual   Professionals who offer services to persons who are troubled, who are in need of having their situation understood and treated, or who require some other kind of help focus more on the individual than on group trends or statistical relations. In psychology this surely is true of direct service providers such as clinical, counseling, and school psychologists, psychoanalysts, and other therapists.

At an earlier time, however, when psychologists were *testers,* the relationship with clients was largely through the medium of tests, and "test results" were pretty much the be-all and end-all of that relationship.

> We not only did just what we were asked to do, without taking a clinical interest in the patient, but actively encouraged referrers to believe in the special powers of our instruments and the unique qualities of our results. . . . How far the tester is from clinical responsibility is seen in his indifference to the way the referrer plans to use his answer. (Towbin, 1964)

Today we know that a psychologist cannot carry out a good psychological assessment without taking a clinical interest in the client. And how the assessment report is shaped is closely tailored to the problem that is under investigation.

A particularly troublesome fact that hampers the tailoring of psychological data to a client's problem is information overload. Typically, the battery approach to evaluation leads to volumes of data, a sizable portion of which has no evident relation to the question at hand. All too often, not knowing what to do with a mass of facts and impressions, the psychologist just jams them all into a "shotgun report."

The alternative is a time-consuming process of winnowing. A series of judgments are made on how useful discrete findings are in addressing the problem of a specific individual. The data that are judged to be relevant are then phrased to make the findings of the assessment accessible.

The extent to which focusing is crucial to assessment is seen in the therapist who accepts that it is useful to conceptualize assessment as "the treatment process in microcosm" (Allen, 1981). With the understanding that "one cannot diagnose without treating," he or she might make typical therapeutic issues—for example, alliance, transference, countertransference—the foci of the assessment, particularly when it is being carried out in conjunction with therapy.

Conclusion   From the foregoing discussion we conclude that computer-generated psychological reports are in the tradition of testing and do not follow sufficiently closely the proposed criteria for psychological assessment to merit this designation.

Working into the algorithm such nontest variables as demographic data can make the computer product a bit more like an assessment. More important, the psychologist computer test user is constrained by American Psychological Association ethics, provider standards, and testing standards (as interpreted in *Guidelines*) to improve upon the product that issues "raw" from the machine. You will note that a number of the inputs into this process are similar to the procedures a psychologist uses to prepare an assessment (for example, responding to the reason for carrying out an evaluation, eliminating data he or she judges not to be pertinent to the case at hand, and reframing the focus in terms of clinical judgment). Hence, when the psychologist is conscientious, the final product is likely to evidence more of the characteristics of an assessment.

The interaction of the psychologist computer test user with the computer test report and with the consumer of the computer product is the topic of the next section. It is an explication of the "middleman" role of the psychologist.

FUNCTIONING AS A TEST USER

Using the report as is   The computer report may serve as a self-contained document holding sufficient information to contribute to decision making directed to the problem for which testing was ordered. When the test user is a psychologist, she or he is expected to carry out the responsibilities listed in *Guidelines,* that is, to ascertain that the report is adequate for its intended purpose.

When the person who orders computerized testing does not meet the criteria for being a "qualified professional" to use reports responsibly (p. 185; *Guidelines,* p. 8), it is strongly recommended that a qualified psychologist serve as a consultant to the report consumer. Matarazzo (1983) points out that computerized testing is utilized by "employers, physicians, psychologists, social workers, counselors, nurse practitioners, and other licensed health care providers." Many of these consumers do not meet the criteria of a "qualified professional" and use computer services uncritically in the absence of qualified psychological consultants. This can result in serious errors, and even unnecessary human suffering. Such practice is at marked variance with the goals of psychology.

Using the computer report in a battery   Rather than being used as an adequate document, the computer report may be employed as a tool (as a test is employed as a tool) in an assessment battery. In this approach the statements of the report are considered to be hypotheses—just as the psychologist's initial interpretations of scores and response content are hypotheses. These are then incorporated into a report in accordance with the psychologist's assessment schema, such matters as the reason for assessment and the psychologist's frame of reference shaping the statements and the organization of the report.

"A second opinion"   Psychological reports contribute importantly to solving problems; hence, the accuracy of the information they convey can be crucial. For this reason a test user might wish to compare his or her report with an independent report based on both objective material and the input of a test expert.

Appropriateness of computer testing for the client   Whenever computer psychological testing is contemplated, there are a number of questions that should be asked: Will the test whose use is being contemplated be applicable to the problem under investigation; will it yield the sort of information that is needed? Does the test have adequate validity? Will the circumstances of testing, including computer administration, yield valid data? Are the test norms appropriate to the test subject? Is the test under consideration economical and convenient to use? The *Standards for Educational and Psychological Testing* (American Psychological Association, 1985) emphasizes the importance of consulting technical manuals and user's guides to deal with such necessary questions: "Publishers should provide enough information for a qualified user or a reviewer of a test to evaluate the appropriateness and technical adequacy of the test. . . . A manual should be evaluated on the basis of its completeness, accuracy, and clarity" (p. 35). A manual that falls short in any of these requirements may not provide the information that is needed to make a decision about using a test.

Does the report adequately address the topic for which testing was done?   Computer programs are designed to contribute answers to questions for which testing frequently is employed. It is common, for example, for computer reports to offer a diagnosis or to suggest several possible diagnoses with which the test data are consistent. Suicidality, a prognosis, or information pertinent to treatment or rehabilitation can also be programmed.

Some older tests adapted to computer use (such as the MMPI) have been extensively researched as to their ability to yield information concerning personality and pathological trends. Thus the bulk of the report statements generated from the use of these tests emphasizes those issues in personality functioning that are historically of widespread interest, such as sociability, trustfulness, somatization tendencies, mood, and activity level. These may or may not be pertinent to the problem presented by a particular client. Only a "qualified professional," as defined by *Guidelines,* is equipped to separate irrelevant or erroneous statements from those that are potentially useful.

Report statements that are stereotyped, nondifferentiating, and nonindividualized are of special concern. These, commonly, are Aunt Fanny- or Barnum-type statements (pp. 51–55). Such report content can be well composed and confidently expressed, and therefore seductive. Though they may be quite accurate, statements of this variety tell you nothing, and they certainly do not address the topic for which testing was done.

Disjointed, even if accurate, statements about an individual tend to be less informative than integrated statements. Insights about the same topic— for example, what arouses a person to anger and how he or she deals with angry feelings—should be tied together rather than appearing as a number of discrete, self-contained statements, widely separated in the report.

Competent integration is the hallmark of the effective use of the battery approach, where scores, patterns, or responses from any part of the battery may contribute to the interpretation of scores, patterns, or responses in any other part of the battery. A hypothesis stemming from data on one test may be strengthened or weakened by the data of another instrument. Example: A person who, in response to a Beck Depression Inventory item, acknowledges having plans to commit suicide may be less credible to the psychologist as a suicidal risk if his or her TAT themes involve concern for the future and there are themes of constructive planning.

Simply combining in one report data from different tests is not extracting from the battery the useful information that is there. Such is the case with computer reports that contain information selected from various tests, information that is not integrated into central themes of interest (pp. 129–132). Units of data thus presented do not mutually interact with and modify one another as commonly happens when themes of a report are developed.

Some specifics to look for: accuracy, consistency, contradictions, potential confusion, shotgun effects   Some computer reports are easy to evaluate; others are less so. But easy or not, "Professionals who provide assessment services bear the ultimate responsibility for providing accurate judgments about the clients they evaluate" (*Guidelines,* p. 21). In addition to accuracy, the professional must also be concerned with the usefulness and accessibility to the client of the information provided to her or him.

Let us start with report length, it being a common complaint that reports are too long (p. 37). Such is often the case with computer reports. Matarazzo (1983) despairs of reports that number up to 50 pages in length, and Butcher (1978) reviews a computer service whose report gives you "everything you could possibly tell about a person from the test." Perhaps the machine is comfortable with this much information, but the human handles volumes of information best when it is purged of trivialities, "boiled down," categorized, and focused. The "shotgun report" does not provide a basis for making sharp judgments. Even when it is accurate, it contains little that is useful.

Inconsistency or contradiction may find its way into reports in various ways. The source may be inconsistency in the client's test-taking attitude or mood, particularly if testing is done over a period of time. As computer reports come to be based on an increasing number of tests, we can expect increasing opportunities for inconsistent, even contradictory, statements to appear in reports. In the example of inconsistent statements on page 191, we note that if the Beck Depression Inventory were the sole instrument used there would be no basis to challenge the conclusion that the test taker had plans for suicide. But the TAT, tapping as it does a different level of functioning and permitting the test taker a lesser awareness of what she or he is disclosing, yielded information to question the conclusions reached from the Beck Inventory alone.

Further, inconsistency among test results is not necessarily an error. It can be a valuable bit of diagnostic information. Arnow and Cooper (1984), for example, share the observation that when borderline personality disorder patients are administered the Rorschach, "the testing situation actively precipitates the emergence of a host of regressive and primitive processes." This observation fits well with Singer's (1977) data that demonstrate that borderlines do well on highly structured tasks but regress to a more primitive cognitive mode on the Rorschach, an important matter in view of new conceptualizations of borderline pathology.

The educational role of the test user   Still standing between the computer and the client is the test user in the role of educator. Interpreting the report to the client, and making sure that it is understood, is, of course, an educational role. The test user also presents to the client, in the context of such understanding, practical suggestions for utilizing the report. He or she often must be shown how the report relates to the reason for psychological evaluation, and to nuances and idiosyncracies in the test taker and in the situation.

It is also helpful to explain to the client how the report was derived from testing (and other input). A little information about psychometric theory and how algorithms are derived can help to demystify the computer testing process and make for a more realistic understanding of computer reports. It is especially important to explain that the report was not written about the particular test taker who hopes to benefit from the testing, but rather about persons who produce the test taker's psychometric pattern and that all the statements made in the report are probabilities.

Reflections on the role of the test user   The foregoing discussion on functioning as a test user is in full agreement with *Guidelines'* position regarding the need for high-level training and skill mastery for those who take on this role (p. 185; *Guidelines,* p. 8). Spelling out this role can be disquieting, however, since many of those who make regular use of computer reports are not "qualified professionals" (cf. Matarazzo, 1983, 1986).

Guidelines, in calling for the "final decision" regarding report content to be made by a "qualified professional," indicates that professional knowledge and judgment should be brought to bear on the raw computer product. As a result of such scrutiny it may become necessary for professionals who review the material, and we repeat this important point, "to edit or amend the computer report to take into account their own observations and judgments and to ensure that the report is comprehensible, free of jargon, and true to the person evaluated."

Hofer and Green (1985), publishing before the American Psychological Association issued *Guidelines,* anticipated that the application of ethical principles could give rise to some practical difficulties. Thus,

> There is a certain tension between the requirements of professional standards and the practical usefulness of computerized interpretation systems. Most people are interested in computerized interpretation because they see it as saving time and effort, especially in the more routine aspects of testing.

Arguing from a positive approach to computer evaluation drawing on the outcome of Meehl's (1954) statistical versus clinical prediction controversy, and bringing in some more recent considerations pertaining to predictive validity, they express concern that

> The current professional ethical guidelines and the proposals for new ones emphasize that each interpretation must be carefully reviewed for its appropriateness to each examinee in the light of new research, additional information about the test taker, and sound professional judgment. This requirement, if taken to an extreme, would seriously erode the usefulness of the test because reviewing the validity of each interpretive statement could be comparable to writing the entire report oneself.

Hofer and Green raise a difficult issue. Few, perhaps, would care to sacrifice accuracy and clinical utility in the interest of such goals as saving time and avoiding tedium. The ethical injunction is too clear. Another question is whether it is worth the expenditure of professional time to modify what is essentially a testing report to one that more nearly resembles assessment. The distinction between the two should be clear in the mind of the professional who must make this choice.

VALIDITY

Validity should always be a matter of concern to both those who create psychological reports and those who use them. With computer evaluation now prominent on the scene, the issue of the validity of computer reports seemingly overrides older clinical concerns about the validity of psychological evaluation.

In general, the validity status of computer evaluation is still less than promising. Computer services publish validity data for tests that have been designed for computer interpretation, but Matarazzo (1983) reminds us that "to date, there is no evidence published in peer-reviewed journals that one full page of the narrative descriptions is valid." *Guidelines* sounds a similarly disenchanting note with respect to well-established instruments that have been adapted to computer use: "At present, there is no extensive evidence about the validities of computerized versions of conventional tests."

It should also be pointed out that conventional (idiographic) reports, constructed as they are from multiple inputs of test data and nontest data, do not have easily demonstrable validity. That is, they lack psychometric evidence, or "evidential grounds" for validity (Messick, 1980). Messick proposes that determination of validity may, in addition to psychometric evidence, rest on social and ethical issues. He suggests that "questions of the appropriateness of test use in proposed applications are answerable on ethical grounds by appraising potential social consequences of the testing," and he concludes, "By thus considering both the evidential and consequential bases of both test interpretation and test use, the roles of evidence and social values in the overall validation process are illuminated, and test validity comes to be based on ethical as well as evidential grounds."

COMPUTER REPORTS AND THE LAW

Computerized testing is a still-emerging technology. With the potential to have influence on many lives, it seems likely that numerous lawsuits will eventually involve large numbers of persons at all levels of the computer testing enterprise. Additionally many test users will have contact with the law when they are called as expert witnesses.

It is in the role of expert witness that the psychologist is likely to experience the full force of cross-examination, with particularly heavy interrogations directed at his or her instruments and the manner of using them. Test validity has long been a target of opportunity when evidence based on testing is presented. The technology of computer-generated reports and the validity of computer-derived statements present attorneys with further subject matter for intense and potentially devastating cross-examination.

The scrutiny under which a psychologist's evidence and opinions might be put in the legal arena is further discussed in Chapter 9, Forensic Psychological Evaluations.

8
Psychological Reports and the Psychotherapeutic Process

Psychological reports have long been sought to clarify issues in psychotherapy. This is in spite of inadequate rationale and of the fact that historically the relevant literature revealed widespread disagreement over the practice. Currently trends seeking to link assessment with psychotherapy follow theses that seek support in research and/or clinical experience. Paradigms for reporting psychological information have been developed in such diverse areas as conventional psychotherapy, behavior therapy, psychoanalysis, group therapy, marital/family therapy, and neuropsychology. The oral reporting of clinical findings directly to clients is in widespread use.

The application of psychological assessment to intervention, particularly psychotherapy, rests largely on clinical experience, tradition, scattered case studies, and professional opinion. As with much of psychological diagnostic work and psychotherapy—indeed much of clinical psychological practice—hard evidence for the validity of the practice is difficult to come by.

Prout (1986, p. 611), after reviewing the pertinent literature, offers this paradoxical position:

> It appears that the actual utility of assessment (behavioral or traditional) in planning and conducting treatment programs is unclear and has not been empirically demonstrated at this time. Despite this equivocal situation, good clinical practice still dictates that assessment remain an important part of a comprehensive treatment approach.

Clearly there is need to review how psychological material is developed and applied in the interest of bringing about therapeutic change. Of high priority is identifying the sort of content that is most likely to be useful in various therapeutic situations. The mechanics of sharing therapeutic information with clients and therapists can be particularly important.

CONTENT AND FOCUS
OF TREATMENT-ORIENTED REPORTS

According to Brown (1965), Blank's (1965) *Psychological Evaluation in Psychotherapy: Ten Case Histories* is the "first book . . . to document the direct relationship between a patient's response patterns on a battery of psychological tests and his subsequent behavior in psychotherapy." The relationships between test and psychotherapy response patterns that are drawn by Blank range from highly general observations to recommendations that are more or less specific. Subsequent research also presents findings with varying degrees of generality or specificity.

    General implications for treatment in psychological reports   The general use of psychological information is set forth by Brown (1965), who conceptualizes the psychological report as a "road map." "It is seldom that the therapist is taught to regard the psychological report as a road map or itinerary of the terrain he is to traverse with the patient." Those who shun the contribution that psychodiagnostics can make "fail to formulate a therapeutic plan, and often embark on 'blind' therapy without psychological charts, compass or sextant"—Klopfer's (1964) theme of "the blind leading the blind."

    Need for a personality overview   Cooper and Wittenberg (1985) present a similar general view on the value of psychological information in the conduct of psychotherapy. They postulate a basic need to formulate a coherent overview of the psychotherapy client, an overall picture as opposed to a collection of fragments about the client (for example, a diagnostic label—pieces of transference behavior, assorted dynamics, and other limited areas of personality functioning, such as oedipal dynamics or masochistic impulses). They compare such a coherent overview with "the underlying theme in a psychological novel."

    When treatment appears to bog down in chaos or inertia, Cooper and Wittenberg call for "a new set of lenses through which to view the patient." Such "lenses" are provided by an understanding of how the patient perceives his world, his experiences in living, what the patient is trying to accomplish in life, and central themes of life, such as the "secret plot" as conceived by Fromm (Maccoby, 1972) or the "core issue" of Saul (1958).

    Thus, the identification of large areas of functioning that are central to a client's personality structure may be crucial in setting the focus of treatment. Discussions by Mortimer and Smith (1983) and De La Cour (1986) point up not only the importance of focus in psychotherapy, but also what is involved in selecting the proper focus and use and misuse of the focus. The Mortimer and Smith paper is particularly helpful in defining the key role that psychological tests may play in setting the focus of psychotherapy, and how use of the focus can improve the outcome of therapy.

Accent on character   Everly (1986) summarizes current thinking about the issue of whether psychotherapy should focus on the presenting symptoms (or syndromes) or on character (or personality styles). His conclusion is that information on personality style is central to understanding psychopathology, which he regards as an extension of dysfunctional personality styles. Thus, "The real target of intermediate and long term psychotherapeutic efforts becomes the personality dysfunction." Such emphasis on basic personality processes, as identified by psychological tests, results in a psychological report whose content differs significantly from the symptom-centered approaches that are in widespread use in the mental health field.

The identification of cognitive style, particularly of abstract versus concrete thinking, is commonly observed in psychological reports. By contrast, Weiner and Crowder (1986) point out that "psychotherapists rarely assess . . . patients' ability to reason abstractly," though these authors attach great importance to understanding their patients along the concrete-abstract dimension of thinking. Concrete thinkers, they suggest, do not do well in insight-oriented therapy. Nor would the use of metaphors, evidently a common practice (Barker, 1985), be appropriate for those who think concretely. On the other hand, concrete thinking "is no obstacle to changing attitudes and behaviors by means that do not involve the development of insight into unconscious conflict or motivation."

In a comprehensive discussion of concreteness and its various subtypes, Brown (1985) illustrates the impact on therapy of various modes of concrete thought patterns. He provides some clues for identifying concreteness in psychological test productions, but generally the psychologist is thrown on his or her own resources to detect concreteness that might affect the course of therapy. He describes, for example, a class of "interactionally concrete patients. . . . These patients may appear dense and unable to grasp the significance of the analyst's interventions despite abstractive capabilities in other areas of their lives." In an illustrative case, Brown identifies the dynamics of such concrete thinking. Indicators of such idiosyncratic patterns commonly appear in projective material and can be used to alert the therapist so that they might more readily be dealt with.

An overall approach to therapy-related issues   The value of general information, then (general in the sense of encompassing large segments of personality), is to (1) help set an overall approach to therapy, such as setting treatment goals and adopting strategies, and (2) consult when a hitch in therapy develops. At such times rereading the psychological report may provide insights as to what is "going on" and what changes in goals or technique may be in order. Rereading the report, in the light of what the therapist has observed in the treatment situation, may cause it to take on a new significance for the conduct of therapy.

Knoff (1986) also emphasizes that psychological information is of value in the clinical situation primarily as it relates to meeting therapeutic goals. The psychological report, along with the feedback conference of the therapist and the psychological assessor, is mainly "(a) to answer and discuss the initial referral's questions and concerns," and "(b) to analyze the intrapersonal and interpersonal issues and circumstances which cause, support, or maintain the identified referral behaviors or affects."

Another value of the psychological report is that it can be made available early in therapy, anytime the therapist feels ready for an overview of what are likely to be salient issues of concern. Cooper and Wittenberg quote Sullivan to the effect that the understanding needed to move therapy forward could be gained in the course of treatment within seven to fifteen sessions. Might not therapy proceed more directly and smoothly, with less stumbling down blind alleys, if the road map suggested by Brown (p. 196) were routinely used by therapists?

Thus, Arnow and Cooper (1984) alert us to their finding that psychological testing has the power efficiently to bring forth for observation regressive behaviors that are less likely to be seen in other situations. In particular they stress the diagnostic value of the Rorschach with borderline patients, the lack of structure of this instrument paralleling that which exists in classical psychoanalysis and various life situations that precipitate regression. Arnow and Cooper express "hope that the clinical usefulness of the Rorschach can be enhanced with a deeper understanding of the dynamic interactions between properties of the testing situation and specific developmental vulnerabilities, which together shape the response process." Further, "A grasp of the psychological impact of the testing situation provides additional data for clarifying the kinds of situations likely to stimulate regressions or exacerbations of a borderline patient's psychopathology."

Suggestions for Dealing with Circumscribed Therapeutic Issues

More specific than the foregoing views are a broad range of inputs into the therapy process. These have not been systematically classified, and they may enter the psychological report as widely varied content intended to have various uses. Frequently the content presented is to alert the therapist to some anticipated problem, or even to "warn" the therapist of some potential hazard.

Classes of content thus presented to the therapist range from present behaviors to predictions of future behavior, from the intrapsychic to socially objective behaviors. Predictions of outcome are frequently made, and tips for the conduct of therapy are common.

Blank's case studies   A review of Blank's (1965) 10 cases illustrates this lack of uniformity of content. To the extent that clients have different problems and needs, and personality structures that will respond differently to therapy, uniformity is not to be expected. Case-focused reports properly vary widely in terms of the content they present.

Thus, one of Blank's cases focuses heavily on social issues, all of which, with greater or lesser directness, have meaning for psychotherapy. This is despite the fact that Blank's reports were routine evaluations and not geared to the patient's eventual involvement in individual psychotherapy. The report

1. Warned the therapist of the client's morbid distress.
2. Warned of her tendency to test relationships with seduction.
3. Suggested the client's need to focus on her sense of inability to give.
4. Especially underscored her need to make commitments—with respect to relationships in general, and to treatment in particular.

In another case, where the time available for therapy was limited, the report was addressed to therapeutic issues and the outcome was highly favorable. Report recommendations were

1. To focus on reality.
2. To capitalize on the transference relationship.

In a case judged to have a poor prognosis (seemingly confirmed by a negative outcome), the report writer gave attention to understanding the morbid processes, even though the therapeutic possibilities were limited. Thus, the report suggested

1. A poor prognosis.
2. Poorly integrated defenses with potentiality for regression to severe psychopathology.
3. The possibility of suicide.
4. Markedly distorted perception of self and others.
5. Morbid preoccupations, rage, and helplessness.

Other items of therapy-related content gleaned from Blank's study include

1. The need to encourage expressions of anger.
2. The need to foster independent, autonomous behavior.
3. Alerting therapist to a "stumbling block" posed by the "weaning process."
4. A discussion of defenses.
5. Basic mistrust in the patient.
6. The fear of self-examination.
7. The patient's need to examine family relationships.
8. A neurotic relationship with family members.

9. The need to tap rage that is confused with sexual concepts.
10. Tendencies to somatization.
11. Tendency not to confront conflicts.
12. Discussion of social defenses and related problems.
13. Inaccessible tendency to act out.
14. Need for special effort to promote secure, warm relationship in therapy.
15. Prediction of behavior in therapy.
16. Ego strength.
17. Social needs.
18. Need to understand and work with impulses.
19. Identity issues.
20. Need to proceed cautiously.

Prout's assessment scheme   Prout (1986), focusing on the function of psychological assessment in therapeutic intervention with children and adolescents, presents a comprehensive seven-part scheme.

1. *Establish a baseline.* In this first step, the assessor records the extent or the severity of the problem in both descriptive and quantitative terms. These data form a basis for initiating treatment and evaluating the efficacy of treatment as it proceeds.
2. *Pinpoint treatment targets.* "Pinpoint," or *focus,* is the key concept here. Themes or content to be dealt with are sharply defined.
3. *Assess developmental status.* Judgments of normality or abnormality are made relative to a client's age. Cognitive and language levels and social and emotional development must all be considered in treatment planning.
4. *Assess children's view of the problem.* Does the child perceive that he or she has a problem? If so how does he or she understand the problem? The answers help to determine the nature of treatment or whether treatment is possible at all.
5. *Assess relevant environmental factors.* The impact of environmental factors (school, family, peers) on the child is defined, and plans for dealing with disruptive factors are made.
6. *Select appropriate treatment strategy.* Prout advocates an eclectic approach, the role of assessment being to enable the therapist to tailor treatment to specific identified issues.
7. *Evaluate efficacy.* The purpose of this step is to evaluate program efficacy and/or to conduct research. The goal is to understand the effectiveness of various treatments with different disorders.

Appelbaum's contributions   Calling on his experience and insight as both a psychological assessor and a psychotherapist, and having reference to a list of assessment goals compiled by Dr. Herbert J. Schlesinger for the purpose of training in psychological testing, Appelbaum (1969) presents a list of questions that might be addressed in a report written for a psychotherapist.

1. The illness from an adaptive point of view.
   a. Positive and negative consequences of the illness.
   b. The effect of the illness on object relations and transference paradigms.
   c. The identities the illness is modeled on.
2. The possibilities for other "choices," growth, and change.
   a. Strength of drive.
   b. Commitment to infantile patterns, and areas of "openness."
   c. Resiliency, acceptability of substitutes, possibilities for sublimation.
   d. Utilizability of anxiety or pain, and anxiety tolerance.
   e. Ability of the ego to function and grow under frustration.
3. Possibilities of further decompensation.
   a. Likely course of decompensation.
   b. Resiliency, ability to take distance.
   c. Capacity to withstand regression.
   d. Special areas of vulnerability—intolerant "superego," ego-weakness, specific conflicts and their associated trigger words and ideas.
4. Ego capacities.
   a. Psychological-mindedness.
   b. Humor.
   c. Objectivity.
5. Subjective experience.
   a. Moods.
   b. Attitudes.
   c. Emotional quality with which the environment is invested.
   d. Psychosexual level of experience which is most likely under what conditions.
   e. Repertoire of roles and identity fragments.[1]

In a later work, stemming from extensive research at The Menninger Foundation, Appelbaum (1977) lists a number of benefits of adequate psychological assessment, these over and above the major conclusion that those therapists who ignored the contributions of the psychological report stood the greatest risk of making faulty clinical judgments.

Among the more specific benefits of psychological assessment, Appelbaum lists providing information

1. Leading to better decisions as to who should get treatment—and who should not. Psychological data on ego strength point up the extent of improvement that can be anticipated and are highly pertinent to this decision.
2. For determining what kind of intervention would benefit different people.
3. Pertaining to the setting of goals and formulating strategies for reaching those goals.
4. Concerning a useful way of organizing data about people—that is, whether they need greater access to, or more control over, their thoughts and feelings.

---

[1]From "Psychological Testing for the Psychotherapist" by Stephen A. Appelbaum, *Dynamic Psychiatry*, 1969, *2*, 158–163. Copyright © 1969 by Pinel-Verlags GmbH, Munich, West Germany, and reproduced by permission of the author and publisher.

5. Concerning the meaning of change to a client, whether it is beneficial or harmful in a given personal and social context.

Kissen's position on the usefulness of the psychological report in therapy   Concerned with "pragmatic" haste in the initiation of therapy, it is Kissen's (1973) thesis that

> A skillful and clinically-focused test report can be of immense practical useful-
> ness to the psychotherapist—if it is appropriately addressed to relevant treatment
> issues. A good test report . . . can alert the therapist to such important clinical
> factors as the character structure and characteristic defensive maneuvers of his
> patient, his expressive style, his salient psycho-dynamic conflicts, his psycholog-
> ical-mindedness and motivation for treatment, and perhaps most importantly his
> typical interpersonal interaction tendencies which may very well be enacted in
> the form of a transference-countertransference interaction with the therapist.
> Other factors such as the patient's impulsive potential, possibility for further
> decompensation, and subjective experience of himself are also useful for the
> therapist to know at the beginning point of therapy.

Assessment in psychoanalysis   In psychoanalysis a rethinking of the scope of treatment may have implications for psychological assessment, par-ticularly on the focus of the content that is to be reported. Paolino's work (1981a,b) is particularly germane. He observes, "It is now widely recognized that the alliance and transference are not the only meaningful relationships in psychoanalysis." Rather than being exclusively concerned with these two im-portant variables, Paolino suggests that it is important to assess the patient's *analyzability* as a contribution to making a decision on whether the prospec-tive analysand is a suitable candidate for psychoanalysis. By analyzability he means that the patient experiences ". . . a state of readiness that involves the capacity to cognitively and emotionally understand psychoanalysis plus the capacity for constructive psychological and behavioral change as a result of that understanding." From his discussion of this position the following re-quirements for analyzability of prospective patients are abstracted.

1. A "need" for analysis in the sense that symptoms are sufficiently troublesome to warrant the sacrifices that analysis entails.
2. A good "fit" between the patient and the particular analyst who is involved.
3. An intact ego that will not be overwhelmed and still be able to maintain trust and a therapeutic alliance in the face of crises.
4. A close relationship with one who is sufficiently supportive and flexible to adjust to the personality changes that result from a successful analysis.
5. A skeptical attitude that is based on a relative lack of knowledge of psychoa-nalysis, this skepticism later to give way to an attitude of trust in the analyst and in analytic methods (Freud, 1913).
6. The quality of "psychological mindedness" (Appelbaum, 1973).
7. The capacity for insight, a quality related to psychological mindedness.

8. An understanding of the harmful role of symptoms (not just that they are painful) and the holding of a realistic view on ridding oneself of them.

9. The capacity to experience [painful] feelings [and thoughts] within the session rather than just describe them.

10. The ability . . . to bear . . . painful feelings and thoughts without acting them out.

To be able to supply such information demands considerable flexibility and skill on the part of the psychological assessor. Most test data cannot directly be translated into these variables. It is expected that interview data, thorough knowledge of the analytic process, and considerable clinical skill would be necessary to make the sort of judgments that are required by Paolino's criteria.

APPROACHES TO SHARING THERAPEUTIC INFORMATION

Increasingly, psychological information is being shared by professionals and clients (pp. 47–50). Such information may be transmitted to the client in written or oral reports. Or it may be jointly developed by psychologist and client in the context of psychological testing sessions. Indeed, it is an old technique (Bettelheim, 1947; Luborsky, 1953) to ask clients to take on the psychologist's role, interpreting their own psychological productions (for example, TAT stories) for self-edification and for the edification of the examining psychologist.

Berg (1984, 1985) discusses "expanding the parameters of psychological testing" and the use of shared understandings in the feedback process. The flexible application of tests that he describes is consistent with the trend of using psychological instruments as "less of a test" than a psychometric instrument (Korchin & Schuldberg, 1981) and more of an interview (Zubin, Eron, & Schumer, 1965) or a tool to help develop a transaction between psychologist and client from which both parties might derive insights (Singer, 1977).

The current use of oral and written psychological reports as feedback to clients is an approach that is based on precedent (Harrower, Vorhaus, Roman, & Bauman, 1960). The application of the feedback technique by Roman and Bauman to marriage therapy is of particular interest. The introduction by Harrower et al. of the concept that each marriage has a "personality" defines a rich source of diagnosable material that can profitably be examined. The observation that what the different partners contribute to a marriage by virtue of the fact that each has "a different 'way of looking at the world' [which] can be presented in *projective counseling* [their expression] through the study of a single Rorschach card by both partners simultaneously," focuses an approach to studying the interaction in the nuptial dyad. Klopfer (1984) has extended the use of the Rorschach to disclose to clients their interpersonal dynamics. His *consensus Rorschach* can be the basis of feedback for two or more people, such as a married couple, an entire family, a parent and child, siblings, classmates, and roommates. When applied to a therapist-client dyad important insights can be gained on how these persons interact. Many instruments, however, can yield data to study personality and the interaction of persons in an intimate relationship. These include projective techniques, standardized psychometric instruments, and forms for observation by self and others.

Dorr (1981) builds on such approaches, citing specifically the work of Loveland, Wynne, and Singer (1963), Levy and Epstein (1964), Willi (1969), Araoz (1972), Floyd (1974), and Williams (1974). His own procedure consists of three phases. The initial phase is given to the administration of a comprehensive battery of five instruments. Each marriage partner completes the examination independently, following which a consensus Rorschach is administered. The major feature here is the offering of joint responses by the couple, these coming into being on the basis of the partners' agreement on what are the "best" responses.

The psychological report is presented to the couple in the next two phases. In the first, an oral report is given by the therapist in the context of a give-and-take conversation, with some of the interpretations reached being developed by the couple with the therapist's guidance. In the final phase a written psychological "report letter," a rather lengthy document of five to eight pages, is prepared and sent to the couple, with provision made for continuing therapy with the examiner or elsewhere. Dorr notes that "the follow-up letter encapsulates what has transpired and provides an opportunity for me to clarify any errors or ambiguous interpretations that I may have made." He explains further that "the couple cannot possibly absorb all that is said in the feedback session, much less metabolize it effectively."

A number of advantages are claimed for this procedure. Testing is seen as cutting through defenses that are destructive to the therapeutic process and that have also created tensions in the marriage. The contributions of testing to the therapist's understanding of the case are seen as even greater than the gains that accrue from more typical examination: "The abundance of information yielded by a full, individual battery is geometrically expanded when integrated with an identical battery administered to the marriage partner." Dorr observes further that in the procedure described the tests may "take on the quality of a separate therapeutic agent," an agent that "paradoxically fosters both objectivity and extreme emotionality." And finally, although the procedure exercises a therapeutic function, the clients cannot develop a transference to the tests, nor can the tests develop a countertransference to the clients!

The development and sharing of information with the client is generally regarded as of therapeutic value. Assessor/therapists, including Berg (1985), Fischer (1970, 1979), Mosak and Gushurst (1972), and Richman (1967), regard sharing of information with the client as therapeutic in itself or as a means of setting the stage for therapy.

Berg presents excerpts of the feedback process that illustrate the development of insights, from which we may conclude that the feedback process itself is a therapeutic transaction. He also suggests that "Such testing can guide the future treatment process at strategic points by clarifying how the patient must be helped and how the help must be delivered to maximize the likelihood that he will experience this assistance as help indeed."

Mosak and Gushurst suggest that it is helpful to begin with a psychological evaluation. Such a procedure defines the issues so they are "immediately clear and specific," opens up the client, divests the client of the "secrecy, shame, and incoherence" that have become attached to him or her, and stimulates self-awareness. The therapeutic gain may be achieved by referring to the client's responses to test stimuli. For example, the client may gain insight into an aspect of his life style when the examiner suggests to him that he has revealed his typical life posture by attacking the validity of testing. The goal of such examiner-client interaction is to impart to the client the feeling of being understood. The major use of psychological testing is conceived by Mosak and Gushurst, however, "as an introduction to the therapeutic process." Consider, for example, that the transference/countertransference first manifested in the testing transaction may be expected to generalize to the therapy process.

There is no meaningful dividing line between diagnosis and therapy, and the therapeutic use and potential of diagnostic instruments need to be emphasized. When therapeutic ends are actively pursued in the context of psychological testing, we may wonder whether testing should be regarded primarily as diagnosis or as therapy. Allen (1981) regards diagnosis as treatment in microcosm—a more time-limited procedure than what is formally structured as therapy—and observes that "one cannot diagnose without treating." Schlesinger's (1973) position is that "one can view the interaction between the patient and the clinician as a *diagnostic* process or a *treatment* process depending upon one's purpose in making the discrimination."

The substance of psychological reporting is not tests—assessment can be done without testing or with minimal testing. Nor is writing a necessary feature of the psychological report. Reports can be delivered orally, as in the context of verbal feedback as just discussed. The essence of the psychological report is the communication of essential psychological information—such as to bring about improvement in a client's condition.

The wide latitude of psychological reporting implicit in such a view compels us to examine ways of communicating psychological information in novel situations. The emphasis of this book being on professional practice, a question arises as to how different a psychological report should be when the recipient is not a professional. The answer should be evident to the book's readers: Not at all. We have emphasized that reports—at least those that focus on personality—should be written (or spoken) in plain English, avoiding technical words, jargon, and theory. Now that nonprofessionals, including clients and their families, are likely to read reports prepared primarily for professionals, there is double reason to abide by this injunction. As suggested earlier (p. 48), reports written about clients might well also be written for clients.

Other writers are in accord. Fischer (1970) and Mosak and Gushurst (1972) suggest "the style of communication should be simple, direct, and easily comprehensible. Technical concepts should be translated into everyday common-sense terminology, and psychological jargon should be scrupulously avoided." The language in the reports to clients by Dorr (1981) and by Yalom et al. (1975), which are presented in the next section of this chapter, are conversational in tone.

Allen et al. (1986) advise that there are yet other considerations in how to present information to clients. How understandable, meaningful, useful will it be? "The way the truth is told will influence how well the patient can hear, retain, and use it." Special concern is also expressed by these authors for preserving the self-esteem of psychiatric patients. In this regard they point out, "The nuances of language are important; some patients are likely to feel *assaulted* by references to 'brain damage,' 'brain lesions,' and 'cognitive deficits'" (emphasis added).

EXEMPLIFICATION OF THERAPEUTIC REPORTING

Feedback About Test Performance

The following brief excerpt is from a session in which the psychologist feeds back to a client information about his test performance (Fischer, 1970). Pointing up the egalitarian nature of the transaction that Fischer refers to as "sharing impressions," she observes that "the tester must now dialogue rather than diagnose in order to approximate the client's experience." The goal is that both the psychologist and the client increase their understandings with a view to the psychologist's making suggestions to the client for some life changes that might enhance his adjustment.

> P: Did you notice you didn't do as well on the arithmetic part and the part where you said numbers back to me? You know, on both those kinds of problems, you had to figure in your head. I wonder if you have trouble with those same things out in life, like on the job?
> C: Well, yeah, that's right. But it doesn't matter about numbers—it's doing it in my head. I just always know that I can't get things to work out when I've got to keep numbers in my head, or like those block pictures.
> P: I hadn't thought of that. I guess you did do better on the first half of the test where you were telling me answers about everyday things than you did on the last half where you had to quietly figure out the answers to abstract, new kinds of problems, and then tell me the answer.

C: Sure, I'm always at my best when I'm talking to people. It's like I know where I stand. Like in a business conference, I can talk up a really great idea, and everybody's impressed. But I'm sure not the guy to write it out by myself, or figure out a cost analysis. I just know I'm beat before I start—so I don't.

P: So when jobs call for you to work on your own you see that as equivalent to certain failure. Therefore, you never try to do them?

C: That's what I just said.

Interestingly, although test performance provides the basis for discussion between psychologist and client, the focus of the discussion is on the client, not on the tests; the interaction is client-centered, not test-centered. Psychologists currently are inclined to view performance on tests as a microcosm of the client's life (for example, Allen, 1981), but it is the macrocosm that is the client's life that holds the psychologist's interest. It is also worth noting that the raw material for discussion in this example is performance on intelligence tests, yet the conclusions and the implications for remediation are in the domain of "personality."

This fact holds a lesson for psychological reporting in general. It would be conceptually wrong, were this a written report, to confine information concerning the client's performance on a test of intelligence, such as the examiner comments on here, to a section of the report labeled "Intelligence" or "Intellectual Assessment."

Neuropsychological Reports to Clients and Families

Allen et al. (1986) stress that providing written feedback to a client who has taken a battery of neuropsychological tests—or to the family of the client—is a custom job. Of particular concern to these authors is the hazard that the client will not understand correctly the information that the examiner provides; these clinicians "learned the hard way about the complexities of providing feedback." The general rule is that "the content of the feedback, the way it is communicated, when it is conveyed to the patient, and who conveys it depend as much on the psychological and cognitive functioning of the individual patient as they do on the test findings."

Both verbal feedback and a written report letter in a conversational tone should be provided to the client. Allen et al. believe that the actual neuropsychological report written for professional use would be too technical and confusing for clients. To further guard against misunderstanding, the client initially reads the letter in the presence of the examiner so that the issues set forth may be discussed and clarified.

Following are excerpts from such a letter.

I am writing to summarize the findings of the neuropsychological testing you completed recently. You may recall that you were concerned about some problems with your memory. . . . Your performance on a battery of memory tests was significantly better than that observed previously. . . . Your scores on several tasks were in the mildly impaired range and there was no single area of major difficulty.

While your cognitive problems are relatively mild, they are likely to affect several areas of performance. That is, you have difficulty paying attention and concentrating, along with difficulty catching on to complicated tasks and staying on track. Because these problems are not severe, you can perform almost any task adequately, as long as you are given enough time and instruction and you are under a minimum of psychological stress. . . . Your psychological reactions to the difficulties you have in performing tasks are also important to consider. As soon as you run into difficulty, you are liable to become frustrated or sad, only adding to your problems with attention, concentration, and staying on track. As you know, this emotional reaction can develop into a vicious circle of frustration and increasingly ineffective performance.

Because your emotional reactions to your difficulties play such an important part in the problems you are having, psychological treatment has good prospects for helping you to function more effectively. . . . It is important for you to develop realistic expectations which will enable you to effectively cope with stressful demands.[2]

Response to a Psychotherapist

The written report that follows is in response to a referral from a psychiatrist who had scheduled the client for once-a-week appointments. The client, a 38-year-old male combat veteran, held the diagnosis posttraumatic stress disorder. He had also been diagnosed as having a bipolar disorder, mixed, and alcohol and polysubstance abuse had contributed to additional diagnoses. His history revealed multiple infractions of the law, mostly for assault and battery, driving while intoxicated, and larceny. His job history was poor. He had never married but had experienced multiple unstable heterosexual relationships.

Reason for Assessment The consultation request read: "For diagnosis and personality picture. Evaluate reality testing and ego strength. Please make recommendations for psychotherapy."

The client was interviewed, following which he completed a battery of tests. The psychologist then prepared the following report addressed to the above concerns.

Descriptive and Diagnostic Overview. The client's appearance—articles of camouflage clothing, campaign ribbons, and other military insignia complement his ready disclosure of a string of problems commonly reported by Vietnam combat veterans: nightmares, flashbacks, depression and recurrent suicidal thoughts and attempts, bodily tension, fear of being in crowds and buildings, mistrust, and often uncontrollable anger. On questioning he describes his substance abuse and out-of-control behaviors, such as car stealing, that often are linked with his alcohol use. He also describes periods of elevated mood. My diagnostic impression is post-traumatic stress disorder, histrionic personality disorder, and bipolar disorder, mixed.

Core Conflicts. Mr. B. is struggling with a severe conflict over defining his personal identity, and with specific conflicts associated with this central issue of his life. These involve a sense of inadequacy with respect to maleness, and a general all around lack of self-esteem. These are underlying reasons for self-recrimination, of fearfulness, of a sense of helplessness and hopelessness in facing the world, and resentment against those toward whom he takes a dependent attitude. He feels that people should, but do not, help him to more adequate functioning.

Defenses. Mr. B. attempts at several levels, to be, or at least to appear, more adequate than he feels when he is in touch with his feelings. Unable to accept his perceived limitations in the above conflict areas, he denies the reality of what is real and very pertinent in his life—the existence of a discrepancy between what he feels he is and what he feels he should be. He rationalizes, makes excuses to himself, anything to shield himself from recognizing himself as the inadequate, undermanly person he experiences himself to be.

Lifestyle, Symptoms. He also compensates for his felt shortcomings in exaggerated, stereotyped manly behaviors, and in similar fantasy, and he indulges in role playing designed both to impress himself and to gain social reinforcement for the image of himself that he seeks to establish. These behaviors have now crystallized into a lifestyle that stands out in its demands for acceptance and attention; it is a means of trying to influence others to define him along the lines he is unsuccessfully trying to define himself, and to relate to him in terms of that definition. Overall, and over any period of time, he is unsuccessful in getting people to meet his needs, and he reacts both with the subjective symptoms of which he complains, and a repertoire of socially negative behaviors involving hostility, withdrawal (including chemically assisted withdrawal), or both. The expression of anger, and blaming others, are confessions of his inability to cope as he would like to.

Assets. Despite the negative social features of his life, I find Mr. B. capable of developing rapport. He recognizes that he needs to change and he is hurting enough to work at it. He is of superior intelligence (though quite naive in his understanding of life). He can be quite rigid in his intellectual and behavioral patterns; nevertheless he is capable of making modest, but significant changes when he fully understands they are necessary. He is comfortable with abstract thinking and can react to subtleties. He has good respect for reality and is in no particular danger of developing a psychotic adjustment. Finally, I should point out that Mr. B's pretrauma adjustment was generally good.

Recommendations for Treatment. In the context of an accepting therapeutic relationship the patient is capable of achieving and accepting insights that he now resists. During our contact he volunteered that a previous mental health worker had suggested that he is really "a marshmallow," and he looked to me for my reaction. He seemed comforted by my suggestion that being "macho" (his term) may have some drawbacks in today's society. I think he can recognize that his "macho" goals are counterproductive, but that at the same time he needn't settle for less than what is realistic personally and socially in the way of manhood and adequacy. Probably a number of sessions will revolve about this manhood and adequacy issue.

As therapy progresses Mr. B. should be encouraged once more to become involved with employment and personal relationships. With close support and guidance I believe he can be more successful than he has been in recent years. I anticipate that Mr. B. will require a long term therapeutic relationship for the support it can offer as he seeks to make a transition to a modified lifestyle.

Concurrent with psychotherapy I would be supportive of referral to an alcohol and drug rehabilitation program, and to AA. His mood states will require monitoring and stabilization.

Psychological Reports
In Marital Counseling

A "report letter," written to "John and Mary Jones," exemplifies an approach used in marital counseling as developed by Dorr (1981). The function and the form of such reports are quite unlike classical reports. The function is atypical in that reports are written directly to the clients as a therapeutic tool. The form is atypical not only because the report is fashioned in such a way as to provide an understandable summary of the counseling interaction, feedback, and an opportunity to contemplate and "digest" earlier clinical contacts, but also because the report writer uses the report as a means of interacting with the clients: Objective appraisal alone does not appear to be adequate to achieve the purpose that Dorr seeks. His personal compassion, insight, and "understanding" seem to be built into the report.

John and Mary's relationship does not exist in the best of all possible worlds, and John and Mary are not the best of all possible people—whatever that might mean. Dorr seeks to teach a couple endowed with common frailties and living in a less than perfect world how to live together. In so doing he is frank and open, yet he discusses the couple's problems in a way that is meant to be both constructive and palatable (it might be that much more difficult to make the message constructive were it not palatable). John and Mary need to know what the significant forces in their life are. We would guess that they came to therapy knowing that they differ significantly from one another, that in some ways they are rather opposites. Yet it is possible to be encouraging: "This is not insurmountable," "This is not necessarily a problem, however." The approach seems to be to convey the message that John and Mary can enhance their relationship by realistically understanding who they are.

Mr. and Mrs. John Jones
Street and Number
City, State, Zip

Dear John and Mary:

I hope this letter finds you well. I talked to (my cotherapists) during and after your work with them in (another city). They informed me that you did an enormous amount of work and appeared to be moving in a positive direction. In this letter, I will summarize the results of the conjoint psychological testing. I will report on each test in turn and offer some concluding remarks.

The juxtaposed Edwards profiles are appended, together with scale definitions. You will recall that the Edwards is a psychometric instrument that is based on Murray's needs system. The scores are reported in terms of percentiles, hence a score at the 50th percentile is higher than about half of the individuals in the norm group and lower than the other half.

On John's profile we see that the highest need score was for Affiliation; to be associated with other people, to have friends, and this sort of thing. We also see high scores on Abasement which reflects a tendency to accept blame and to take on others' responsibilities. He was relatively high on Nurturance which is to give nurturance to others, and his steadfastness is revealed by the high score on Endurance. His Autonomy score was extremely low which in some ways complements the high Affiliation score although these scales are largely independent. He also had a relatively low Dominance score and a low Change score. The Aggressiveness score was very low suggesting that he avoids expression of hostility and aggression. Overall, the profile is consistent with what I observed in the feedback session; a quiet, retiring, gentle man who likes to avoid conflict.

Heterosexuality and Exhibitionism were the two highest scores on Mary's scale which is consistent with the history of fashion modeling. A model who doesn't have exhibitionistic needs probably would not do very well. Further, Mary says that she has gotten along better with men in the past than with women. The high Heterosexuality score reflects this. She had a very low Affiliation need score. Very high or very low need scores usually reflect a transitory emotional state. Mary confirmed that she is very wary of closeness and lives as a psychological "recluse" out of fear of being hurt or betrayed.

In comparing the two profiles I saw some possibility for conflict. For example, the Affiliation scores deviate significantly from the norm and in opposite directions. The absolute difference between the two scores is very large. I am sure this would lead to conflict in marriage. Another factor is that John has fairly high nurturance and succorance needs. Succorance is the need to receive nurturance. Mary is not especially low on nurturance, but in comparison to John's high succorance need, we see that John may feel unsatisfied, unsupported, and generally unnurtured.

The juxtaposed MMPI profiles are appended together with some scale definitions. *Please remember my caution that these scales were labeled according to the psychiatric norm group and may therefore sound overly pathological.*

Mary's profile is that of a woman who hurts very much. This profile reveals a hurt person, a cautious person, who is probably using an enormous amount of psychological energy to protect, defend, and project, leaving little for personal growth or joy. The repressive defenses are not working well and in view of her accomplishments in life, her self-esteem is really quite low. When we are hurt our basic defensive strategies tend to become exaggerated. This is the picture we see before us. One of Mary's defenses is to be angrily impulsive and another is to resort to externalization and projection. Hence, we see an exaggerated elevation on the Paranoia scale. This is not exactly clinical paranoia, but rather a kind of all-seeing, overly sensitive stance toward life. The "feelers" are out just waiting to get stepped on. The problem with paranoia is that it tends to feed on itself. The more sensitive you get the more you find to feed the paranoia. Mary described herself on the Intake Booklet as a very sensitive person. Sensitivity can be a good personal trait. While it is desirable to be sensitive regarding other peoples emotions we have to learn to grow some "alligator skin" around our own personalities so that we are not easily hurt ourselves.

John's MMPI profile is "ultranormal." The MMPI does not measure normality except in the statistical sense. Hence, the scores don't mean that he does not have paranoid or impulsive, or other kinds of traits, it merely reveals that these traits are closer to the statistical norm.

When comparing the two profiles, the major problem will be that John might find it hard to empathize with his more emotional, volatile, and sensitive spouse. This is not insurmountable. Furthermore, we know that Mary is in a personal crisis at this time and when the crisis begins to resolve her emotionality will settle considerably.

Now let me turn to the Rorschach. John's Rorschach was that of a man who does his best to keep his life simple, smooth, and relaxed. Obviously, he is extremely bright but he does not choose to exercise his mind in emotional areas. This is not to say that he is not thoughtful. He is very sensitive and thoughtful. However, his major strategy in life is to keep emotional reactions under wrap. The Rorschach was consistent with the Sentence Completion response "When the going gets rough . . . I get quiet."

The Rorschach suggests that while his "life strategy" helps his stability he may be cutting himself off from psychological growth in certain areas. Is it possible to be too stable? Perhaps. Oversimplification of life's complex problems can lead to as many errors as overreaction. A person can be wrong in either direction. The Rorschach would suggest that in his attempts to maintain psychological equilibrium he may be minimally utilizing certain internal psychological resources such that his problem-solving capability may become stereotyped and ineffective.

Mary's Rorschach reveals a unique mind. She has an extensive associational process and the creativity can lead her in two directions. She can either be very original and clever in perception and problem-solving, or she may be way "offbase." Interestingly, the Rorschach suggests that both of you may at times be way off base in dealing with life's problems but for different reasons; John because he may be overly constricted and Mary because she is overly reactive.

Mary's Rorschach is that of a highly emotional individual. She has a good reservoir of psychological strengths but these strengths are not well organized and may not be particularly accessible to her at this time. With continued work and treatment, of course, these strengths will become more available.

On Mary's Rorschach I see many signs of emotional pain including depression and anxiety. Some of the distress is clearly related to losses in life, but also they may be related to some erroneous assumptions about the way life is to be. I will comment more on this later.

When I look at the Rorschachs together I see two people who are psychologically very different. This is not necessarily a problem, however. I would suggest to Mary that she enjoy her looseness. Looseness is not a weakness. It is a virtue to be built on. I would encourage Mary to think like an artist. Art is disciplined emotion. The artist must risk and then evaluate dispassionately. As a legitimate singer, I am an artist of sorts. I am sure you know the enormous risk of self-esteem that I face everytime that I stand up in front of anywhere from 1 to 300 people, and wager that both sides of my brain will work together so that I can get the words and music straight and hope that the small pieces of gristle in my throat will work the way they did in practice. When I go to sing I must think that I am the hottest thing going. I must not doubt myself but when it is all over and I listen to the tape or go back to my teacher, ego must stay outside the door. I must view the performance dispassionately; neither being too harsh on myself (if I don't quite sound like Robert Merrill) or unrealistic in my appraisal of my limitations. John is cautious, guarded, and also stable. While I am encouraging him to explore more the looser side of his nature, I also encourage him to rejoice in his own conservative characteristics as well.

Now let me turn to the TAT. As I mentioned the TAT interpretation is the most speculative aspect of the feedback.

On Card I (which shows the boy looking at a violin) John told a story about a little boy who had been scolded by his teacher. He settles down and doggedly goes on and becomes a very accomplished violinist. Is this the discipline that allowed John to excel? In Mary's story the little boy looked at the violin and seemed to be rather overwhelmed by the strangeness and the magnitude of the task. However, little by little he whittled the task down to something that he felt he could deal with and decided that he would at least try. This may be the way Mary views a lot of things in life. At first they are rather overwhelming but as she uses those strong psychological resources within her she begins to regain her self-confidence and go on.

Card 2 is a pastoral scene which shows a young woman in the foreground and a man plowing the background, and an older woman over on the side. John's story was about the girl in the foreground going on to continue her schooling so that she will hopefully "free her unborn sibling of the farm." The rescue theme is obvious. On the other hand, we see more gloom in Mary's story. The young girl had dreams but now merely becomes "resigned." Accepting life's reality is one thing but, to me, resignation is very depressing. I am enough of a romantic to believe that we can face certain of life's limitations and still reach for magic.

Card 4 depicts a woman clutching the shoulders of a man whose face and body are averted as though pulling away. Ninety percent of the people who respond to this card tell the story about conflict. John, however, chose to project a story in which this man and lady are friends. He is leaving and she is trying to get him to stay. There is no negative affect expressed. When asked what the people feel he responded; "Happy." There is no right answer to these stories but it struck me that John managed to duck out of the potential conflict of this story as he did in response to Card 13 MF (which shows the woman nude to the waist in bed and the man turned away). This card also "pulls" negative emotion. He started a story about a prostitute who overdosed on drugs but after the police were called John focused on the way in which the hero "covers his eyes" because he has never seen anyone dead. Of course, the man is covering his eyes in the picture but almost no one comments on it. Am I overinterpreting in suggesting that this reflects a great reluctance to see hurt in a person. This may be a major dynamic in the marriage. Let me explain.

John met Mary when she was hurting greatly. He could satisfy his nurturance needs in playing the wonderful professional who took care of Mary's mother *and Mary*. He protected her and nurtured her. That sounds like a beautiful way to start a marriage but it really isn't because it starts off confirming Mary's vulnerability and weakness. Perhaps Mary has weakness and vulnerability, but she also has strength and toughness.

On the Intake Booklet John said in response to the sentence completion root "I am . . . what I am." But this is not really true, at least when he is around Mary. John tiptoes around trying not to get Mary mad, trying not to hurt Mary, to avoid conflict etc., etc. I believe this is done because of a genuine concern for her feelings and welfare. But in so doing he diminishes himself and also diminishes Mary. Mary is no longer a patient. John is not Mary's therapist. John has a right to be who he is and to say what he thinks and feels. As long as he continues to squelch who he is he will lessen both himself and Mary. If Mary is upset over what John is feeling that is Mary's problem, not John's. This is a matter of personal space. Mary can grow only when she is given the space to grow. If she feels that John *must* be this, *must* be that, *should* do this, *should* do that, and he allows her to continue to think that this is true Mary may not grow. He can only genuinely love her when he is honest about who he is. Then she must make a choice whether to love the reality or not love it. But to try to be something else is to be a phony. One cannot love an image very long.

I think Mary's response to the last blank card is the most revealing. I will quote it verbatim.

> I had a dream—I dreamed of a world filled with beauty and love. The dream began as it should—or as I had pictured it would. As I grew older the dream began to shatter. Some things I once thought as beautiful were not so. The things I loved became fewer and fewer. Then one day I awoke and found the world could once again be beautiful and I once again could find much of the love I thought forever lost. With each passing year—this time—I clutched dearly the beautiful things and the love I at last had again. But at the last—even with my constant struggle to hold on dearly—the clouds started drifting in one by one covering the beauty and trying to draw up with them—the love. The ending is although I feel like it is time

to put the dreams aside and either drift with the clouds or stay behind, I still struggle for my dream.

Mary let me comment on this by quoting from a paper that I am working on.

Beth's silky black hair tumbles over her boney shoulders in defiance of the paralyzing depression that reigns within her. Her dark brown eyes plead through long, black lashes. The gaze is without malice or strength. Only raw need shows. The concaves of her scrawny body are deepened by the skin's olive hue, and its frailness describes her ego. Hurt Beth, child Beth, pathetic Beth. Her quiet scared eyes scream her loneliness. Though in years an adult, she is very young, vulnerable, dependent; afraid like a new fawn waiting quietly and anxiously in the woods for its mother to return with warm milk.

Carol comes to us differently. She is arrogant, cocky, and aggressive. She doesn't walk, she swaggers. She is cruel, slashing and ripping all that crosses her path. Our reaction is to get away from her as fast as possible.

Though different in style, Beth and Carol are very similar. Each is a part person, each is unwhole. Each possesses a personality that is imperfectly integrated, incomplete and static. Each is starving because she cannot drink the milk of love and kindness that is offered. The styles differ. Beth regurgitates nourishment, Carol spits it out petulantly. The reasons are the same and may be understood in the context of personality structure. Parts are split apart; they do not function in concert, do not speak to each other; thus they are not whole. Carol wrote, "even God didn't deny evil its right to existence—he only split it off."

But did he? John Steinbeck says that "underneath the topmost layers of frailty, men want to be good and want to be loved. Indeed most of their vices are attempted shortcuts to love."

God gave us what we are and it sometimes comes out as evil. Jealousy, hatred, spitefulness, greed are God-given drives, probably set within us to help us survive. To be real we must not deny these parts. Rather they must interact with each other.

Beth and Carol were both patients of mine. Another patient whom I will call Sue once asked me how one attained contentment and a feeling of wholeness in life—how one overcame the horrible feeling of loneliness that she felt all the time. She was a pianist and we discussed music. Together we discovered that a piece of music is only a combination of noise and time. *In its movement it becomes real.*

The parts interact in time and become a new whole. To be of beauty it must have dissonance and resolution. As an art form it must possess and stir emotion, and not always pretty emotion. The emotion may be hate, rage, fear, sorrow, love, or compassion. There can be no body of art that is mere prettiness. It would not by wholly human, thus it would not be art. There is a place for ugliness in art because art is the reflection of the completeness of life.

But what do we do in our own lives? Do we embrace with equal zest our dullness and our nobleness; our stupidity and our faithfulness; our vileness and our compassion; our goodness and our badness? In my experience we do not. We float the pretty parts to the top but we sequester the not so pretty parts. We rarely know each other and thus we find it so hard to truly love each other. One cannot love a part for very long and when we show to the world only the pretty we live in constant fear that the ugly will be discovered and we will lose those whom we love. So we do not risk revealing ourselves and paradoxically we diminish ourselves and our lovers.

Let me tell you about another patient of mine whom I will call Bret. For five years Bret struggled with the terrible conflict. He wanted so badly to live in a world of beauty and gentleness and he wanted so badly to be this himself. Yet there were other parts about him that he despised. You see, the world he saw was a projection of himself, both beautiful and not so beautiful.

On the fifth anniversary of our work together he brought me a butterfly as a graduation present. He no longer needed me. The black and white butterfly was beautiful. The black symbolized what he thought was the evil—the ugly. The white symbolized what he saw as the pure and the good. What he learned was that when put together true beauty emerged. Life is beautiful in its completeness as he came to accept all parts of himself he also came to rejoice in the fullness of his universe.

Bret was very much like the little girl you told about in the TAT whose mother was reading to her. She was daydreaming about "the way she would like it to be." Bret used to think as you expressed in your response to the last TAT card— "the dream began as it should." He embraced the dream with all of his might. He "shouldered" with the tenacity of a bull dog. But when he finally let go of these myths, the true beauty of life emerged. With the butterfly he gave me a card that said "Thank you for your love, your patience, for believing in me, your friendship. . . . but most of all for helping me become the person I am . . . for freedom!"

Barbara and I extend to you best wishes in your quest to achieve wholeness and true beauty in life together. If you ever wish to discuss any of this please call.

Sincerely,

Darwin Dorr, Ph.D

Darwin Dorr, Ph.D.
Director of Psychological Services

DD:lc

Psychological Reports
as a Group Psychotherapy Tool

Noting trends toward an egalitarian relationship between therapist and client, Yalom, Brown, and Bloch (1975) and Yalom (1985) describe a new form of psychological report that facilitates the group psychotherapy process. Similar to the manner in which Fischer (1970), Craddick (1972, 1975), and Mosak and Gushurst (1972) share psychological data with clients, each report, consisting of a summary of the group meeting, is made available to the client prior to the next meeting. The typical report consists of three to seven pages, double spaced, of narrative and commentary. It requires 20 to 40 minutes to dictate and is done immediately following the session. The typed report is then mailed to the clients.

A number of benefits, as perceived either by the therapists or by the clients, are described.

1. Revivification of the meeting. A report of the happenings of the meeting refresh the memory and make for continuity between meetings. The next meeting is likely to continue on the theme of the previous one.

2. The participant observer role. In reading the summary report the clients become observers as well as participants in the therapy process. The therapists have an opportunity to repeat interpretations they deem to be important, particularly those that clients may not have adequately attended to because of personal or sociodynamic reasons. Some interpretations are repeated because they are regarded as exceedingly important or exceedingly complex.

3. A second chance. The therapists point out what should have happened in the meeting but didn't, thus encouraging, sometimes goading clients to participate or to follow through.

4. Construction of group norms. The report is used to give structure to the group, a set of rules for the functioning of the group to maximize its effectiveness. Thus, the therapists may focus on the need for here-and-now content, or for the need of the group members to take responsibility for the conduct of the sessions. Certain practices of the group or its members may be questioned, or the members may be criticized.

5. Therapeutic leverage. Important content may be repeated and emphasized. Thus, one client evaded participation by entertaining the other group members. At one point, however, he remarked, "When you see me smiling like this in the group, it means I'm covering up pain; don't let me keep getting away with it." This crucial statement was tagged for reuse.

6. New contributions. The report provides an opportunity for the therapist to offer new observations, clarifications, or interpretations. It may be that the therapist misses certain insights during the session but arrives at them afterward. Or the timing may not have been right to make comments, or a client for various reasons may have been unreceptive. Or the introduction of cognitive material during a crucial experiential period might have been destructive.

7. Transmission of the therapist's temporal perspective. Typically the therapist has a better temporal perspective than the clients who are involved in the here and now of their own problems. The therapist must therefore become the "group

historian, the time-binder.'' Here is what a therapist wrote into a report about a client who failed to grasp the progress she was making:

> Delores described the despair she had been experiencing. In some ways it sounded almost identical to the kinds of despair Delores described in the group when she first entered—having to do with loneliness, with the feeling that she always had to ask people to be with her and do things with her, that there was no one in the world who cared about her.
>
> However, there is an important difference in her state now and her condition at that time. Several months ago Delores presented these things as though that's the way the world *was*—that there *was* no one in the world for her. This time she has a more realistic view of it. She realizes that this is the way she is thinking right now. She feels discouraged and angry because she knows that there is so much more work to do. She is upset at the fact that her center of self-regard is not inside but still outside of herself, and that she allows others to define her, to tell her whether she is worthwhile rather than having a stable, internal sense of self-worth. In a sense then, at some level Delores recognizes that she is responsible for her bad feelings about herself, and hence can change these feelings.

8. Therapist self-disclosure. The authors feel strongly that group therapy should be demystified, that their views of the process be disclosed for the purpose of ''model setting, deepening the therapist-patient relationship, demonstrating a personal belief in therapy and a trust in the group, and facilitating transference resolution.'' Faith healing and placebo techniques are shunned as the therapists discuss their ''here-and-now feelings in the group—puzzlement, discouragement, pleasure, and annoyance.'' The following brief excerpt discloses some of the feelings of therapists Dave and Lena:

> Dave and Lena both felt considerable strain in the meeting. We felt caught between our feelings of wanting to continue with Delores, but also being very much aware of Bob's obvious hurting in the meeting. Therefore, even at the risk of Delores's feeling that we were deserting her, we felt strongly about bringing in Bob before the end of the meeting.

9. Filling gaps. The report is helpful to clients and therapists in keeping them informed when meetings are missed because of illness or vacations. It is also the authors' impression that new patients enter the group more smoothly if given reports of the three or four previous meetings.

10. The summary as an event in the group. Individual clients react to the reports in their own idiosyncratic manners. For example, there may be paranoid distortions or feelings of rejection when attention is focused on other members of the group. The feelings aroused by the report may then be dealt with in therapy.

11. Therapist uses. The report facilitates the supervisory process as both supervisor and trainee react to the same material. More important, as in the writing of all psychological reports, the very act of writing can help us to shape and sharpen our conclusions. Writing a report—as opposed to an offhand verbal report—can force us to think more about the case. This is of particularly great importance when the writer is also the therapist.

Psychological Reports
for Behavior Therapy

The relation between behavioral diagnosis and treatment is a tighter one than in other established therapies. Lazarus (1973) conceptualizes more or less discrete elements of behavior into seven categories—*Behavior, Affect, Sensation, Imagery, Cognition, Interpersonal relationships,* and *Drugs (and Biological)*—from which he derived the acronym *Basic Id.* Prescriptive interventions may then be paired with each of the elements of the Basic Id, a neat linking of psychological assessment with treatment. In the following out-of-context report prepared by Lazarus,[3] six of the seven elements of the Basic Id are addressed.

Modality	Problem	Proposed Treatment
Behavior	Inappropriate withdrawal responses	Assertive training
	Frequent crying	Nonreinforcement
	Unkempt appearance	Grooming instructions
	Excessive eating	Low-calorie regimen
	Negative self-statements	Positive self-talk assignments
	Poor eye contact	Rehearsal techniques
	Mumbling of words with poor voice projection	Verbal projection exercises
	Avoidance of heterosexual situations	Reeducation and desensitization
Affect	Unable to express overt anger	Role playing
	Frequent anxiety	Relaxation training and reassurance
	Absence of enthusiasm and spontaneous joy	Positive imagery procedures
	Panic attacks (usually precipitated by criticism from authority figures)	Desensitization and assertive training
	Suicidal feelings	Time projection techniques
	Emptiness and aloneness	General relationship building
Sensation	Stomach spasms	Abdominal breathing and relaxing
	Out of touch with most sensual pleasures	Sensate focus method
	Tension in jaw and neck	Differential relaxation
	Frequent lower back pains	Orthopedic exercises
	Inner tremors	Gendlin's focusing methods

[3]From "Multimodal Behavior Therapy: Treating the Basic Id" by Arnold A. Lazarus, *Journal of Nervous and Mental Disease,* 1973, *156,* 404–411. Copyright © 1973 by The Williams & Wilkins Co., Baltimore, and reproduced by permission of the author and publisher. See also *The Practice of Multi-Modal Therapy* by A. A. Lazarus (New York: McGraw-Hill, 1981).

Modality	Problem	Proposed Treatment
Imagery	Distressing scenes of sister's funeral	Desensitization
	Mother's angry face shouting, "You fool!"	Empty chair technique
	Performing fellatio on God	Blow up technique (implosion)
	Recurring dreams about airplane bombings	Eidetic imagery invoking feelings of being safe
Cognition	Irrational self-talk: "I am evil." "I must suffer." "Sex is dirty." "I am inferior."	Deliberate rational disputation and corrective self-talk
	Syllogistic reasoning, overgeneralization	Parsing of irrational sentences
	Sexual misinformation	Sexual education
Interpersonal relationships	Characterized by childlike dependence	Specific self-sufficiency assignments
	Easily exploited/submissive	Assertive training
	Overly suspicious	Exaggerated role taking
	Secondary gains from parental concern	Explain reinforcement principles to parents and try to enlist their help
	Manipulative tendencies	Training in direct and confrontative behaviors

The following report was contributed by Dr. Paul Lapuc, following the logical approach of Lazarus. Lapuc prepared these initial progress reports, to be updated and revised as treatment is initiated and carried out.

HENRY J. DIAGNOSIS: SCHIZOPHRENIA, CHRONIC UNDIFFERENTIATED TYPE

This 37-year-old separated male was admitted in an intoxicated state. A review of his history and present condition has delineated several problem areas. These, together with proposed treatment plans, are as follows:

Problem #1: Excessive drinking, blackout spells, and associated physical acting out. Through self-admission and baseline data of a week's duration, it is ascertained that the patient drinks daily between 6 and 18, 12 oz. beers.

Proposed Treatment: A written contractual agreement limiting the number of days he will drink and expected behavior demonstrated upon return to the ward. Violation of contract will lead to restriction in p.j.'s for a period of one week.

Problem #2: Tremors of hand, other unpleasant physiological sensations that disturb him, i.e., the feeling that he can't breathe, headaches, insomnia, tightening sensations in the stomach and other muscular aches.

Proposed Treatment: Relaxation training and biofeedback.

Problem #3: Tearfulness. Occurs whenever he does not get his own way or begins to feel sorry for himself.

Proposed Treatment: Nonreinforcement.

Problem #4: Affective disorders marked by feelings of being ready to explode and then being unable to control his behavior. Feelings of anger. Depression, i.e., entertaining of suicidal thoughts.

Proposed Treatment: Time projection techniques, relaxation and desensitization.

Problem #5: Cognitive disorders marked by thoughts of not being able to do the right thing; inability to accept success; thoughts of letting his family down.

Proposed Treatment: Deliberate rational disputation and corrective self-talk.

Problem #6: Intuitive dysfunctions marked by auditory hallucinations, i.e., hearing father's voice "calling my name" and "I feel that people are out to get me."

Proposed Treatment: Psychodrama and/or role playing involving images of self; rational disputation.

Problem #7: Poor interpersonal relationships marked by dependency upon others to make decisions for him, exploitiveness, submissiveness, and manipulative tendencies.

Proposed Treatment: Specific self-sufficiency assignments: corrective training and training in direct and confrontative behaviors.

9

Forensic Psychological Evaluations

Psychologists are finding increasing acceptance in the legal forum, particularly as expert witnesses. Both research and judicial decisions support this relatively new role. To function in this forum the psychologist must acquire additional knowledge, including an understanding of the legal culture and a specialized body of legal guidelines. Psychological reports in forensic settings may in some respects differ strikingly from reports in clinics and schools, and the clinician needs special preparation to move from one area of practice to the other. A particular caution pertains to the pitfalls that are commonly encountered in psychological reporting: In the courtroom they can be a potent hazard to competent practice.

Forensic psychology is a well-established specialty that appeals to numerous practicing psychologists and psychology students. Psychology and the Law became an APA division in 1981 and has enrolled over 1,000 members in its first five years.

Two landmark court decisions have especially contributed to the advancement of forensic psychology and to the growing acceptance of the psychologist as an *expert witness*. These are *People* v. *Hawthorne* (1940)[1] and *Jenkins* v. *United States* (1962).[2]

In *People* v. *Hawthorne* the issue was whether anyone but a licensed physician should be allowed to testify as an expert with respect to insanity. The judicial opinion in that case was that it cannot be said that the psychologist's "ability to detect insanity is inferior to that of a medical man whose experience along such lines is not so extensive." The presiding judge further observed that "there is no magic in particular titles or degrees, and, in our age of intense scientific specialization, we might deny ourselves the use of the best knowledge available by a rule that would immutably fix the educational qualifications to a particular degree."

[1]People v. Hawthorne (1940). *Michigan Reports,* 293, 15–26.
[2]Jenkins v. United States (1962). *Federal Reporter* (2d series), 307, 637–52.

In the Jenkins case Judge David Bazelon of the United States Court of Appeals, District of Columbia Circuit, made several points about the qualifications of an expert. Membership in a particular profession, or holding a particular degree, or having undergone a specific course of training is not among them. Rather, an expert witness is a person who has the skill to draw conclusions from a set of facts from which a jury is not competent to draw conclusions. The subject matter from which the expert witness draws conclusions relates to specialized learning, such as an area of science, that is beyond the experience of the average layperson. And finally, the expert's skill, knowledge, and experience is such as to make it appear that his or her testimony will contribute to the search for truth.

Petrella and Poythress (1983) report findings that contradict the "conventional wisdom" that nonmedically trained clinicians make "second-rate" experts when testifying on forensic issues. Their study concludes that nonmedical examiners (psychologists and social workers) produce more thorough reports than their medical colleagues. And they could not establish that physicians' reports are otherwise qualitatively superior, as many believe. The authors suggest that "these findings . . . support an expanded and more aggressive role in expert testimony by psychologists properly trained in the relevant legal issues."

In today's climate of widespread judicial acceptance of psychologists in the expert witness role, cross-examining attorneys still may be inclined to challenge a psychologist's qualifications. "You are not a medical doctor, you are just a doctor of philosophy. Is that correct?" "Then you do not have an M.D.?" are examples of remarks that attorneys may make in an attempt to have the psychologist disqualified as a witness or to cast doubt on the testimony that the psychologist will offer.

This chapter emphasizes responsible and effective psychological reporting in the judicial system. The material that follows evidences concern for the soundness and the effectiveness of the psychological report in forensic settings and also for the credibility of the psychologist as an expert witness. How to cope with gambits of cross-examining attorneys, such as the remarks noted in the preceding paragraph, is therefore one of the important skills that must be mastered by the psychologist who practices in the legal forum.

BEING A FORENSIC PSYCHOLOGIST

Before broaching the issue of preparing forensic psychological reports, it is well to look at the competencies of the psychologist who prepares those reports. What special skills and knowledge must the psychologist bring to this task? What personal qualities must the forensic psychologist have?

Most apparent, the psychologist who functions in a legal context needs to have an understanding of the content of the law and how it functions. *How much* understanding? The belief is widespread that the forensic psychologist just can't know too much law, although a working familiarity with certain areas (for example, family law) is likely to be more useful than knowledge of other specialized branches (for example, corporate law). Thus, a number of forensic psychologists have earned a law degree as well as a degree in psychology. Poythress (1979) is an advocate of graduate curricula that lead to a combined J.D.-Ph.D. degree.

The forensic psychologist must also be well grounded and up to date in relevant areas of psychological theory and practice. For much forensic work, assessment concepts and instruments used in assessment should be thoroughly understood. The psychologist must be skilled in selecting instruments that are appropriate to the questions raised, and he or she must be able to respond effectively to challenges of validity and interpretation. Knowledge of periodical literature that pertains to the foregoing issues should be current.

The practicing forensic psychologist should have ready access to pertinent current literature in psychology and law. The following books and technical publications are especially useful:

AMERICAN EDUCATIONAL RESEARCH ASSOCIATION, AMERICAN PSYCHOLOGICAL ASSOCIATION, & NATIONAL COUNCIL ON MEASUREMENT IN EDUCATION. (1985) *Standards for Educational and Psychological Testing.* Washington, D.C.: American Psychological Association.
AMERICAN PSYCHOLOGICAL ASSOCIATION. (1986) *Guidelines for Computer-Based Tests and Interpretations.* Washington, D.C.: Author.
BLAU, T. H. (1984) *The Psychologist as Expert Witness.* New York: John Wiley.
MALONEY, M. P. (1985) *A Clinician's Guide to Forensic Psychological Assessment.* New York: Free Press.
MALONEY, M. P., & WARD, M. P. (1976) *Psychological Assessment: A Conceptual Approach.* New York: Oxford University Press.
NIETZEL, M. T., & DILLEHAY, R. C. (1986) *Psychological Consultation in the Courtroom.* Elmsford, N.Y.: Pergamon Press.
SCHWITZGEBEL, R. L., & SCHWITZGEBEL, R. K. (1980) *Law and Psychological Practice.* New York: John Wiley.
SHAPIRO, D. L. (1984) *Psychological Evaluation and Expert Testimony.* New York: Van Nostrand Reinhold
ZISKIN, J. (1981) *Coping with Psychiatric and Psychological Testimony* (3rd ed., 2 vols.). Venice, Calif.: Law and Psychology Press.
ZISKIN, J. (1983) *Coping with Psychiatric and Psychological Testimony* (3rd ed., 1983 Supplement). Venice, Calif.: Law and Psychology Press.

Forensic Culture

When you start to practice in the legal forum, the experience can be like taking up practice in a new land. There are new language and new knowledge to acquire, new traditions to learn, new procedures to become acclimated to, and a rough-and-tumble route to seeking justice known as the adversarial system. Writing psychological reports calls for an approach different from that used in clinics and schools. But the psychologist who chooses to work in this culture must adapt to its ways. "When in Rome, do as the Romans do" is more than just good advice; it is mandatory. To ignore the requirements of the legal system is to invite the ignoring of one's expert testimony by the judge or the jury.

Further on the cultural theme, Poythress (1979) cautions, "Many psychologists who function competently and effectively in the classroom or clinic may flounder in the courtroom." The problem is one of lack of acculturation. One must have specialized training and the opportunity to gain experience in the legal setting. The books by Shapiro (1984), Blau (1984b), and Maloney (1985), suggested on the previous page, are good places to begin, as are Brodsky (1977) and two short, but highly informative, articles by Brodsky and Robey (1972) and Nash (1974).

A body of knowledge   New words and new meanings for old words are quick to greet the newcomer to the legal forum. These are words that pertain to procedures and to concepts of legal questions. They pertain also to very practical implications for the dispensing of justice. Thus, the psychologist as expert witness must be careful to avoid impeachment (not in the everyday sense of placing charges against a public official)—that is, not being allowed to give testimony because of being found by the court to be lacking in qualifications; having one's procedures or opinions or conclusions successfully challenged; or even being personally discredited.

Legal tests, or definitions, of questions the psychologist is to address must be a matter of the psychologist's working knowledge. Competency to stand trial (the ability of the accused to understand the charges and to participate with the lawyer in the defense) is commonly confused with the issue of criminal responsibility (pertaining to the mental state of the accused at the time the crime was committed). Dealing with the mental state of the accused at the time of the crime—generally revolving around the issue of insanity—provides more fertile soil in which confusion may flourish.

Insanity is often conceived in mental health terms (that is, as mental illness), and mental health experts may be called upon to testify when an accused criminal uses the insanity defense. In particular, insanity is commonly equated with psychosis. But neither definitions of mental illness nor of psychosis meet the legal definition of insanity.

The traditional definition in the United States is the McNaughten rule, which holds that an accused person is insane and not morally responsible if at the time of the crime the accused "was labouring under such a defect of reason, from disease of the mind, as not to know the nature and the quality of the act he was doing; or, if he did know it, that he did not know he was doing what was wrong." The Durham rule, in use in the District of Columbia, states that "an accused is not criminally responsible if his unlawful act was the product of mental disease or defect." The American Law Institute (ALI) Model Code definition sets forth that "a person is not responsible for criminal conduct if at the time of such conduct as a result of mental disease or defect he lacks substantial capacity either to appreciate the criminality of his conduct or to conform his conduct to the requirements of the law.''

In addressing the insanity question, then, the psychologist must be aware of what particular standard is in effect in the jurisdiction in which testimony is being given. In the United States the McNaughten rule and the ALI standard are both popular. Twenty-two states abide by the McNaughten definition of insanity, and 22 use the ALI Model Code (Blau, 1984b).

A body of practice   There are a number of traditions and customs, courtesies, and rules in the judiciary system. Familiarity with most of these will be readily acquired by those who spend much time in forensic practice. Blau (1984) feels it appropriate to share the following with his readers:

"On being seated [in the witness-box], the witness should turn to the judge, only two or three feet away, smile, and quietly say, 'Good morning (or good afternoon), your Honor.' This acknowledgement of the judge is good manners and helps to establish the witness's credibility with the bench.'' Before testifying, the expert witness should not, under any circumstances, converse with persons who are associated with the opposing side in the case, lest the judge declare a mistrial. And if, during a brief recess, the witness has need to use the restroom the procedure is to gain the assistance of a bailiff. Again the concern is that the witness might have proscribed contacts, such as with opposing counsel, witnesses for the opposition, or witnesses who have not yet testified.

Central to our system of seeking justice is the adversary model, a long-established procedure in which opposing attorneys carry out strategies calculated to win the case for their side. In so doing they seek to present whatever evidence is favorable to the case and ignore or challenge or play down evidence that is not.

Particularly during the cross-examination phase, the opposing attorney is likely to attack the expert witness, the expert witness's testimony, or both. The objective may be to impeach the expert's qualifications, procedures, or opinions, or to destroy the credibility of the expert. For example, if the cross-examiner can point out contradictions in a psychologist's report, the attorney argues that it follows as a logical conclusion that here is a person whose opinions cannot be trusted. Among the more unpalatable questions that a cross-examiner may put to an expert are questions pertaining to sex, or sex preference, or life style. Or the attorney may hurl innuendo of faulty ethical practice: "How much are you being paid to testify in this case?" (Ethical expert witnesses do not sell their testimony; they are paid for their time.) Against this background it is easy to understand why carefulness and thoroughness are crucial to the practice of forensic psychology.

Ziskin's (1981) advice to attorneys on conducting the cross-examination of expert psychological and psychiatric witnesses, fleshed out in four chapters of examples and suggestions, is entirely consistent with the adversarial foundation of law. Throughout two volumes (and in seminars, also), he hammers on the theme that "psychiatry and clinical psychology lack firmly established knowledge," and he presents chapters full of evidence to support this contention. His purpose is "to attack," "hold up to ridicule," "find flaws and vulnerabilities," "illuminate problems or deficiencies," and "impair, destroy and diminish the credibility of the expert and the evidence." In harsh metaphor, he advises his readers to "draw the noose tight."

Large numbers of attorneys have been "Ziskinized," and Ziskin's is but one of several "canned attacks on psychological testimony that are available to the legal profession" (King & Leli, 1979). The psychologist who writes forensic reports might do well to study the ways in which professional opinions can be vulnerable—or made to appear vulnerable—which will also provide grounds for a courtroom victory.

Understandably, a psychologist can feel uncomfortable, intimidated, or angry when confronted by a lawyer using such an approach, and might develop a negative attitude toward the procedure. But such response indicates a failure to understand the adversary model and can detract from the effectiveness with which the psychologist functions as an expert witness. A psychologist in this situation clearly must learn to better understand the adversary process and how to cope with it.

Although immersed in adversarial proceedings, the psychologist's own role is not adversarial. The psychologist's goal, rather, is to make findings available accurately and conscientiously, presenting data to support conclusions and not concealing evidence that may be contrary to the position of the side that has retained his or her services.

The court wants "just the facts"—that is, observations, inferences, conclusions, or opinions—from the expert witness. Making legal decisions in a case (for example, whether a defendant was insane at the time the crime was committed) is not a function of the expert; that duty is vested in the judge or the jury. Nor should the expert embellish findings or otherwise seek to influence decisions. Thus, the needs and the requirements of the courts are fully consistent with the *Ethical Principles of Psychologists* (American Psychological Association, 1981), particularly Principle 4g, which states:

> Psychologists present the science of psychology and offer their services, products, and publications fairly and accurately, avoiding misrepresentation through sensationalism, exaggeration, or superficiality. Psychologists are guided by the primary obligation to aid the public in developing informed judgments, opinions, and choices.

Material that the psychologist presents must therefore be both convincing and ethical, and within the concrete understanding of judges and jurors. Cohen (1979) quotes from the writings of no less an authority than Freud (1913/1959b) to illustrate the sort of testimony that should *not* be offered.

The first . . . chance actions of the patient . . . will betray one of the governing complexes of the neurosis. A clever young philosopher, with leanings toward aesthetic exquisiteness, hastens to twitch the crease in his trousers into place before lying down for the first sitting; he reveals himself as an erstwhile coprophiliac of the highest refinement, as was to be expected of the developed aesthete. A young girl on the same occasion hurriedly pulls the hem of her skirt over her exposed ankle; she has betrayed the kernel of what analysis will discover later, her narcissistic pride in her bodily beauty and her tendencies to exhibitionism.

Cohen suggests that an attorney would have little difficulty in successfully challenging the *credibility* of Freud were he to present such clinical insights by way of testimony.

The substance of an attorney's attack on testimony will likely not be on the psychologist's conclusions per se but more on the procedures and theories that give rise to those conclusions (Schwitzgebel & Schwitzgebel, 1980). It is "scientific adequacy" that is likely to be challenged. Hence the need for the psychologist to be fully knowledgeable about the instruments used in arriving at conclusions. Such issues as validity, reliability, techniques of administration, scoring, interpretation, cultural and other bias, behavioral norms, and various tangential issues may be raised by the cross-examining attorney, and the psychologist had better be deft in reciting current pertinent knowledge.

The well-read attorney may be expected to raise questions on quite technical matters, such as the F-K Index, the standardization of the MMPI, the validity or reliability coefficients of instruments, or the conclusions of particular studies. Ziskin, for example, cites abundant evidence from the literature that impugns the validity and the legal usefulness of the psychological armamentarium of tests in general and also of a number of widely used instruments such as the WAIS-R, the Rorschach, the TAT, the MMPI, the Bender, and Figure Drawing. Unmentioned, of course, are those studies whose conclusions support their use or even those aspects of "negative" studies that are favorable to the instruments. The responsible psychologist will be familiar with these. Also helpful are compilations, such as those by Gilbert (1978, 1980) and Ogdon (1981), that list research relating test data with possible interpretations. Although such material normally would not be recommended for inclusion in the written report, the psychologist might draw on such material in the courtroom to support the manner in which conclusions were gained.

Poythress (1980) recommends a similar defensive mode for psychologists whose opinions are challenged with "learned treatises." He cites the sort of evidence with which psychologists might be confronted and then suggests rebuttal tactics and rebuttal sources. For example, the assertion that "mental health professionals (psychiatrists or psychologists) cannot distinguish the mentally ill or insane person from the normal or sane person" likely would rest on Rosenhan's (1973) widely known study. Poythress recommends "absolute denial that Rosenhan's paper has any relevance for the judgment of legal insanity" and suggests as a rebuttal source the critique of a recognized authority (Spitzer, 1976). The responsible psychologist, however, will not seek to defend indefensible positions. Regarding the issue of future dangerousness, which tends to be overpredicted by psychologists and other clinicians, if there is need to make such a prediction it should be done with appropriate qualification or be stated in probability terms. Two of Poythress's suggestions may be helpful:

> Your Honor, my clinical impression is that the defendant may be physically assaultive in the near future if not hospitalized and treated soon; however, I should warn the court that predictions in this area are highly inaccurate and there is risk of hospitalizing a nondangerous person.
>
> [Also,] Your Honor, while the absolute risk for suicide in this patient is low, his disorder of psychotic depression places him in a relatively high-risk group for suicides; some studies (e.g., Pokorny, 1964) indicate a suicide risk level 53 times that of the suicide risk level for the "normal person."

There are many occasions in which the psychologist must be cautious. Morse (1978) suggests that the sort of data that courts seek from mental health professionals is primarily social, moral, or legal, not scientific. Clinicians should therefore attempt to answer only those questions that pertain to areas where they have expertise and adequately validated tools.

DIAGNOSTIC REPORTS AND FORENSIC REPORTS: SIMILARITIES AND DIFFERENCES

Forensic psychological reports, like diagnostic reports, need follow no prescribed format. Personal qualities of the report writer, the purpose of assessment, and specific needs of the case determine both the style and the organization of the report. The content of the report is to an extent a matter of personal judgment but should *always* respond to the questions that have been asked and to the special needs or mandates of the setting. For example, the content of a psychological report may be partly prescribed by statute (pp. 230–231).

Clarity of presentation is *always* a must, but it is even more important in forensic reports than in reports written for school or clinic use. Terminology and syntax are the greatest offenders. Jargon and poorly explained concepts or conclusions are decidedly unwelcome in the legal setting. (If you must use technical terms, define them.) Do the same with multiple-meaning words or technical words that have found their way into common usage. *Paranoid,* for example, is used in different clinical senses, which in turn tend to differ from lay usages.

In the clinic or school setting where team members regularly interact with one another or with students, parents, or guardians, there are opportunities for these persons to meet with the report writer to clarify communications.

Judges and juries, however, do not have the time or the inclination to engage in such exchanges. Expert opinion that does not communicate well and that may irritate the judge and the jury cannot be expected to receive the attention and respect it might otherwise merit.

The forensic report needs to be far more comprehensive, careful, and detailed than reports in other settings. As a result it tends to be a longer document than reports prepared for diagnostic/therapeutic interventions, and length in forensic reports is not the vice it is considered to be in Chapters 2 and 3. Rather, it is the price to pay for a report that is written with as much concern for legal requirements as for psychological soundness.

Whether the psychologist is gathering data for a written report or for an oral report (testimony, such as during courtroom or deposition proceedings), he or she seeks out data in anticipation of the cross-examination. Records are compiled with care and in detail. Dates, times, places, significant events—such as accidents or treatment for emotional problems—and other materials pertinent to the case must be on tap when needed.

Both the content and the sources of content of forensic reports tend to be broader and more extensive than those of diagnostic/therapeutic reports. In nonforensic settings it is not uncommon for the psychologist to rely solely on test data or on test data and interview. This may be unwise when an assessment is done in connection with a case at law. Poythress (1979) thus discusses the coming to grief of a psychologist who testified under cross-examination that he based his testimony entirely on his findings using projective techniques. The literature, however, did not support such a practice, and Poythress believes that "one must question whether a well-trained clinical psychologist, with no special forensic training and armed only with traditional psychological tests, can conduct a competent forensic evaluation."

Indeed, forensic reports might include content whose purpose is to teach. The psychologist may present a discourse on theory that is relevant to a case, or may reference studies that support his or her thesis. Where ability to predict dangerousness, for example, is at issue before the court, the psychologist might cite recent research and informed opinion that bear on this perennial problem. Such a direct teaching approach seems out of place and exhibitionistic in most settings where psychological reports are written.

Certain classes of content to be included in forensic reports are prescribed by statute. "Each state specifies, with a greater or lesser degree of exactness, what is required in the way of an opinion or report from an expert appointed to advise the court on the competency of a witness to stand trial" (Blau, 1984a). Blau sets forth in this paper the requirements of the State of Florida with respect to issues of competency.

> (1) In considering the issue of competence to stand trial, the examining experts should consider and include in their report, but are not limited to, an analysis of the mental condition of the defendant as it affects each of the following factors:

     (i)   Defendant's appreciation of the charges;
    (ii)   Defendant's appreciation of the range and nature of possible penalties;
   (iii)   Defendant's understanding of the adversary nature of the legal process;
   (iv)   Defendant's capacity to disclose to attorney pertinent facts surrounding the alleged offense;
    (v)   Defendant's ability to relate to attorney;
   (vi)   Defendant's ability to assist attorney in planning defense;
  (vii)   Defendant's capacity to realistically challenge prosecution witnesses;
 (viii)   Defendant's ability to manifest appropriate courtroom behavior;
   (ix)   Defendant's capacity to testify relevantly;
    (x)   Defendant's motivation to help himself in the legal process;
   (xi)   Defendant's capacity to cope with the stress of incarceration prior to trial.

In general, what is necessary as report content follows from the type of report being written or the specific questions that are addressed in the report. Thus Hoffman (1986) sets forth and discusses the areas of content to be included in a report for litigation following a personal injury. When the question is of insanity Maloney (1985) teases out and defines five content areas that must be included in the report if the McNaughten standard applies, and five different but partly overlapping concepts that must be taken into account in jurisdictions that are guided by the American Law Institute standard.

For dealing with the McNaughten standard the report should include a discussion of the following topics:

Disease of the Mind	The Nature and Quality of the Act
Defect of Reason	Wrong
Knowing	

In the case of the ALI standard the psychologist's report should discuss the following concepts:

Resulting from Mental Disease or Defect	Criminality/Wrongfulness
Lack Substantial Capacity	Lacks Substantial Capacity to Conform Conduct to the Requirements of the Law
Appreciation	

SCIENCE AND PERSUASION

Functioning in an adversarial system, the forensic psychologist is neither adversary nor advocate. "One is an advocate only for one's own opinion" (Shapiro, 1984). Does this view allow for the use of persuasion along with science (Appelbaum, 1970)? Might persuasion be inconsistent with presentation of "just the facts"?

Brodsky and Robey (1972) describe both an ideal role and an undesirable role for an expert witness: "The ideal role of the expert witness is that of a detached, thoroughly neutral individual who simply and informatively presents the true facts as he sees them; the undesirable role is that of a partisan, seeking to undermine the opponent, acting deceptively to present his case more favorably and behaving in a variety of unethical, inappropriate ways for reasons of greed, maladjustment, or personal aggrandizement." Again Principle 4g of the *Ethical Principles of Psychologists* (p. 227) is relevant here.

The psychologist has an obligation to be responsible, which includes being effective. He or she must, then, present opinions that have a chance to be fairly received by judge and jury, and that won't be tarnished by an unmerited lack of credibility brought about by a cross-examiner or by the psychologist's own doing.

How best to defend one's credibility and one's testimony is a topic for a workshop that Jay Ziskin (not further referenced) conducts. His position is quoted by Nietzel and Dillehay (1985):

> Mental health professionals who provide psychiatric and psychological testimony are often challenged by well-prepared attorneys as to their evidence, opinions and expert status. This workshop is designed to acquaint mental health professionals with various types of challenges and how to best defend against attack in psychiatric and psychological testimony.

To help to establish credibility, the expert witness may read in books how to dress and how to behave. Clothing must be conservative, even if he or she favors more informal garb at the office or on campus. Practicing courtroom etiquette and carrying out the expected amenities, such as smiling and greeting the judge, is a good idea. It is also well to appear knowledgeable and correct with respect to courtroom procedures, such as checking in with the secretary or the bailiff when arriving to give testimony. And, very important, the expert must always answer straightforwardly and appear calm and self-assured no matter how intense the cross-examination or how challenged he or she might feel. Don't get ruffled, defensive, angry, or flip is good advice. If you understand and accept the adversary process, this advice may be easier to implement.

Whether or not the expert witness feels defensive, the fact is that the cross-examiner's questions force him or her into a defensive role. Forceful challenges may be hurled at the expert's qualifications, credibility, knowledge, procedures, and reasoning. Some attorneys come to this task particularly well armed.

Poythress (1980) views the courtroom struggle of defending one's expert opinion as at times a "fight fire with fire" situation in which the expert has the opportunity to show that he or she is knowledgeable, up to date, and competent with respect to the opinion that is being challenged. The judge and the jury are favorably impressed by a display of competence and are inclined to be persuaded that the expert's opinion is credible. Poythress cautions, however, that the expert not be exhibitionistic of his or her expertise or appear too authoritative.

> It is not particularly desirable for the discussion to turn into a high-level academic debate fraught with conceptually abstract, professional jargon, which is meaningless to the judge or jury. Even in dealing with professional or technical papers, the expert witness should translate the meaning of these data into everyday, understandable language for the court audience. Similarly, it is not necessary to inundate the audience with your knowledge of all the literature by citing author, title, volume, and page number of every paper ever printed on the topic.

Zusman (1983) suggests that, quite innocently, the expert may move from a position of detachment and neutrality to an adversary role. Under the stresses of courtroom procedure the witness might (unconsciously) identify with the side that has retained him or her, may come to feel that this is "his side." Zusman labels this occurrence *forensic identification*. An expert witness so identified is likely to stray beyond the boundaries of legitimate and necessary persuasion.

WHEN PITFALLS ARE DOWNFALLS

Pitfalls of psychological reporting, such as those discussed in Chapter 2, in varying degrees detract from the mission of the assessment psychologist. In the forensic situation, pitfalls in a psychologist's report may be the most direct route for an opposing attorney to follow in the interest of impeaching the psychologist's credibility and conclusions. "I have almost invariably found the clinician's report to be a gold mine of material with which to challenge his conclusions," advises Ziskin (1981).

Of the five categories of pitfalls identified in Chapter 2, Ziskin directs his heaviest fire on "Problems of Science and Profession." He builds his general assault strategy on psychological and psychiatric testimony on the position that there is "a lack of validated knowledge or data base and deficiencies of evaluation methodology that at the present time are inherent in the mental health or behavioral science fields." He is further impressed that clinical reports tend to include deficiencies that are the fault of the report writer. These include errors of omission and of commission, misconstruction of the data, and examiner bias. The latter two problems are discussed in Chapter 2 as irresponsible interpretation, a very prevalent pitfall. However, all the pitfalls discussed in Chapter 2 can be downfalls in the legal arena.

Problems of content   Report topics that are addressed, not addressed, or slighted may all invite attack. It is crucial that the psychologist have adequate opinions for all the legal questions that are raised, and for which psychological expertise is pertinent. When there is a question of insanity, for example, in a jurisdiction in which the McNaughten rule is the standard, it is appropriate to address the five components of this standard detailed by Maloney (1985) and summarized on page 231 in this chapter.

The inclusion of raw data, or of too much raw data, is a frequent criticism that is made of clinical reports. In the legal system raw data are likely to be viewed differently. Opinions unsupported by data are likely to be poorly received and challenged. Opinions must not appear to be the product of a hunch, or even the outcome of the extensive experience of the examiner "with this type of case." The court wants solid data.

Problems of interpretation   Faulty interpretation, which may stem from personal ideas, bias, inadequate assessment skills, and so on, are grounds to attack the credibility of the expert witness. A criterion for the acceptability of expert opinion is found in the court ruling of *Frye* v. *United States* (1923),[3] which includes the statement "While courts will go a long way in admitting expert testimony deduced from a well recognized scientific principle or discovery, the thing from which the deduction is made must be sufficiently established to have gained general acceptance in the particular field in which it belongs." Neither in court nor in clinic are idiosyncratic interpretations welcome.

Speculation is less acceptable in a report that is written as a contribution to a legal question than it is in a clinical report. In the latter, speculation may point up a need for additional investigation, as, for example, in therapy. Speculation is not evidence and does not provide a basis for making a legal decision.

Just how vulnerable to cross-examination a psychologist's faulty conclusions might be in the courtroom may be inferred from the following criticisms that were made of a forensic psychological report. Excerpted from a much longer evaluation, the following three paragraphs are representative of the sort of grievous errors and improprieties uncovered by Dr. David L. Shapiro in response to an attorney's request for a qualified opinion on the technical soundness of a psychological report submitted by an expert witness. The material is reproduced with the permission of Dr. Shapiro.

> Dr. K. speaks of the test results that he obtained on both Mr. and Mrs. W. as being valid, but he failed to administer any instruments which have built-in validity scales, a prerequisite for doing a careful forensic evaluation. The possibility of deception exists in any forensic setting, but there is no indication of any of the well-recognized tests, such as the Minnesota Multiphasic Personality Inventory or the Millon Clinical Multiaxial Inventory being used, both of which have scales which specifically address the truthfulness of the self-presentation.

[3]Frye v. United States. 293 Fed 1013 (D.C. Cir. 1923).

Initially, in looking at the overall findings on the Wechsler Adult Intelligence Scale, Revised Form, Dr. K. makes reference to the disparity between the Verbal and Performance Subtests as being "suggestive of organically related cognitive disturbance." While this is one possible explanation for the data, there are a number of others. For example, some of the variability could well be consistent with the fact that Mr. W. may be more verbally oriented than behaviorally oriented. That is, some, though perhaps not all, of the variability could be accounted for by personality style and not by an organic deficit. The only way of telling whether this discrepancy does represent an organic deficit is to perform neuropsychological evaluation. Another way would be, through history, to find out what any previous test results would be, if any, and see whether the current scores represent a significant discrepancy or decrement from previous evaluations. It is my opinion that, to make a statement such as Dr. K. did, about this being an organically related cognitive disturbance is going far beyond the data presented.

Perhaps even more striking, in terms of misrepresenting data, is Dr. K.'s discussion, on Page 3 of his report, of the difficulties on Verbal subtests which Mr. W. has. Dr. K. basically tries to state that Mr. W. has a neurological problem called transcortical aphasia, implicating the frontal or parietal areas of the dominant hemisphere. The testing which he does, once again, the WAIS-R, cannot be used to make such inferences. There are a variety of tests and examinations for aphasia on the market, but Dr. K. uses none of them. There is even an aphasia screening test, which takes less than ten minutes to administer, which he did not even use. Once again, he has tried to over-interpret data from a test which simply does not provide the data that he is describing. The use of the WAIS-R in this manner is clearly a departure from accepted professional practice. He also describes tasks of "auditory discrimination" and tasks of deductive and inductive reasoning. To put it very bluntly, such tasks do not exist on the WAIS-R. If Dr. K. is interpreting certain tests as providing data for these two areas, once again, he is misrepresenting the test results.

Problems of psychologist's attitude and orientation   Too many reports are written by simply gathering up and putting on paper the information that the data seem to provide, with little or no attention given to the purpose for which the psychological report is requested. Hence, the criticism is frequently made that reports are not practical or useful, obviously not an acceptable quality of report when legal decisions might rest on the psychologist's findings.

The psychologist's attitude is frequently captured by judgments made about his or her reports. Terms like *exhibitionism, too authoritative, too theoretical, too abstract* suggest that the psychologist's focus is on something other than meeting the practical needs of the case. Judge and jury may react negatively to a psychologist who may appear more bent on overwhelming than on informing.

The frequent criticism made of clinical reports, that they are too test-oriented and not sufficiently client-oriented, is less likely to be made of forensic reports. In legal cases there is great interest in the data from which the psychologist reaches an opinion. On the other hand, it is possible to confuse the report consumer with too much data. When the psychologist's judgment calls for the inclusion of large quantities of data, it might be best to place the material in an appendix.

Problems of communication   Offenses against the King's English, vague, unclear, or ambiguous reports, poorly organized reports, reports that are too technical or too complex to be understood by lay readers or listeners, or reports that are written in an offensive or undercommunicative style simply do not convey the material that is called for. Additionally, such poor use of the language is likely to contribute to a negative impression of the psychologist's credibility.

Hedging is not acceptable in either clinic or courtroom. In each setting the need is for dependable information, not appearances of dependable information. The psychologist who is prone to hedge should not anticipate "getting away with it" in the legal setting. When Ziskin (1981) spots qualifications like "perhaps," "may," "seems," "some," or "tends," he prepares an attack on the expert's uncertainty.

Lengthy reports are not the pitfall in the courtroom that they are in the clinic. Legal decisions rest on data and detail. This fact, of course, is not a license to ramble.

Problems of science and profession   There are serious issues and problems not yet solved in the science of psychology and in its application. The area of test validity is representative of our present state of scientific psychological achievement. Many of our widely used tests, particularly in the personality area, fall short of desirable criteria for psychometric validity or applicability to forensic work. This shortcoming may be expected to be alleviated when "psycho-legal assessment instruments," such as discussed by Lanyon (1986), come into more general use. These include instruments for use in the assessment of competency, insanity, dangerousness, child custody issues, homicide, and sex offenders.

On the basis of such fact, Ziskin (1981) takes the position that "psychiatry and clinical psychology lack firmly established knowledge." Elsewhere in the same work Ziskin, in effect, indicates that he might be overstating the case: "The book consists almost entirely of the literature which negates the expertise of these professionals. The lawyer should be aware that there is some literature supportive of psychiatric and psychological evaluation. I have not included such literature because I view it as irrelevant in the legal context."

Faced by an attorney who is thus armed with but a small fraction of the literature that is pertinent to the point at issue, the psychologist is at an advantage. The psychologist is more thoroughly trained and experienced in psychology than the well-prepared lawyer. The psychologist's knowledge is balanced, not one-sided, thus permitting him or her to present opinions fairly, ethically, and convincingly.

The superior knowledge of the psychologist can be used to put in an accurate perspective what could be a devastating attack on the validity of procedures. When the Rorschach is thus challenged, the psychologist might admit that, yes, the instrument yields poor psychometric data, but rich idiographic data (Aronow, Reznikoff, & Rauchway, 1970). Or the psychologist might point out that many studies of Rorschach validity have been faulty and that *conceptual* studies of the instrument yield significantly more favorable results than *empirical* studies (Atkinson, Quarrington, Alp, & Cyr, 1986). (The expert witness should, of course, be prepared to explain these concepts in simple terms.) It can be helpful to the court to interpret significant studies in a meaningful framework.

Maloney (1985) presents a case for the proper use of psychological diagnostic opinion in forensic matters. His approach is predicated on the conceptualization of psychological diagnostic work as assessment, rather than the more limited approach of testing (Maloney, 1985; Maloney & Ward, 1976. See also Chapters 5 and 7 of this book.) Tests are viewed as merely tools that provide just a part of the input into the assessment process, along with various other data obtained from a number of sources. Maloney submits:

> Presenting a clear and comprehensive case evaluation is an excellent way to meet the legal requirements of the court for psychiatric information. If the examiner offers observations in a logically consistent manner, the processes of assessment can be readily appreciated and understood by the court. In short, the examiner simply presents the observations, how and why he or she developed his or her inferences, and the reasons for his or her conclusions.

FORENSIC PSYCHOLOGICAL EVALUATION: A QUESTION OF CRIMINAL RESPONSIBILITY

The following forensic psychological report from the files of Dr. David L. Shapiro illustrates an effective approach to developing and supporting an expert opinion addressed to the question of criminal responsibility. In this case the defendant was charged with rape and assault, and excessive alcohol intake had been introduced by the defendant as a factor related to his alleged criminal behavior.

The heavy detailing of the presentation and the citing of numerous sources of information that are in addition to test data are characteristic of forensic reporting. Test results, police reports, statements from the victim of the crime, interview data from the defendant, and input from others who knew the defendant personally or through professional contact all flow together in the buildup to the conclusion. The elements of the conclusion (for example, paranoid thinking, lack of evidence of malingering, and schizoid personality features) are clearly supportable, as is the reasoning from data to the conclusion, a sequence that judge or jury may readily follow (cf. Maloney, above). Note, for example, the facts that Shapiro garners, and how he uses them, to cast doubt on the possibility that paranoid thinking might have been a factor in the perpetration of the offenses with which the defendant is charged.

Pursuant to your request I examined Mr. Len Jones, at my office on two separate occasions, and in addition interviewed by phone, Mr. Jones' girl friend, with whom he had been living at the time of the offense. In addition, I reviewed the materials which you had sent me, which included a letter to defense counsel by Diane Erwine, Ph.D., a series of reports from the police department, a report of an investigation, and statements from the victim of the sexual assault, from an employee at the medical center, from Matthew Barnes, who had been with Mr. Jones in an automobile immediately preceding the offense, and a statement from Mr. Jones himself. In addition, I received and reviewed accounts of Mr. Jones' two previous arrests, one on a charge of assault, and one on a charge of petit larceny. As you know, Mr. Jones is charged with the rape, and assault, with a hammer, on an employee at the medical center, the rape allegedly occurring within her van. According to her statement, when she entered the van, the side door opened, a man entered, who was later identified as Mr. Jones, and the woman asked him to leave. He apparently had a hammer in his hand and told her to get undressed. She refused, and Mr. Jones allegedly threw her to the floor of the van, and pulled off her clothes. He proceeded to hit her in the face and the head with the hammer, and then proceeded to have sexual intercourse with her. He then choked her until she passed out.

During the course of examination, Mr. Jones indicated that he was aware of the charge against him, but stated that he was *under the influence of alcohol at the time*. He stated that he had no memory at all of the assault, stating only that he recalls only being at the medical center. He stated that he had had a fifth of wine, and a half gallon of Wild Irish Rose. He stated that of that Wild Irish Rose, he had consumed approximately a fifth. He started drinking at 11:30 that morning, but stated that he had not taken any drugs. *He stated that the behavior is very unlike him, since he is "not usually violent," but will usually "pass out and go to sleep."* He indicated that in the past he has never hurt anybody, when drinking, nor does drinking tend to intensify his interest in sexual relationships. According to Mr. Jones, during the course of examination, his last memory is getting out of the automobile in order to urinate, in the underground parking structure at the medical center. He stated that he *recalled urinating by the side of the car,* then got back into the car, laid the seat back, lay down, and that his friend, who had gone into the center, came back, and "we drove home."

What is somewhat striking in this account of the offense is that it *is at variance with Mr. Jones' previous statement which he made to the police.* In that statement, he stated that he recalls a girl walking towards a van, and that when he looked back around "she wasn't there no more." He stated that he saw the girl putting something into the van, and that he had gone to the van "because I admired it, it was a pretty color, it was an odd color, the design on it." He also stated that the girl was white, that she was sitting in the van, that she had pants on, that he had probably gotten into the van by the double doors on the side.

Mr. Jones also stated "I remember having the hammer in my hand while I was in the van. I don't remember hitting the girl or having sex with the girl in the van." When confronted, during the course of the examination, with the discrepancy between his statement at that time, and his current version, Mr. Jones indicated that he could not remember making that initial statement, and feels very puzzled at the details involved in that statement.

Regarding previous criminal records, Mr. Jones indicated that he had never been convicted before, but recounted the assault charge, which he maintained was self defense, and a juvenile charge of rape, in which the complaining witness "never showed up in court."

Mental status examination revealed a neatly dressed, cooperative, punctual, well oriented individual, whose attention, perception and memory were intact. His affect was somewhat blunted, but his speech was coherent, and *he denied any experiences of hallucinatory phenomena, though he indicated that he had "the shakes" during a period of alcohol withdrawal, on one occasion.* He did report, however, *significant paranoid ideation, a feeling that "people are talking about me."* He stated that when he feels this way, he thinks that other people are thinking that he is begging and asking things when he really is not. He stated, however, that this *paranoid ideation occurs exclusively at work, and does not spread to the rest of his life.* He did note that *when he drinks, the paranoid thinking becomes far more intense, and that he wants to jump on the people that he feels are talking about him.* Mr. Jones denied any suicidal ideation, or any attempts at suicide, and noted, rather spontaneously, "if I do have a problem I'd like to catch it before it gets too bad."

Interview with Mr. Jones girl friend, Ms. Howell, revealed the impression that Mr. Jones is generally "quiet, helpful and basically good, but has a *nasty temper when he is drinking."* Ms. Howell indicated, however, that even when angered, Mr. Jones has never hit her, but resembles "a child with a temper tantrum." She verified Mr. Jones' *paranoid ideation, when he is drinking,* that he feels that people are talking about him. She indicated that on the evening of the offense, he had left the home at approximately 5:50 P.M. and returned at 7:30 in the evening, at which point "he just came in and went to bed." Ms. Howell recalls that *Mr. Jones was so intoxicated, that she was concerned, and "asked him not to go out."* She did speak about his having alcohol blackouts, when he is unaware of what he is doing for quite some time, indicating that this has happened on five or six occasions. She indicated that on at least one occasion, he has become violent, toward objects, breaking a punch bowl set of hers while he was drinking. However, she stated that other than the drinking he does not manifest any violent behavior whatsoever.

Mr. Jones was born in California, the third of four siblings. He indicated that his parents are alive, and that he has not seen his father since he was a baby. He was raised by his mother, and indicated that he had a good relationship with his mother. He denied having any serious illnesses or injuries as a young child.

Mr. Jones went as far as the tenth grade in school, at which point he indicated that he dropped out, to get a job to help his mother. He began working for the public school system, and indicated that he has held that same job for approximately ten years. He stated that he consistently would drink during the course of his employment, but it never interfered with his performance on the job. He indicated that he did have difficulty in both reading, and in mathematics. When asked exactly what the difficulty with reading was, he stated that he would get mixed up trying to pronounce words, because "the letters would switch around." This does suggest, of course, the possibility of a learning disability, which does need to be further investigated. Mr. Jones described a rather isolated existence, stating that he was never really close to any friends, and if anyone said anything wrong, "I would snap them up or walk away." This was in reference, of course, to the quick temper noted above. He indicated that he does this to some extent at the present, though primarily when he is drinking, and states that it is more under control. He indicated that he has never been really close to any girl, with the exception of his present girl friend. He indicated that he has only had sexual relationships with two women in his life, and again stated *"that's because I kept to myself." He denied any homosexual involvement,* "I don't want no man." He began drinking when he was fifteen years of age, and the heavy drinking commenced following his dropping out of school at age eighteen. He stated that he would spend the money made from his job primarily on "booze and clothes." He denied ever being involved in drugs.

Mr. Jones has never been in the military service.

At the age of twenty-one, Mr. Jones was married, to a girl with whom he had gone ever since he left high school. He stated that they were married for one year, but that the marriage broke up, because "her family was always visiting, and we had no privacy." He also indicated that the house was not clean, and that this bothered him a great deal. He indicated that he has four children, two by his former wife, and two by his girl friend. He stated that he met his girl friend, that is Ms. Howell, one year after he left his wife. He stated that he plans to marry Ms. Howell if he is able to obtain a divorce. He stated that his relationship with Ms. Howell is "beautiful."

Regarding psychiatric treatment, he indicated that he is not involved in any regular treatment program at present, but had been involved in an alcohol program. He had not had any prior mental health contact. He indicated that his *oldest brother, had been committed, following his acquittal by reason of insanity on a murder charge.* He indicated that his older brother had been there for two-and-a-half years.

Regarding head trauma, he indicated that he had been hit in his head and knocked unconscious, by a chair, and had been treated for one day at a hospital. That occurred in 1973, according to Mr. Jones, though the records from that hospitalization were not available at the time that this report was prepared.

Mr. Jones indicated that he has occasional severe headaches in the left frontal area, but denies any evidence of blackouts, or seizures. Phenomena which sound like *"absence" states occur frequently, according to Mr. Jones, with coworkers asking him "why he goes into space." This particular phenomenon was verified by Ms. Howell in interview with her.* He denies any other phenomena, suggestive of temporal lobe involvement, and also denies a variety of other symptoms suggestive of neurological dysfunction.

The psychological testing revealed an individual with a *verbal IQ of 73, a performance IQ of 76, and a resultant full scale IQ of 73, placing him within the borderline range of intellectual functioning.* The most *notable decrement in his verbal functioning are those measuring acquired knowledge, speaking to perhaps some educational deficiencies. There is some impairment of his social judgment by his impulsivity,* and some indication, consistent with a tendency to withdraw in a schizoid manner from social interaction, that he has difficulty manipulating the environment to his own advantage.

Mr. Jones' profile on the Minnesota Multi-Phasic Personality Inventory is a *valid one, revealing no evidence whatsoever of malingering.* At the same time, *it does not present the picture of any major impairment in reality testing,* but *is consistent, rather, with the schizoid somewhat withdrawn personality described above, with prominent features of anxiety and depression.* The projective testing reveals some evidence of body image distortion, and *some transparencies suggestive of an underlying mental disorder.* There is also evidence of many *paranoid concerns, sexual confusion, and many attempts to avoid emotional stimulation at all costs. While his reality testing is completely intact, his defensive structure is exceedingly rigid and constricted.* He tends to be rather preoccupied with internal concerns, and avoids and withdraws from the world around him.

The screening test for central nervous system dysfunction does reveal *a borderline score, suggesting the possibility of an organic brain syndrome.* This of course is consistent with the history of head injury related by Mr. Jones, and some of the symptoms described both by him and his girl friend. Nevertheless, confirmation of this would certainly require further neurological and neuropsychological input.

In summary, then, Mr. Jones is an individual with a *schizoid personality, tending to withdraw from and avoid interpersonal contact as much as possible.* There is consistent evidence of a paranoid orientation, though this *appears to be related primarily to Mr. Jones' intake of alcohol. That is, he only manifests these paranoid ideas at times when he is drinking.* There is in addition a rather pervasive element of depression, and Mr. Jones' excessive drinking may well be a response to his basically depressive nature. Finally, there is the evidence of some mild, though pervasive brain damage, which needs further investigation.

Despite the presence of the schizoid withdrawal, the paranoia, depression and the possible brain damage, there does not appear to be any clear connection between those elements and the alleged offense. The schizoid withdrawal, of course, would result in behavior exactly the opposite of assaultive, namely, withdrawal, and avoidance of situations. The brain damage could conceivably result in a hyper-sensitivity, and a tendency to over react to environmental stimulation, which of course would also be consistent with the paranoia. *However, in the absence of any indication that there was a prior interaction between the rape victim, and Mr. Jones, which would have aroused the paranoid thinking, such a possibility is pure speculation.* Finally, of course, the *depression is also far more consistent with a tendency to withdraw, and be introverted, rather than act out in an antisocial manner.* Therefore, the constellation of Mr. Jones' personality disorder does not, in any way, "add up" to behavior consistent with the alleged offense.

Therefore, it is my opinion, that the behavior at the time of the alleged offense, if committed by Mr. Jones, was *the product of his alcoholism, rather than of any underlying mental disease or defect.* Therefore, it appeared, that with the exception of the alcohol, Mr. Jones possessed the capacity to appreciate the wrongfulness of his behavior, and to conform his behavior to the requirements of the law. The alleged offense, if committed by Mr. Jones, was not the product of a mental disease or defect.

I trust the above analysis is of some assistance to you. If I may be of further help, please do not hesitate to call on me.

Very truly yours,[4]

---

[4]Reproduced from unpublished workshop materials with the permission of Dr. David L. Shapiro.

Appendix

A GUIDE TO CHECKING THE REPORT

The following Quality Check of the Psychological Report is based on the cardinal principles of report writing that are set forth in the text. It may be used by the student independently as an approach to reviewing the adequacy of reports. It may also be used by the supervisor and the student together as an instructional tool.

The items are worded in a general or an inclusive way. Different discrete shortcomings may point up problems in particular aspects of report writing. It should also be pointed out that judgment based on experience is helpful in responding to the items. Some clinical acumen is needed, for example, in deciding whether a report meets ethical and legal responsibilities or whether it is too speculative.

The checklist may be particularly helpful in reviewing computer-generated reports. This is consistent with the ethical constraints placed on the psychologist who uses these reports, or who "stands between the computer and the client." With the high quality of syntax that has become characteristic of many computer reports, certain errors may be difficult to detect when reading is more casual than critical. Such is not likely to be the case in many circumstances where computer reports are submitted–in forensic settings, for example.

Quality Check of the Psychological Report

	Yes	No
Does the report meet all responsibilities, ethical and legal, to the client, and to the community, and, as applicable, to other professionals and agencies?	☐	☐
Is the completion of the report timely?	☐	☐
Is the report properly focused in terms of the reason for assessment, data on the client, and a frame of reference?	☐	☐
Does the content unnecessarily duplicate that of others? (Is there encroachment on the established role of other professions?)	☐	☐
If raw data are presented, is the material also interpreted or used for illustration?	☐	☐
Is all appropriate illustrative material presented?	☐	☐
Is all of the content relevant and significant?	☐	☐
Is content presented with appropriate emphasis?	☐	☐
Are diagnoses, prognoses, and recommendations given as necessary?	☐	☐
Is all other essential material included?	☐	☐
Is interpretation sufficiently focused (not too general, differentiating among clients)?	☐	☐
Are conclusions adequately supported by data?	☐	☐
Is speculation within reason?	☐	☐
Is speculation properly labeled as such?	☐	☐
Are all interpretations within acceptable levels of responsibility?	☐	☐
Is the report written so as to be meaningful and useful?	☐	☐
Are exhibitionistic, authoritative, or similarly offensive statements avoided?	☐	☐
Is the report client-oriented rather than test-oriented?	☐	☐
Are concepts that are too theoretical or too abstract avoided?	☐	☐
Is word usage appropriate (absence of jargon, stereotyped, esoteric, overly technical, or complex language)?	☐	☐
Is the language used clear and unambiguous?	☐	☐
Is the report too long (padded, redundant, rambling, unfocused, offering useless content, or in the manner of a "shotgun approach")?	☐	☐
Is the style appropriate for the mission, for the setting, and for those who may read it?	☐	☐
Is the report logically and effectively organized?	☐	☐
Are the conclusions of the report set forth without hedging?	☐	☐
Is the report adequately persuasive in terms of needs and forcefulness of the data?	☐	☐
Is the report self-contradictory?	☐	☐

B

Appendix

RECOMMENDED READINGS

Adjunctive text and reference works may be assigned by the instructor or supervisor as helpful in learning the assessment–report writing function. The author has found the following titles of value for the purpose, but other works might also be appropriate.

General Reference Works

AMERICAN PSYCHIATRIC ASSOCIATION. (1987). *Diagnostic and Statistical Manual of Mental Disorders* (3rd ed., rev.) (DSM-III-R). Washington, D.C.: Author.

    DSM-III is *the* official diagnostic classification used in psychiatric settings and by psychiatrists in private practice. It is also widely recognized outside the psychiatric profession. Psychologists who render services in collaboration with psychiatrists or where psychiatric authority is recognized must be familiar with the classification and must be able to use it with facility.

CAMPBELL, R. J. (Ed.). (1981). *Psychiatric Dictionary* (5th ed.). New York: Oxford University Press.

    This dictionary is the leading source of technical definitions used by psychiatrists and allied professionals whose work is related to psychiatry. Psychologists use many psychiatric terms, and overlap in the vocabularies of psychologists and psychiatrists makes a good psychiatric dictionary a valuable reference work for psychological report writers.

CHOCA, J. (1980). *Manual for Clinical Psychology Practicums*. New York: Brunner/Mazel.

"The purpose of this *Manual* is to provide practical and easily understandable guidelines." Presented in outline form, there is an abundance of information on such topics as basics of clinical practice, diagnosis, record keeping, and treatment. The student psychologist might occasionally consult the manual when "working up" a case.

ENGLISH, H. B., & ENGLISH, A. C. (1958). *A Comprehensive Dictionary of Psychological and Psychoanalytic Terms*. New York: D. McKay.

Obviously, a quarter century brings many changes in scientific and professional terminology. But what this work loses in obsolescence it more than compensates for in scholarliness that often provides information and shades of meaning not to be found in any other current psychological dictionary.

GOLDENSON, R. M. (Ed.). (1984). *Longman Dictionary of Psychology and Psychiatry*. New York: Longman.

This up-to-date dictionary draws on broad areas of psychology and related disciplines such as psychiatry, physiology, neurology, and medicine. The straightforward definitions offered should be helpful to the report writer in developing case presentations.

PARASHAR, O. D. (1977). *Dictionary of Special Education*. Freeport, NY: Educational Activities, Inc.

This dictionary is most likely to be useful to school psychologists and others working with handicapped children. Definitions are clear and minimally technical. In addition to psychological terms there are numerous entries pertaining to handicapped children, terms concerned with such matters as medical and neurological disorders.

WOLMAN, B. B. (Ed.). (1973). *Dictionary of Behavioral Science*. New York: Van Nostrand Reinhold.

"The motto of the Dictionary is *Concision and Precision.*" Involving the collaboration of almost a hundred distinguished behavioral scientists and covering such diverse areas as genetics, psychopathology, educational psychology, industrial psychology, and psychiatry, we are inclined to expand the motto to include *comprehensive.*

And . . . A good dictionary of the English language.

Assessment

AMERICAN EDUCATIONAL RESEARCH ASSOCIATION, AMERICAN PSYCHOLOGICAL ASSOCIATION, NATIONAL COUNCIL ON MEASUREMENT IN EDUCATION. (1985). *Standards for Educational and Psychological Testing*. Washington, DC: American Psychological Association.

This compilation meets perceived needs to set testing standards in accordance with social needs and ethical requirements, and to incorporate in these standards recent technical advances in testing and related fields. Foci are on test construction and evaluation, and on the application of tests for particular uses and in particular circumstances. Because these standards deal with issues of what is proper and appropriate in testing, they can be of forensic interest.

AMERICAN PSYCHOLOGICAL ASSOCIATION. (1986). *Guidelines for Computer-Based Tests and Interpretations*. Washington, DC: Author.

This 24-page booklet, part of a sequence of guides to test makers and test users that includes *Ethical Principles of Psychologists* (1981), *Standards for Educational and Psychological Testing* (1985), and *Standards for Providers of Psychological Services* (1977) will help psychologists decide how computers might fit into their testing or assessment practices. Cast in an ethical framework, the booklet defines the participants in the computer testing enterprise, spells out the specific responsibilities of test users, and provides guidelines for the users of computer-based tests and interpretations.

ANASTASI, A. (1982).   *Psychological Testing* (5th ed.). New York: Macmillan.

From basic concepts to specific tools, a thorough and widely accepted book that may serve as a refresher and a reference work. The information in such a text can be useful in forensic work to make sure one is on solid ground in the selection of instruments and their proper use and interpretation. A conscientious lawyer might also turn to this book in building a case, and the psychologist in the role of expert witness should be prepared to answer the questions this book might inspire.

BARLOW, D. H. (Ed.). (1981).   *Behavioral Assessment of Adult Disorders.* New York: Guilford.

"This book, unlike most of its predecessors, is not a book on how to do behavioral assessment, listing the various procedures available at this time and the philosophies underlying them. The purpose of this book is to provide an up-to-date, state-of-the-art description of the assessment procedures and strategies for the most common adult clinical problems. . . . "

BECK, S. J. (1952).   *Rorschach's Test, Vol. 3: Advances in Interpretation.* New York: Grune & Stratton.

Beck first presents his views on personality as gained from clinical observation and experience with the Rorschach. He then illustrates the functioning of actual persons as seen in the Rorschach. Whether or not one is working in the context of Beck's "system," to follow this expert's interpretation of data can be nothing but an enriching experience. His approach can be considered a model.

BECK, S. J. (1961).   *Rorschach's Test, Vol. 1: Basic Processes* (3rd ed.). New York: Grune & Stratton.

Administration of the Rorschach is presented following Hermann Rorschach's view of his test as an *experiment* or *experimental procedure.* The remainder of the book sets forth and explicates Beck's scoring system.

BLAU, T. H. (1984).   *The Psychologist as Expert Witness.* New York: John Wiley.

Blau's book is far-ranging in bringing to the reader an understanding of legal principles and practices, and the integration of psychological knowledge and procedures into such a framework. The approach is practical and instructive. Blau offers a number of pointers and insights that might preclude frustration and grief in the neophyte forensic psychologist.

CONE, J. D., & HAWKINS, R. P. (1977).   *Behavioral Assessment: New Directions in Clinical Psychology.* New York: Brunner/Mazel.

The focus of this book is on concepts, principles, and issues in behavioral assessment and is in contrast to books centered on specific assessment approaches and their application to problem areas that may be behaviorally assessed.

CRONBACH, L. J. (1984).   *Essentials of Psychological Testing* (4th ed.). New York: Harper & Row, Pub.

An excellent basic text covering the principles and applications of testing. Much information is given on a number of selected instruments. Professionals, as well as students, might have occasion to consult this work.

DAHLSTROM, W. G., WELSH, G. S., & DAHLSTROM, L. E. (1972).   *An MMPI*

Handbook: Clinical Interpretation, Vol. I (rev. ed.). Minneapolis: University of Minnesota Press.

This book is a comprehensive guide to the clinical use of the MMPI, with considerable attention given to administration, scoring and profiling, procedures for coding and configural analysis, interpretative considerations, and questions of validity. Various of 15 appendixes may from time to time be useful.

EXNER, J. E., JR. (1978). *The Rorschach: A Comprehensive System, Vol. II: Current Research and Advanced Interpretation.* New York: John Wiley.

This integrated system as set forth in this and the previous listing, in the words of Exner, draws on the "best of the Rorschach," i.e., on the contributions of a number of distinguished workers, particularly Beck, Klopfer, Hertz, and Piotrowski. Emerging is a new system of scoring and interpretation that has won wide acceptance even though this has meant considerable homework for instructors schooled in one of the earlier systems. A number of useful tables are included.

EXNER, J. E., JR. (1986). *The Rorschach: A Comprehensive System* (2nd ed.). New York: John Wiley.

This revision of Exner's basic statement on the Rorschach is updated with the significant research findings that have become available since the first appearance of the comprehensive system. Dubbed the *comprehensive system* because it seeks to incorporate the best elements of the five earlier leading systems, the work is also comprehensive in its coverage of the Rorschach, from administration and scoring through interpretation.

FISCHER, C. T. (1985). *Individualizing Psychological Assessment.* Monterey, CA: Brooks/Cole.

This book is a wide-ranging approach to its announced subject matter, an in-depth treatment from philosophical and theoretical roots in European existential/phenomenological thinking, to an exploration of the art of Andrew Wyeth, to classroom questions and answers. An individualized report may start with a highly individualized title—for example, "Melvin, The Iron Bunny."

GILBERT, J. (1978). *Interpreting Psychological Test Data, Vol. I: Test Response Antecedent.* New York: Van Nostrand Reinhold.

Test performance, scores, and relationships among scores are listed along with possible interpretations on the basis of cited research. Instruments for which data are reported are the Bender-Gestalt, human figure drawing, the WAIS, and the Rorschach.

GILBERT, J. (1980). *Interpreting Psychological Test Data, Vol. II: Behavioral Attributes Antecedent.* New York: Van Nostrand Reinhold.

Personality characteristics and behaviors are associated with test performance, scores, and relationships among scores on the basis of cited research. Instruments for which data are reported are the Bender-Gestalt, human figure drawing, the WAIS, and the Rorschach. The presentation is the reverse of the arrangement of test data to interpretation that is the format of Gilbert, Vol. I (see preceding).

GOLDEN, C. J., HAMMEKE, T. A., & PURISCH, A. D. (1980). *A Manual for the Luria-Nebraska Neuropsychological Battery* (rev. ed.). Los Angeles: Western Psychological Services.

This very practical work holds the complete instructions for administration of all 269 items of the battery. The chapter on interpretation deals with rationale and offers specific guidelines to the clinical diagnosis of brain dysfunction.

GRAHAM, J. R. (1977). *The MMPI: A Practical Guide.* New York: Oxford University Press.

The title of this book sums up its content and its goals, which it meets nicely. A student unfamiliar with the MMPI who studies this book will gain a working knowledge of the instrument, from its format and content through administration, scoring, profiling, and interpretation. Special features include discussions of a number of research scales and the use of computerized reports.

HUTT, M. L. (1977). *The Hutt Adaptation of the Bender-Gestalt Test* (3rd ed.). New York: Grune & Stratton.

Hutt's work shows how "The Bender," a test of developmental level, can also be used effectively to gain data on a wide variety of personality features. Useful information concerning psychotic disorganization, depressed mood, elevated mood, anxiety, compulsivity, impulsivity, and negativism commonly is disclosed. The instrument frequently can be used as an aid to the diagnosis of brain dysfunction.

KAUFMAN, A. S. (1979). *Intelligent Testing with the WISC-R*. New York: John Wiley.

Kaufman has given his book a fortunate title that is descriptive of an approach to assessment and an understanding of how best to use the WISC-R. Going beyond the psychometric approach, Kaufman discusses how to extract from test scores and patterns the maximum amount of meaningful information that can be developed from them. His interpretations rest on observations of the child and developmental and cognitive theory, as well as on test performance.

KNOFF, H. M. (Ed.). (1986). *The Assessment of Child and Adolescent Personality*. New York: Guilford.

This book presents a comprehensive theoretical and practical approach to child and adolescent assessment. It is both a useful text and a reference work that can be helpful to school psychologists and clinical psychologists who do psychological assessments of children and adolescents. A number of instruments and non-test approaches to assessment are discussed, and report-writing principles and other areas of application are dealt with.

LEZAK, M. D. (1983). *Neuropsychological Assessment* (2nd ed.). New York: Oxford University Press.

This is a practically oriented text, with a basic concern for training students for communicating about the psychological aspects of brain dysfunction. The author deals with basic neuropsychological concepts, with neuroanatomy and the relation of brain to behavior, with diagnostic issues, and with a number of the instruments used in neuropsychological assessment.

LURIA, A. R. (1973). [*The Working Brain: An Introduction to Neuropsychology*] B. Haigh, (trans.). New York: Basic Books.

The contributions of this distinguished psychologist linking brain to behavior provide a basis for the enlightened practice of neuropsychology.

MALONEY, M. P. (1985). *A Clinician's Guide to Forensic Psychological Assessment*. New York: Free Press.

Maloney presents chapter-length discussions of such basic forensic issues as standards of legal insanity, competency to stand trial, and child custody and dependency evaluations. Also dealt with is the ability of the mental health professional to make a contribution to answering questions on the order of a defendant's competency to waive *Miranda* rights. The book is particularly distinguished by its treatment of *psychological assessment* in the forensic situation.

MASH, E. J., & TERDAL, L. G. (1981). *Behavioral Assessment of Childhood Disorders*. New York: Guilford.

Following an extensive introduction to behavioral assessment of childhood disturbance are 15 chapters addressed to the assessment of classes of disorder. These are grouped under four general headings: "Externalizing Disorders" (e.g., hyperactivity, conduct disorders), "Internalizing Disorders" (e.g., anxiety and depression), "Developmental Disorders" (e.g., autism, learning disabilities, psychosexual problems), and "Health-Related Disorders" (e.g., obesity, seizure disorders, elimination problems).

MATARAZZO, J. D. (1972). *Wechsler's Measurement and Appraisal of Adult Intelligence* (5th ed.). New York: Oxford University Press.

Although Matarazzo's discussion of the Wechsler-Bellevue and the WAIS are not fully pertinent to the WAIS-R, certain features retain their value (e.g., content of the newer instrument is similar to that of its predecessors, and the implications for understanding personality functioning to be gained from the W-B, the WAIS, and the WAIS-R are also similar). Matarazzo's views on intelligence and its assessment provide a good background for understanding the intellect of one's clients.

MILLON, T. (1981). *Disorders of Personality: DSM-III, Axis II.* New York: John Wiley.

Personality disorder is one of the several major categories of psychopathology recognized in DSM-III. To comprehend Millon's discourse is to master, to a significant degree, the concept of personality, its function and its dysfunction. Such basic insights are also helpful for understanding other classes of disorder. Covering the topic of personality disorder in much greater detail than the DSM, which is essentially atheoretical, adynamic, and not focused on developmental issues, this book presents views on all these topics.

OGDON, D. P. (1981). *Psychodiagnostics and Personality Assessment: A Handbook* (2nd ed.). Los Angeles: Western Psychological Services.

Test performance, scores, and relationships among scores are related to possible interpretations on the basis of cited research. Instruments reported on are the Wechsler scales, the Rorschach, projective drawings, and the Bender-Gestalt.

RAPAPORT, D., GILL, M. M., & SCHAFER, R. (1968). *Diagnostic Psychological Testing* (rev. ed., R. R. Holt, Ed.). New York: International Universities Press.

In what has been called a "labor of love," Holt has revised and made more usable the 1945 (Vol. I) and 1946 (Vol. II) work that laid the basis for a tradition and orientation in psychological assessment. Particularly helpful are approaches to the uses of such tests as the Rorschach, the TAT, and the adult Wechsler scale (Rapaport et al. used the then-extant Wechsler-Bellevue Scale, but their manner of using this instrument is applicable to the WAIS-R).

REITAN, R. M., & DAVISON, L. A. (Eds.). (1974). *Clinical Neuropsychology: Current Status and Applications.* Washington, D.C.: V. H. Winston.

This book, covering both general and specific topics in neuropsychology, may serve as a textbook and as a reference source. Much of the book is focused on issues of brain dysfunction in children. Some specific problems addressed are the application of neuropsychological techniques to mentally retarded and epileptic patients. Tests and batteries are discussed in an appendix.

RUSSELL, E. W., NEURINGER, C., & GOLDSTEIN, G. (1970). *Assessment of Brain Damage: A Neuropsychological Key Approach.* New York: John Wiley.

The focus of this book is the Halstead-Reitan Neuropsychological Battery. In 100 pages the authors deal with description and rationale of the battery, validation, and the neuropsychological keys—i.e., a key for localizing brain damage and indicating the degree of lateralization of brain damage, and a "process" key to determine the *type* of brain damage. The latter key sorts assessment results into four categories: (1) no brain damage, (2) acute brain damage, (3) static brain damage, and (4) congenital brain damage. Norms and procedures for scoring brain dysfunctional behaviors are supplied.

SATTLER, J. M. (1982). *Assessment of Children's Intelligence and Special Abilities.* Boston: Allyn & Bacon.

This comprehensive approach to assessment may serve as both a text and a reference book to advanced undergraduate and beginning graduate students in school and clinical psychology, and to practitioners in these areas. Sattler discusses psychological instruments in considerable depth, and he treats report writing more thoroughly than do most authors of assessment texts.

SCHAFER, R. (1967). *The Clinical Application of Psychological Tests: Diagnostic Summaries and Case Studies.* New York: International Universities Press.

Originally published in 1948, this book will remain invaluable for the foreseeable future. The diagnostic labels used do not accord well with current nomenclature, the Bellevue Scale (W-B,I) that is much discussed is the grandfather of the WAIS-R, and the Sorting Test that he routinely included in his battery is not one of our leading instruments today, but the grasp of psychopathology and the approach to understanding it that Schafer displays point up a savoir-faire and a paradigm that can serve the modern psychological assessor well.

SHAPIRO, D. (1965). *Neurotic Styles.* New York: Basic Books.

Disregard the publication date of this book. Its topic is *neurosis,* a term that does not receive high billings in DSM-III but that is very much entrenched in clinical practice and in cultural lore. The several neuroses with which Shapiro deals have very real referents both in clinical symptoms and in everyday behavior. He focuses on four neurotic "styles": the obsessive-compulsive, the paranoid, the hysterical, and the impulsive. His formulations can be a solid contribution to insight into many problems of assessment.

SHAPIRO, D. L. (1984). *Psychological Evaluation and Expert Testimony.* New York: Van Nostrand Reinhold.

Shapiro brings pertinent legal knowledge within the ken of the nonforensically sophisticated psychologist. Chapters in such areas of the law as competency to stand trial, criminal responsibility, and family law can be helpful to the psychologist who is to serve as an expert witness. Equally useful are samples of Shapiro's own forensic psychological reports.

SMALL, L. (1980). *Neuropsychodiagnosis in Psychotherapy* (rev. ed.). New York: Brunner/Mazel.

Small alerts the reader to the prevalence—possibly widespread prevalence—of brain dysfunction in clients who are being treated with psychotherapy. Often the relationship between brain dysfunction and the presenting symptom may be inferred only from "soft signs." Although treatment of neuropsychological symptoms is not far advanced, the assessor's determination that brain dysfunction is contributing to a psychological problem may have implications for making recommendations for *psychotherapy.*

WEBB, L. J., DI CLEMENTE, C. C., JOHNSTONE, E. E., SANDERS, J. I., & PERLEY, R. A. (1981). *DSM-III Training Guide.* New York: Brunner/Mazel.

The neophyte in clinical assessment is not the only one in need of training in formal ("official") diagnosis. Seasoned clinicians, too, sometimes are confused, and many have been sent scurrying to such training guides as that produced by Webb et al. This work contributes to understanding the DSM-III system, which is a sharp departure from the two earlier DSMs. The focus is on practical application. It is endorsed by Robert Spitzer, the chief architect of DSM-III.

ZISKIN, J. (1981). *Coping with Psychiatric and Psychological Testimony* (3rd ed., 2 vols). Venice, Calif.: Law and Psychology Press.

Ziskin's work is written for attorneys and is full of information on how to overcome psychological and psychiatric testimony and how to impeach the credibility of the psychologist or psychiatrist expert witness. It is well, therefore, that the expert witness know what he or she might need to defend against. You can cope with Jay Ziskin, but you have to do your homework, mind your p's and q's, and read Jay Ziskin.

References

AFFLECK, D. C., & STRIDER, F. D. (1971). Contribution of psychological reports to patient management. *Journal of Consulting and Clinical Psychology, 37*(2), 177–179.

ALLEN, J. G. (1981). The clinical psychologist as a diagnostic consultant. *Bulletin of the Menninger Clinic, 45*(3), 247–258.

ALLEN, J. G., LEWIS, L., BLUM, S., VOORHEES, S., JERNIGAN, S., & PEEBLES, M. J. (1986). Informing psychiatric patients and their families about neuropsychological assessment findings. *Bulletin of the Menninger Clinic, 50,* 5–21.

ALLPORT, G. (1937). *Personality: A psychological interpretation.* New York: Holt.

AMERICAN EDUCATIONAL RESEARCH ASSOCIATION, AMERICAN PSYCHOLOGICAL ASSOCIATION, & NATIONAL COUNCIL ON MEASUREMENT IN EDUCATION. (1985). *Standards for Educational and Psychological Testing.* Washington, DC: American Psychological Association.

AMERICAN PSYCHIATRIC ASSOCIATION. (1952). *Diagnostic and Statistical Manual, Mental Disorders.* Washington, DC: Author.

AMERICAN PSYCHIATRIC ASSOCIATION. (1980). *Diagnostic and Statistical Manual, Mental Disorders* (3rd ed.) (DSM-III). Washington, DC: Author.

AMERICAN PSYCHIATRIC ASSOCIATION. (1987). *Diagnostic and Statistical Manual of Mental Disorders* (3rd ed., rev.) (DSM-III-R). Washington, DC: Author.

AMERICAN PSYCHOLOGICAL ASSOCIATION. (September 1971). Shared results and open files with the client: Professional irresponsibility or effective involvement? Annual Meeting, Washington, DC.

AMERICAN PSYCHOLOGICAL ASSOCIATION. (1977).   *Standards for Providers of Psychological Services.* Washington, DC: Author.

AMERICAN PSYCHOLOGICAL ASSOCIATION. (1981).   Ethical principles of psychologists. *American Psychologist, 36*(6), 633–638.

AMERICAN PSYCHOLOGICAL ASSOCIATION. (1986).   *Guidelines for Computer-Based Tests and Interpretations.* Washington, DC: Author.

ANASTASI, A. (1982).   *Psychological Testing* (5th ed.). New York: Macmillan.

APPELBAUM, S. A. (1969).   Psychological testing for the psychotherapist. *Dynamic Psychiatry, 2,* 158–163.

APPELBAUM, S. A. (1970).   Science and persuasion in the psychological test report. *Journal of Consulting and Clinical Psychology, 35*(3), 349–355.

APPELBAUM, S. A. (1973).   Psychological mindedness: Word, concept, and essence. *International Journal of Psychoanalysis, 55,* 35–46.

APPELBAUM, S. A. (1977).   *The Anatomy of Change.* New York: Plenum.

ARAOZ, D. L. (1972).   The thematic apperception test in marital therapy. *Journal of Contemporary Psychotherapy, 5,* 41–48.

ARNOW, D., & COOPER, S. H. (1984).   The borderline patient's regression on the Rorschach test. *Bulletin of the Menninger Clinic, 48,* 25–36.

ARONOW, E., & REZNIKOFF, M. (1971).   Application of projective tests to psychotherapy: A case study. *Journal of Personality Assessment, 35*(4), 379–393.

ARONOW, E., REZNIKOFF, M., & RAUCHWAY, A. (1970).   Some old and new directions in Rorschach testing. *Journal of Personality Assessment, 43,* 227–234.

ATKINSON, L., QUARRINGTON, B., ALP, I. E., & CYR, J. J. (1986).   Rorschach validity: An empirical approach to the literature. *Journal of Clinical Psychology, 42,* 360–362.

AUGER, T. J. (1974).   Mental health terminology—A modern Tower of Babel? *Journal of Community Psychology, 2*(2), 113–116.

BARKER, P. (1985).   *Using Metaphors in Psychotherapy.* New York: Brunner/Mazel.

BARLOW, D. H. (Ed.). (1981).   *Behavioral Assessment of Adult Disorders.* New York: Guilford.

BECK, S. J. (1952).   *Rorschach's Test, Vol. 3: Advances in Interpretation.* New York: Grune & Stratton.

BECK, S. J. (1961).   *Rorschach's Test, Vol. I: Basic Processes* (3rd ed.). New York: Grune & Stratton.

BERG, M. (1984).   Expanding the parameters of psychological testing. *Bulletin of the Menninger Clinic, 48,* 10–24.

BERG, M. (1985).   The feedback process in diagnostic psychological testing. *Bulletin of the Menninger Clinic, 49,* 52–69.

BERNE, E. (1964).   *Games People Play.* New York: Grove Press.

BERSOFF, D. N. (1975).   Professional ethics and legal responsibilities on the horns of a dilemma. *Journal of School Psychology, 13*(4), 359–376.

BETTELHEIM, B. (1947).   Self-interpretation of fantasy: The Thematic Apperception Test as an educational and therapeutic device. *American Journal of Orthopsychiatry, 37,* 80–100.

BLANK, L. (1965).   *Psychological Evaluation in Psychotherapy: Ten Case Histories.* Chicago: Aldine.

BLAU, T. H. (1984).   Psychological tests in the courtroom. *Professional Psychology: Research and Practice, 15,* 176–186. (a)

BLAU, T. H. (1984).   *The Psychologist as Expert Witness.* New York: John Wiley. (b)

BLOCK, J. (1961).   *The Q-Sort Method in Personality Assessment and Psychiatric Research.* Springfield, IL: Chas. C. Thomas.

BRADLEY, G. W., & BRADLEY, L. A. (1977).   Experimenter prestige and feedback related to acceptance of genuine personality interpretations and self-attitude. *Journal of Personality Assessment, 41*(2), 178–185.

BREGER, L. (1968).   Psychological testing: Treatment and research implications. *Journal of Consulting and Clinical Psychology, 32*(2), 178–181.

BRODSKY, S. L. (1977).   The mental health professional on the witness stand: A survival guide. In B. D. Sales (Ed.), *Psychology in the Legal Process*. Jamaica, NY: Spectrum Publ.

BRODSKY, S. L. (Chair). (1972).   Shared results and open files with the client. *Professional Psychology, 3*(4), 362–364.

BRODSKY, S. L., & ROBEY, A. (1972).   Becoming an expert witness: Issues of orientation and effectiveness. *Professional Psychology, 3,* 173–176.

BROWN, F. (1965).   Foreword. In L. Blank, *Psychological Evaluation in Psychotherapy: Ten Case Histories*. Chicago: Aldine.

BROWN, L. J. (1985).   On concreteness. *Psychoanalytic Review, 72,* 379–402.

BUTCHER, J. N. (1978).   Review of Minnesota Multiphasic Personality Inventory: Behaviordyne Psychodiagnostic Laboratory Service. In O. K. Buros (Ed.), *Eighth Mental Measurements Yearbook*. Highland Park, NJ: Gryphon Press.

CAMPBELL, R. J. (Ed.). (1981).   *Psychiatric Dictionary* (5th ed.). New York: Oxford University Press.

CARR, A. C. (1968).   Psychological testing and reporting. *Journal of Projective Techniques and Personality Assessment, 32*(6), 513–521.

CARRIER, N. A. (1963).   Need correlates of "gullibility." *Journal of Abnormal and Social Psychology, 66*(1), 84–86.

CHOCA, J. (1980).   *Manual for Clinical Psychology Practicums*. New York: Brunner/Mazel.

COHEN, L. J. (1980).   The unstated problem in a psychological testing referral. *American Journal of Psychiatry, 137*(10), 1173–1176.

COHEN. R. J. (1979).   *Malpractice: A Guide for Mental Health Professionals*. New York: Free Press.

COLE, J. K., & MAGNUSSEN, M. G. (1966).   Where the action is. *Journal of Consulting Psychology, 30*(6), 539–543.

COMTOIS, R. J., & CLARK, W. D. (1976).   A framework for scientific practice and practitioner training. *JSAS Catalog of Selected Documents in Psychology, 6,* 74 (Ms. No. 1301).

CONE, J. D., & HAWKINS, R. P. (1977).   *Behavioral Assessment: New Directions in Clinical Psychology*. New York: Brunner/Mazel.

CONRAD, H. S. (1932).   The validity of personality ratings of preschool children. *Journal of Educational Psychology, 23,* 671–680.

COOPER, A., & WITTENBERG, E. G. (1985).   The "bogged down" treatment: A remedy. *Contemporary Psychoanalysis, 21,* 27–41.

CRADDICK, R. A. (1972).   Humanistic assessment: A reply to Brown. *Psychotherapy: Theory, Research and Practice, 9*(2), 107–110.

CRADDICK, R. A. (1975).   Sharing oneself in the assessment procedure. *Professional Psychology, 6*(3), 279–282.

CRONBACH, L. J. (1984).   *Essentials of Psychological Testing* (4th ed.). New York: Harper & Row, Pub.

CUADRA, C. A., & ALBAUGH, W. P. (1956).   Sources of ambiguity in psychological reports. *Journal of Clinical Psychology, 12,* 108–115.

DAHLSTROM, W. G., WELSH, G. S., & DAHLSTROM, L. E. (1972).   *An MMPI Handbook: Clinical Interpretation, Vol. I* (rev. ed.). Minneapolis: University of Minnesota Press.

DAILEY, C. A. (1953).   The practical utility of the psychological report. *Journal of Consulting Psychology, 17,* 297–302.

DANA, R. H. (1966).   Eisegesis and assessment. *Journal of Projective Techniques, 30*(3), 215-222.

DANA, R. H., HANNIFIN, P., LANCASTER, C., LORE, W., & NELSON, D. (1963).   Psychological reports and juvenile probation counseling. *Journal of Clinical Psychology, 19*(3), 352-355.

DAVENPORT, B. F. (1952).   The semantic validity of TAT interpretation. *Journal of Consulting Psychology, 16,* 171-175.

DE LA COUR, A. T. (1986).   Use of the focus in brief dynamic psychotherapy. *Psychotherapy: Theory, Research and Practice, 23,* 133-139.

DELLA CORTE, M. (1980).   Psychobabble: Why do we do it? *Psychotherapy: Theory, Research and Practice, 17,* 281-284.

DE NELSKY, G. Y., & BOAT, B. W. (1986).   A coping skills model of psychological diagnosis and treatment. *Professional Psychology: Research and Practice, 17,* 322-330.

DOLLIN, A., & REZNIKOFF, M. (1966).   Diagnostic referral questions in psychological testing. *Psychological Reports, 19,* 610.

DORR, D. (1981).   Conjoint psychological testing in marriage therapy: New wine in old skins. *Professional Psychology, 12*(5), 549-555.

ENGLISH, H. B., & ENGLISH, A. C. (1958).   *A Comprehensive Dictionary of Psychological and Psychoanalytical Terms.* New York: Longman, Green and Co.

EVERLY, G. S., JR. (1986).   The MCMI in treatment planning. *Responses, 2*(2), 3.

EXNER, J. E., JR. (1969).   *The Rorschach Systems.* New York: Grune & Stratton.

EXNER, J. E., JR. (1978).   *The Rorschach: A Comprehensive System, Vol. II: Current Research and Advanced Interpretation.* New York: John Wiley.

EXNER, J. E., JR. (1986).   *The Rorschach: A Comprehensive System* (2nd ed.). New York: John Wiley.

FAUST, D., & MINER, R. A. (1986).   The empiricist and his new clothes: DSM-III in perspective. *American Journal of Psychiatry, 143,* 962-967.

FILER, R. N. (1952).   The clinician's personality and his case reports. *American Psychologist, 7,* 336.

FISCHER, C. T. (1970).   The testee as co-evaluator. *Journal of Counseling Psychology, 17*(1), 70-76.

FISCHER, C. T. (1972).   Paradigm changes which allow sharing of "results" with the client. *Professional Psychology, 3*(4), 364-369.

FISCHER, C. T. (1979).   Individualized assessment and phenomenological psychology. *Journal of Personality Assessment, 43,* 115-122.

FISCHER, C. T. (1985).   *Individualizing Psychological Assessment.* Monterey, Calif.: Brooks/Cole.

FLESCH, R. (1972).   *Say What You Mean.* New York: Harper & Row, Pub.

FLESCH, R. (1974).   *The Art of Readable Writing* (25th anniversary ed.). New York: Harper & Row, Pub. (Originally published, 1949.)

FLOYD, W. A. (1974).   The use of the MMPI in marital counseling and research. *Journal of Family Counseling, 2,* 16-21.

FORER, B. R. (1949).   The fallacy of personal validation: A classical demonstration of gullibility. *Journal of Abnormal and Social Psychology, 44,* 118-123.

FOSTER, A. (1951).   Writing psychological reports. *Journal of Clinical Psychology, 7,* 195.

FOWLER, R. D. (1985).   Landmarks in computer-assisted psychological assessment. *Journal of Consulting and Clinical Psychology, 53,* 816-825.

FOWLER, R. D., & BUTCHER, J. N. (1986).   Critique of Matarazzo's views of computerized testing: All sigma and no meaning. *American Psychologist, 41,* 94-96.

FREUD, S. (1959).   [On beginning the treatment. Further recommendations in the technique of psycho-analysis.] In E. Jones & J. Riviere (Trans.), *Collected Papers, Vol. II.* New York: Basic Books. (Originally published, 1913.)

GARFIELD, S. L. (1957). *Introductory Clinical Psychology.* New York: Macmillan.

GARFIELD, S. L., HEINE, R. W., & LEVENTHAL, M. (1954). An evaluation of psychological reports in a clinical setting. *Journal of Consulting Psychology, 18,* 281–286.

GILBERT, J. (1978). *Interpreting Psychological Test Data, Vol. I: Test Response Antecedent.* New York: Van Nostrand Reinhold.

GILBERT, J. (1980). *Interpreting Psychological Test Data, Vol. II: Behavioral Attribute Antecedent.* New York: Van Nostrand Reinhold.

GOLDEN, C. J., HAMMEKE, T. A., & PURISCH, A. D. (1980). *A Manual for the Luria-Nebraska Neuropsychological Battery* (rev. ed.). Los Angeles: Western Psychological Services.

GOLDENSON, R. M. (Ed.). (1984). *Longman Dictionary of Psychology and Psychiatry.* New York: Longman.

GRAHAM, J. R. (1977). *The MMPI: A Practical Guide.* New York: Oxford University Press.

GRAYSON, H. M., & TOLMAN, R. S. (1950). A semantic study of concepts of clinical psychologists and psychiatrists. *Journal of Abnormal and Social Psychology, 45,* 216–231.

GREENE, R. L. (1977). Student acceptance of generalized personality interpretations: A reexamination. *Journal of Consulting and Clinical Psychology, 45,* 965–966.

GREENE, R. L. (1978). Can clients provide valuable feedback to clinicians about their personality interpretations?: Greene replies. *Journal of Consulting and Clinical Psychology, 46*(6), 1496–1497.

HAMMER, E., & PIOTROWSKI, Z. A. (1953). Hostility as a factor in the clinician's personality as it affects his interpretation of projective drawings (H-T-P). *Journal of Projective Techniques, 17,* 210–216.

HAMMITT, K. B. (1982). Does your patient understand? The implications of functional illiteracy. *Frontiers of Psychiatry, 12*(1), 14.

HAMMOND, K. R., & ALLEN, J. M. (1953). *Writing Clinical Reports.* Englewood Cliffs, N.J.: Prentice-Hall.

HARROWER, M., VORHAUS, P., ROMAN, M., & BAUMAN, G. (1960). *Creative Variations in the Projective Techniques.* Springfield, Ill.: Chas. C. Thomas.

HARTLAGE, L. C., FREEMAN, W., HORINE, L., & WALTON, C. (1968). Decisional utility of psychological reports. *Journal of Clinical Psychology, 24*(4), 481–483.

HARTLAGE, L. C., & MERCK, K. H. (1971). Increasing the relevance of psychological reports. *Journal of Clinical Psychology, 27,* 459–460.

HARTY, M. K. (1986). Action language in the psychological test report. *Bulletin of the Menninger Clinic, 50,* 456–463.

HATHAWAY, S. R., & MEEHL, P. E. (1951). *An Atlas for the Clinical Use of the MMPI.* Minneapolis: University of Minnesota Press.

HEADRICK, L. B. (1956). From W. O. Hadlock, Engineer as author. *RCA Engineer,* August–September.

HOFER, P. J., & GREEN, B. F. (1985). The challenge of competency and creativity in computerized psychological testing. *Journal of Consulting and Clinical Psychology, 53,* 826–838.

HOFFMAN, B. F. (1986). How to write a psychiatric report for litigation following a personal injury. *American Journal of Psychiatry, 143,* 164–169.

HOLT, R. R. (1967). Diagnostic testing: Present status and future prospects. *Journal of Nervous and Mental Disease, 144*(6), 444–465.

HOLTZMAN, W. H. (1964).   Recurring dilemmas in personality assessment. *Journal of Projective Techniques and Personality Assessment, 28*(2), 144–150.

HOLZBERG, J., ALLESSI, S. L., & WEXLER, M. (1951).   Psychological case reporting at psychiatric staff conferences. *Journal of Consulting Psychology, 5,* 425–429.

HOWE, H. E., JR. (1981).   Description and application of an evaluative scheme for assessment from a decision-making perspective. *Journal of Clinical Psychology, 37*(1), 110–117.

HUTT, M. L. (1977).   *The Hutt Adaptation of the Bender-Gestalt Test* (3rd ed.). New York: Grune & Stratton.

IVNIK, R. J. (1977).   Uncertain status of psychological tests in clinical psychology. *Professional Psychology, 8*(2), 206–213.

JACKSON, D. E. (1978).   The effect of test taking on acceptance of bogus personality statements. *Journal of Clinical Psychology, 34*(1), 63–68.

JOHNSON, W. (1945).   The degree of extensional agreement among twenty psychologists in their use of the labels "hypothesis," "theory," and "law." *Iowa Academy of Science, 52,* 255–259.

KAUFMAN, A. S. (1979).   *Intelligent Testing with the WISC-R.* New York: John Wiley.

KELLER, C. W. (1971).   *Characteristics of Rorschach Interpreter Types: An Exploratory Study.* Unpublished doctoral dissertation, Texas Tech University.

KIDDER, T. (1981).   *The Soul of a New Machine.* Boston: Little, Brown.

KING, R. D., & LELI, D. (1979).   Teaching mental health and law: A reply to Goldenburg. *Professional Psychology, 10*(6), 771–772.

KISSEN, M. (1973).   The importance of psychological testing for the psychotherapy process. *The Journal of Clinical Issues in Psychology, 5,* 11–13.

KLOPFER, B., & KELLEY, D. M. (1946).   *The Rorschach Technique: A Manual for a Projective Method of Personality Diagnosis.* New York: Collins Publishers.

KLOPFER, W. G. (1954).   Principles of report writing. In B. Klopfer, M. D. Ainsworth, W. G. Klopfer, & R. R. Holt (Eds.), *Developments in the Rorschach Technique, Vol. I: Technique and Theory.* New York: Collins Publishers.

KLOPFER, W. G. (1960).   *The Psychological Report.* New York: Grune & Stratton.

KLOPFER, W. G. (1964).   The blind leading the blind: Psychotherapy without assessment. *Journal of Projective Techniques and Personality Assessment, 28*(4), 387–392.

KLOPFER, W. G. (1984).   Application of the Consensus Rorschach to couples. *Journal of Personality Assessment, 48,* 422–440.

KNOFF, H. M. (Ed.). (1986).   *The Assessment of Child and Adolescent Personality.* New York: Guilford.

KNOFF, H. M. (1986).   A conceptual model and pragmatic approach toward personality assessment referrals. In H. M. Knoff (Ed.), *The Assessment of Child and Adolescent Personality.* New York: Guilford.

KORCHIN, S. J., & SCHULDBERG, D. (1981).   The future of clinical assessment. *American Psychologist, 36,* 1147–1158.

KORNER, I. N. (1962).   Test report evaluation. *Journal of Clinical Psychology, 18,* 194–197.

KUDER, G. F. (1948).   *Kuder Preference Record.* Chicago: Science Research Associates.

LACEY, H. M., & ROSS, A. O. (1964).   Multidisciplinary views on psychological reports in child guidance clinics. *Journal of Clinical Psychology, 20*(4), 522–526.

LACKS, P. B., HORTON, M. M., & OWEN, J. D. (1969).   A more meaningful and practical approach to psychological reports. *Journal of Clinical Psychology, 25,* 383–386.

LANYON, R. I. (1986). Psychological assessment procedures in court-related settings. *Professional Psychology: Research and Practice, 17,* 260–268.

LAYNE, C. (1978). Relationships between the "Barnum Effect" and personality inventory responses. *Journal of Clinical Psychology, 34*(1), 94–97.

LAYNE, C. (1979). The Barnum effect: Rationality versus gullibility? *Journal of Consulting and Clinical Psychology, 47*(1), 219–221.

LAYNE, C., & ALLY, G. (1980). How and why people accept personality feedback. *Journal of Personality Assessment, 44*(5), 541–546.

LAZARUS, A. A. (1973). Multimodal behavior therapy: Treating the "Basic Id." *Journal of Nervous and Mental Disease, 156,* 404–411.

LAZARUS, A. A. (1981). *The Practice of Multimodal Therapy.* New York: McGraw-Hill.

LEVY, J., & EPSTEIN, N. B. (1964). An application of the Rorschach test in family investigation. *Family Process, 3,* 344–376.

LEVY, L. (1963). *Psychological Interpretation.* New York: Holt, Rinehart & Winston.

LEZAK, M. (1983). *Neuropsychological Assessment* (2nd ed.). New York: Oxford University Press.

LOVELAND, N. T., WYNNE, L. C., & SINGER, M. T. (1963). The family Rorschach: A new method for studying family interaction. *Family Process, 2,* 187–215.

LUBORSKY, L. (1953). Self-interpretation of the TAT as a clinical technique. *Journal of Projective Techniques, 17,* 217–223.

LURIA, A. R. (1973). [*The Working Brain: An Introduction to Neuropsychology*] (B. Haigh, Trans.). New York: Basic Books.

MACCOBY, M. (1972). Developments in Erich Fromm's approach to psychoanalysis. *Address to William Alanson White Psychiatric Society,* (Referenced in Cooper & Wittenberg, 1985.)

MALONEY, M. P. (1985). *A Clinician's Guide to Forensic Psychological Assessment.* New York: Free Press.

MALONEY, M. P., & WARD, M. P. (1976). *Psychological Assessment: A Conceptual Approach.* New York: Oxford University Press.

MANNING, E. J. (1968). "Personal validation": Replication of Forer's study. *Psychological Reports, 23,* 181–182.

MASH, E. J., & TERDAL, L. G. (1981). *Behavioral Assessment of Childhood Disorders.* New York: Guilford.

MASLING, J. (1960). The influence of situational and interpersonal variables in projective testing. *Psychological Bulletin, 57*(1), 65–85.

MATARAZZO, J. D. (1965). Postdoctoral residency program in clinical psychology. In Conference Committee. *Preconference Materials Prepared for the Conference on the Professional Preparation of Clinical Psychologists,* pp. 71–73, American Psychological Association, Washington, D.C.

MATARAZZO, J. D. (1972). *Wechsler's Measurement and Appraisal of Adult Intelligence* (5th ed.). New York: Oxford University Press.

MATARAZZO, J. D. (1981). Obituary: David Wechsler (1896–1981). *American Psychologist, 36*(12), 1542–1543.

MATARAZZO, J. D. (1983). Computerized psychological testing. *Science, 221,* July 22, p. 323.

MATARAZZO, J. D. (1986). Computerized psychological test interpretations: Unvalidated plus all mean and no sigma. *American Psychologist, 41,* 14–24.

MAYMAN, M. (1959). Style, focus, language and content of an ideal psychological test report. *Journal of Projective Techniques, 23,* 453–458.

MEEHL, P. E. (1954). *Clinical Versus Statistical Prediction: A Theoretical Analysis and a Review of the Evidence.* Minneapolis: University of Minnesota Press.

MEEHL, P. E. (1956).   Wanted—A good cookbook. *American Psychologist, 11,* 263–272.

MESSICK, S. (1980).   Test validity and the ethics of assessment. *American Psychologist, 35,* 1012–1027.

MILLON, T. (1981).   *Disorders of personality: DSM-III, Axis II.* New York: John Wiley.

MOORE, C. H., BOBLITT, W. E., & WILDMAN, R. W. (1968).   Psychiatric impressions of psychological reports. *Journal of Clinical Psychology, 24*(3), 373–376.

MORSE, S. J. (1978)   Law and mental health professionals: The limits of expertise. *Professional Psychology, 9*(3), 389–399.

MORTIMER, R. L., & SMITH, W. H. (1983).   The use of the psychological test report in setting the focus of psychotherapy. *Journal of Personality Assessment, 47,* 134–138.

MOSAK, H. H., & GUSHURST, R. S. (1972).   Some therapeutic uses of psychologic testing. *American Journal of Psychotherapy, 26*(4), 539–546.

MUSSMAN, M. C. (1964).   Teachers' evaluation of psychological reports. *Journal of School Psychology, 3*(1), 35–37.

NASH, M. M. (1974).   Parameters and distinctiveness of psychological testimony. *Professional Psychology, 5,* 239–243.

NATIONAL ASSOCIATION OF SCHOOL PSYCHOLOGISTS. (1974).   *Principles for Professional Ethics* (Mimeo).

NEWMAN, E. B. (1966).   Proceedings of the American Psychological Association, Incorporated, for the year 1966. *American Psychologist, 21,* 1125–1153.

NIETZEL, M. T., & DILLEHAY, R. C. (1986).   *Psychological Consultation in the Courtroom.* Elmsford, NY: Pergamon Press.

ODOM, C. L. (1950).   A study of the time required to do a Rorschach examination. *Journal of Projective Techniques, 14,* 464–468.

OGDON, D. P. (1981).   *Psychodiagnostics and Personality Assessment: A Handbook* (2nd ed.). Los Angeles: Western Psychological Services.

OLIVE, H. (1972).   Psychoanalysts' opinions of psychologists' reports: 1952 and 1970. *Journal of Clinical Psychology, 28*(1), 50–54.

PAOLINO, T. J. (1981).   Analyzability: Some categories for assessment. *Contemporary Psychoanalysis, 17*(3), 321–340. (a)

PAOLINO, T. J. (1981).   *Psychoanalytic Psychotherapy: Theory, Technique, Therapeutic Relationship and Treatability.* New York: Brunner/Mazel. (b)

PARASHAR, O. D. (1977).   *Dictionary of Special Education.* Freeport, NY: Educational Activities, Inc.

PETERSON, D. R. (1968).   *The Clinical Study of Social Behavior.* New York: Appleton-Century-Crofts.

PETRELLA, R. C., & POYTHRESS, N. G., JR. (1983).   The quality of forensic evaluations: An interdisciplinary study. *Journal of Consulting and Clinical Psychology, 51,* 76–85.

PETTY, R. E., & BROCK, T. C. (1979).   Effects of Barnum personality assessments on cognitive behavior. *Journal of Consulting and Clinical Psychology, 47*(1), 201–203.

PLOTKIN, R. (December 1978).   Through the looking glass: Clients' access to their own records. *APA Monitor,* p. 10.

POKORNY, A. D. (1964).   Suicide rates in various psychiatric disorders. *Journal of Nervous and Mental Disease, 139,* 499–506.

POYTHRESS, N. G., JR. (1979).   A proposal for training in forensic psychology. *American Psychologist, 36,* 612–621.

POYTHRESS, N. G., JR. (1980).   Coping on the witness stand: Learned responses to "learned treatises." *Professional Psychology, 11*(1), 139–149.

PROUT, A. T. (1986).   Personality assessment and individual therapeutic interventions. In H. M. Knoff, *The Assessment of Child and Adolescent Personality*. New York: Guilford.

RAKOFF, V. M., STANCER, H. C., & KEDWARD, H. B. (1977). *Psychiatric Diagnosis*. New York: Brunner/Mazel.

RAPAPORT, D., GILL, M. M., & SCHAFER, R. (1968). *Diagnostic Psychological Testing* (rev. ed., R. R. Holt, Ed.). New York: International Universities Press.

RICHARDS, W. S., & MERRENS, M. R. (1971). Student evaluation of generalized personality interpretations as a function of method of assessment. *Journal of Clinical Psychology, 27*(4), 457–459.

RICHMAN, J. (1967). Reporting diagnostic test results to patients and their families. *Journal of Projective Techniques and Personality Assessment, 31*, 62–70.

ROBINSON, J. T. (1951). *Some Indications of Personality Differences Among Clinical Psychologists as Revealed in their Reports on Patients*. Unpublished master's thesis, Duke University.

ROBINSON, J. T., & COHEN, L. D. (1954). Individual bias in psychological reports. *Journal of Clinical Psychology, 10*, 333–336.

ROSEN, M. (1973). Alice in Rorschachland. *Journal of Personality Assessment, 37*(2), 115–121.

ROSENHAN, D. L. (1973). On being sane in insane places. *Science,* 179, 250–258.

ROSENWALD, G. C. (1963). Psychodiagnostics and its discontents. *Psychiatry, 26*(3), 222–240.

ROTH, L. H., WOLFORD, J., & MEISEL, A. (1980). Patient access to records: Tonic or toxin? *American Journal of Psychiatry, 137*(5), 592–596.

RUCKER, C. N. (1967). Technical language in the school psychologist's report. *Psychology in the Schools, 4*, 146–150.

RUSSELL, E. W., NEURINGER, C., & GOLDSTEIN, G. (1970). *Assessment of Brain Damage: A Neuropsychological Key Approach*. New York: John Wiley.

SARBIN, T. R., TAFT, R., & BAILEY, D. E. (1960). *Clinical Inference and Cognitive Theory*. New York: Holt, Rinehart & Winston.

SARGENT, H. D. (1951). Psychological test reporting: An experiment in technique. *Bulletin of the Menninger Clinic, 15*, 175–186.

SATTLER, J. M. (1982). *Assessment of Children's Intelligence and Special Abilities*. Boston: Allyn & Bacon.

SAUL, L. (1958). *Technique and Practice of Psychoanalysis*. Philadelphia: Lippincott.

SCHAFER, R. (1949). Psychological tests in clinical research. *Journal of Consulting Psychology, 13*, 328–334.

SCHAFER, R. (1954). *Psychoanalytic Interpretation in Rorschach Testing*. New York: Grune & Stratton.

SCHAFER, R. (1976). *A New Language for Psychoanalysis*. New Haven: Yale University Press.

SCHLESINGER, H. J. (1973). Interaction of dynamic and reality factors in the diagnostic testing interview. *Bulletin of the Menninger Clinic, 37*, 495–517.

SCHWITZGEBEL, R. L., & SCHWITZGEBEL, R. K. (1980). *Law and Psychological Practice*. New York: John Wiley.

SHAPIRO, D. (1965). *Neurotic Styles*. New York: Basic Books.

SHAPIRO, D. L. (1984). *Psychological Evaluation and Expert Testimony*. New York: Van Nostrand Reinhold.

SHECTMAN, F. (1979). Problems in communicating psychological understanding: Why won't they listen to me?! *American Psychologist, 34*(9), 781–790.

SHECTMAN, F., & SMITH, W. H. (1984). *Diagnostic Understanding and Treatment Planning: The Elusive Connection*. New York: John Wiley.

SHENKEL, R. J., SNYDER, C. R., BATSON, C. D., & CLARK, G. M.

(1979). Effects of prior diagnostic information on clinicians' causal attributions of a client's problems. *Journal of Consulting and Clinical Psychology, 47,* 404-406.

SHEVRIN, H., & SHECTMAN, F. (1973). The diagnostic process in psychiatric evaluations. *Bulletin of the Menninger Clinic, 37*(5), 491-494.

SHIVELY, J. J., & SMITH, A. E. (1969). Understanding the psychological report. *Psychology in the Schools, 6,* 272-273.

SINGER, M. T. (1977). The borderline diagnosis and psychological tests: Review and research. In P. Hartocollis (Ed.), *Borderline Personality Disorders: The Concept, the Syndrome, the Patient.* New York: International Universities Press.

SISKIND, G. (1967). Change of attitude? *The Clinical Psychologist, 20*(4), 158. (a)

SISKIND, G. (1967). Fifteen years later: A replication of "a semantic study of concepts of clinical psychologists and psychiatrists." *The Journal of Psychology, 65,* 3-7. (b)

SLOVES, R. E., DOCHERTY, E. M., & SCHNEIDER, K. C. (1979). A scientific problem-solving model of psychological assessment. *Professional Psychology, 10*(1), 28-35.

SMALL, L. (1980). *Neuropsychodiagnosis in Psychotherapy* (rev. ed.). New York: Brunner/Mazel.

SMITH, M. B. (1986). The plausible assessment report: A phrenological example. *Professional Psychology: Research and Practice, 17,* 294-295.

SMITH, W. H. (1978). Ethical, social, and professional issues in patients' access to psychological test reports. *Bulletin of the Menninger Clinic, 42*(2), 150-155.

SMITH, W. H., & GABBARD, G. (1980). Psychological testing and the psychiatric resident. *Bulletin of the Menninger Clinic, 44*(6), 647-652.

SMYTH, R., & REZNIKOFF, M. (1971). Attitudes of psychiatrists toward the usefulness of psychodiagnostic reports. *Professional Psychology, 2*(3), 283-288.

SNYDER, C. R. (1974). Acceptance of personality interpretations as a function of assessment procedures. *Journal of Consulting and Clinical Psychology, 42*(1), 150.

SNYDER, C. R., & COWLES, C. (1979). Impact of positive and negative feedback based on personality and intellectual assessment. *Journal of Consulting and Clinical Psychology, 47*(1), 207-209.

SNYDER, C. R., HANDELSMAN, M. M., & ENDELMAN, J. R. (1978). Can clients provide valuable feedback to clinicians about their personality interpretations? A reply to Greene. *Journal of Consulting and Clinical Psychology, 46*(6), 1493-1495.

SNYDER, C. R., & LARSON, G. R. (1972). A further look at student acceptance of general personality interpretations. *Journal of Consulting and Clinical Psychology, 38*(3), 384-388.

SNYDER, C. R., SHENKEL, R. J., & LOWERY, C. R. (1977). Acceptance of personality interpretations: The "Barnum Effect" and beyond. *Journal of Consulting and Clinical Psychology, 45*(1), 104-114.

SOUTHER, J. W. (1957). *Technical Report Writing.* New York: John Wiley.

SOUTHER, J. W., & WHITE, M. L. (1977). *Technical Report Writing.* New York: John Wiley.

SPITZER, R. L. (1976). More on pseudoscience in science and the case for psychiatric diagnosis: A critique of D. L. Rosenhan's "On being sane in insane places" and "The contextual nature of psychiatric diagnosis." *Archives of General Psychiatry, 33,* 459-470.

SPITZER, R. L. (Chairperson). (1980). *Diagnostic and Statistical Manual of Mental Disorders* (3rd ed.) (DSM-III). Washington, D.C.: American Psychiatric Association.

STEIN, E. J., FUREDY, R. L., SIMONTON, M. J., & NEUFFER, C. H. (1979). Patient access to medical records on a psychiatric inpatient unit. *American Journal of Psychiatry, 136*(3), 327–332.

STRONG, E. K., JR., & CAMPBELL, D. P. (1974). *Strong Vocational Interest Blank.* Stanford, CA: Stanford University Press.

STURM, I. E. (1974). Toward a composite psychodiagnostic report outline. *Newsletter for Research in Mental Health and Behavioral Science, 16*(3), 6–7.

SUGARMAN, A. (1981). The diagnostic use of countertransference reactions in psychological testing. *Bulletin of the Menninger Clinic, 45,* 473–490.

SUNDBERG, N. D. (1955). The acceptability of "fake" versus "bona fide" personality test interpretations. *Journal of Abnormal and Social Psychology, 50,* 145–147.

SUNDBERG, N. D. (January 14, 1976). Completely blind analysis of the case of a schizophrenic veteran. Presented at Oregon Psychological Association Meeting.

TALLENT, N. (1956). An approach to the improvement of clinical psychological reports. *Journal of Clinical Psychology, 12,* 102–109.

TALLENT, N. (1958). On individualizing the psychologist's clinical evaluation. *Journal of Clinical Psychology, 14,* 243–244.

TALLENT, N. (1980). *Report Writing in Special Education.* Englewood Cliffs, NJ: Prentice-Hall.

TALLENT, N. (1987). Computer-generated psychological reports: A look at the modern psychometric machine. *Journal of Personality Assessment, 51,* 95–108.

TALLENT, N., KENNEDY, G., SZAFIR, A., & GROLIMUND, B. (1974). An expanded role for psychiatric nursing personnel: Psychological evaluation and interpersonal care. *Journal of Psychiatric Nursing and Mental Health Services, 12*(3), 19–23.

TALLENT, N., & RAFI, A. A. (1965). National and professional factors in psychological consultation. *British Journal of Social and Clinical Psychology, 4,* 149–151.

TALLENT, N., & REISS, W. J. (1959). Multidisciplinary views on the preparation of written clinical psychological reports: I. Spontaneous suggestions for content. *Journal of Clinical Psychology, 15,* 218–221. (a)

TALLENT, N., & REISS, W. J. (1959). Multidisciplinary views on the preparation of written clinical psychological reports: II. Acceptability of certain common content variables and styles of expression. *Journal of Clinical Psychology, 15,* 273–274. (b)

TALLENT, N., & REISS, W. J. (1959). Multidisciplinary views on the preparation of written clinical psychological reports: III. The trouble with psychological reports. *Journal of Clinical Psychology, 15,* 444–446. (c)

TALLENT, N., & REISS, W. J. (Winter 1959–1960). A note on an unusually high rate of returns for a mail questionnaire. *The Public Opinion Quarterly, 23*(4), 579–581.

TAYLOR, J. L., & TEICHER, A. A. (1946). A clinical approach to reporting psychological test data. *Journal of Clinical Psychology, 2,* 323–332.

THORNE, F. C. (1961). *Clinical Judgment: A Study of Clinical Errors.* Brandon, VT: Journal of Clinical Psychology.

TOWBIN, A. P. (1960). When are cookbooks useful? *American Psychologist, 15,* 119–123.

TOWBIN, A. P. (1964). Psychological testing from end to means. *Journal of Projective Techniques and Personality Assessment, 28,* 86–91.

TREHUB, A., & SCHERER, I. W. (1958). Wechsler-Bellevue scatter as an index of schizophrenia. *Journal of Consulting Psychology, 22,* 147–149.

ULRICH, R. E., STACHNIK, T. J., & STAINTON, N. R. (1963). Student acceptance of generalized personality interpretations. *Psychological Reports, 13,* 831–834.

VAN REKEN, M. K. (1981).   Psychological assessment and report writing. In C. E. Walker (Ed.), *Clinical Practice of Psychology.* Elmsford, NY: Pergamon Press.

VERNON. W. H. D. (Spring 1955).   Diagnostic testing and some problems of communication between psychiatrists and clinical psychologists. *Bulletin of the Maritime Psychological Association,* 12–29.

WEBB, L. J., DI CLEMENTE, C. C., JOHNSTONE, E. E., SANDERS, J. L., & PERLEY, R. A. (1981).   *DSM-III Training Guide.* New York: Brunner/Mazel.

WECHSLER, D. (1944).   The psychologist in the psychiatric hospital. *Journal of Consulting Psychology, 8,* 281–285.

WEINER, M. F., & CROWDER, J. D. (1986).   Psychotherapy and cognitive style. *American Journal of Psychotherapy, 40,* 17–25.

WERTHEIMER, M. (1945).   *Productive Thinking.* New York: Harper & Row, Pub.

WIENER, D. N., & RATHS, O. N. (1959).   Contributions of the mental hygiene clinic team to clinic decisions. *American Journal of Orthopsychiatry, 29,* 350–356.

WILLI, J. (1969).   Joint Rorschach testing of partner relationships. *Family Process, 8,* 64–78.

WILLIAMS. T. (1974).   Family resemblance in abilities: The Wechsler scales. *Behavior Genetics, 5,* 405–409.

WIRT, R. D., LACHAR, D., KLINEDINST, J. K., & SEAT, P. D. (1977).   *Multidimensional Description of Child Personality: A Manual for the Personality Inventory for Children.* Los Angeles: Western Psychological Services.

WOLMAN, B. B. (Ed.). (1973).   *Dictionary of Behavioral Science.* New York: Van Nostrand Reinhold.

WOODY, R. H. (1972).   The counselor-therapist and clinical assessment. In R. H. Woody & J. D. Woody, *Clinical Assessment in Counseling and Psychotherapy.* New York: Appleton-Century-Crofts.

WRIGHT, R. H. (1981).   What to do until the malpractice lawyer comes: A survivor's manual. *American Psychologist, 36*(12), 1535–1541.

WYATT *v.* ADERHOLT, (1974).   503 F. 2nd 1305 *Federal Reporter,* 2d Series, 1311–1312.

YALOM, I. D. (1985).   *The Theory and Practice of Group Psychotherapy* (3rd ed.). New York: Basic Books.

YALOM, I. D., BROWN, S., & BLOCH, S. (1975).   The written summary as a group psychotherapy technique. *Archives of General Psychiatry, 32*(5), 605–613.

ZISKIN, J. (1981).   *Coping with Psychiatric and Psychological Testimony* (3rd ed., 2 vols.). Venice, CA: Law and Psychology Press.

ZISKIN, J. (1983).   *Coping with Psychiatric and Psychological Testimony* (3rd ed., 1983 Supplement). Venice, CA: Law and Psychology Press.

ZUBIN, J. (1972).   Newer approaches to personality assessment: Discussion of symposium on newer approaches to personality assessment. *Journal of Personality Assessment, 36,* 427–434.

ZUBIN, J., ERON, L. D., & SCHUMER, F. (1965).   *An Experimental Approach to Projective Techniques.* New York: John Wiley.

ZUSMAN, J. (1983).   Differences in repeated psychiatric examinations of litigants to a lawsuit. *American Journal of Psychiatry, 140,* 1300–1304.

Author Index

Subject Index